W9-CCD-356

GIRL ON FILM

A Graphic Novel Memoir

Written by **Cecil Castellucci**

Illustrated by **Vicky Leta**, **Melissa Duffy**,
V. Gagnon & **Jon Berg**

Colored by **Kieran Quigley**
& **Joana Lafuente**

Lettered by **Mike Fiorentino**

ARCHAIA™
Los Angeles, California

Page 2 photo by **Cordelia Lawton**

Page 5 photo by **Carla Folwell**

Pages 7-11, 16-19, 39-44, 53-54, 72, 84-86, 98, 111-113, 146, 151-156 illustrated by **Vicky Leta**

Pages 12-15, 20-38 illustrated by **Melissa Duffy**

Pages 45-52, 55-71, 73-83, 87-97, 99-102 illustrated by **V. Gagnon**

Pages 103-110, 114-145, 147-150 illustrated by **Jon Berg**

Pages 7-11, 16-19, 39-44, 53-54, 72, 84-86, 98, 111-113, 146, 151-156 colored by **Joana Lafuente**

Pages 12-15, 20-38, 45-52, 55-71, 73-83, 87-97, 99-110, 114-145, 147-150 colored by **Kieran Quigley**

Page 159 photo by **Paule Girardin**

Cover photos by **Caz Westover**

Cover illustrations by **Grace Park**

Designer **Scott Newman**

Associate Editor **Sophie Philips-Roberts**

Editor **Sierra Hahn**

Ross Richie CEO & Founder
Joy Huffman CFO
Matt Gagnon Editor-in-Chief
Filip Sablik President, Publishing & Marketing
Stephen Christy President, Development
Lance Kreiter Vice President, Licensing & Merchandising
Arune Singh Vice President, Marketing
Bryce Carlson Vice President, Editorial & Creative Strategy
Scott Newman Manager, Production Design
Kate Henning Manager, Operations
Spencer Simpson Manager, Sales
Elyse Strandberg Manager, Finance
Sierra Hahn Executive Editor
Jeanine Schaefer Executive Editor
Dafna Pleban Senior Editor
Shannon Watters Senior Editor
Eric Harburn Senior Editor
Chris Rosa Editor
Matthew Levine Editor
Sophie Philips-Roberts Associate Editor
Amanda LaFranco Associate Editor
Gavin Gronenthal Assistant Editor

Gwen Waller Assistant Editor
Allyson Gronowitz Assistant Editor
Jillian Crab Design Coordinator
Michelle Ankley Design Coordinator
Kara Leopard Production Designer
Marie Krupina Production Designer
Grace Park Production Designer
Chelsea Roberts Production Design Assistant
Samantha Knapp Production Design Assistant
Paola Capalla Senior Accountant
José Meza Live Events Lead
Stephanie Hocutt Digital Marketing Lead
Esther Kim Marketing Coordinator
Cat O'Grady Digital Marketing Coordinator
Amanda Lawson Marketing Assistant
Holly Aitchison Digital Sales Coordinator
Morgan Perry Retail Sales Coordinator
Megan Christopher Operations Coordinator
Rodrigo Hernandez Mailroom Assistant
Zipporah Smith Operations Assistant
Breanna Sarpy Executive Assistant

ARCHAIA

GIRL ON FILM, November 2019. Published by Archaia, a division of Boom Entertainment, Inc. Girl On Film is ™ & © 2019 Cecil Castellucci. All rights reserved. Archaia™ and the Archaia logo are trademarks of Boom Entertainment, Inc., registered in various countries and categories. All characters, events, and institutions depicted herein are fictional. Any similarity between any of the names, characters, persons, events, and/or institutions in this publication to actual names, characters, and persons, whether living or dead, events, and/or institutions is unintended and purely coincidental.

For information regarding the CPSIA on this printed material, call: (203) 595-3636 and provide reference #RICH – 865882.

BOOM! Studios, 5670 Wilshire Boulevard, Suite 400, Los Angeles, CA 90036-5679. Printed in USA. First Printing.

ISBN: 978-1-68415-453-1, eISBN: 978-1-64144-570-2

Mission Viejo Library
100 Civic Center
Mission Viejo, CA 92691
November 2019

G I R L

O N

F I L M™

A Graphic Novel Memoir

Published by
ARCHAIA™

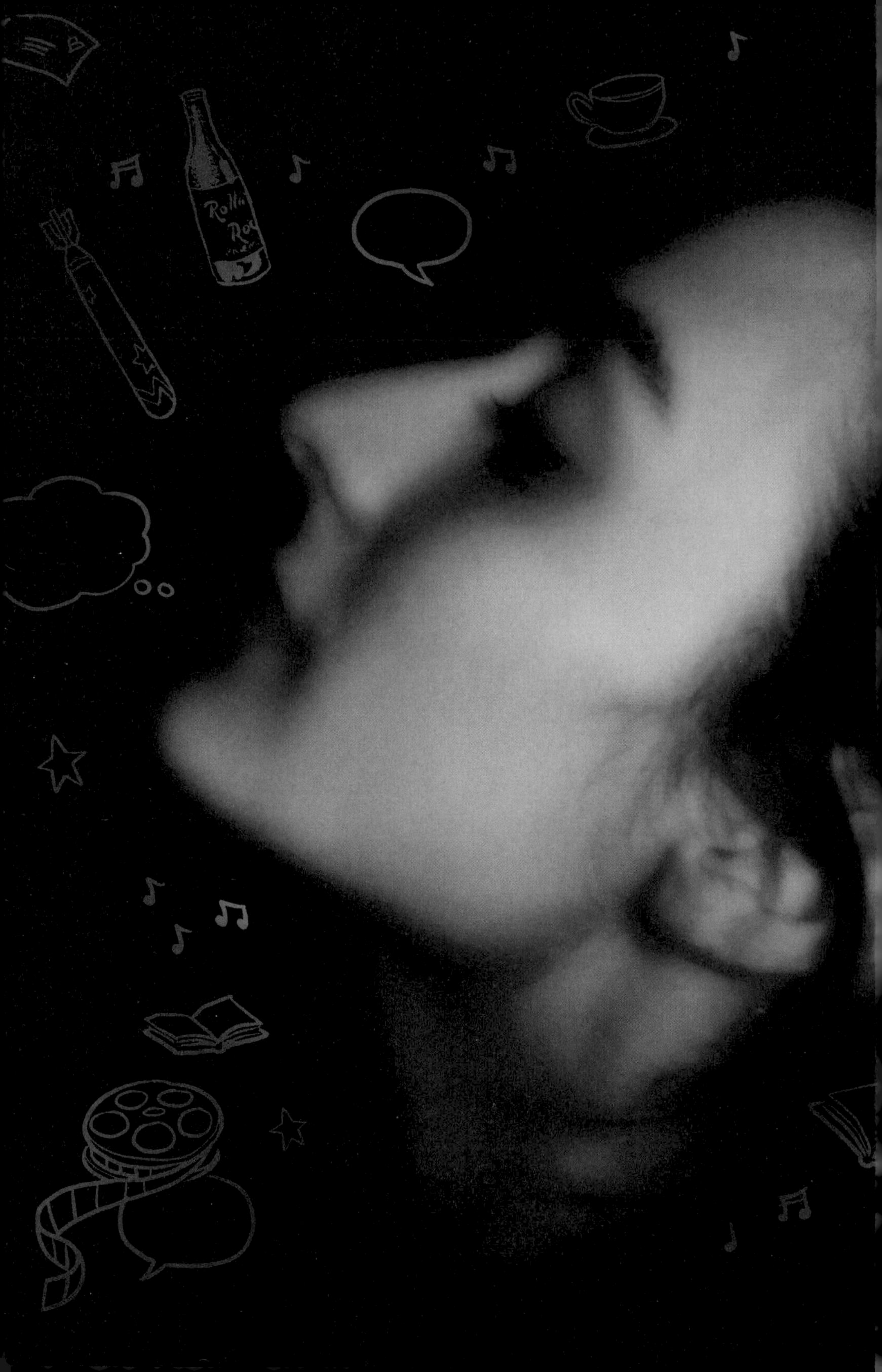

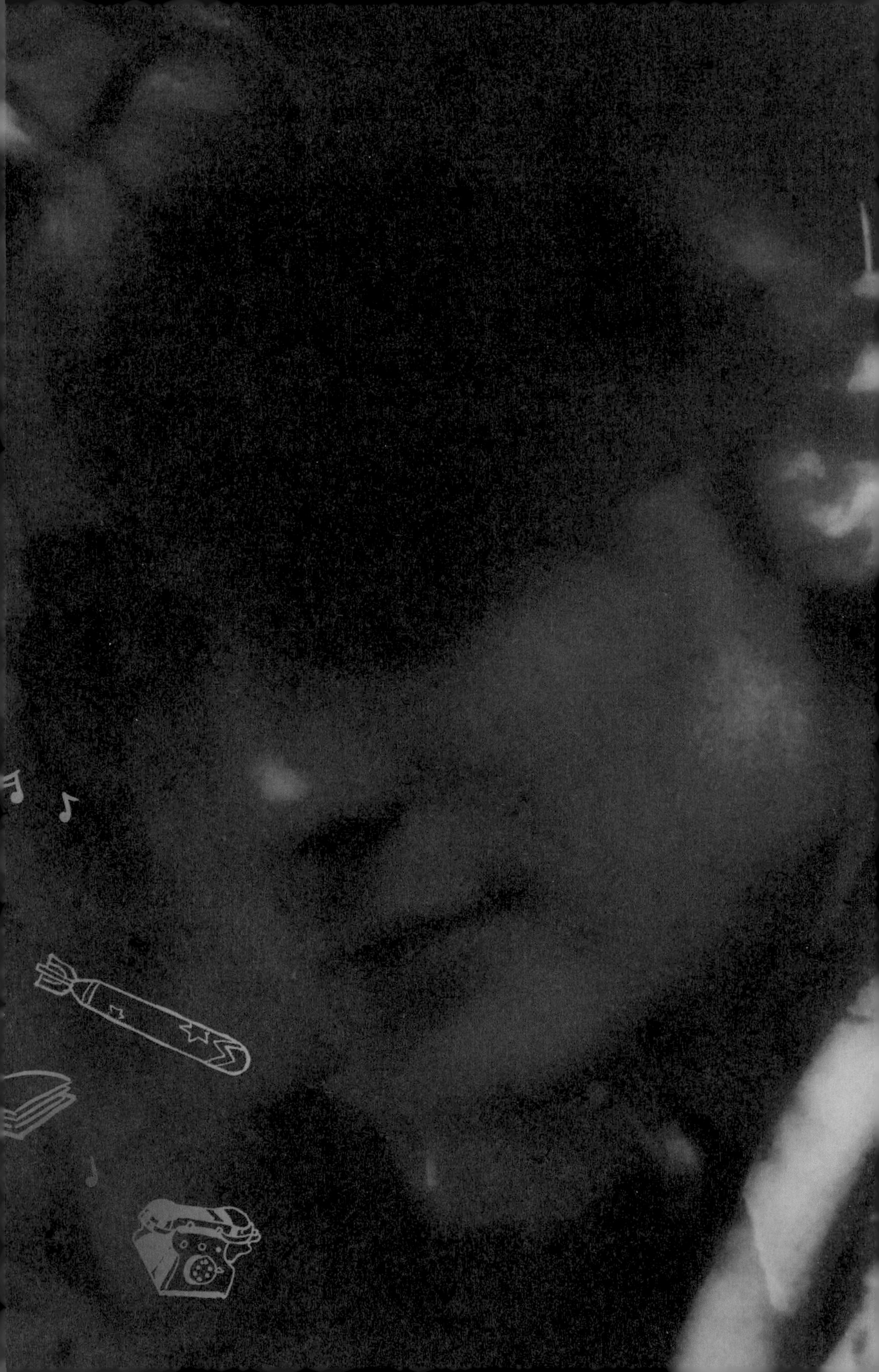

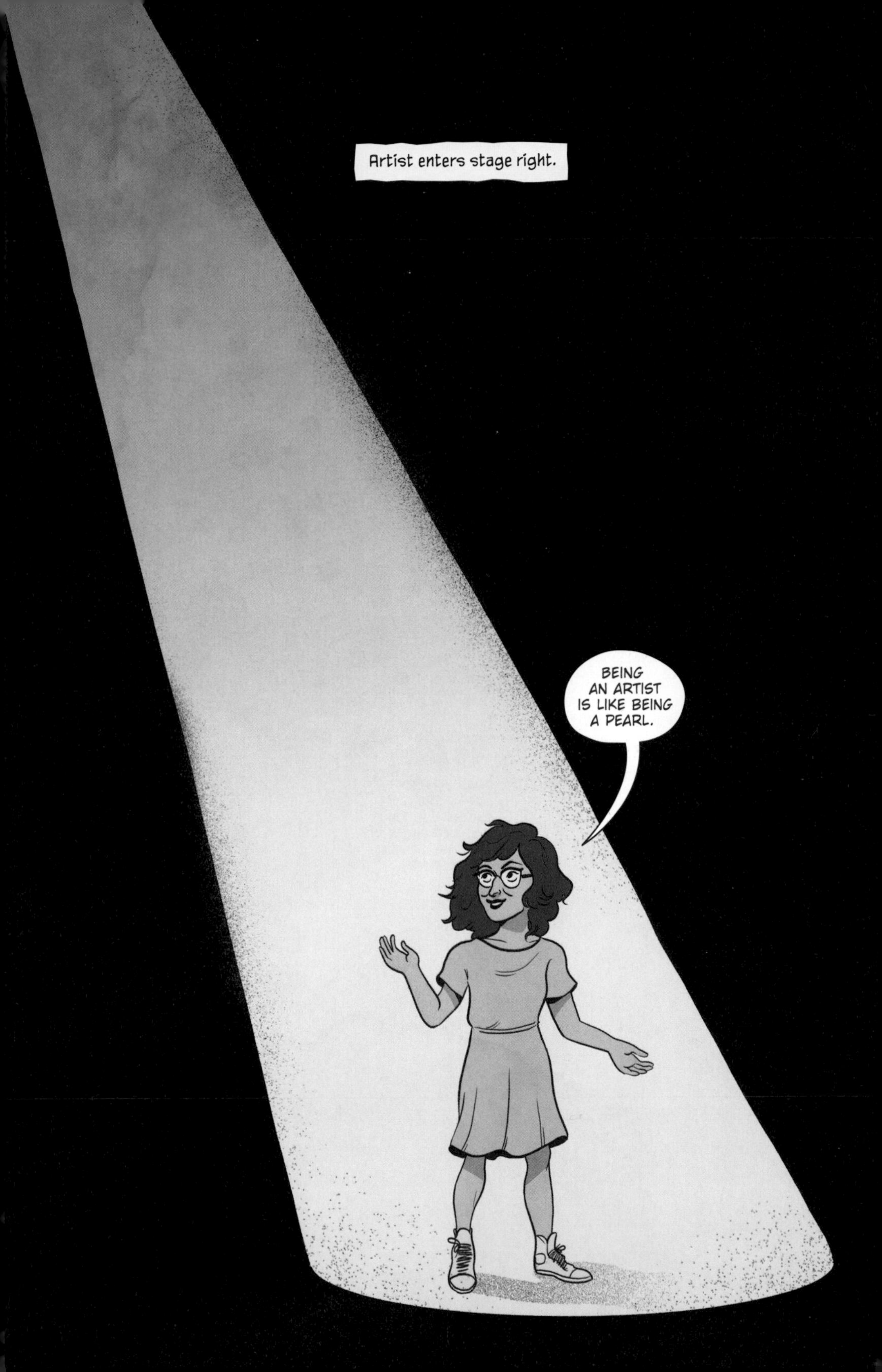
Artist enters stage right.
BEING AN ARTIST IS LIKE BEING A PEARL.

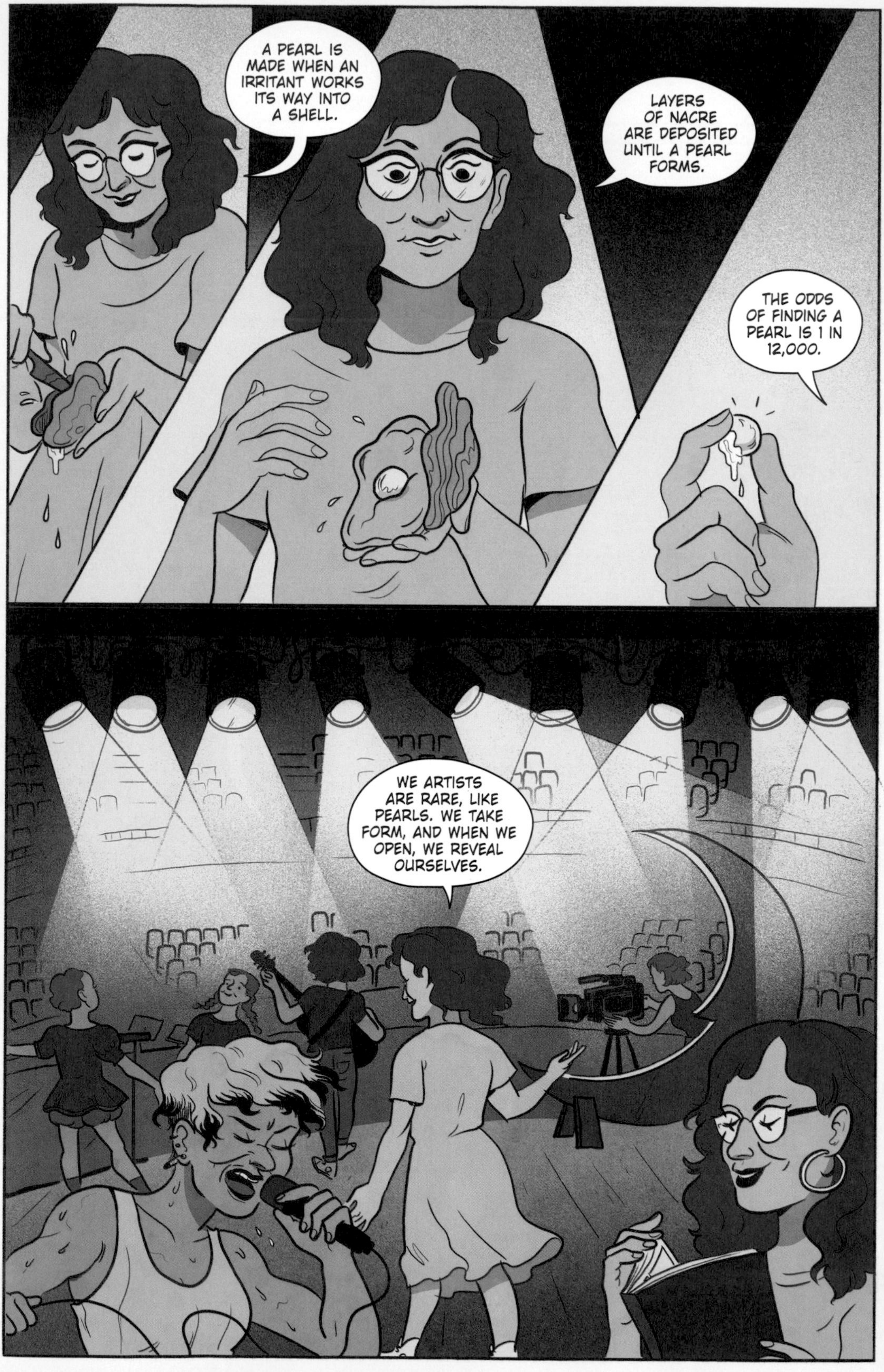
A PEARL IS MADE WHEN AN IRRITANT WORKS ITS WAY INTO A SHELL.
LAYERS OF NACRE ARE DEPOSITED UNTIL A PEARL FORMS.
THE ODDS OF FINDING A PEARL IS 1 IN 12,000.
WE ARTISTS ARE RARE, LIKE PEARLS. WE TAKE FORM, AND WHEN WE OPEN, WE REVEAL OURSELVES.

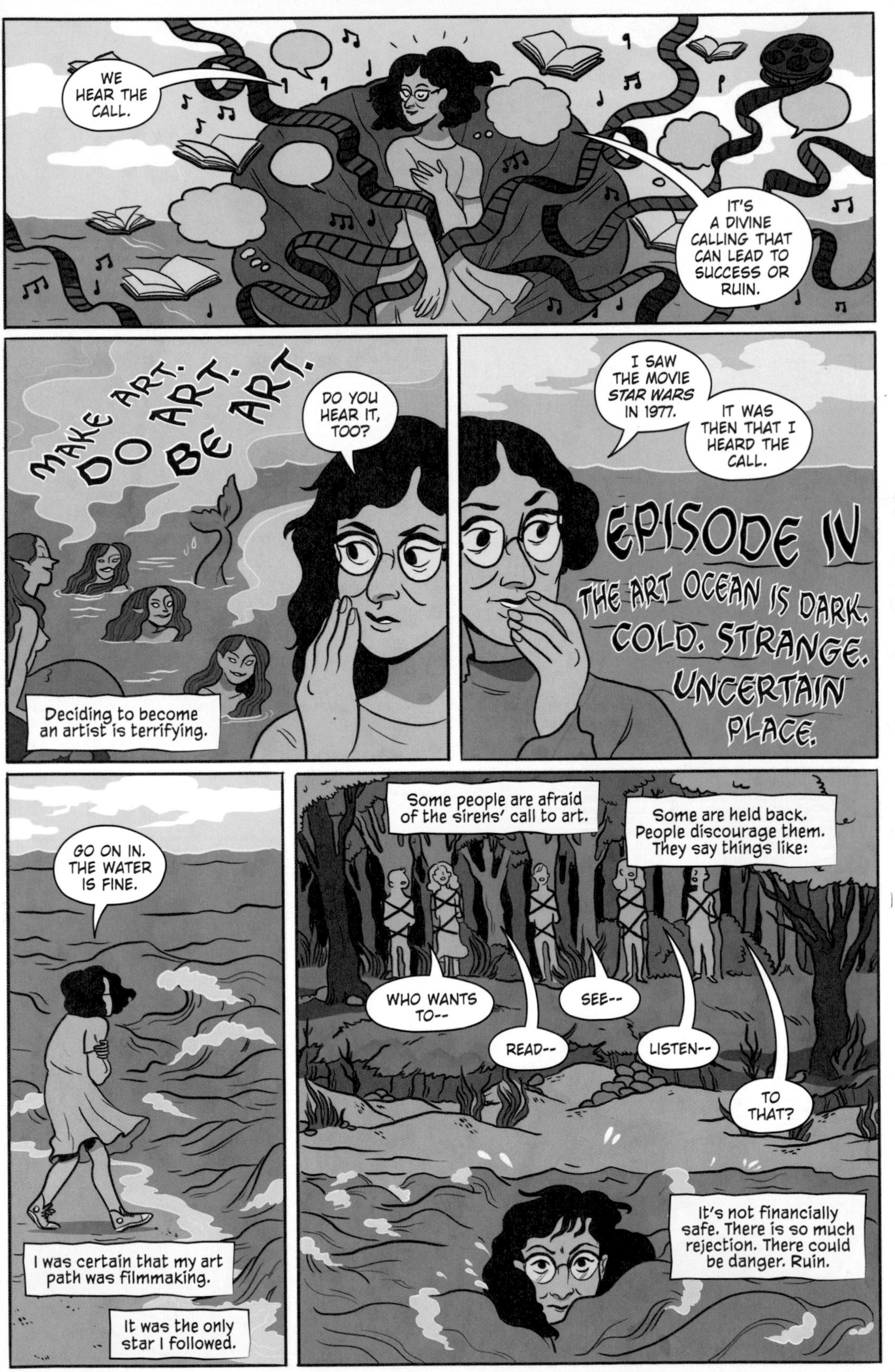
WE HEAR THE CALL.
IT'S A DIVINE CALLING THAT CAN LEAD TO SUCCESS OR RUIN.
MAKE ART. DO ART. BE ART.
DO YOU HEAR IT, TOO?
Deciding to become an artist is terrifying.
I SAW THE MOVIE STAR WARS IN 1977.
IT WAS THEN THAT I HEARD THE CALL.
EPISODE IV
THE ART OCEAN IS DARK. COLD. STRANGE. UNCERTAIN PLACE.
GO ON IN. THE WATER IS FINE.
I was certain that my art path was filmmaking.
It was the only star I followed.
Some people are afraid of the sirens' call to art.
Some are held back. People discourage them. They say things like:
WHO WANTS TO--
READ--
SEE--
LISTEN--
TO THAT?
It's not financially safe. There is so much rejection. There could be danger. Ruin.

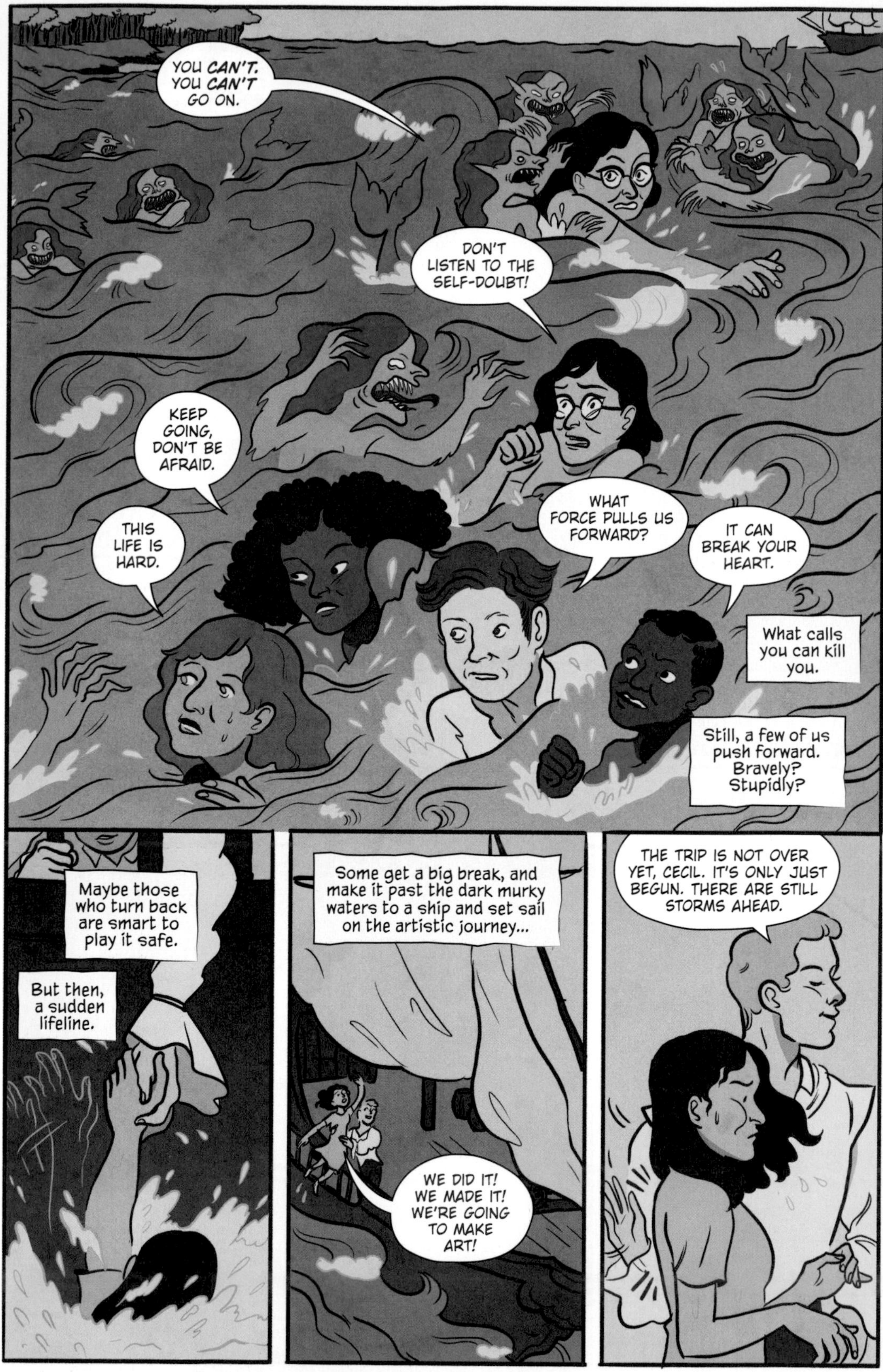

YOU CAN'T. YOU CAN'T GO ON.
DON'T LISTEN TO THE SELF-DOUBT!
KEEP GOING, DON'T BE AFRAID.
THIS LIFE IS HARD.
WHAT FORCE PULLS US FORWARD?
IT CAN BREAK YOUR HEART.
What calls you can kill you.
Still, a few of us push forward. Bravely? Stupidly?
Maybe those who turn back are smart to play it safe.
But then, a sudden lifeline.
Some get a big break, and make it past the dark murky waters to a ship and set sail on the artistic journey...
WE DID IT! WE MADE IT! WE'RE GOING TO MAKE ART!
THE TRIP IS NOT OVER YET, CECIL. IT'S ONLY JUST BEGUN. THERE ARE STILL STORMS AHEAD.

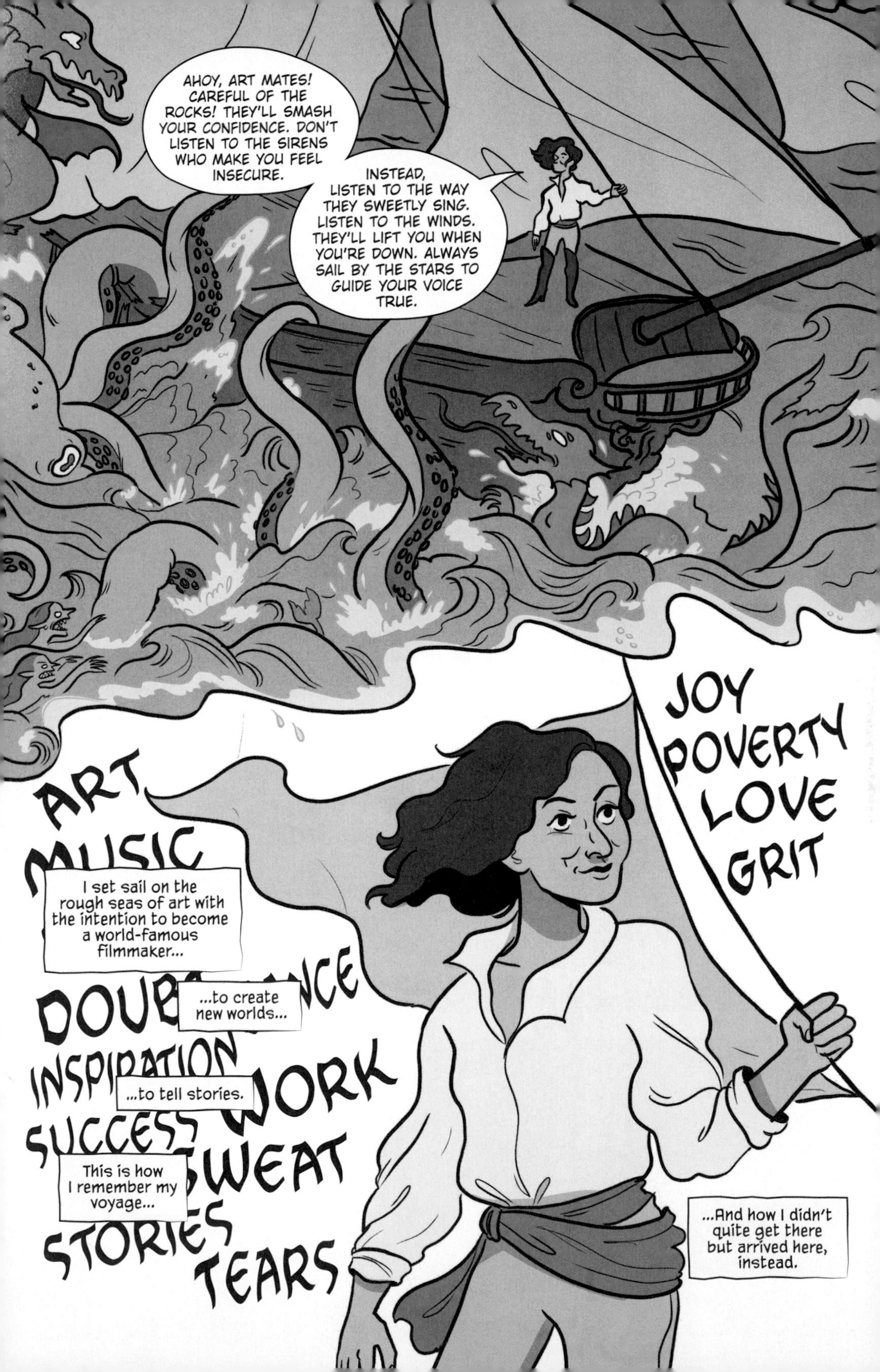
AHOY, ART MATES! CAREFUL OF THE ROCKS! THEY'LL SMASH YOUR CONFIDENCE. DON'T LISTEN TO THE SIRENS WHO MAKE YOU FEEL INSECURE.
INSTEAD, LISTEN TO THE WAY THEY SWEETLY SING. LISTEN TO THE WINDS. THEY'LL LIFT YOU WHEN YOU'RE DOWN. ALWAYS SAIL BY THE STARS TO GUIDE YOUR VOICE TRUE.
JOY
POVERTY
LOVE
GRIT
ART
MUSIC
I set sail on the rough seas of art with the intention to become a world-famous filmmaker...
...to create new worlds...
INSPIRATION
...to tell stories.
WORK
SUCCESS
SWEAT
This is how I remember my voyage...
STORIES
TEARS
...And how I didn't quite get there but arrived here, instead.

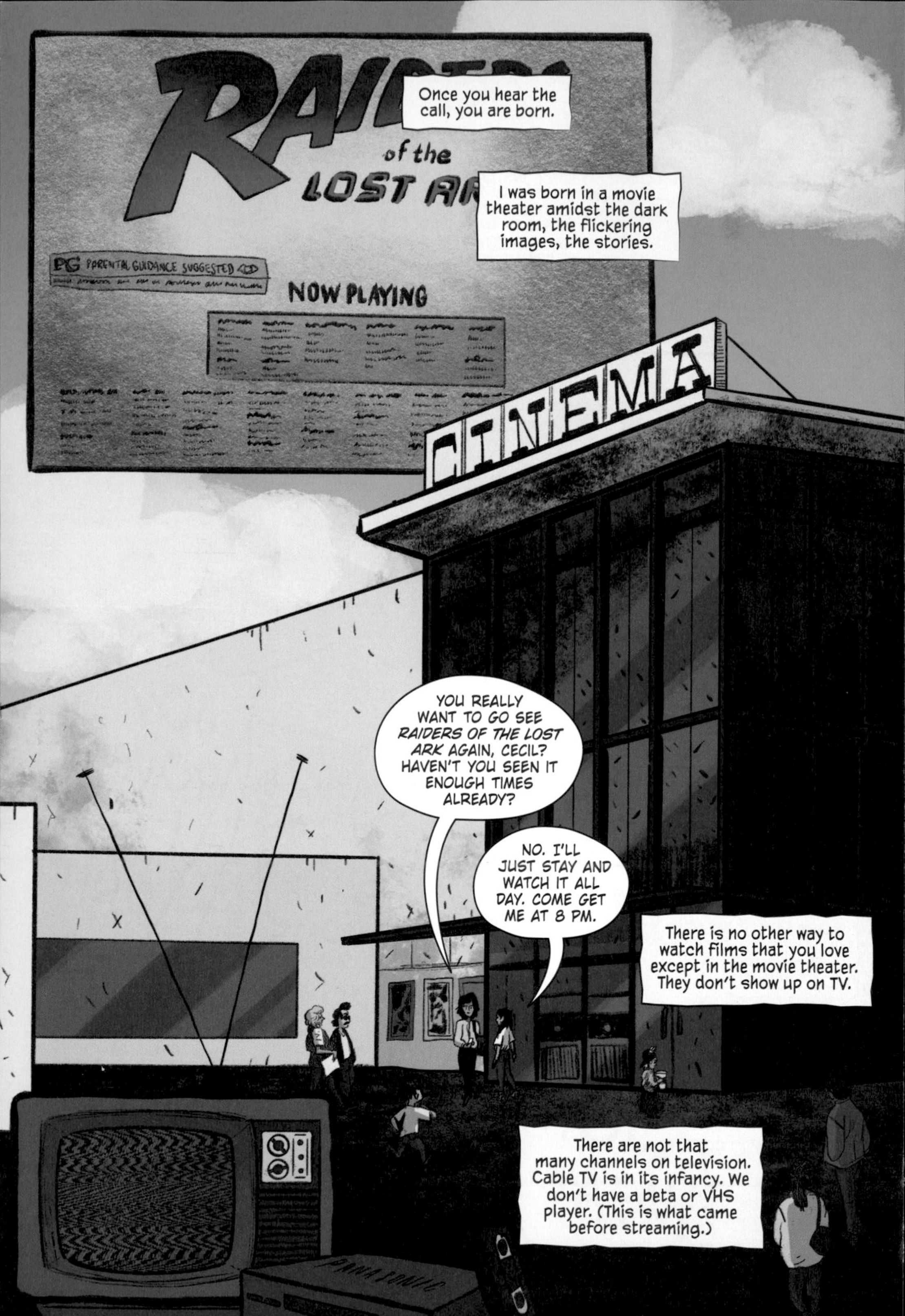
RAIDERS of the LOST ARK
PG PARENTAL GUIDANCE SUGGESTED
NOW PLAYING
Once you hear the call, you are born.
I was born in a movie theater amidst the dark room, the flickering images, the stories.
CINEMA
YOU REALLY WANT TO GO SEE *RAIDERS OF THE LOST ARK* AGAIN, CECIL? HAVEN'T YOU SEEN IT ENOUGH TIMES ALREADY?
NO. I'LL JUST STAY AND WATCH IT ALL DAY. COME GET ME AT 8 PM.
There is no other way to watch films that you love except in the movie theater. They don't show up on TV.
There are not that many channels on television. Cable TV is in its infancy. We don't have a beta or VHS player. (This is what came before streaming.)
PANASONIC

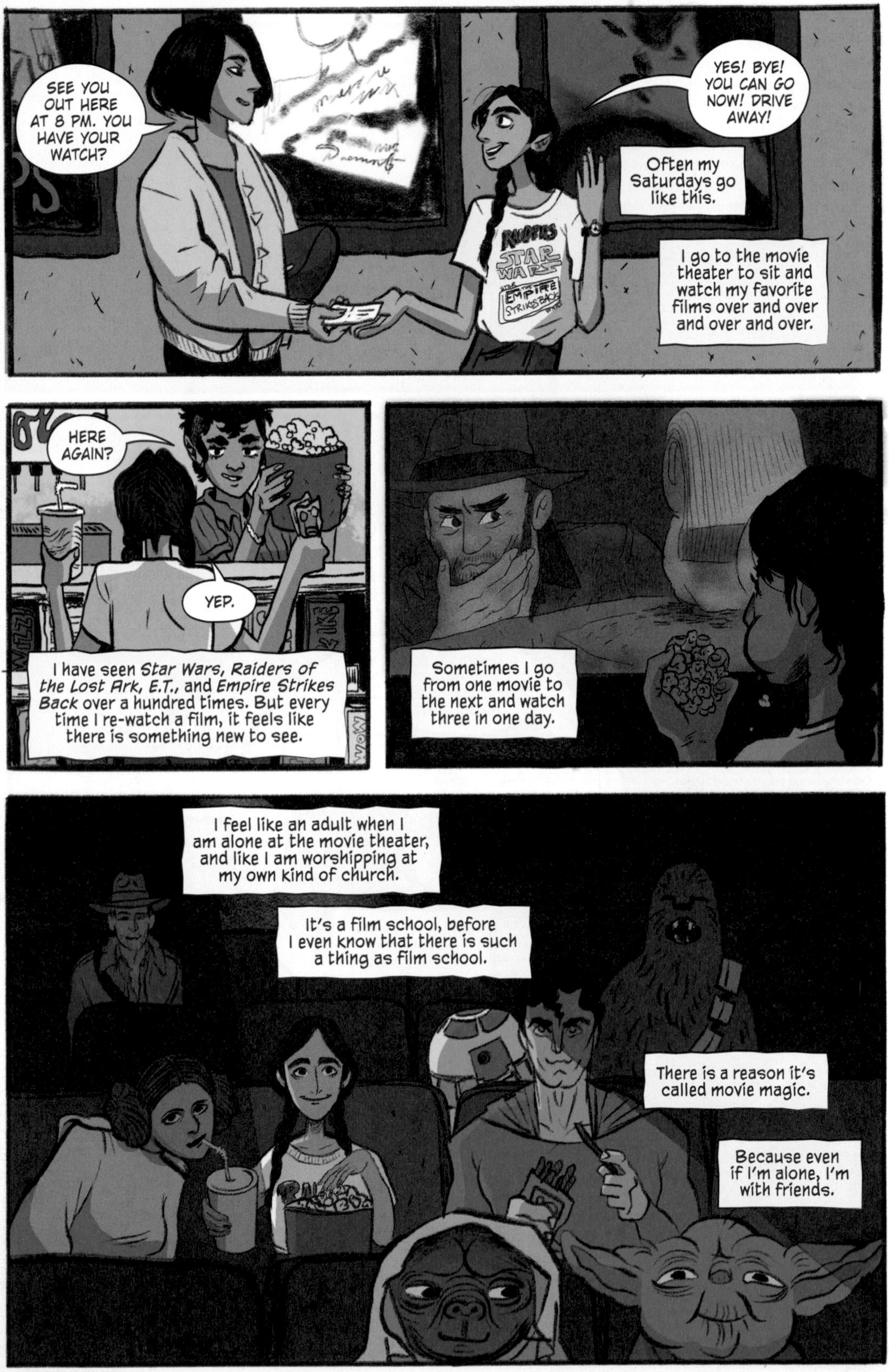

SEE YOU OUT HERE AT 8 PM. YOU HAVE YOUR WATCH?
YES! BYE! YOU CAN GO NOW! DRIVE AWAY!
Often my Saturdays go like this.
I go to the movie theater to sit and watch my favorite films over and over and over and over.
STAR WARS
THE EMPIRE STRIKES BACK
HERE AGAIN?
YEP.
I have seen *Star Wars*, *Raiders of the Lost Ark*, *E.T.*, and *Empire Strikes Back* over a hundred times. But every time I re-watch a film, it feels like there is something new to see.
Sometimes I go from one movie to the next and watch three in one day.
I feel like an adult when I am alone at the movie theater, and like I am worshipping at my own kind of church.
It's a film school, before I even know that there is such a thing as film school.
There is a reason it's called movie magic.
Because even if I'm alone, I'm with friends.

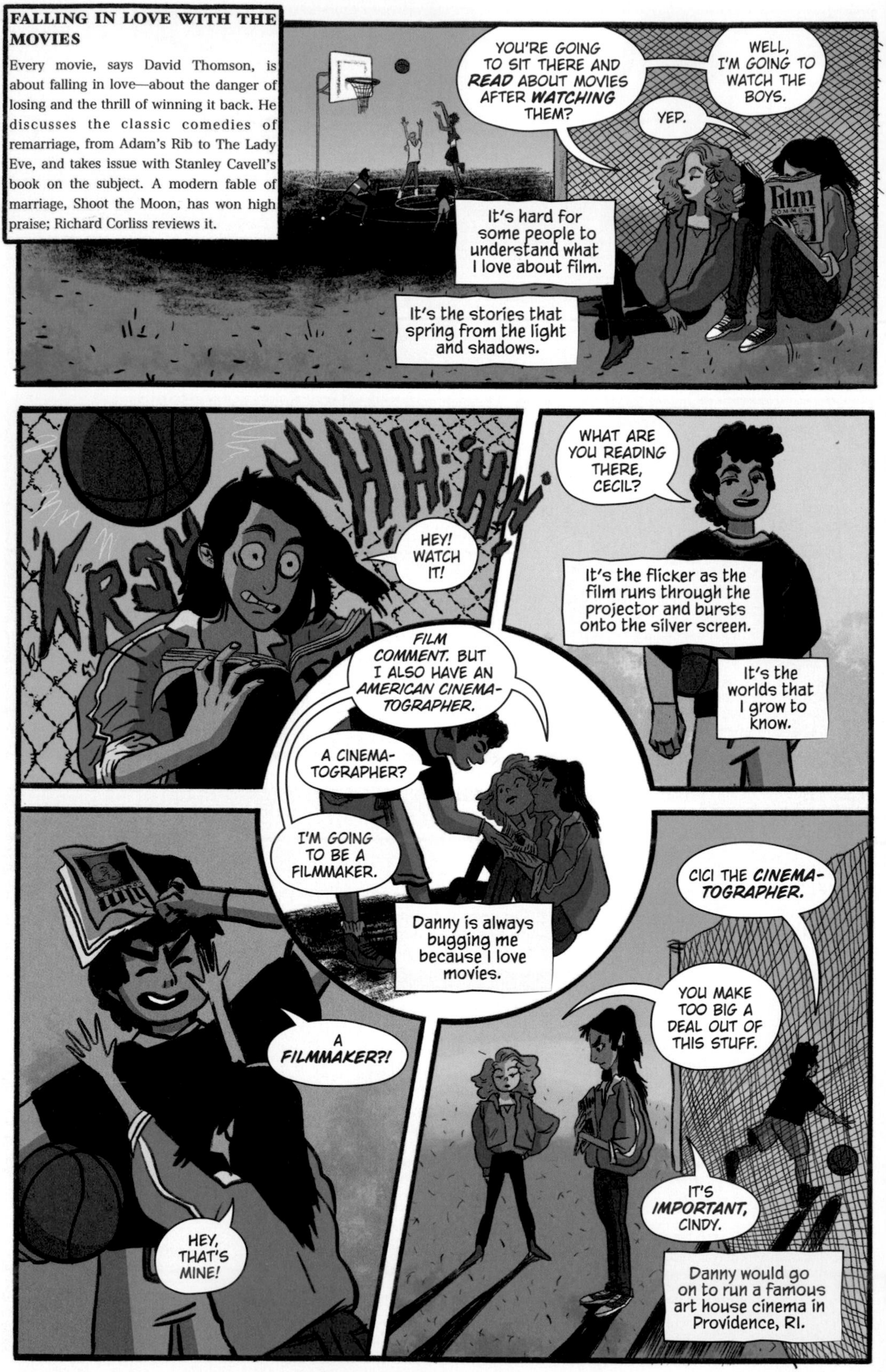
FALLING IN LOVE WITH THE MOVIES
Every movie, says David Thomson, is about falling in love—about the danger of losing and the thrill of winning it back. He discusses the classic comedies of remarriage, from Adam's Rib to The Lady Eve, and takes issue with Stanley Cavell's book on the subject. A modern fable of marriage, Shoot the Moon, has won high praise; Richard Corliss reviews it.
YOU'RE GOING TO SIT THERE AND READ ABOUT MOVIES AFTER WATCHING THEM?
WELL, I'M GOING TO WATCH THE BOYS.
YEP.
Film Comment
It's hard for some people to understand what I love about film.
It's the stories that spring from the light and shadows.
HEY! WATCH IT!
WHAT ARE YOU READING THERE, CECIL?
It's the flicker as the film runs through the projector and bursts onto the silver screen.
It's the worlds that I grow to know.
FILM COMMENT. BUT I ALSO HAVE AN AMERICAN CINEMATOGRAPHER.
A CINEMATOGRAPHER?
I'M GOING TO BE A FILMMAKER.
Danny is always bugging me because I love movies.
A FILMMAKER?!
HEY, THAT'S MINE!
CICI THE CINEMATOGRAPHER.
YOU MAKE TOO BIG A DEAL OUT OF THIS STUFF.
IT'S IMPORTANT, CINDY.
Danny would go on to run a famous art house cinema in Providence, RI.

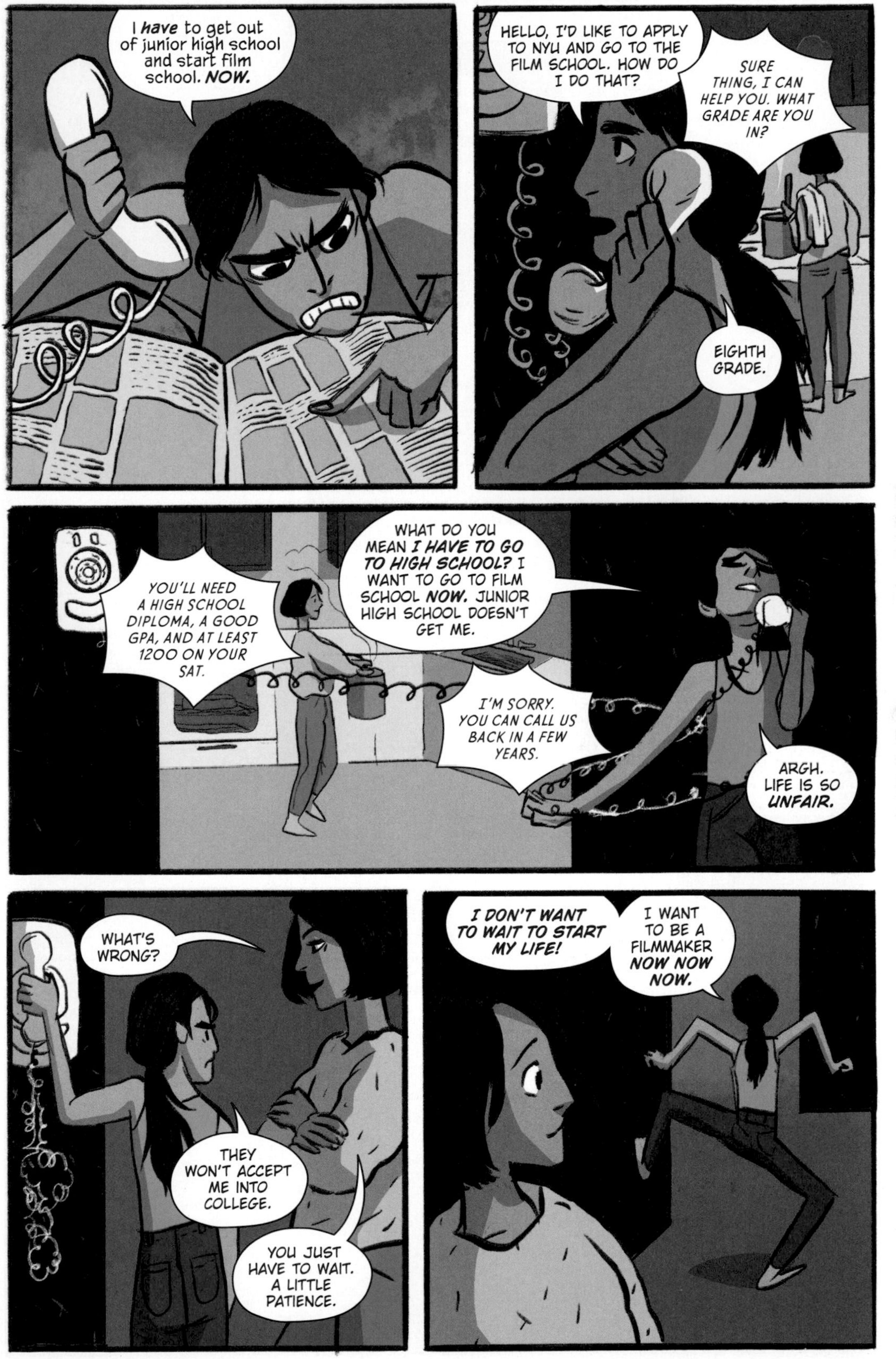
I *have* to get out of junior high school and start film school. ***NOW.***
HELLO, I'D LIKE TO APPLY TO NYU AND GO TO THE FILM SCHOOL. HOW DO I DO THAT?
SURE THING, I CAN HELP YOU. WHAT GRADE ARE YOU IN?
EIGHTH GRADE.
YOU'LL NEED A HIGH SCHOOL DIPLOMA, A GOOD GPA, AND AT LEAST 1200 ON YOUR SAT.
WHAT DO YOU MEAN ***I HAVE TO GO TO HIGH SCHOOL?*** I WANT TO GO TO FILM SCHOOL ***NOW.*** JUNIOR HIGH SCHOOL DOESN'T GET ME.
I'M SORRY. YOU CAN CALL US BACK IN A FEW YEARS.
ARGH. LIFE IS SO ***UNFAIR.***
WHAT'S WRONG?
THEY WON'T ACCEPT ME INTO COLLEGE.
YOU JUST HAVE TO WAIT. A LITTLE PATIENCE.
I DON'T WANT TO WAIT TO START MY LIFE!
I WANT TO BE A FILMMAKER ***NOW NOW NOW.***

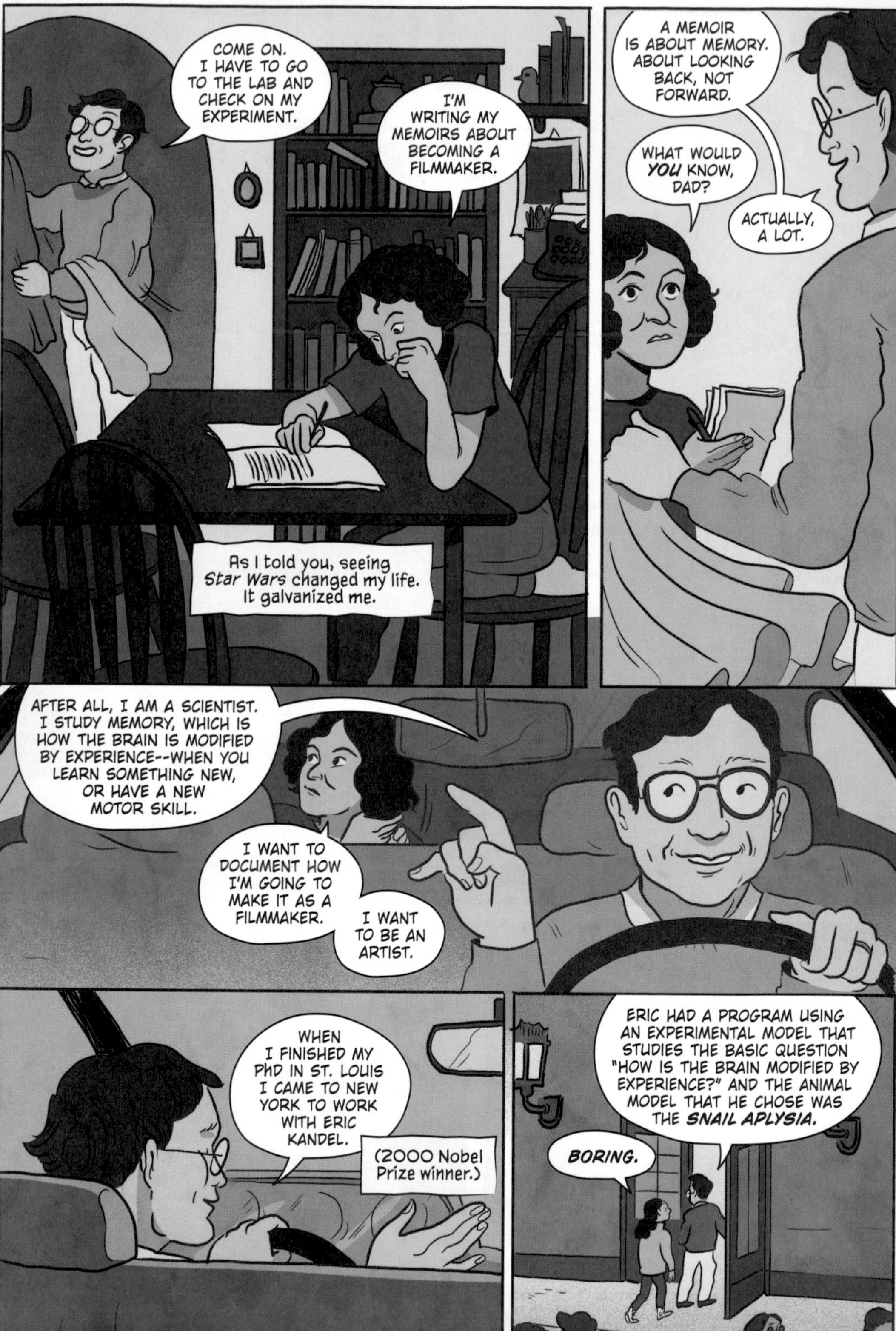
COME ON. I HAVE TO GO TO THE LAB AND CHECK ON MY EXPERIMENT.
I'M WRITING MY MEMOIRS ABOUT BECOMING A FILMMAKER.
As I told you, seeing *Star Wars* changed my life. It galvanized me.
A MEMOIR IS ABOUT MEMORY. ABOUT LOOKING BACK, NOT FORWARD.
WHAT WOULD ***YOU*** KNOW, DAD?
ACTUALLY, A LOT.
AFTER ALL, I AM A SCIENTIST. I STUDY MEMORY, WHICH IS HOW THE BRAIN IS MODIFIED BY EXPERIENCE--WHEN YOU LEARN SOMETHING NEW, OR HAVE A NEW MOTOR SKILL.
I WANT TO DOCUMENT HOW I'M GOING TO MAKE IT AS A FILMMAKER.
I WANT TO BE AN ARTIST.
WHEN I FINISHED MY PhD IN ST. LOUIS I CAME TO NEW YORK TO WORK WITH ERIC KANDEL.
(2000 Nobel Prize winner.)
ERIC HAD A PROGRAM USING AN EXPERIMENTAL MODEL THAT STUDIES THE BASIC QUESTION "HOW IS THE BRAIN MODIFIED BY EXPERIENCE?" AND THE ANIMAL MODEL THAT HE CHOSE WAS THE ***SNAIL APLYSIA.***
BORING.

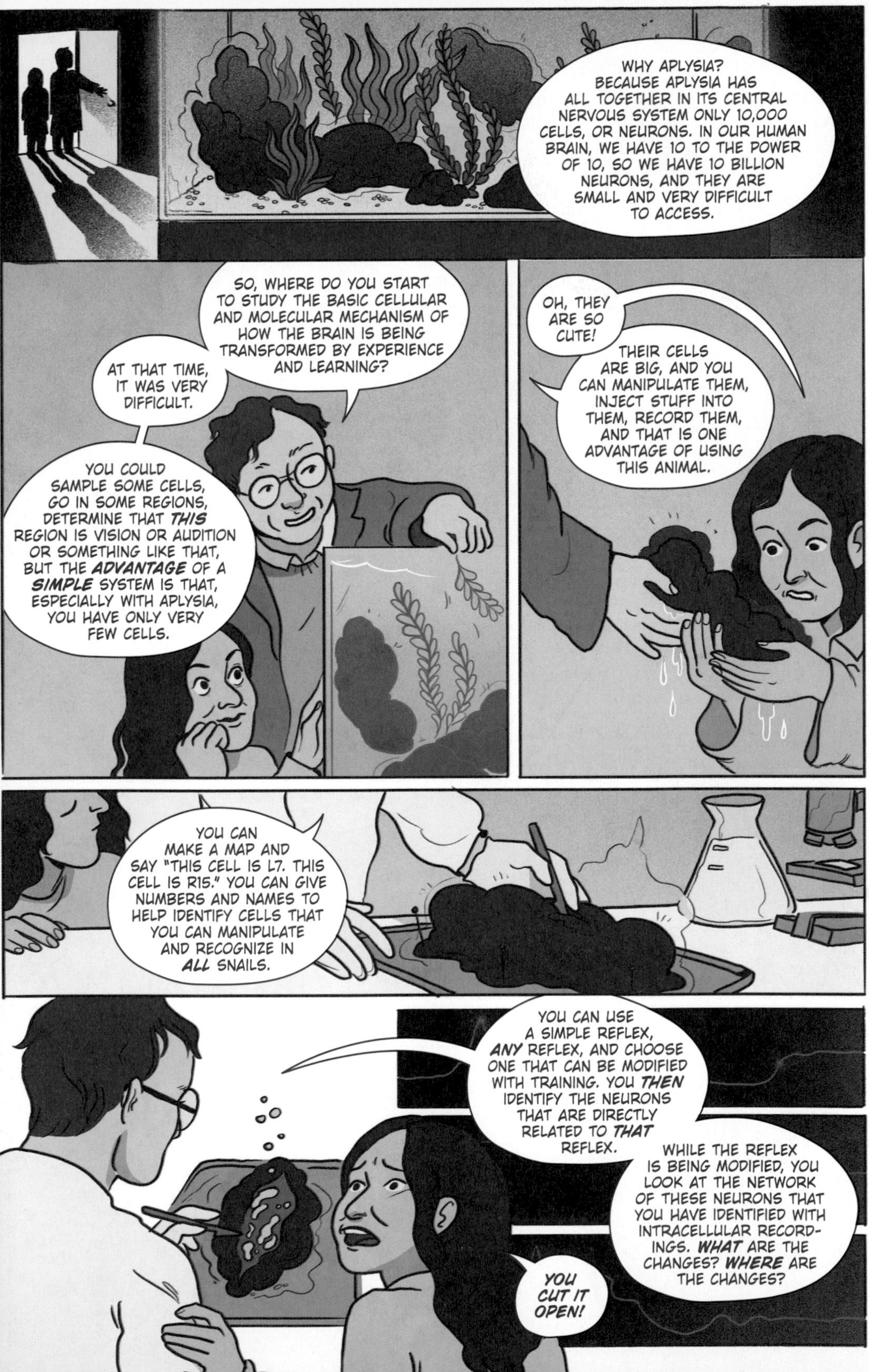
WHY APLYSIA? BECAUSE APLYSIA HAS ALL TOGETHER IN ITS CENTRAL NERVOUS SYSTEM ONLY 10,000 CELLS, OR NEURONS. IN OUR HUMAN BRAIN, WE HAVE 10 TO THE POWER OF 10, SO WE HAVE 10 BILLION NEURONS, AND THEY ARE SMALL AND VERY DIFFICULT TO ACCESS.
SO, WHERE DO YOU START TO STUDY THE BASIC CELLULAR AND MOLECULAR MECHANISM OF HOW THE BRAIN IS BEING TRANSFORMED BY EXPERIENCE AND LEARNING?
AT THAT TIME, IT WAS VERY DIFFICULT.
YOU COULD SAMPLE SOME CELLS, GO IN SOME REGIONS, DETERMINE THAT *THIS* REGION IS VISION OR AUDITION OR SOMETHING LIKE THAT, BUT THE *ADVANTAGE* OF A *SIMPLE* SYSTEM IS THAT, ESPECIALLY WITH APLYSIA, YOU HAVE ONLY VERY FEW CELLS.
OH, THEY ARE SO CUTE!
THEIR CELLS ARE BIG, AND YOU CAN MANIPULATE THEM, INJECT STUFF INTO THEM, RECORD THEM, AND THAT IS ONE ADVANTAGE OF USING THIS ANIMAL.
YOU CAN MAKE A MAP AND SAY "THIS CELL IS L7. THIS CELL IS R15." YOU CAN GIVE NUMBERS AND NAMES TO HELP IDENTIFY CELLS THAT YOU CAN MANIPULATE AND RECOGNIZE IN *ALL* SNAILS.
YOU CAN USE A SIMPLE REFLEX, *ANY* REFLEX, AND CHOOSE ONE THAT CAN BE MODIFIED WITH TRAINING. YOU *THEN* IDENTIFY THE NEURONS THAT ARE DIRECTLY RELATED TO *THAT* REFLEX.
WHILE THE REFLEX IS BEING MODIFIED, YOU LOOK AT THE NETWORK OF THESE NEURONS THAT YOU HAVE IDENTIFIED WITH INTRACELLULAR RECORD-INGS. *WHAT* ARE THE CHANGES? *WHERE* ARE THE CHANGES?
YOU CUT IT OPEN!

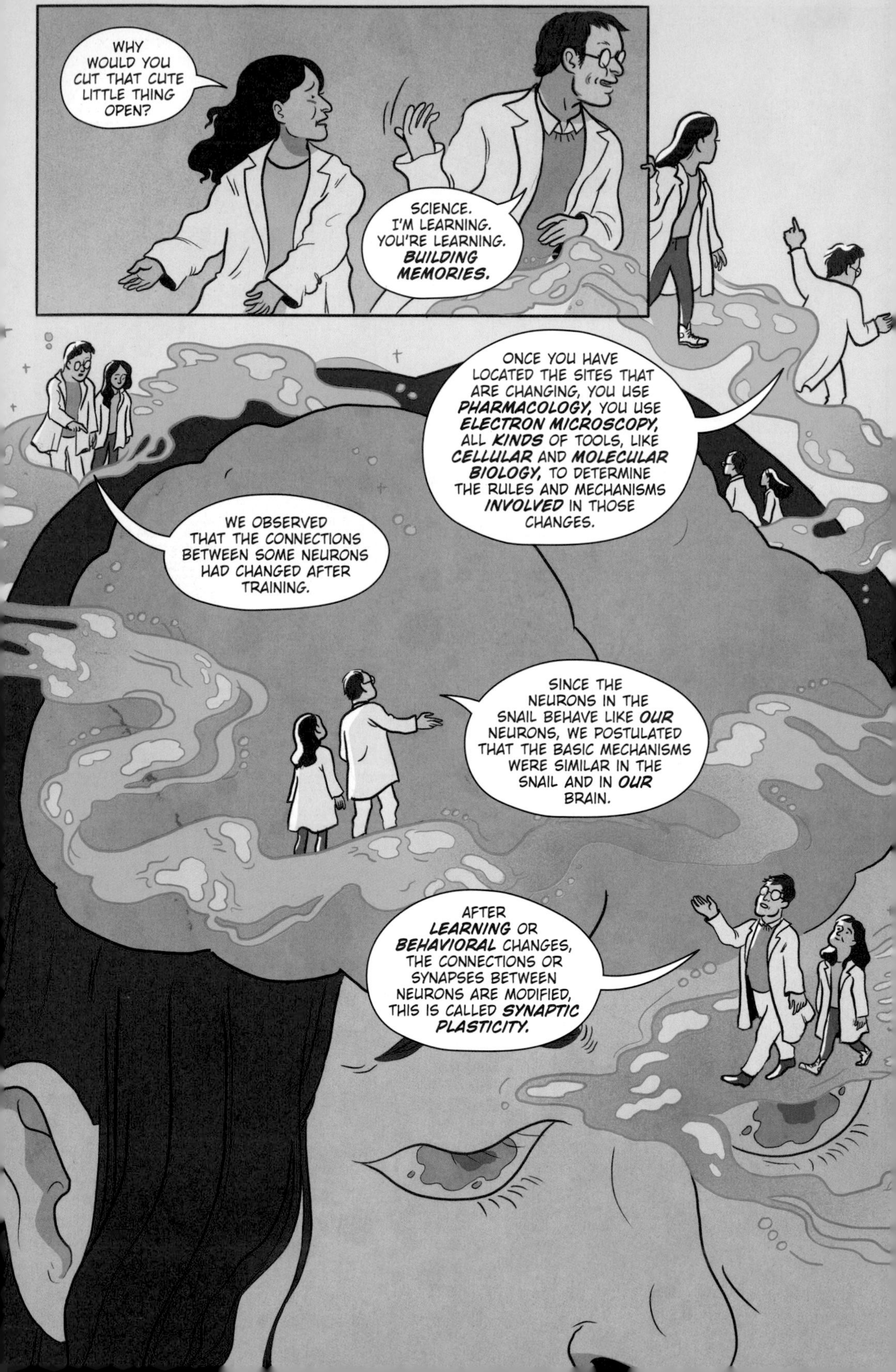
WHY WOULD YOU CUT THAT CUTE LITTLE THING OPEN?
SCIENCE. I'M LEARNING. YOU'RE LEARNING. **BUILDING MEMORIES.**
ONCE YOU HAVE LOCATED THE SITES THAT ARE CHANGING, YOU USE **PHARMACOLOGY,** YOU USE **ELECTRON MICROSCOPY,** ALL **KINDS** OF TOOLS, LIKE **CELLULAR** AND **MOLECULAR BIOLOGY,** TO DETERMINE THE RULES AND MECHANISMS **INVOLVED** IN THOSE CHANGES.
WE OBSERVED THAT THE CONNECTIONS BETWEEN SOME NEURONS HAD CHANGED AFTER TRAINING.
SINCE THE NEURONS IN THE SNAIL BEHAVE LIKE **OUR** NEURONS, WE POSTULATED THAT THE BASIC MECHANISMS WERE SIMILAR IN THE SNAIL AND IN **OUR** BRAIN.
AFTER **LEARNING** OR **BEHAVIORAL** CHANGES, THE CONNECTIONS OR SYNAPSES BETWEEN NEURONS ARE MODIFIED, THIS IS CALLED **SYNAPTIC PLASTICITY.**

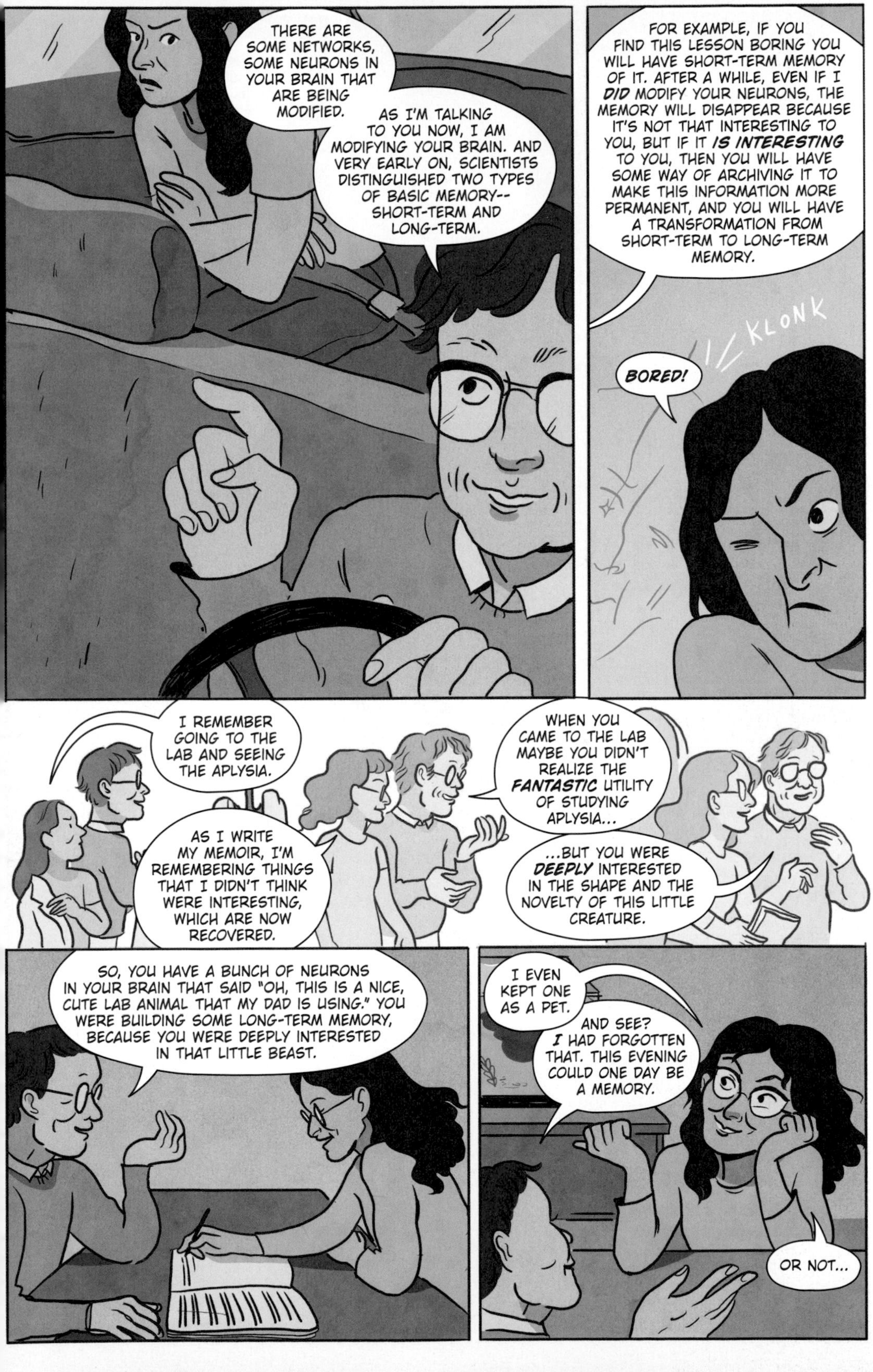
THERE ARE SOME NETWORKS, SOME NEURONS IN YOUR BRAIN THAT ARE BEING MODIFIED.
AS I'M TALKING TO YOU NOW, I AM MODIFYING YOUR BRAIN. AND VERY EARLY ON, SCIENTISTS DISTINGUISHED TWO TYPES OF BASIC MEMORY-- SHORT-TERM AND LONG-TERM.
FOR EXAMPLE, IF YOU FIND THIS LESSON BORING YOU WILL HAVE SHORT-TERM MEMORY OF IT. AFTER A WHILE, EVEN IF I *DID* MODIFY YOUR NEURONS, THE MEMORY WILL DISAPPEAR BECAUSE IT'S NOT THAT INTERESTING TO YOU, BUT IF IT *IS INTERESTING* TO YOU, THEN YOU WILL HAVE SOME WAY OF ARCHIVING IT TO MAKE THIS INFORMATION MORE PERMANENT, AND YOU WILL HAVE A TRANSFORMATION FROM SHORT-TERM TO LONG-TERM MEMORY.
KLONK
BORED!
I REMEMBER GOING TO THE LAB AND SEEING THE APLYSIA.
AS I WRITE MY MEMOIR, I'M REMEMBERING THINGS THAT I DIDN'T THINK WERE INTERESTING, WHICH ARE NOW RECOVERED.
WHEN YOU CAME TO THE LAB MAYBE YOU DIDN'T REALIZE THE *FANTASTIC* UTILITY OF STUDYING APLYSIA...
...BUT YOU WERE *DEEPLY* INTERESTED IN THE SHAPE AND THE NOVELTY OF THIS LITTLE CREATURE.
SO, YOU HAVE A BUNCH OF NEURONS IN YOUR BRAIN THAT SAID "OH, THIS IS A NICE, CUTE LAB ANIMAL THAT MY DAD IS USING." YOU WERE BUILDING SOME LONG-TERM MEMORY, BECAUSE YOU WERE DEEPLY INTERESTED IN THAT LITTLE BEAST.
I EVEN KEPT ONE AS A PET.
AND SEE? *I* HAD FORGOTTEN THAT. THIS EVENING COULD ONE DAY BE A MEMORY.
OR NOT...

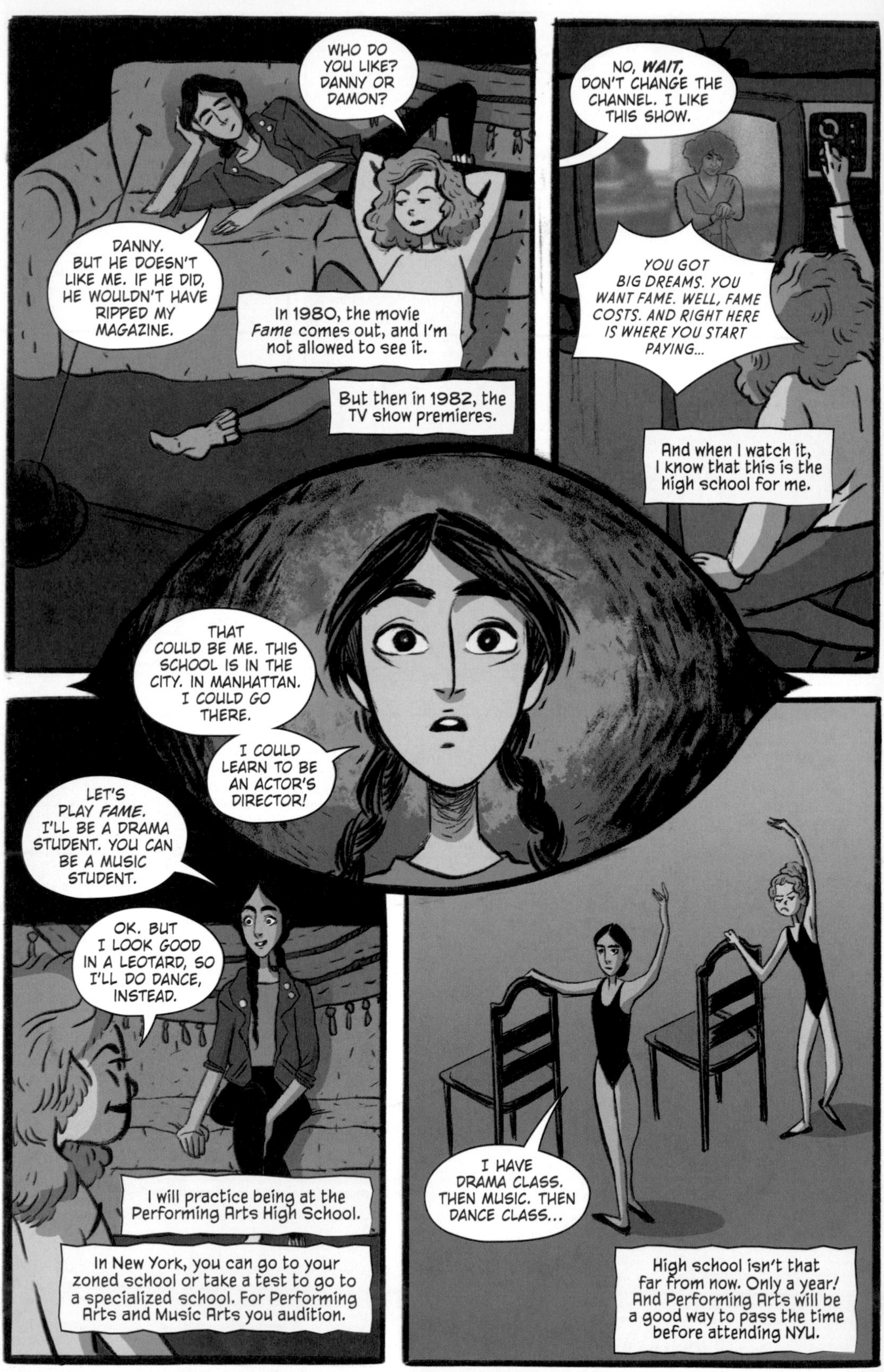

WHO DO YOU LIKE? DANNY OR DAMON?
DANNY. BUT HE DOESN'T LIKE ME. IF HE DID, HE WOULDN'T HAVE RIPPED MY MAGAZINE.
In 1980, the movie *Fame* comes out, and I'm not allowed to see it.
But then in 1982, the TV show premieres.
NO, ***WAIT,*** DON'T CHANGE THE CHANNEL. I LIKE THIS SHOW.
YOU GOT BIG DREAMS. YOU WANT FAME. WELL, FAME COSTS. AND RIGHT HERE IS WHERE YOU START PAYING...
And when I watch it, I know that this is the high school for me.
THAT COULD BE ME. THIS SCHOOL IS IN THE CITY. IN MANHATTAN. I COULD GO THERE.
I COULD LEARN TO BE AN ACTOR'S DIRECTOR!
LET'S PLAY *FAME*. I'LL BE A DRAMA STUDENT. YOU CAN BE A MUSIC STUDENT.
OK. BUT I LOOK GOOD IN A LEOTARD, SO I'LL DO DANCE, INSTEAD.
I will practice being at the Performing Arts High School.
In New York, you can go to your zoned school or take a test to go to a specialized school. For Performing Arts and Music Arts you audition.
I HAVE DRAMA CLASS. THEN MUSIC. THEN DANCE CLASS...
High school isn't that far from now. Only a year! And Performing Arts will be a good way to pass the time before attending NYU.

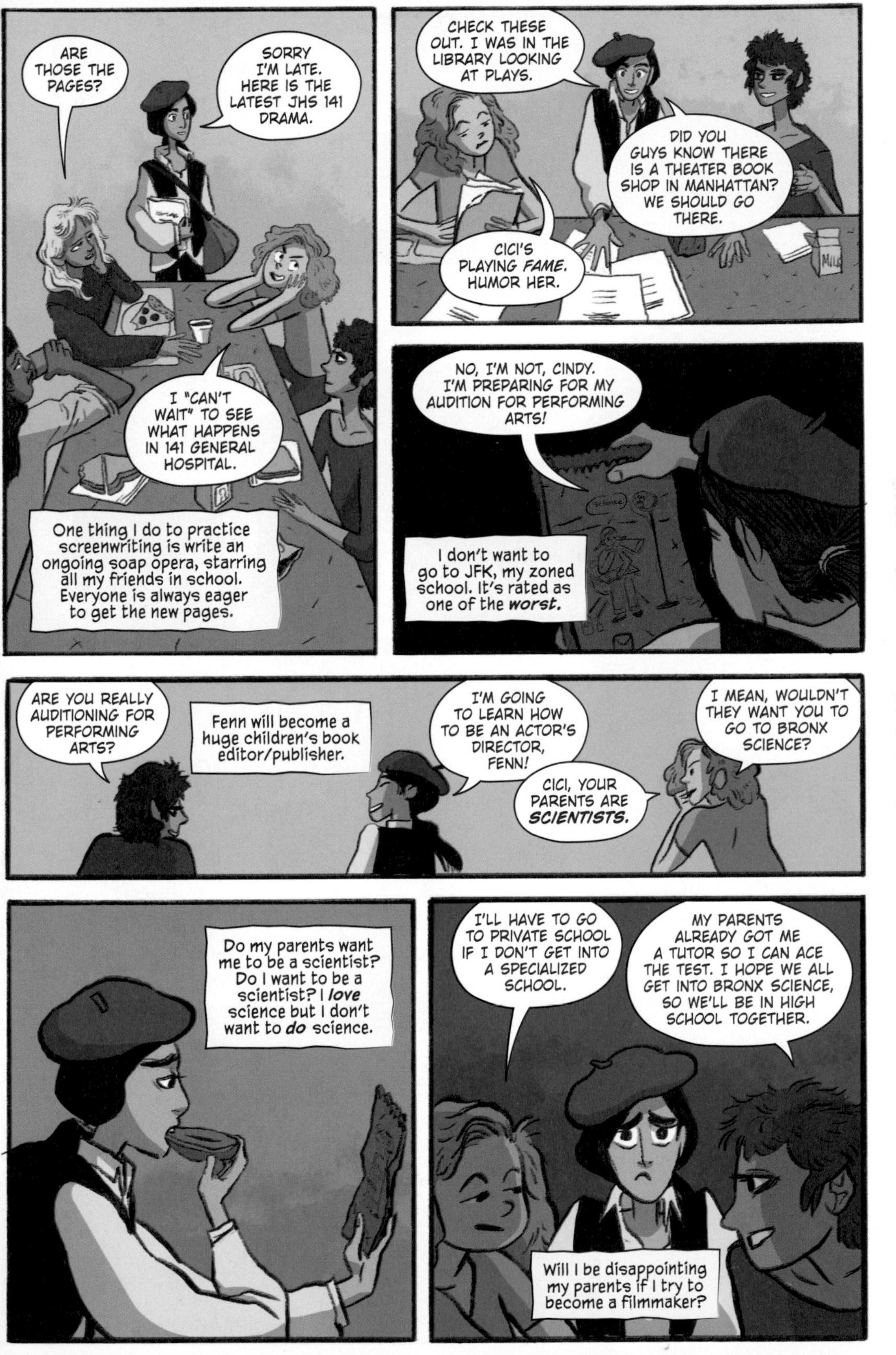
ARE THOSE THE PAGES?
SORRY I'M LATE. HERE IS THE LATEST JHS 141 DRAMA.
I "CAN'T WAIT" TO SEE WHAT HAPPENS IN 141 GENERAL HOSPITAL.
One thing I do to practice screenwriting is write an ongoing soap opera, starring all my friends in school. Everyone is always eager to get the new pages.
CHECK THESE OUT. I WAS IN THE LIBRARY LOOKING AT PLAYS.
DID YOU GUYS KNOW THERE IS A THEATER BOOK SHOP IN MANHATTAN? WE SHOULD GO THERE.
CICI'S PLAYING *FAME*. HUMOR HER.
NO, I'M NOT, CINDY. I'M PREPARING FOR MY AUDITION FOR PERFORMING ARTS!
I don't want to go to JFK, my zoned school. It's rated as one of the ***worst.***
ARE YOU REALLY AUDITIONING FOR PERFORMING ARTS?
Fenn will become a huge children's book editor/publisher.
I'M GOING TO LEARN HOW TO BE AN ACTOR'S DIRECTOR, FENN!
CICI, YOUR PARENTS ARE ***SCIENTISTS.***
I MEAN, WOULDN'T THEY WANT YOU TO GO TO BRONX SCIENCE?
Do my parents want me to be a scientist? Do I want to be a scientist? I ***love*** science but I don't want to ***do*** science.
I'LL HAVE TO GO TO PRIVATE SCHOOL IF I DON'T GET INTO A SPECIALIZED SCHOOL.
MY PARENTS ALREADY GOT ME A TUTOR SO I CAN ACE THE TEST. I HOPE WE ALL GET INTO BRONX SCIENCE, SO WE'LL BE IN HIGH SCHOOL TOGETHER.
Will I be disappointing my parents if I try to become a filmmaker?

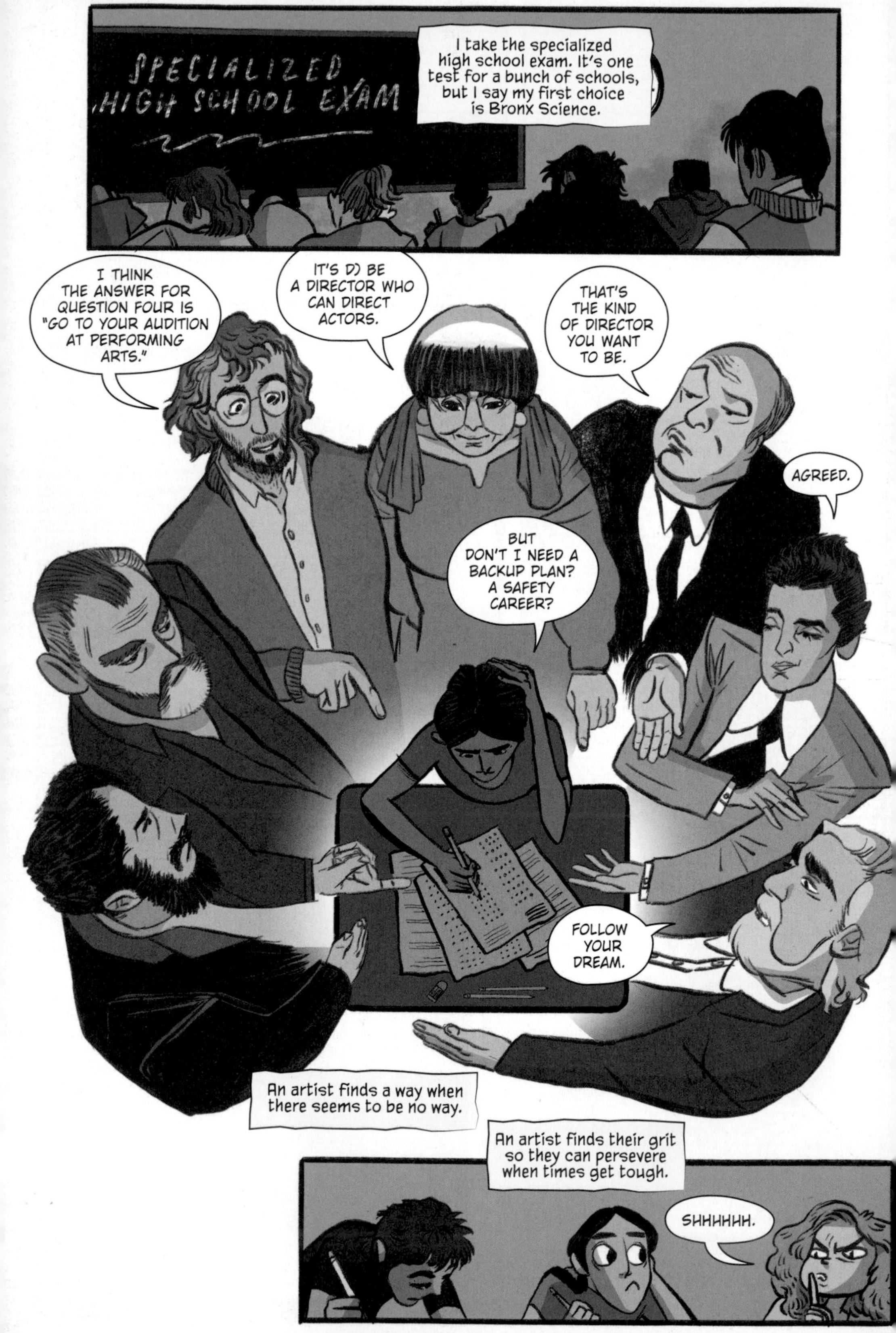
SPECIALIZED HIGH SCHOOL EXAM
I take the specialized high school exam. It's one test for a bunch of schools, but I say my first choice is Bronx Science.
I THINK THE ANSWER FOR QUESTION FOUR IS "GO TO YOUR AUDITION AT PERFORMING ARTS."
IT'S D) BE A DIRECTOR WHO CAN DIRECT ACTORS.
THAT'S THE KIND OF DIRECTOR YOU WANT TO BE.
AGREED.
BUT DON'T I NEED A BACKUP PLAN? A SAFETY CAREER?
FOLLOW YOUR DREAM.
An artist finds a way when there seems to be no way.
An artist finds their grit so they can persevere when times get tough.
SHHHHHH.

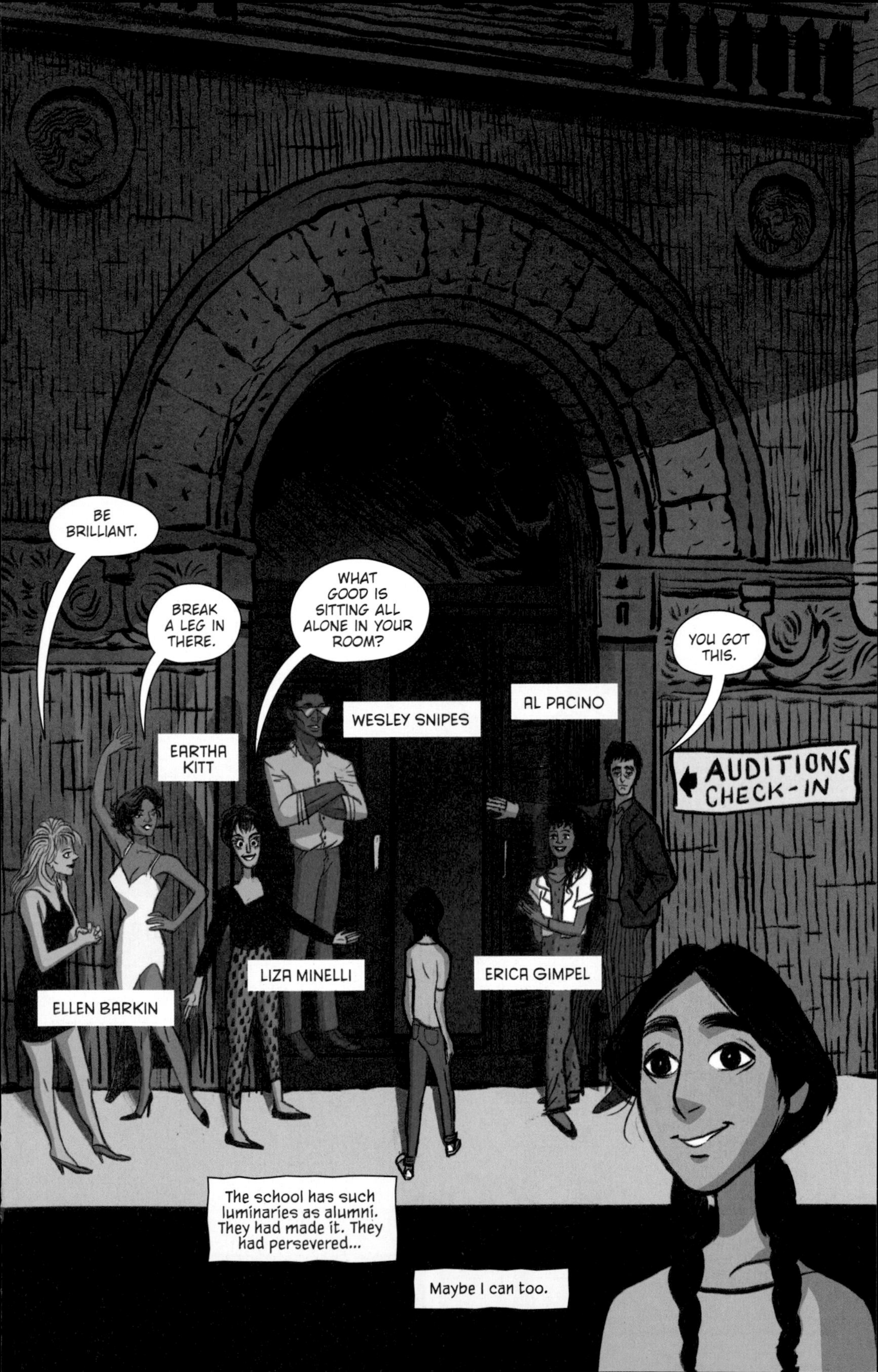
BE BRILLIANT.
BREAK A LEG IN THERE.
WHAT GOOD IS SITTING ALL ALONE IN YOUR ROOM?
YOU GOT THIS.
EARTHA KITT
WESLEY SNIPES
AL PACINO
AUDITIONS CHECK-IN
ELLEN BARKIN
LIZA MINELLI
ERICA GIMPEL
The school has such luminaries as alumni. They had made it. They had persevered...
Maybe I can too.

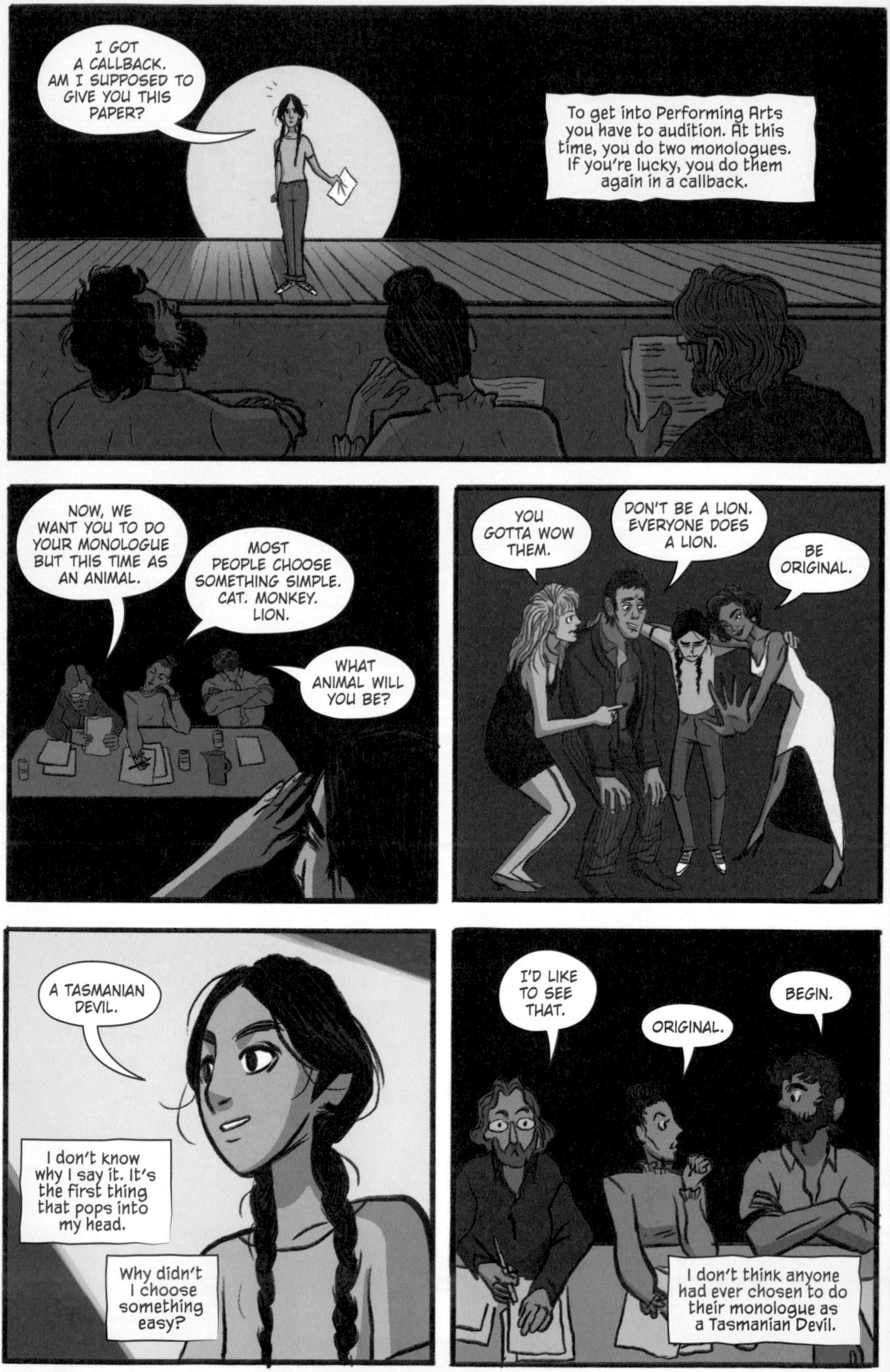
I GOT A CALLBACK. AM I SUPPOSED TO GIVE YOU THIS PAPER?
To get into Performing Arts you have to audition. At this time, you do two monologues. If you're lucky, you do them again in a callback.
NOW, WE WANT YOU TO DO YOUR MONOLOGUE BUT THIS TIME AS AN ANIMAL.
MOST PEOPLE CHOOSE SOMETHING SIMPLE. CAT. MONKEY. LION.
WHAT ANIMAL WILL YOU BE?
YOU GOTTA WOW THEM.
DON'T BE A LION. EVERYONE DOES A LION.
BE ORIGINAL.
A TASMANIAN DEVIL.
I don't know why I say it. It's the first thing that pops into my head.
Why didn't I choose something easy?
I'D LIKE TO SEE THAT.
ORIGINAL.
BEGIN.
I don't think anyone had ever chosen to do their monologue as a Tasmanian Devil.

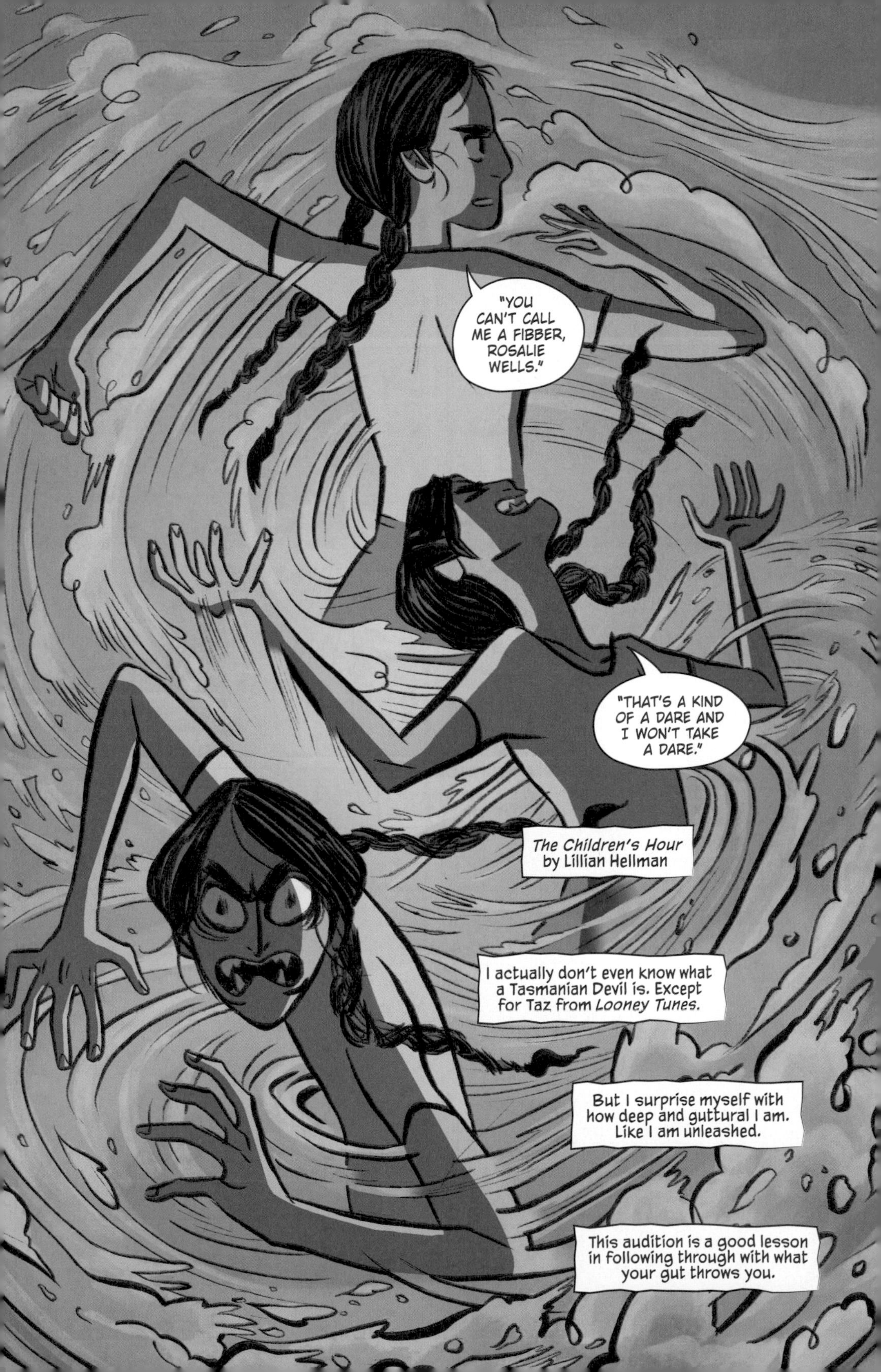
"YOU CAN'T CALL ME A FIBBER, ROSALIE WELLS."
"THAT'S A KIND OF A DARE AND I WON'T TAKE A DARE."
The Children's Hour by Lillian Hellman
I actually don't even know what a Tasmanian Devil is. Except for Taz from *Looney Tunes*.
But I surprise myself with how deep and guttural I am. Like I am unleashed.
This audition is a good lesson in following through with what your gut throws you.

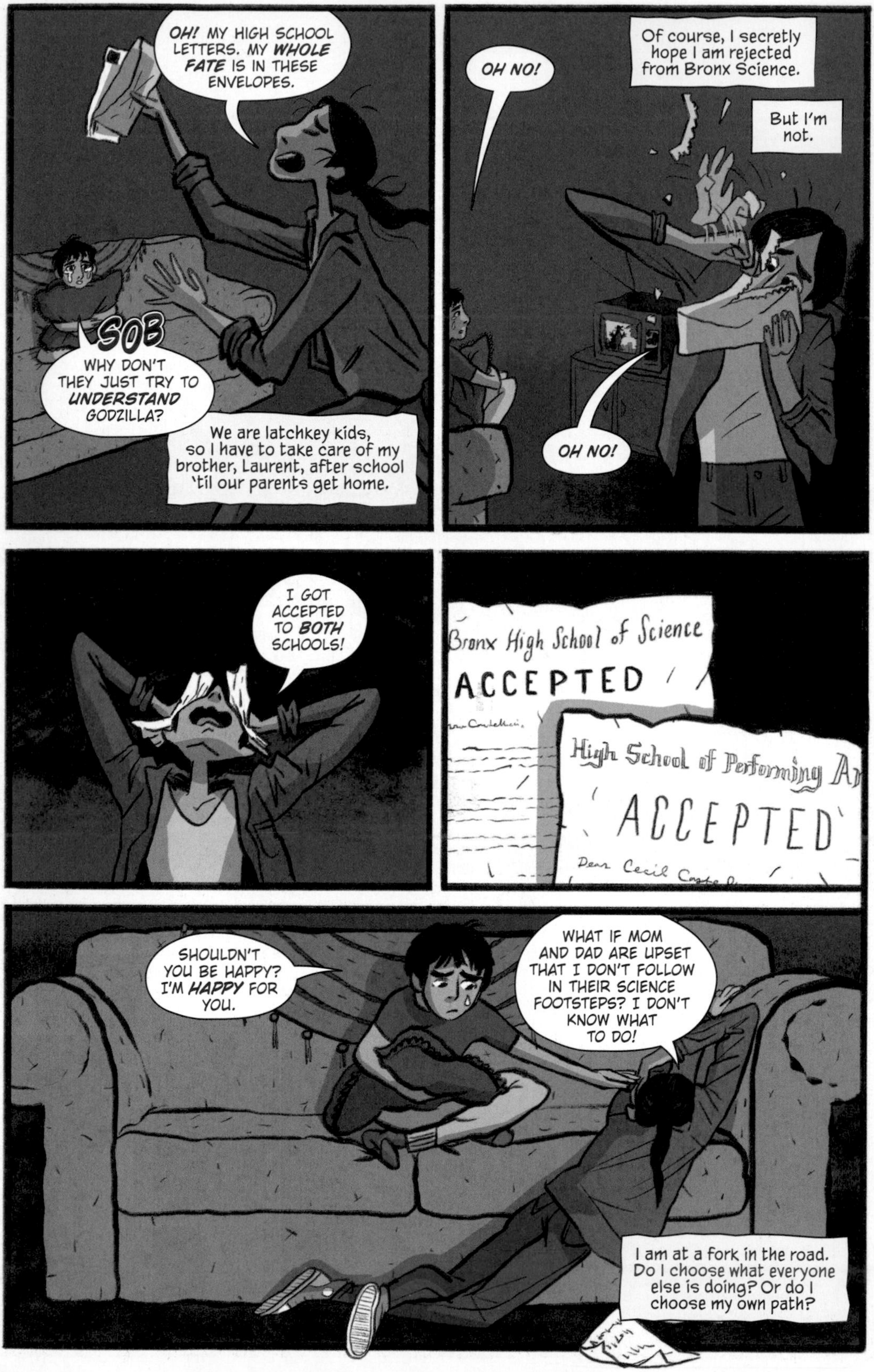
OH! MY HIGH SCHOOL LETTERS. MY WHOLE FATE IS IN THESE ENVELOPES.
SOB
WHY DON'T THEY JUST TRY TO UNDERSTAND GODZILLA?
We are latchkey kids, so I have to take care of my brother, Laurent, after school 'til our parents get home.
Of course, I secretly hope I am rejected from Bronx Science.
OH NO!
But I'm not.
OH NO!
I GOT ACCEPTED TO BOTH SCHOOLS!
Bronx High School of Science
ACCEPTED
High School of Performing Ar
ACCEPTED
Dear Cecil
SHOULDN'T YOU BE HAPPY? I'M HAPPY FOR YOU.
WHAT IF MOM AND DAD ARE UPSET THAT I DON'T FOLLOW IN THEIR SCIENCE FOOTSTEPS? I DON'T KNOW WHAT TO DO!
I am at a fork in the road. Do I choose what everyone else is doing? Or do I choose my own path?

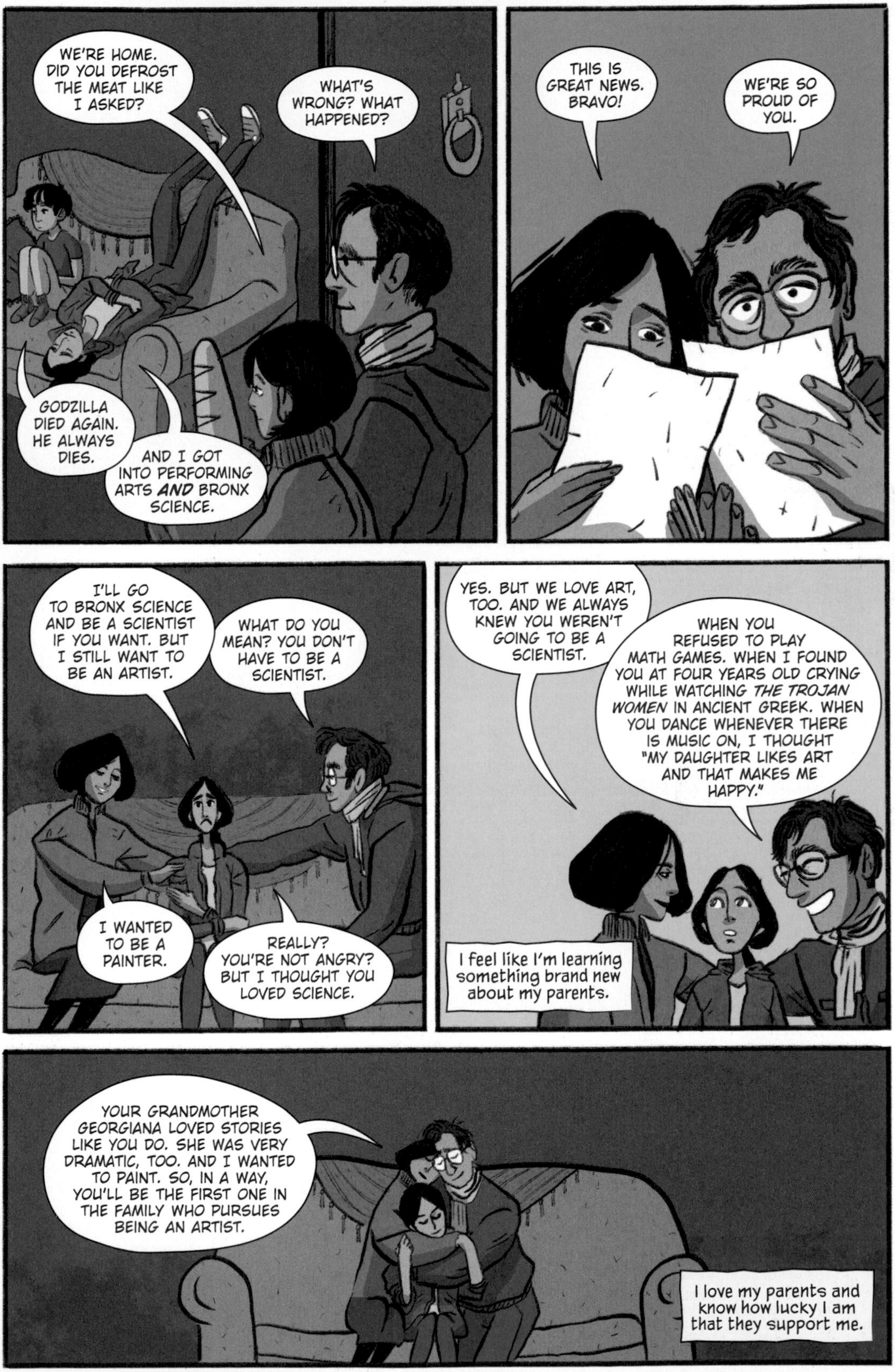
WE'RE HOME. DID YOU DEFROST THE MEAT LIKE I ASKED?
WHAT'S WRONG? WHAT HAPPENED?
GODZILLA DIED AGAIN. HE ALWAYS DIES.
AND I GOT INTO PERFORMING ARTS ***AND*** BRONX SCIENCE.
THIS IS GREAT NEWS. BRAVO!
WE'RE SO PROUD OF YOU.
I'LL GO TO BRONX SCIENCE AND BE A SCIENTIST IF YOU WANT. BUT I STILL WANT TO BE AN ARTIST.
WHAT DO YOU MEAN? YOU DON'T HAVE TO BE A SCIENTIST.
I WANTED TO BE A PAINTER.
REALLY? YOU'RE NOT ANGRY? BUT I THOUGHT YOU LOVED SCIENCE.
YES. BUT WE LOVE ART, TOO. AND WE ALWAYS KNEW YOU WEREN'T GOING TO BE A SCIENTIST.
WHEN YOU REFUSED TO PLAY MATH GAMES. WHEN I FOUND YOU AT FOUR YEARS OLD CRYING WHILE WATCHING *THE TROJAN WOMEN* IN ANCIENT GREEK. WHEN YOU DANCE WHENEVER THERE IS MUSIC ON, I THOUGHT "MY DAUGHTER LIKES ART AND THAT MAKES ME HAPPY."
I feel like I'm learning something brand new about my parents.
YOUR GRANDMOTHER GEORGIANA LOVED STORIES LIKE YOU DO. SHE WAS VERY DRAMATIC, TOO. AND I WANTED TO PAINT. SO, IN A WAY, YOU'LL BE THE FIRST ONE IN THE FAMILY WHO PURSUES BEING AN ARTIST.
I love my parents and know how lucky I am that they support me.

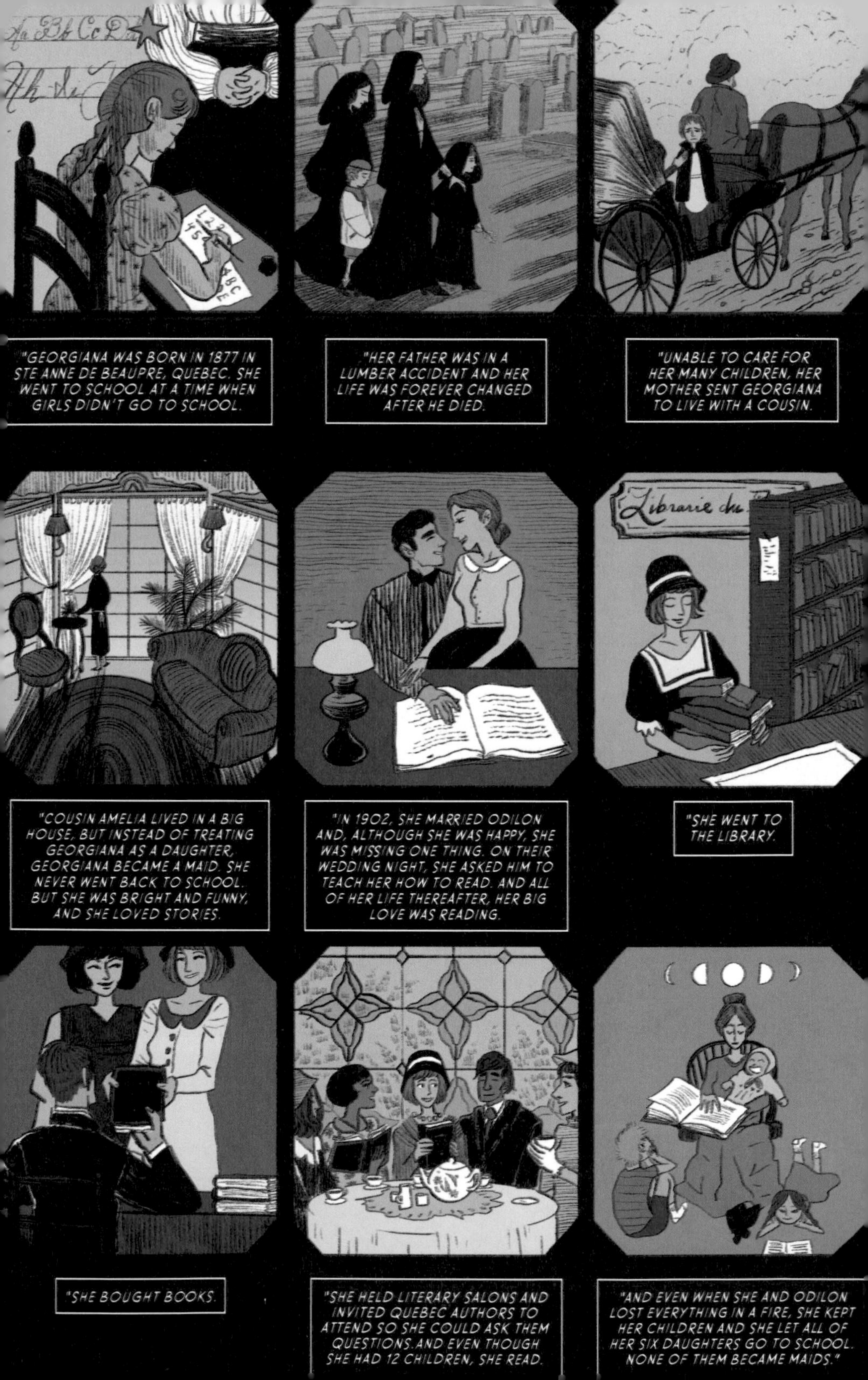
"GEORGIANA WAS BORN IN 1877 IN STE ANNE DE BEAUPRE, QUEBEC. SHE WENT TO SCHOOL AT A TIME WHEN GIRLS DIDN'T GO TO SCHOOL.
"HER FATHER WAS IN A LUMBER ACCIDENT AND HER LIFE WAS FOREVER CHANGED AFTER HE DIED.
"UNABLE TO CARE FOR HER MANY CHILDREN, HER MOTHER SENT GEORGIANA TO LIVE WITH A COUSIN.
"COUSIN AMELIA LIVED IN A BIG HOUSE, BUT INSTEAD OF TREATING GEORGIANA AS A DAUGHTER, GEORGIANA BECAME A MAID. SHE NEVER WENT BACK TO SCHOOL. BUT SHE WAS BRIGHT AND FUNNY, AND SHE LOVED STORIES.
"IN 1902, SHE MARRIED ODILON AND, ALTHOUGH SHE WAS HAPPY, SHE WAS MISSING ONE THING. ON THEIR WEDDING NIGHT, SHE ASKED HIM TO TEACH HER HOW TO READ. AND ALL OF HER LIFE THEREAFTER, HER BIG LOVE WAS READING.
Librarie du
"SHE WENT TO THE LIBRARY.
"SHE BOUGHT BOOKS.
"SHE HELD LITERARY SALONS AND INVITED QUEBEC AUTHORS TO ATTEND SO SHE COULD ASK THEM QUESTIONS. AND EVEN THOUGH SHE HAD 12 CHILDREN, SHE READ.
"AND EVEN WHEN SHE AND ODILON LOST EVERYTHING IN A FIRE, SHE KEPT HER CHILDREN AND SHE LET ALL OF HER SIX DAUGHTERS GO TO SCHOOL. NONE OF THEM BECAME MAIDS."

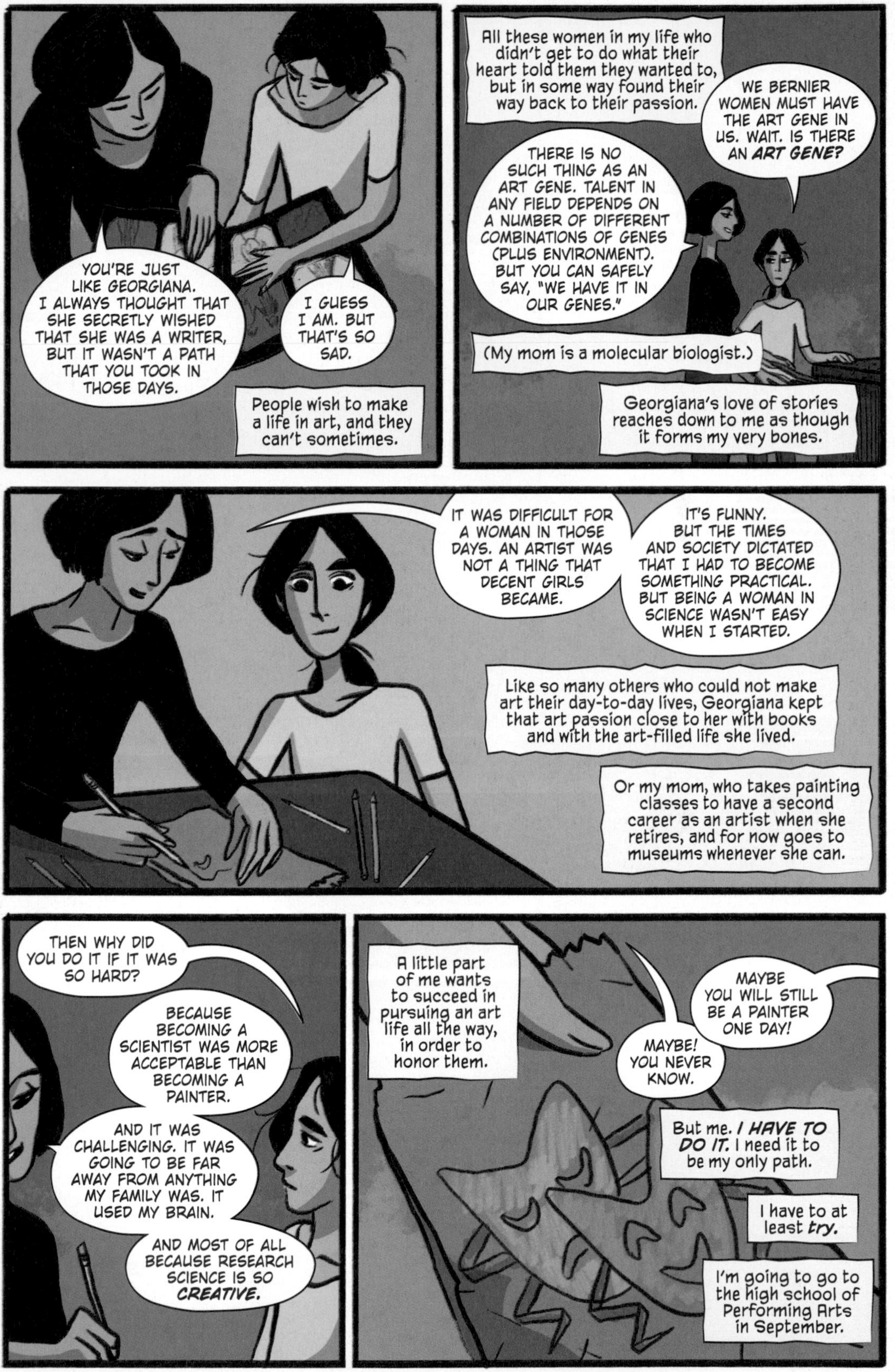

YOU'RE JUST LIKE GEORGIANA. I ALWAYS THOUGHT THAT SHE SECRETLY WISHED THAT SHE WAS A WRITER, BUT IT WASN'T A PATH THAT YOU TOOK IN THOSE DAYS.
I GUESS I AM. BUT THAT'S SO SAD.
People wish to make a life in art, and they can't sometimes.
All these women in my life who didn't get to do what their heart told them they wanted to, but in some way found their way back to their passion.
WE BERNIER WOMEN MUST HAVE THE ART GENE IN US. WAIT. IS THERE AN ***ART GENE?***
THERE IS NO SUCH THING AS AN ART GENE. TALENT IN ANY FIELD DEPENDS ON A NUMBER OF DIFFERENT COMBINATIONS OF GENES (PLUS ENVIRONMENT). BUT YOU CAN SAFELY SAY, "WE HAVE IT IN OUR GENES."
(My mom is a molecular biologist.)
Georgiana's love of stories reaches down to me as though it forms my very bones.
IT WAS DIFFICULT FOR A WOMAN IN THOSE DAYS. AN ARTIST WAS NOT A THING THAT DECENT GIRLS BECAME.
IT'S FUNNY. BUT THE TIMES AND SOCIETY DICTATED THAT I HAD TO BECOME SOMETHING PRACTICAL. BUT BEING A WOMAN IN SCIENCE WASN'T EASY WHEN I STARTED.
Like so many others who could not make art their day-to-day lives, Georgiana kept that art passion close to her with books and with the art-filled life she lived.
Or my mom, who takes painting classes to have a second career as an artist when she retires, and for now goes to museums whenever she can.
THEN WHY DID YOU DO IT IF IT WAS SO HARD?
BECAUSE BECOMING A SCIENTIST WAS MORE ACCEPTABLE THAN BECOMING A PAINTER.
AND IT WAS CHALLENGING. IT WAS GOING TO BE FAR AWAY FROM ANYTHING MY FAMILY WAS. IT USED MY BRAIN.
AND MOST OF ALL BECAUSE RESEARCH SCIENCE IS SO ***CREATIVE.***
A little part of me wants to succeed in pursuing an art life all the way, in order to honor them.
MAYBE YOU WILL STILL BE A PAINTER ONE DAY!
MAYBE! YOU NEVER KNOW.
But me. ***I HAVE TO DO IT.*** I need it to be my only path.
I have to at least ***try.***
I'm going to go to the high school of Performing Arts in September.

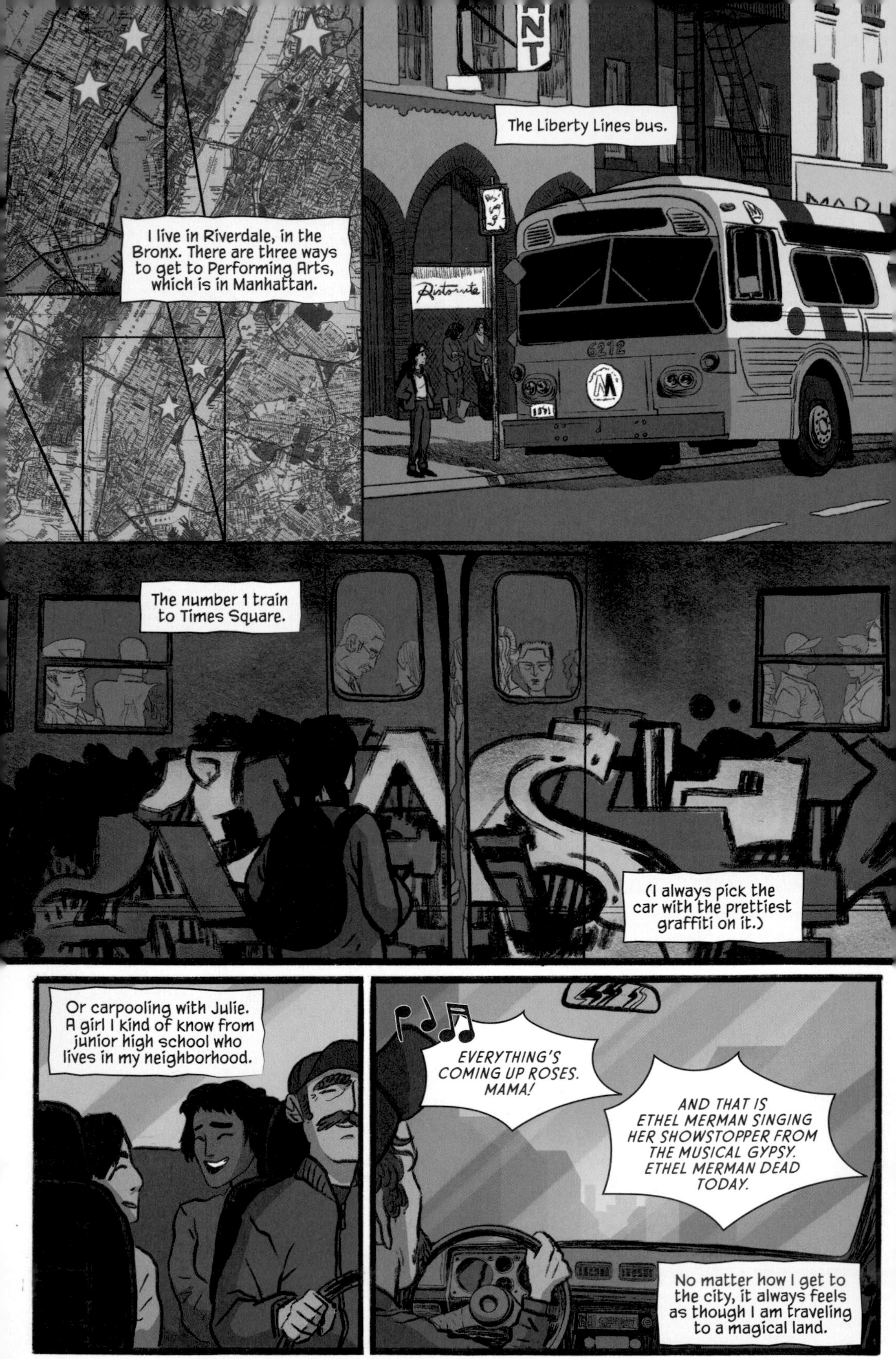
I live in Riverdale, in the Bronx. There are three ways to get to Performing Arts, which is in Manhattan.
The Liberty Lines bus.
6212
The number 1 train to Times Square.
(I always pick the car with the prettiest graffiti on it.)
Or carpooling with Julie. A girl I kind of know from junior high school who lives in my neighborhood.
EVERYTHING'S COMING UP ROSES. MAMA!
AND THAT IS ETHEL MERMAN SINGING HER SHOWSTOPPER FROM THE MUSICAL GYPSY. ETHEL MERMAN DEAD TODAY.
No matter how I get to the city, it always feels as though I am traveling to a magical land.

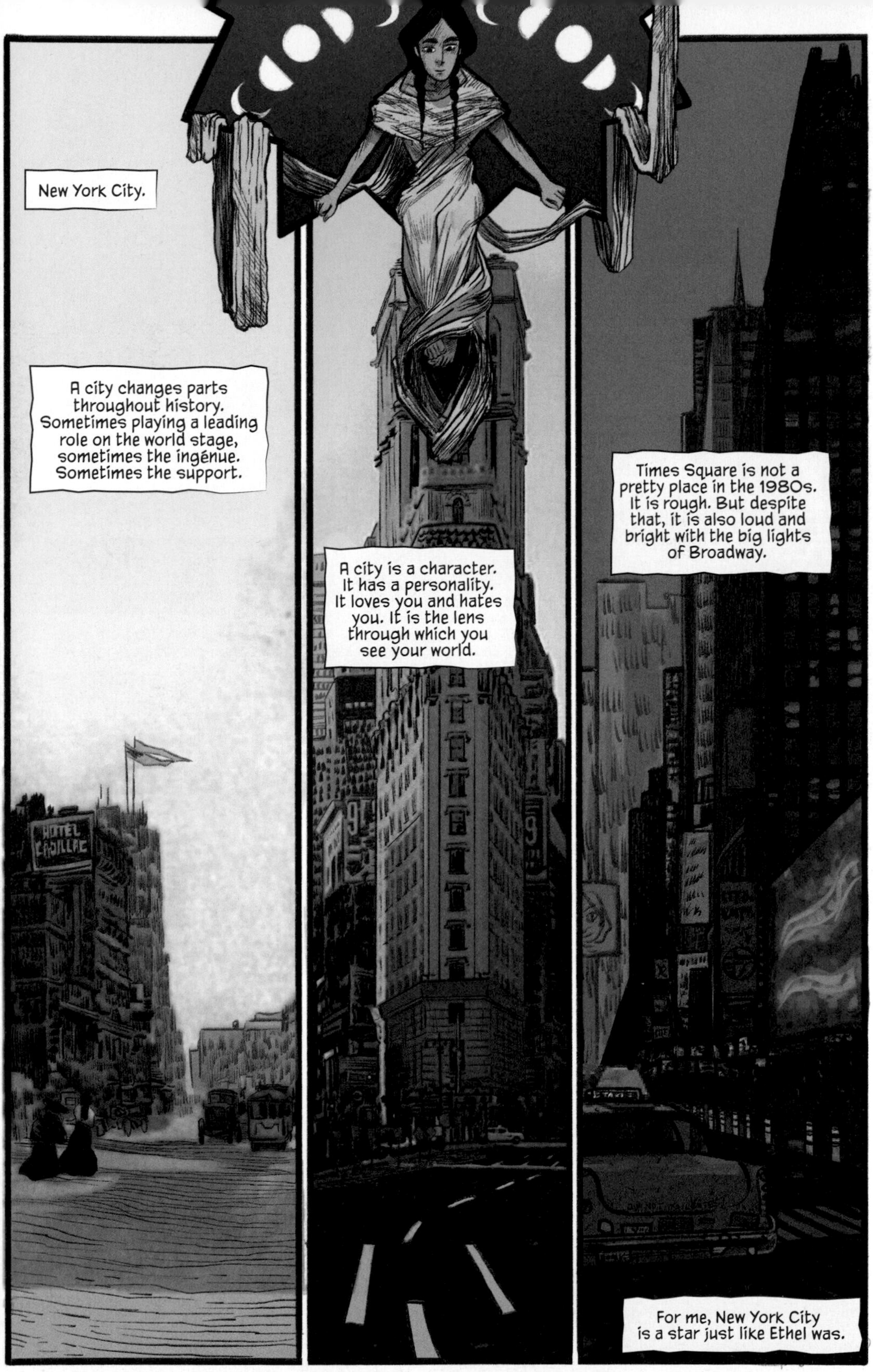
New York City.
A city changes parts throughout history. Sometimes playing a leading role on the world stage, sometimes the ingénue. Sometimes the support.
HOTEL CADILLAC
A city is a character. It has a personality. It loves you and hates you. It is the lens through which you see your world.
Times Square is not a pretty place in the 1980s. It is rough. But despite that, it is also loud and bright with the big lights of Broadway.
For me, New York City is a star just like Ethel was.

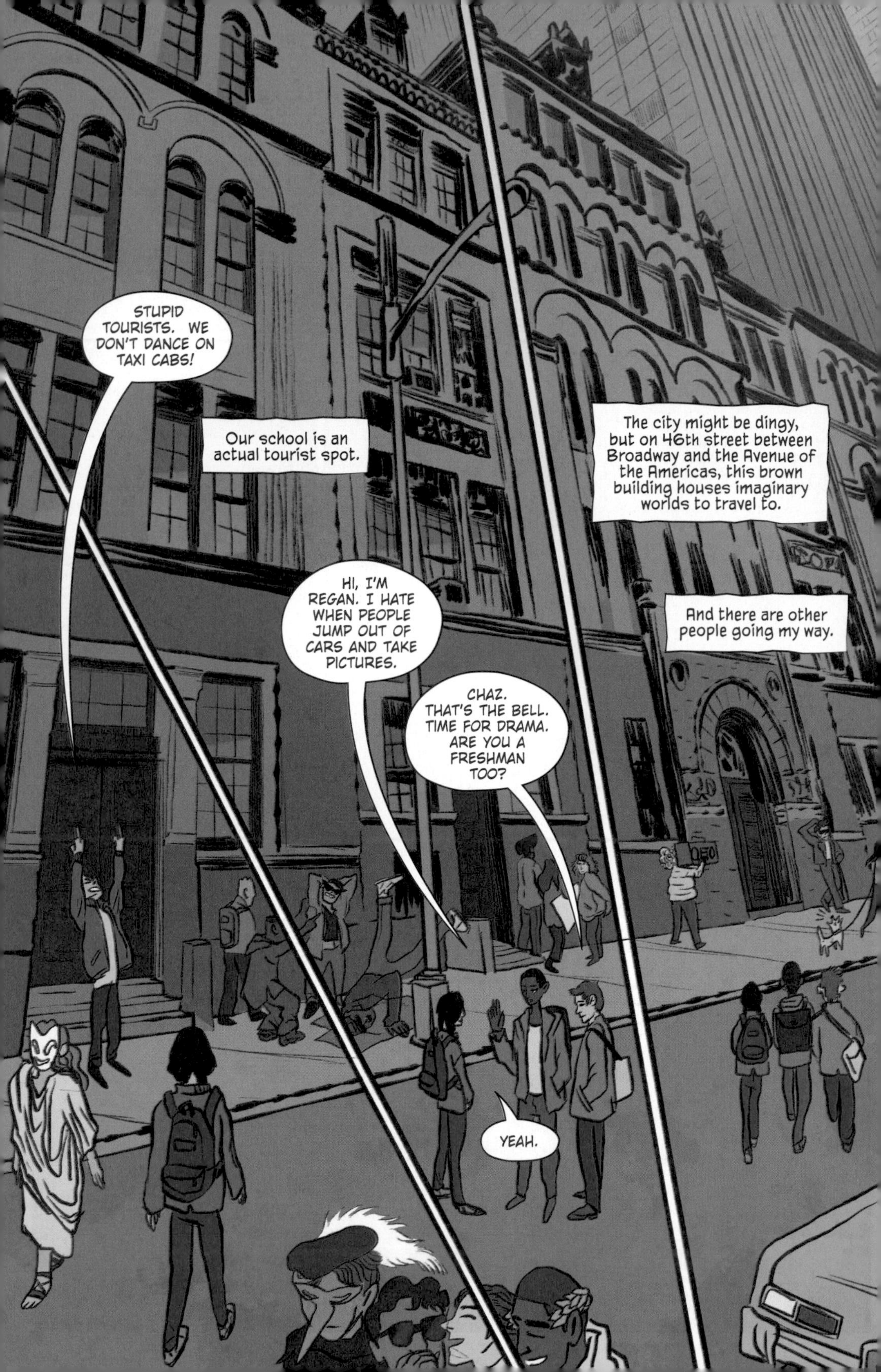
STUPID TOURISTS. WE DON'T DANCE ON TAXI CABS!
Our school is an actual tourist spot.
The city might be dingy, but on 46th street between Broadway and the Avenue of the Americas, this brown building houses imaginary worlds to travel to.
HI, I'M REGAN. I HATE WHEN PEOPLE JUMP OUT OF CARS AND TAKE PICTURES.
And there are other people going my way.
CHAZ. THAT'S THE BELL. TIME FOR DRAMA. ARE YOU A FRESHMAN TOO?
YEAH.

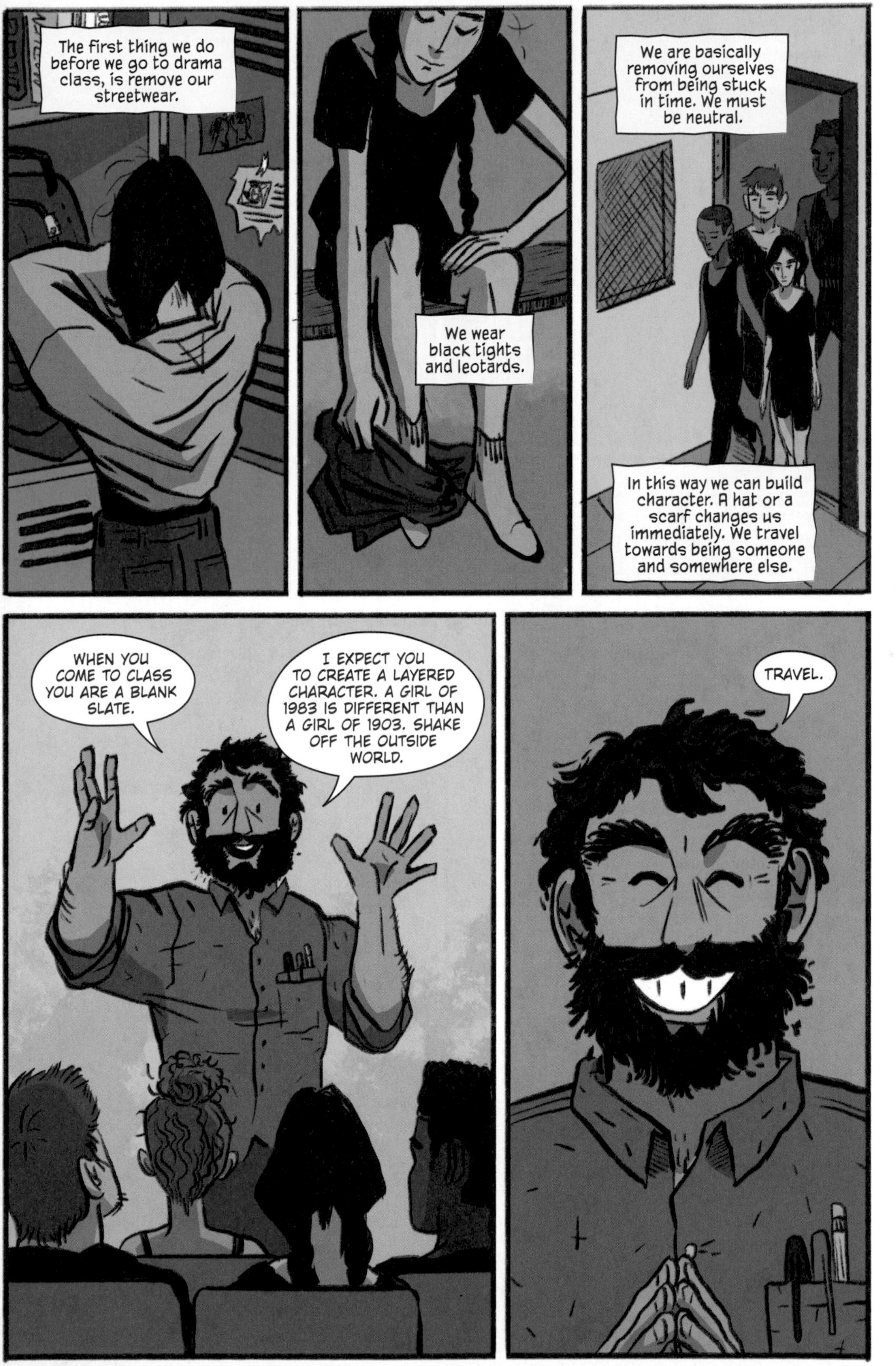
The first thing we do before we go to drama class, is remove our streetwear.
We wear black tights and leotards.
We are basically removing ourselves from being stuck in time. We must be neutral.
In this way we can build character. A hat or a scarf changes us immediately. We travel towards being someone and somewhere else.
WHEN YOU COME TO CLASS YOU ARE A BLANK SLATE.
I EXPECT YOU TO CREATE A LAYERED CHARACTER. A GIRL OF 1983 IS DIFFERENT THAN A GIRL OF 1903. SHAKE OFF THE OUTSIDE WORLD.
TRAVEL.

And travel I do.

You're a Good Man Charlie Brown by Clark Gesner based on the cartoon by Charles M. Schulz

"NAME ONE. JUST TELL ME ONE SINGLE REASON WHY I SHOULD STILL DESERVE TO GO ON LIVING ON THIS PLANET."

"WELL, FOR ONE THING, YOU HAVE A LITTLE BROTHER WHO LOVES YOU."

"EVERY NOW AND THEN I SAY THE RIGHT THING."

Our "exam" for drama class is to present a scene.

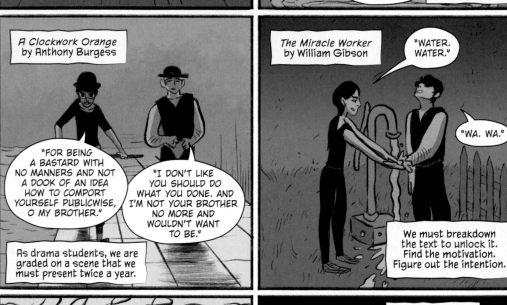

A Clockwork Orange by Anthony Burgess

"FOR BEING A BASTARD WITH NO MANNERS AND NOT A DOOK OF AN IDEA HOW TO COMPORT YOURSELF PUBLICWISE, O MY BROTHER."

"I DON'T LIKE YOU SHOULD DO WHAT YOU DONE. AND I'M NOT YOUR BROTHER NO MORE AND WOULDN'T WANT TO BE."

As drama students, we are graded on a scene that we must present twice a year.

The Miracle Worker by William Gibson

"WATER. WATER."

"WA. WA."

We must breakdown the text to unlock it. Find the motivation. Figure out the intention.

The Madwomen of Chaillot by Jean Giradoux

"I HATE UGLINESS. I LOVE BEAUTY. I HATE MEANNESS. I ADORE KINDNESS. IT MAY NOT SEEM SO GRAND TO SOME TO BE A WAITRESS IN PARIS. I LOVE IT."

We are living, breathing, time-traveling through stories.

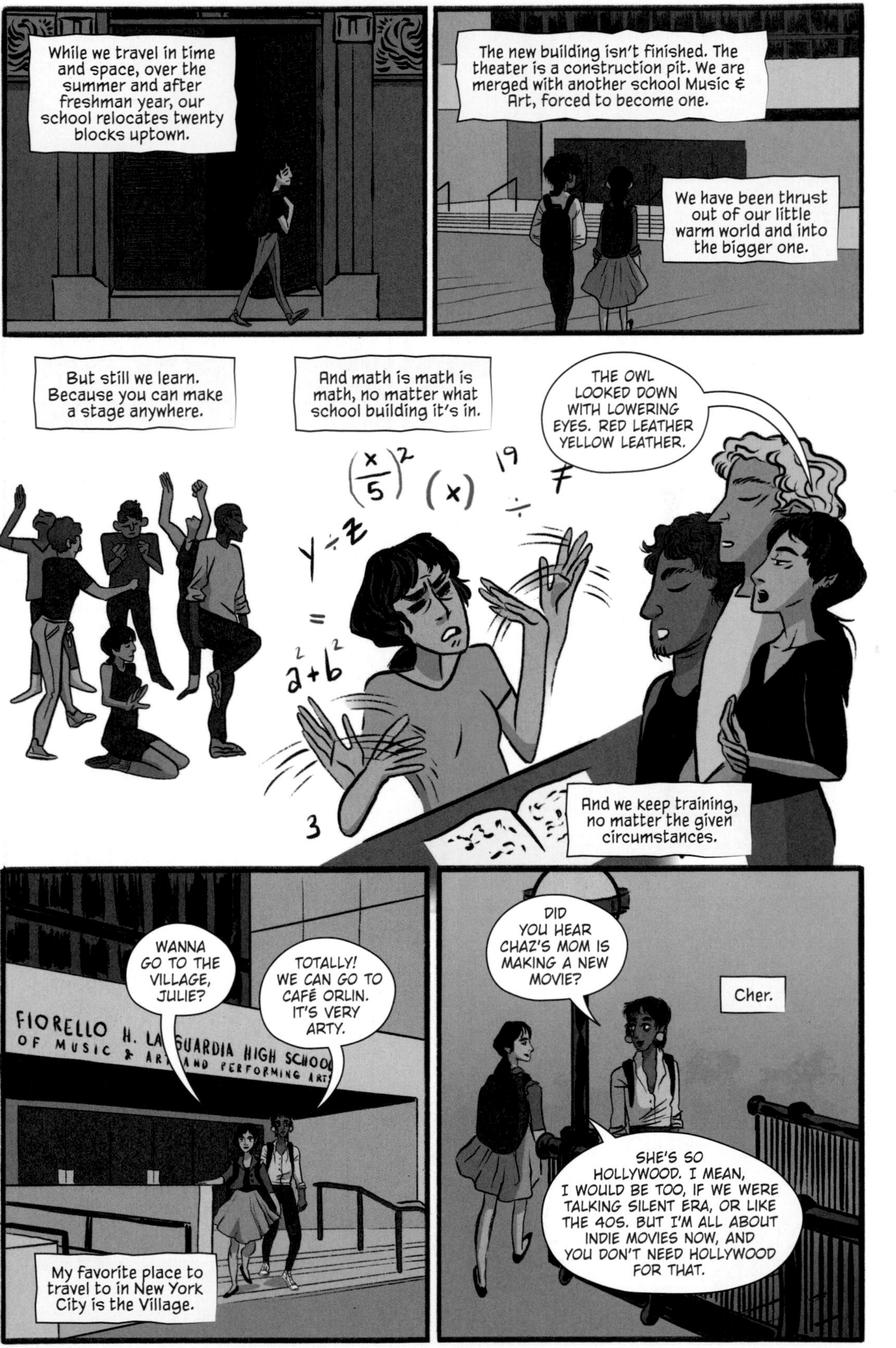

While we travel in time and space, over the summer and after freshman year, our school relocates twenty blocks uptown.
The new building isn't finished. The theater is a construction pit. We are merged with another school Music & Art, forced to become one.
We have been thrust out of our little warm world and into the bigger one.
But still we learn. Because you can make a stage anywhere.
And math is math is math, no matter what school building it's in.
THE OWL LOOKED DOWN WITH LOWERING EYES. RED LEATHER YELLOW LEATHER.
And we keep training, no matter the given circumstances.
FIORELLO H. LAGUARDIA HIGH SCHOOL OF MUSIC & ART AND PERFORMING ARTS
WANNA GO TO THE VILLAGE, JULIE?
TOTALLY! WE CAN GO TO CAFÉ ORLIN. IT'S VERY ARTY.
My favorite place to travel to in New York City is the Village.
DID YOU HEAR CHAZ'S MOM IS MAKING A NEW MOVIE?
Cher.
SHE'S SO HOLLYWOOD. I MEAN, I WOULD BE TOO, IF WE WERE TALKING SILENT ERA, OR LIKE THE 40S. BUT I'M ALL ABOUT INDIE MOVIES NOW, AND YOU DON'T NEED HOLLYWOOD FOR THAT.

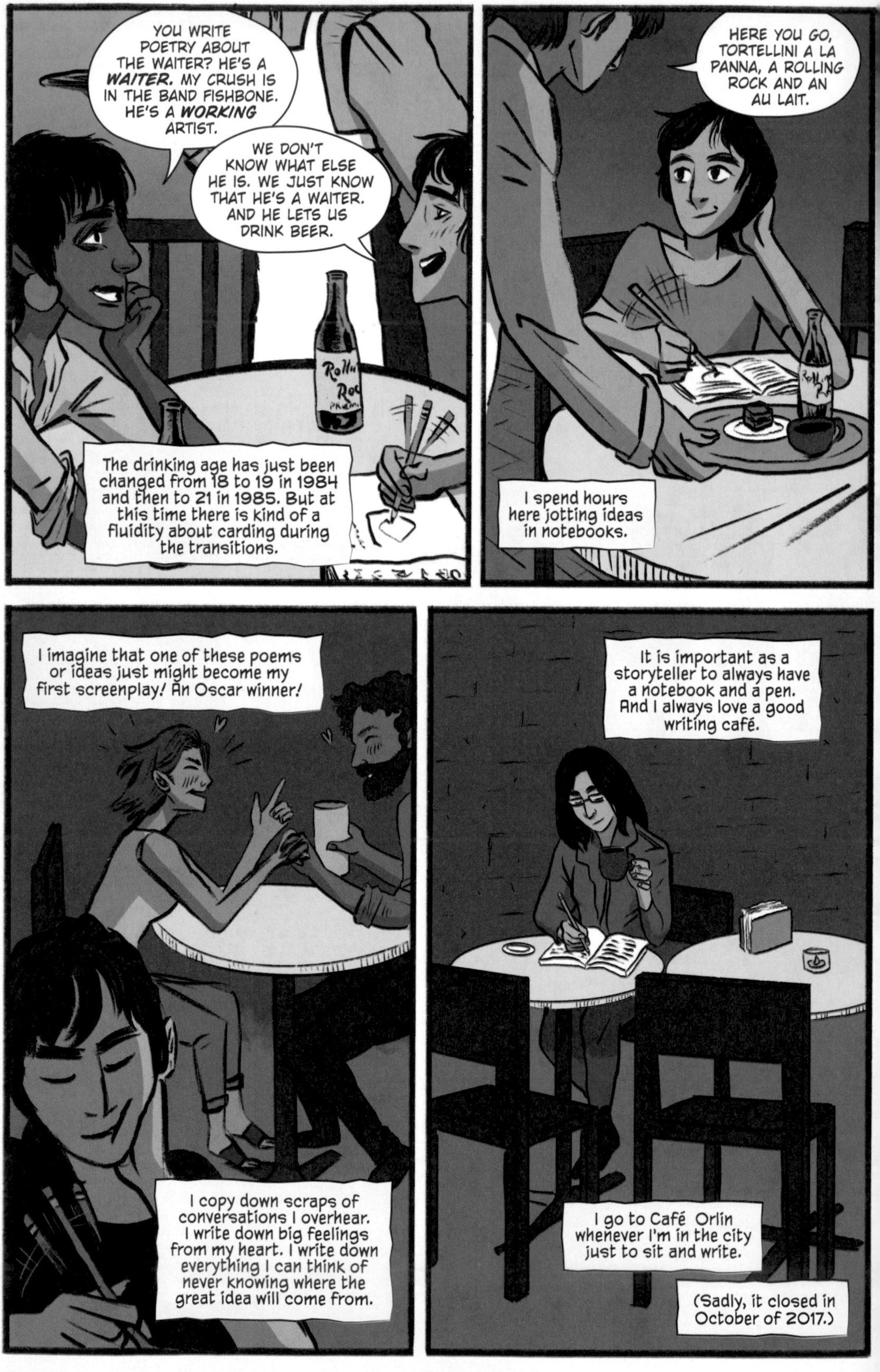
YOU WRITE POETRY ABOUT THE WAITER? HE'S A **WAITER.** MY CRUSH IS IN THE BAND FISHBONE. HE'S A **WORKING** ARTIST.
WE DON'T KNOW WHAT ELSE HE IS. WE JUST KNOW THAT HE'S A WAITER. AND HE LETS US DRINK BEER.
The drinking age has just been changed from 18 to 19 in 1984 and then to 21 in 1985. But at this time there is kind of a fluidity about carding during the transitions.
HERE YOU GO, TORTELLINI A LA PANNA, A ROLLING ROCK AND AN AU LAIT.
I spend hours here jotting ideas in notebooks.
I imagine that one of these poems or ideas just might become my first screenplay! An Oscar winner!
I copy down scraps of conversations I overhear. I write down big feelings from my heart. I write down everything I can think of never knowing where the great idea will come from.
It is important as a storyteller to always have a notebook and a pen. And I always love a good writing café.
I go to Café Orlin whenever I'm in the city just to sit and write.
(Sadly, it closed in October of 2017.)

THE WIDOW CLAIRE BY ...TON ...TE

Theater helps me to travel even further away. Even back in time. I start seeing at least one play a week during my sophomore year.

I discover new favorite storytellers.

Biloxi Blues by Neil Simon

I laugh with masters at the height of their craft.

The Normal Heart by Larry Kramer

And see how stories shout the times and reflect the era they are told in.

The Widow Claire

LAYBILL PLAYBILL PLAYBILL SHOWBILL PLAYBILL SHOWBILL PL

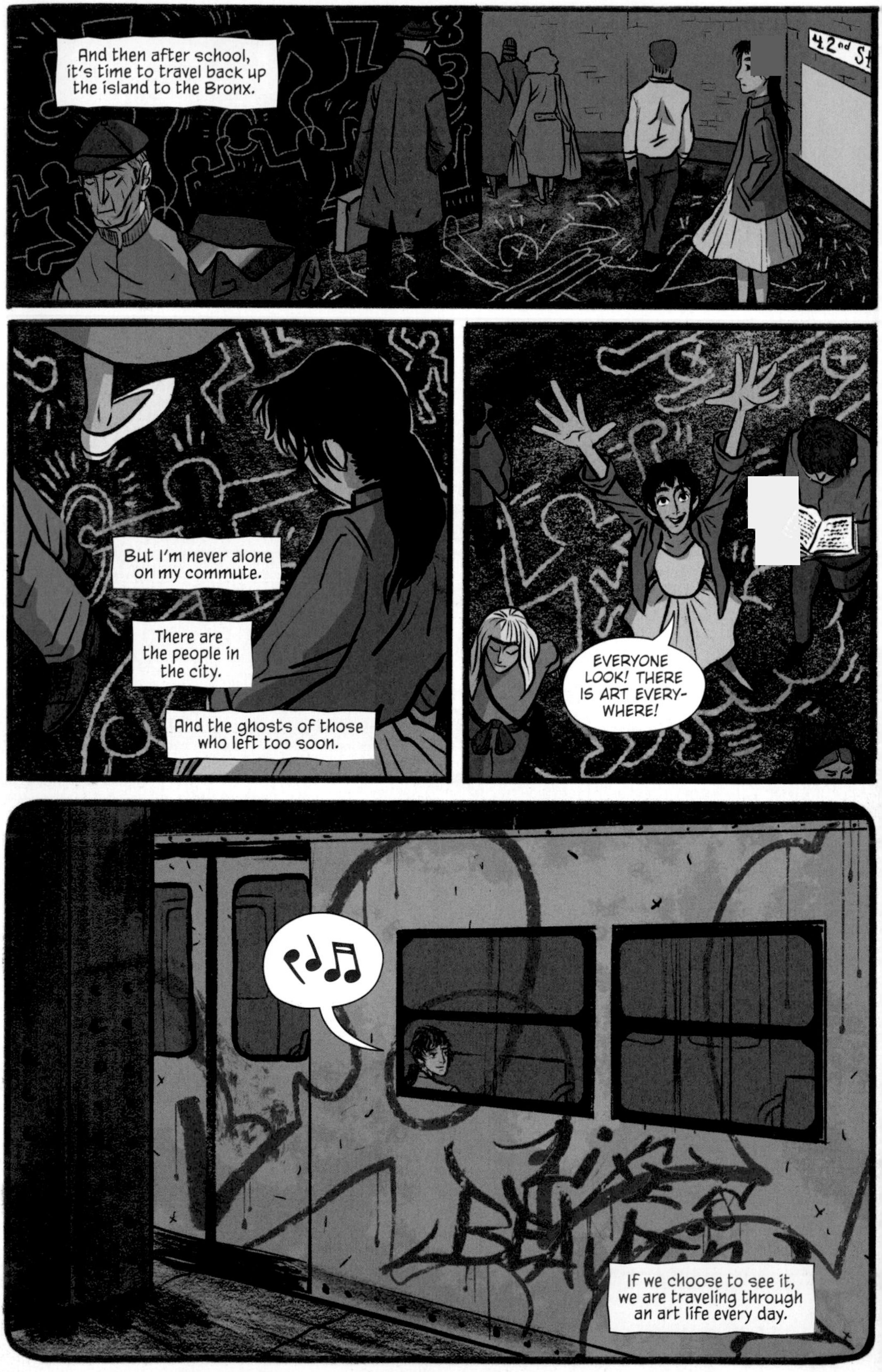
And then after school, it's time to travel back up the island to the Bronx.
But I'm never alone on my commute.
There are the people in the city.
And the ghosts of those who left too soon.
EVERYONE LOOK! THERE IS ART EVERY-WHERE!
If we choose to see it, we are traveling through an art life every day.

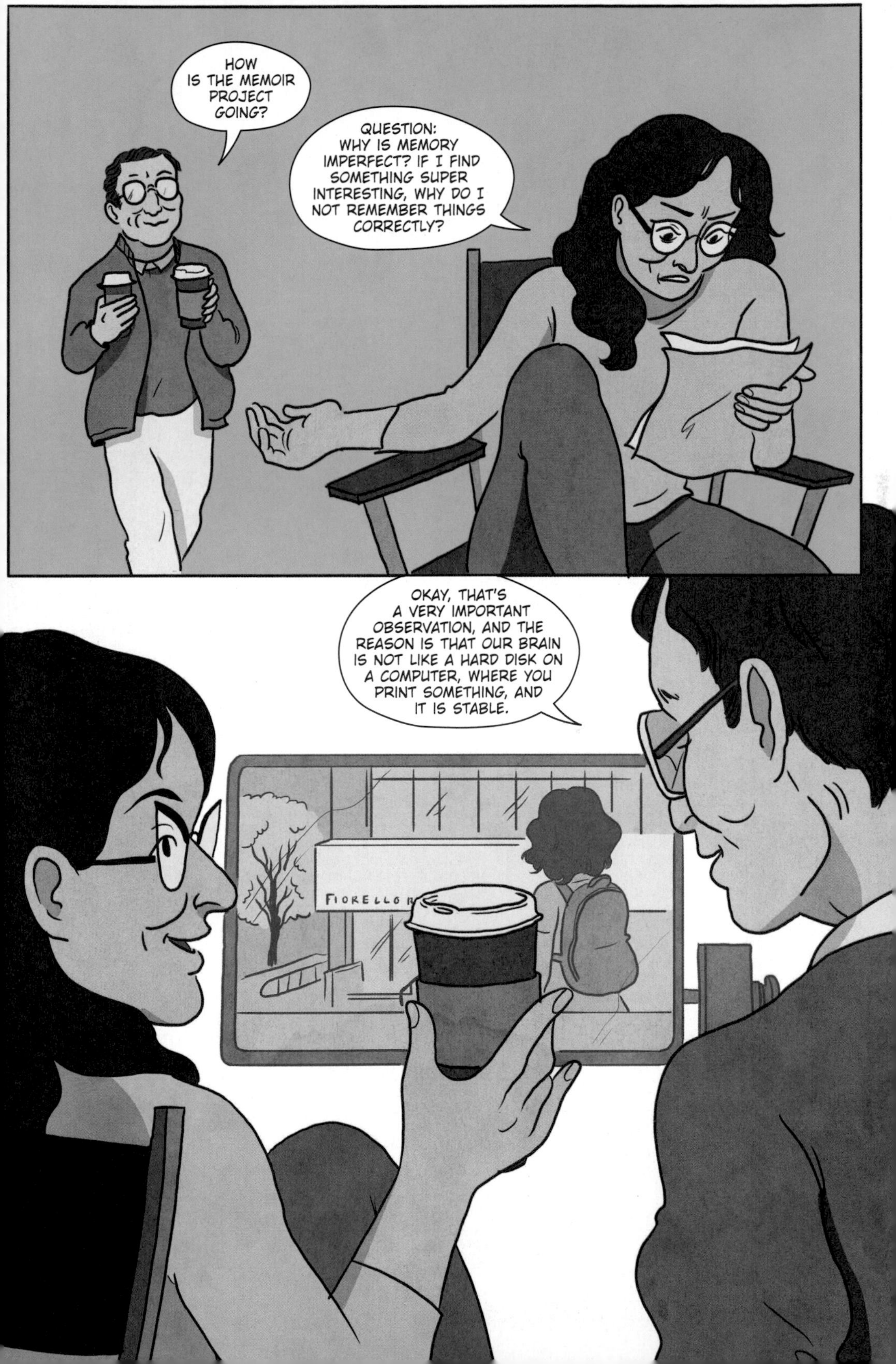
HOW IS THE MEMOIR PROJECT GOING?
QUESTION: WHY IS MEMORY IMPERFECT? IF I FIND SOMETHING SUPER INTERESTING, WHY DO I NOT REMEMBER THINGS CORRECTLY?
OKAY, THAT'S A VERY IMPORTANT OBSERVATION, AND THE REASON IS THAT OUR BRAIN IS NOT LIKE A HARD DISK ON A COMPUTER, WHERE YOU PRINT SOMETHING, AND IT IS STABLE.
FIORELLO

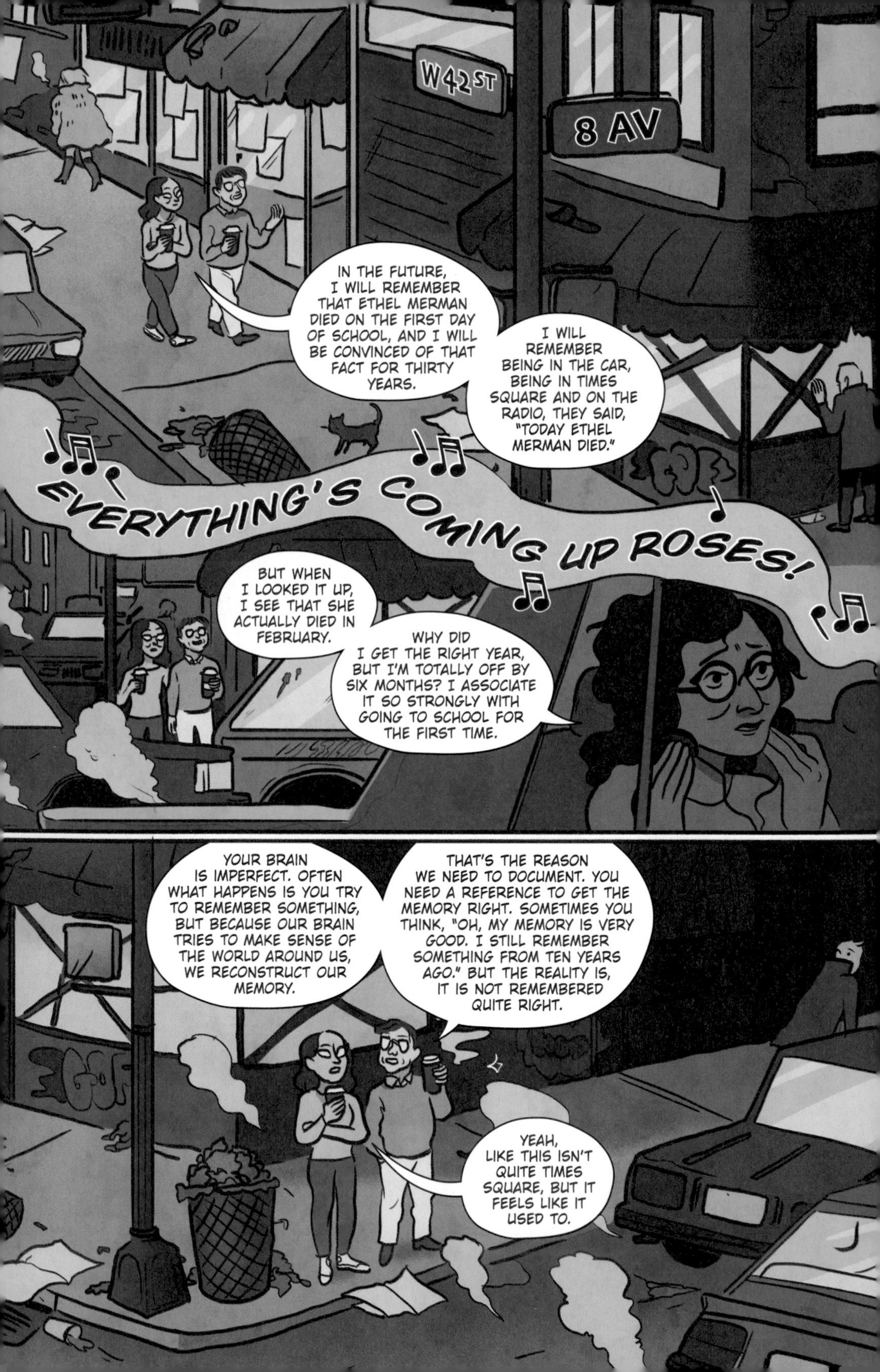
W42ST
8 AV
IN THE FUTURE, I WILL REMEMBER THAT ETHEL MERMAN DIED ON THE FIRST DAY OF SCHOOL, AND I WILL BE CONVINCED OF THAT FACT FOR THIRTY YEARS.
I WILL REMEMBER BEING IN THE CAR, BEING IN TIMES SQUARE AND ON THE RADIO, THEY SAID, "TODAY ETHEL MERMAN DIED."
EVERYTHING'S COMING UP ROSES!
BUT WHEN I LOOKED IT UP, I SEE THAT SHE ACTUALLY DIED IN FEBRUARY.
WHY DID I GET THE RIGHT YEAR, BUT I'M TOTALLY OFF BY SIX MONTHS? I ASSOCIATE IT SO STRONGLY WITH GOING TO SCHOOL FOR THE FIRST TIME.
YOUR BRAIN IS IMPERFECT. OFTEN WHAT HAPPENS IS YOU TRY TO REMEMBER SOMETHING, BUT BECAUSE OUR BRAIN TRIES TO MAKE SENSE OF THE WORLD AROUND US, WE RECONSTRUCT OUR MEMORY.
THAT'S THE REASON WE NEED TO DOCUMENT. YOU NEED A REFERENCE TO GET THE MEMORY RIGHT. SOMETIMES YOU THINK, "OH, MY MEMORY IS VERY GOOD. I STILL REMEMBER SOMETHING FROM TEN YEARS AGO." BUT THE REALITY IS, IT IS NOT REMEMBERED QUITE RIGHT.
YEAH, LIKE THIS ISN'T QUITE TIMES SQUARE, BUT IT FEELS LIKE IT USED TO.

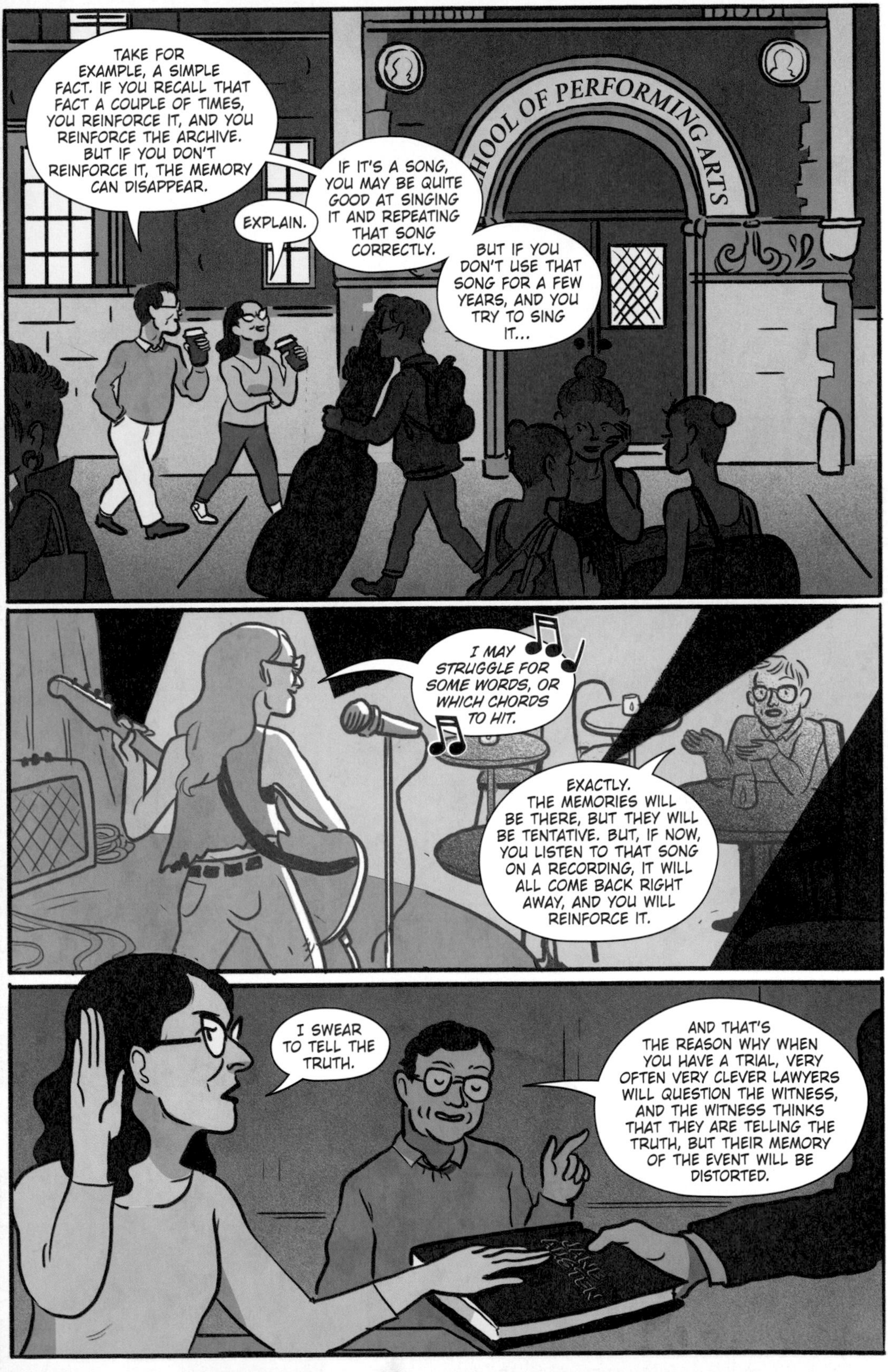
TAKE FOR EXAMPLE, A SIMPLE FACT. IF YOU RECALL THAT FACT A COUPLE OF TIMES, YOU REINFORCE IT, AND YOU REINFORCE THE ARCHIVE. BUT IF YOU DON'T REINFORCE IT, THE MEMORY CAN DISAPPEAR.
EXPLAIN.
IF IT'S A SONG, YOU MAY BE QUITE GOOD AT SINGING IT AND REPEATING THAT SONG CORRECTLY.
HOOL OF PERFORMING ARTS
BUT IF YOU DON'T USE THAT SONG FOR A FEW YEARS, AND YOU TRY TO SING IT...
I MAY STRUGGLE FOR SOME WORDS, OR WHICH CHORDS TO HIT.
EXACTLY. THE MEMORIES WILL BE THERE, BUT THEY WILL BE TENTATIVE. BUT, IF NOW, YOU LISTEN TO THAT SONG ON A RECORDING, IT WILL ALL COME BACK RIGHT AWAY, AND YOU WILL REINFORCE IT.
I SWEAR TO TELL THE TRUTH.
AND THAT'S THE REASON WHY WHEN YOU HAVE A TRIAL, VERY OFTEN VERY CLEVER LAWYERS WILL QUESTION THE WITNESS, AND THE WITNESS THINKS THAT THEY ARE TELLING THE TRUTH, BUT THEIR MEMORY OF THE EVENT WILL BE DISTORTED.

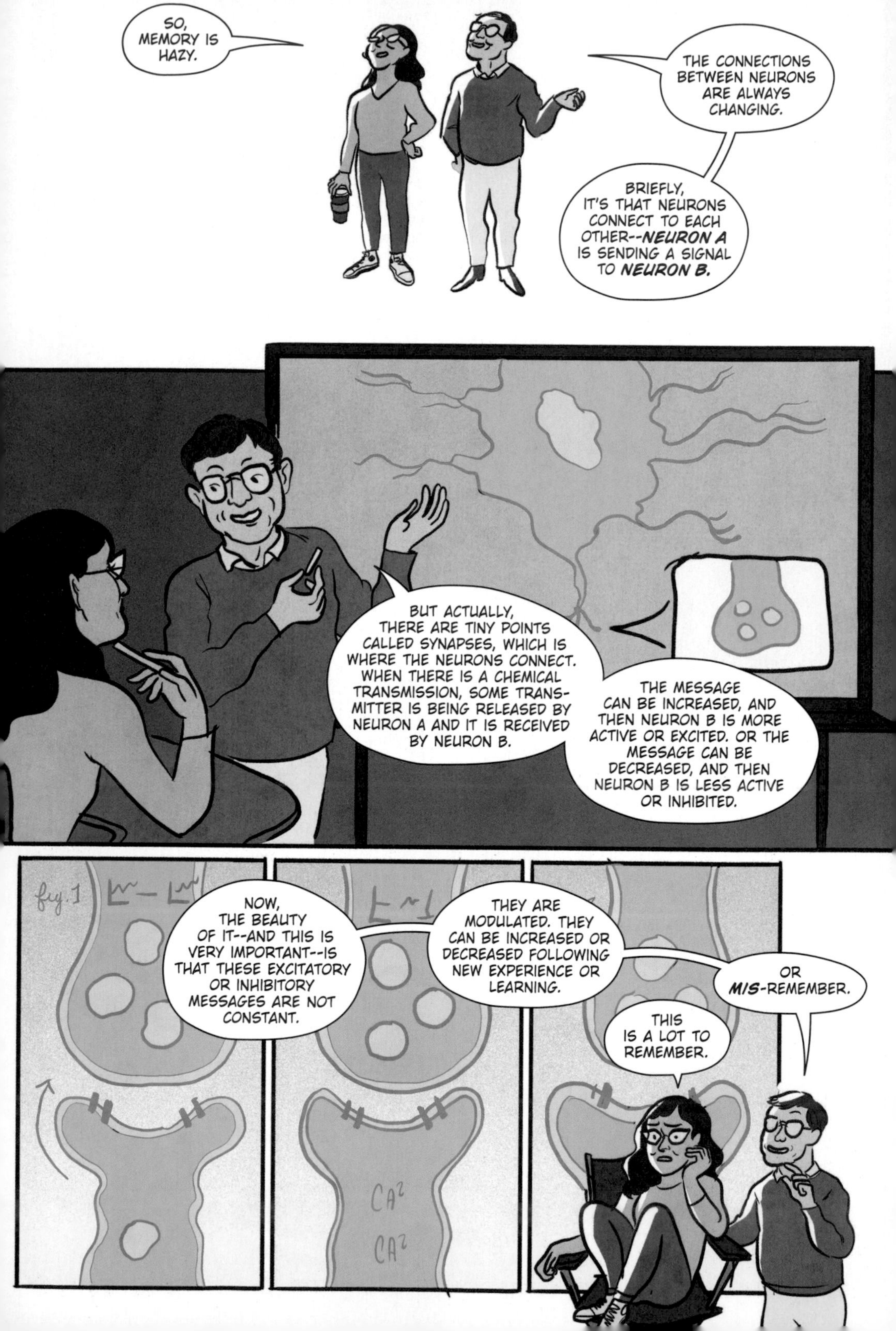
SO, MEMORY IS HAZY.
THE CONNECTIONS BETWEEN NEURONS ARE ALWAYS CHANGING.
BRIEFLY, IT'S THAT NEURONS CONNECT TO EACH OTHER--*NEURON A* IS SENDING A SIGNAL TO *NEURON B.*
BUT ACTUALLY, THERE ARE TINY POINTS CALLED SYNAPSES, WHICH IS WHERE THE NEURONS CONNECT. WHEN THERE IS A CHEMICAL TRANSMISSION, SOME TRANSMITTER IS BEING RELEASED BY NEURON A AND IT IS RECEIVED BY NEURON B.
THE MESSAGE CAN BE INCREASED, AND THEN NEURON B IS MORE ACTIVE OR EXCITED. OR THE MESSAGE CAN BE DECREASED, AND THEN NEURON B IS LESS ACTIVE OR INHIBITED.
fig. 1
NOW, THE BEAUTY OF IT--AND THIS IS VERY IMPORTANT--IS THAT THESE EXCITATORY OR INHIBITORY MESSAGES ARE NOT CONSTANT.
THEY ARE MODULATED. THEY CAN BE INCREASED OR DECREASED FOLLOWING NEW EXPERIENCE OR LEARNING.
CA2
CA2
THIS IS A LOT TO REMEMBER.
OR *MIS*-REMEMBER.

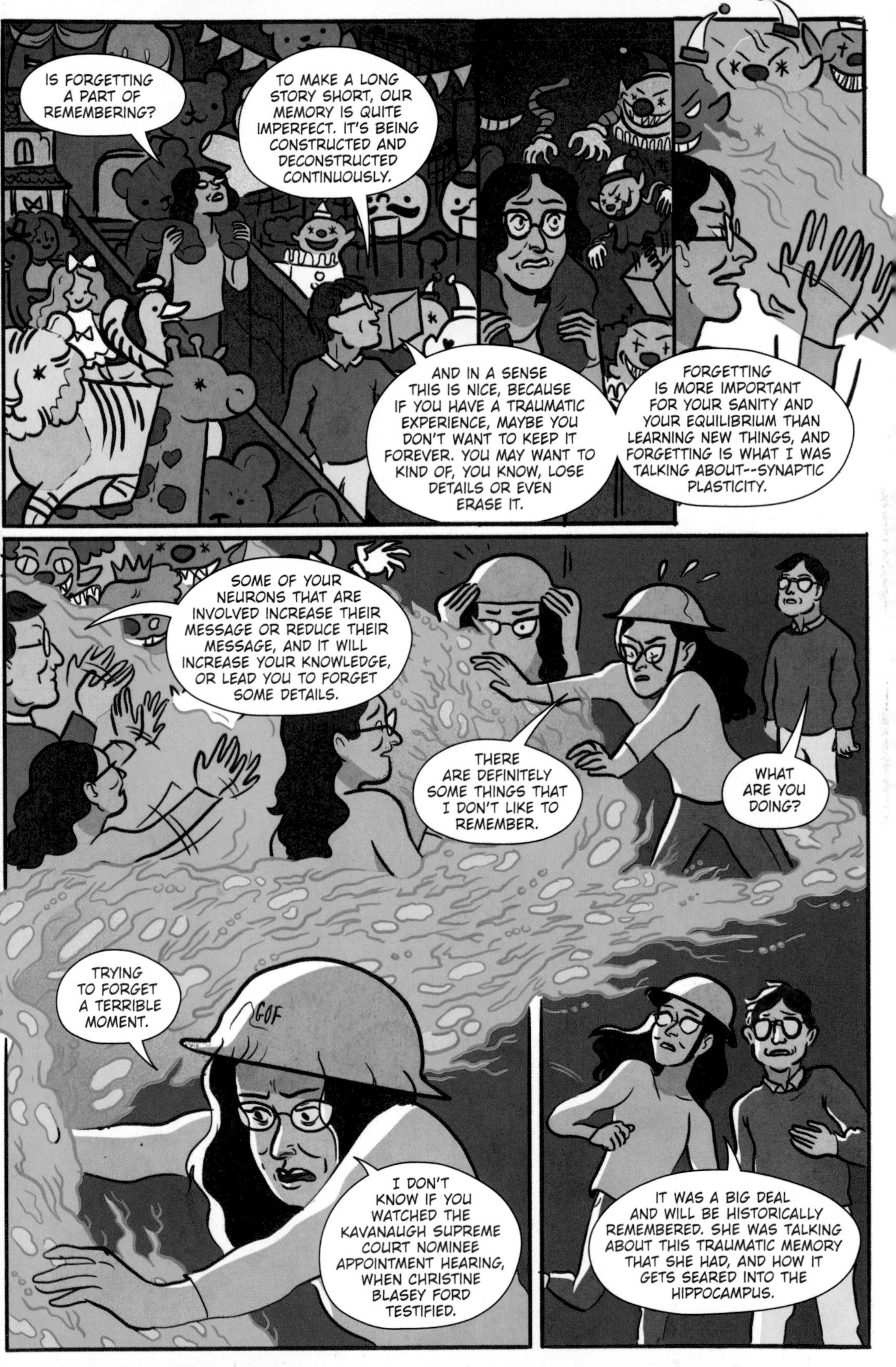
IS FORGETTING A PART OF REMEMBERING?
TO MAKE A LONG STORY SHORT, OUR MEMORY IS QUITE IMPERFECT. IT'S BEING CONSTRUCTED AND DECONSTRUCTED CONTINUOUSLY.
AND IN A SENSE THIS IS NICE, BECAUSE IF YOU HAVE A TRAUMATIC EXPERIENCE, MAYBE YOU DON'T WANT TO KEEP IT FOREVER. YOU MAY WANT TO KIND OF, YOU KNOW, LOSE DETAILS OR EVEN ERASE IT.
FORGETTING IS MORE IMPORTANT FOR YOUR SANITY AND YOUR EQUILIBRIUM THAN LEARNING NEW THINGS, AND FORGETTING IS WHAT I WAS TALKING ABOUT--SYNAPTIC PLASTICITY.
SOME OF YOUR NEURONS THAT ARE INVOLVED INCREASE THEIR MESSAGE OR REDUCE THEIR MESSAGE, AND IT WILL INCREASE YOUR KNOWLEDGE, OR LEAD YOU TO FORGET SOME DETAILS.
THERE ARE DEFINITELY SOME THINGS THAT I DON'T LIKE TO REMEMBER.
WHAT ARE YOU DOING?
TRYING TO FORGET A TERRIBLE MOMENT.
GOF
I DON'T KNOW IF YOU WATCHED THE KAVANAUGH SUPREME COURT NOMINEE APPOINTMENT HEARING, WHEN CHRISTINE BLASEY FORD TESTIFIED.
IT WAS A BIG DEAL AND WILL BE HISTORICALLY REMEMBERED. SHE WAS TALKING ABOUT THIS TRAUMATIC MEMORY THAT SHE HAD, AND HOW IT GETS SEARED INTO THE HIPPOCAMPUS.

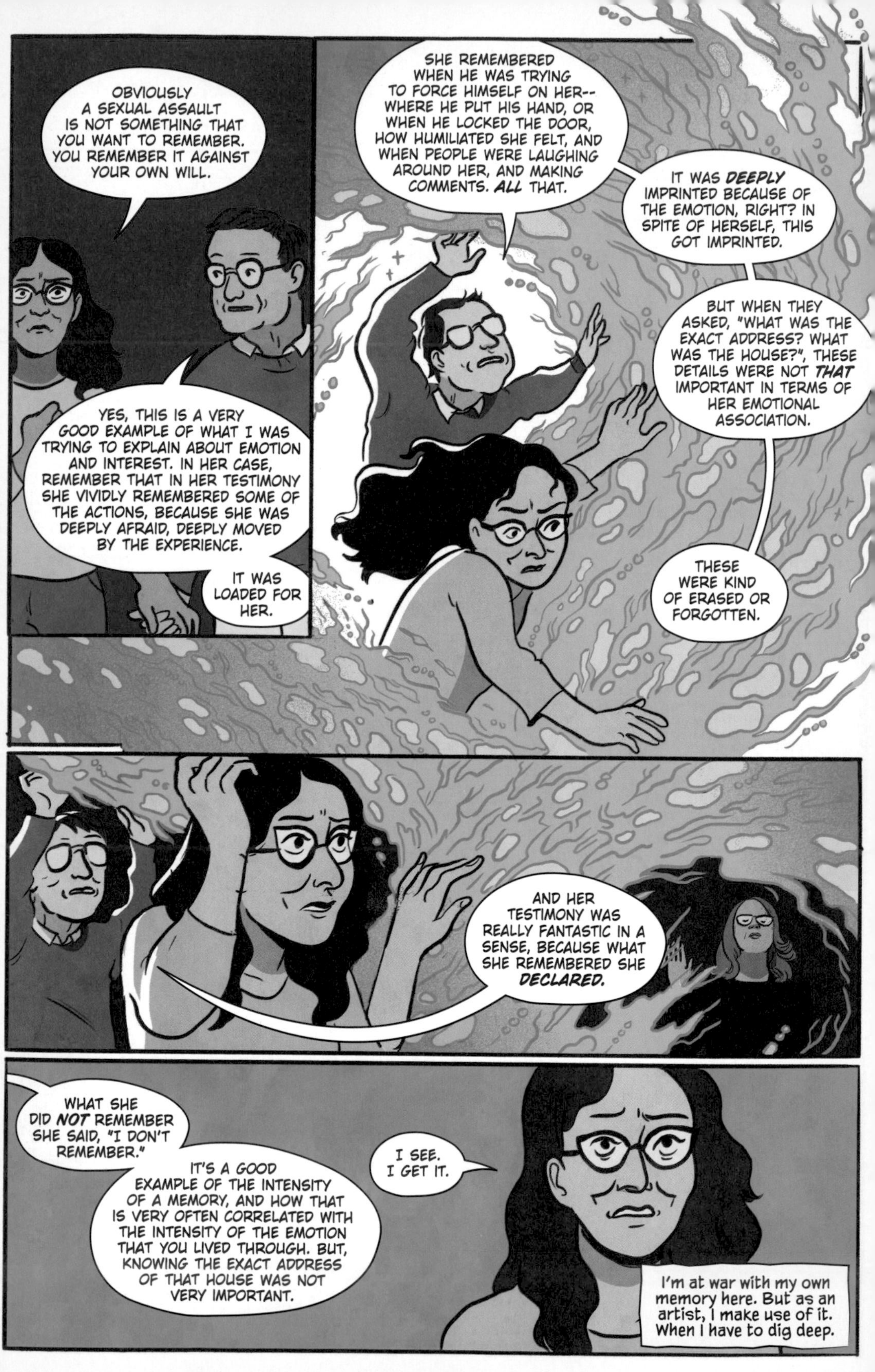
OBVIOUSLY A SEXUAL ASSAULT IS NOT SOMETHING THAT YOU WANT TO REMEMBER. YOU REMEMBER IT AGAINST YOUR OWN WILL.
YES, THIS IS A VERY GOOD EXAMPLE OF WHAT I WAS TRYING TO EXPLAIN ABOUT EMOTION AND INTEREST. IN HER CASE, REMEMBER THAT IN HER TESTIMONY SHE VIVIDLY REMEMBERED SOME OF THE ACTIONS, BECAUSE SHE WAS DEEPLY AFRAID, DEEPLY MOVED BY THE EXPERIENCE.
IT WAS LOADED FOR HER.
SHE REMEMBERED WHEN HE WAS TRYING TO FORCE HIMSELF ON HER-- WHERE HE PUT HIS HAND, OR WHEN HE LOCKED THE DOOR, HOW HUMILIATED SHE FELT, AND WHEN PEOPLE WERE LAUGHING AROUND HER, AND MAKING COMMENTS. ***ALL*** THAT.
IT WAS ***DEEPLY*** IMPRINTED BECAUSE OF THE EMOTION, RIGHT? IN SPITE OF HERSELF, THIS GOT IMPRINTED.
BUT WHEN THEY ASKED, "WHAT WAS THE EXACT ADDRESS? WHAT WAS THE HOUSE?", THESE DETAILS WERE NOT ***THAT*** IMPORTANT IN TERMS OF HER EMOTIONAL ASSOCIATION.
THESE WERE KIND OF ERASED OR FORGOTTEN.
AND HER TESTIMONY WAS REALLY FANTASTIC IN A SENSE, BECAUSE WHAT SHE REMEMBERED SHE ***DECLARED.***
WHAT SHE DID ***NOT*** REMEMBER SHE SAID, "I DON'T REMEMBER."
IT'S A GOOD EXAMPLE OF THE INTENSITY OF A MEMORY, AND HOW THAT IS VERY OFTEN CORRELATED WITH THE INTENSITY OF THE EMOTION THAT YOU LIVED THROUGH. BUT, KNOWING THE EXACT ADDRESS OF THAT HOUSE WAS NOT VERY IMPORTANT.
I SEE. I GET IT.
I'm at war with my own memory here. But as an artist, I make use of it. When I have to dig deep.

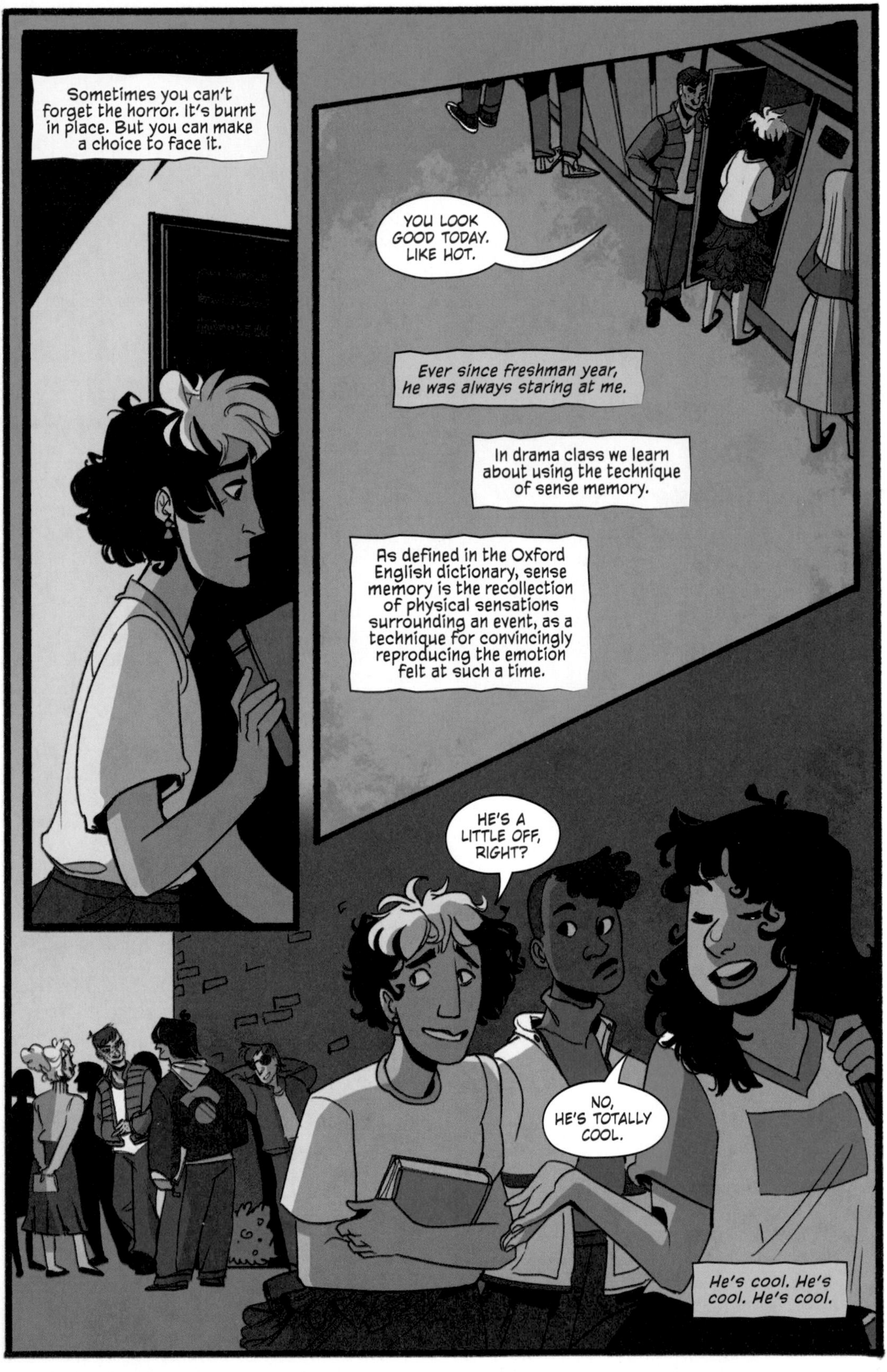

Sometimes you can't forget the horror. It's burnt in place. But you can make a choice to face it.
YOU LOOK GOOD TODAY. LIKE HOT.
Ever since freshman year, he was always staring at me.
In drama class we learn about using the technique of sense memory.
As defined in the Oxford English dictionary, sense memory is the recollection of physical sensations surrounding an event, as a technique for convincingly reproducing the emotion felt at such a time.
HE'S A LITTLE OFF, RIGHT?
NO, HE'S TOTALLY COOL.
He's cool. He's cool. He's cool.

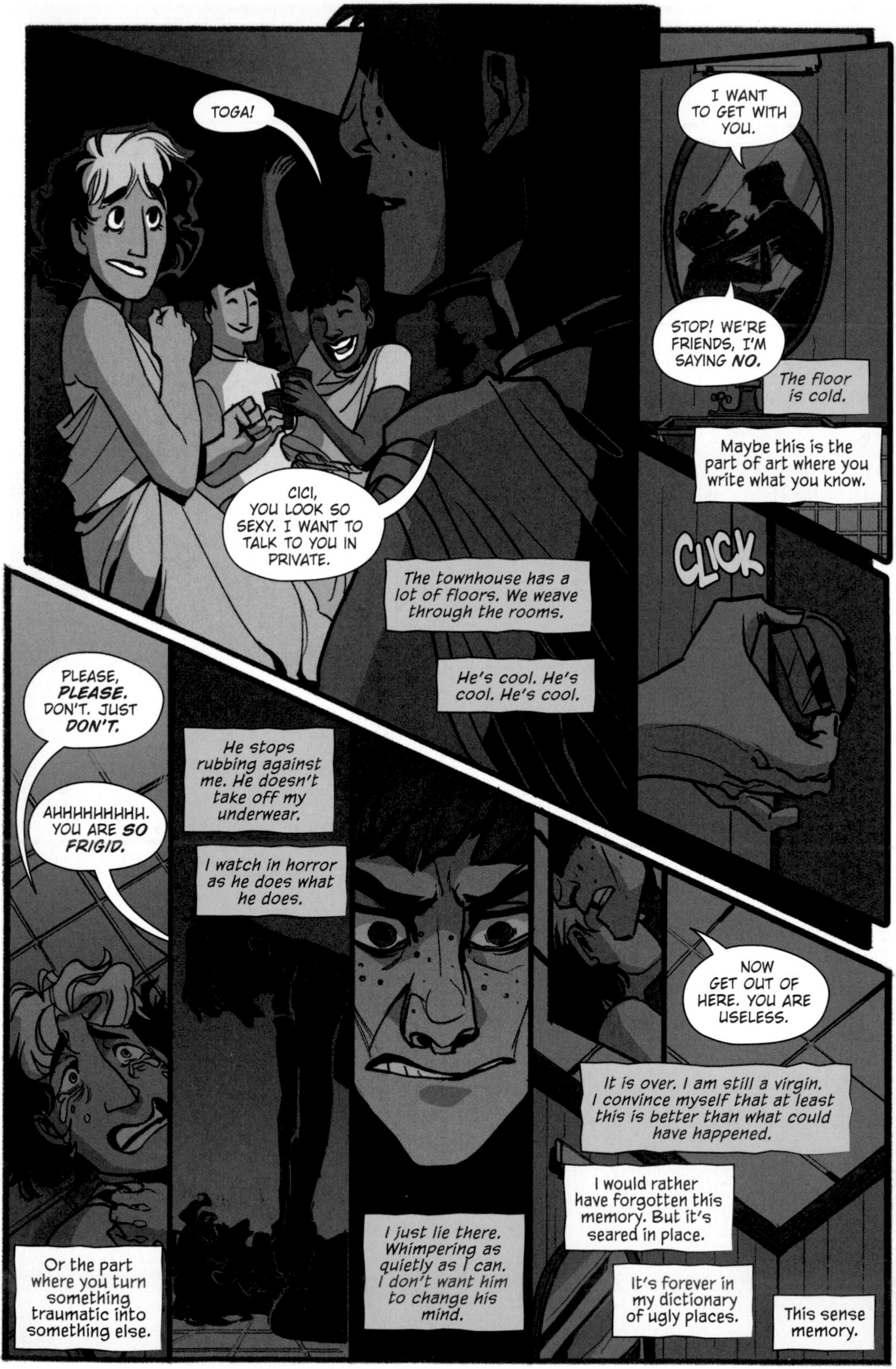
TOGA!
CICI, YOU LOOK SO SEXY. I WANT TO TALK TO YOU IN PRIVATE.
The townhouse has a lot of floors. We weave through the rooms.
He's cool. He's cool. He's cool.
I WANT TO GET WITH YOU.
STOP! WE'RE FRIENDS, I'M SAYING NO.
The floor is cold.
Maybe this is the part of art where you write what you know.
CLICK
PLEASE, PLEASE. DON'T. JUST DON'T.
AHHHHHHHHH. YOU ARE SO FRIGID.
Or the part where you turn something traumatic into something else.
He stops rubbing against me. He doesn't take off my underwear.
I watch in horror as he does what he does.
I just lie there. Whimpering as quietly as I can. I don't want him to change his mind.
NOW GET OUT OF HERE. YOU ARE USELESS.
It is over. I am still a virgin. I convince myself that at least this is better than what could have happened.
I would rather have forgotten this memory. But it's seared in place.
It's forever in my dictionary of ugly places.
This sense memory.

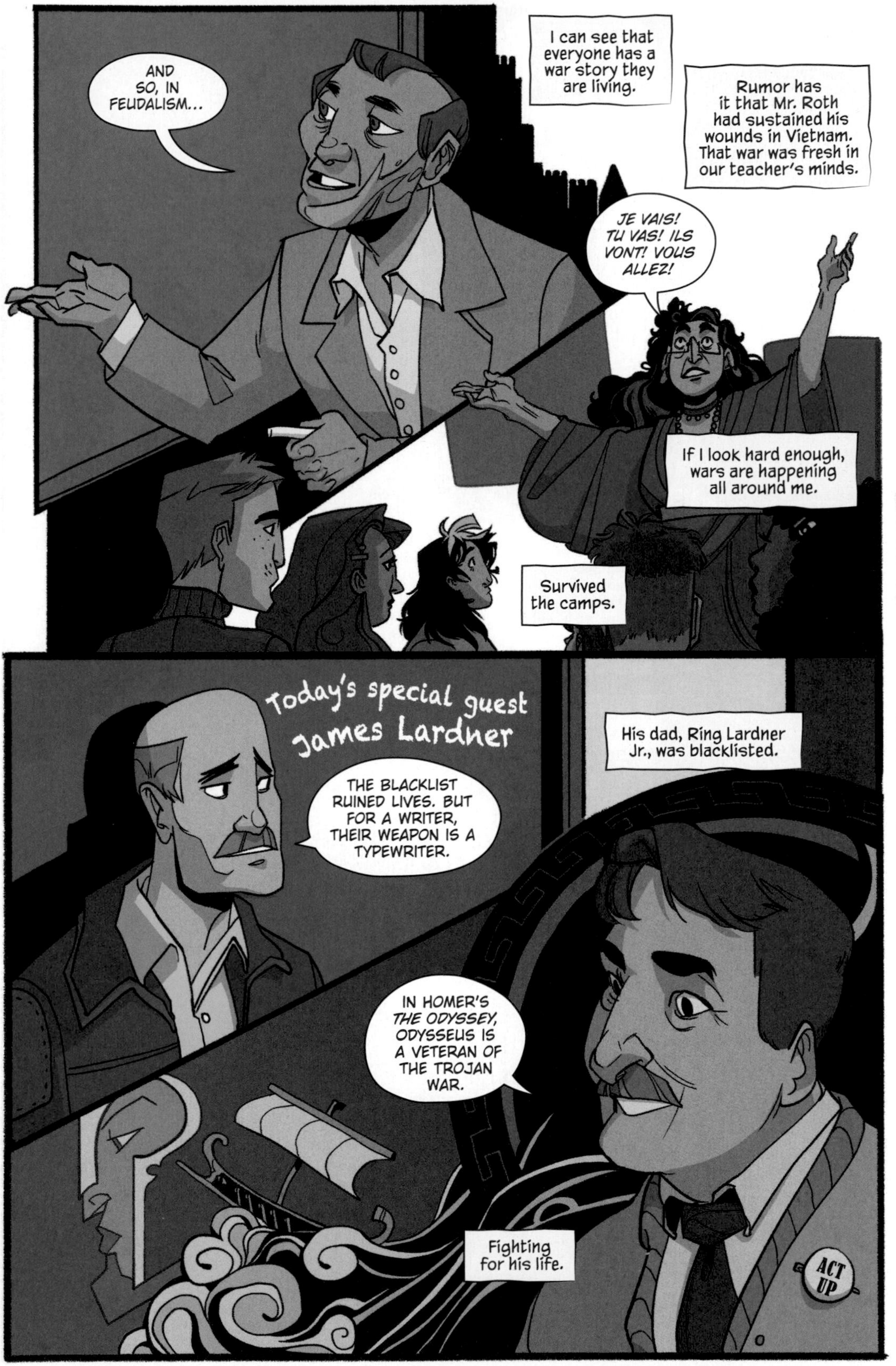
AND SO, IN FEUDALISM...
I can see that everyone has a war story they are living.
Rumor has it that Mr. Roth had sustained his wounds in Vietnam. That war was fresh in our teacher's minds.
JE VAIS! TU VAS! ILS VONT! VOUS ALLEZ!
If I look hard enough, wars are happening all around me.
Survived the camps.
Today's special guest James Lardner
His dad, Ring Lardner Jr., was blacklisted.
THE BLACKLIST RUINED LIVES. BUT FOR A WRITER, THEIR WEAPON IS A TYPEWRITER.
IN HOMER'S THE ODYSSEY, ODYSSEUS IS A VETERAN OF THE TROJAN WAR.
Fighting for his life.
ACT UP

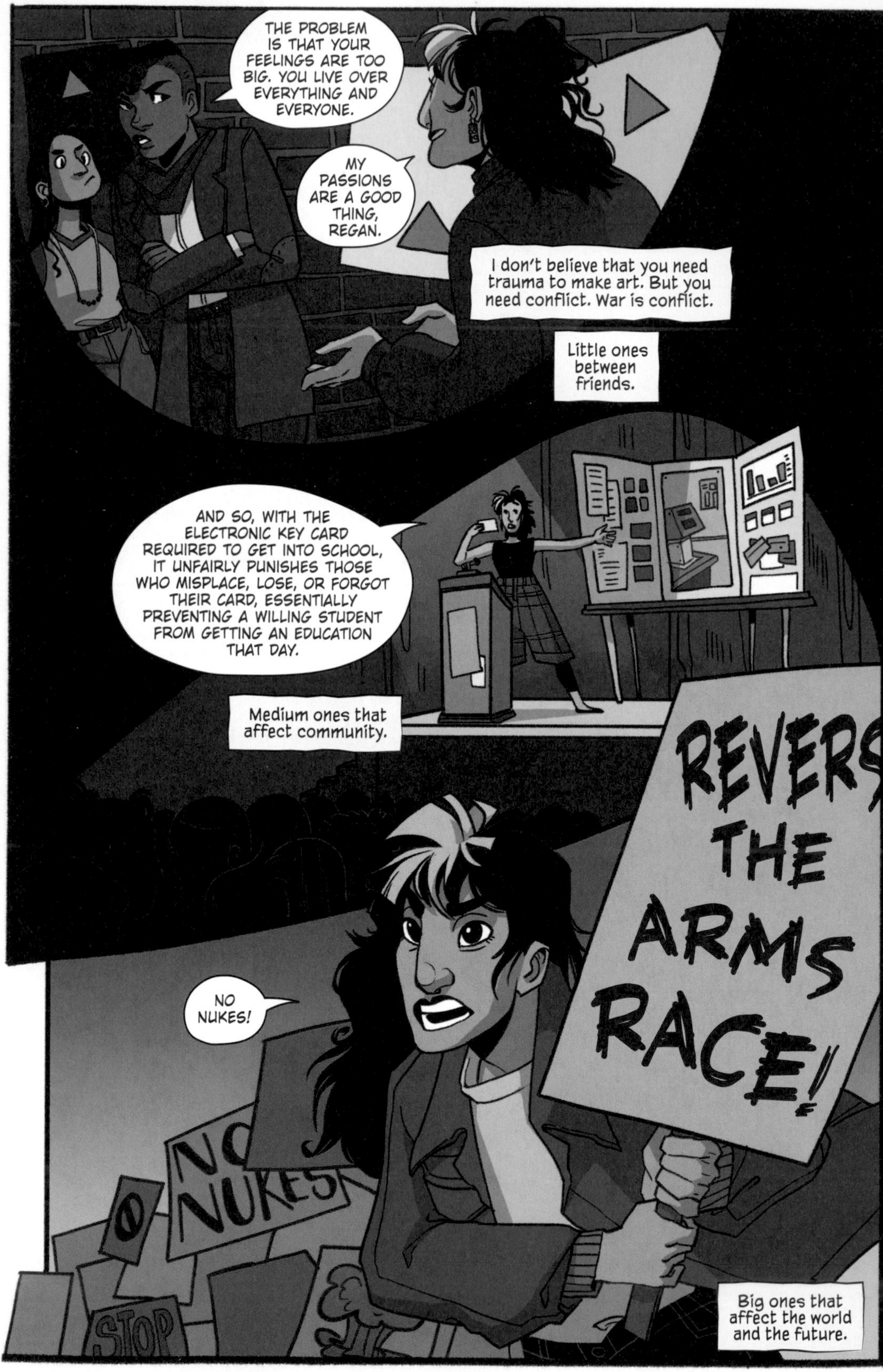

THE PROBLEM IS THAT YOUR FEELINGS ARE TOO BIG. YOU LIVE OVER EVERYTHING AND EVERYONE.
MY PASSIONS ARE A GOOD THING, REGAN.
I don't believe that you need trauma to make art. But you need conflict. War is conflict.
Little ones between friends.
AND SO, WITH THE ELECTRONIC KEY CARD REQUIRED TO GET INTO SCHOOL, IT UNFAIRLY PUNISHES THOSE WHO MISPLACE, LOSE, OR FORGOT THEIR CARD, ESSENTIALLY PREVENTING A WILLING STUDENT FROM GETTING AN EDUCATION THAT DAY.
Medium ones that affect community.
REVERS THE ARMS RACE!
NO NUKES!
NO NUKES
STOP
Big ones that affect the world and the future.

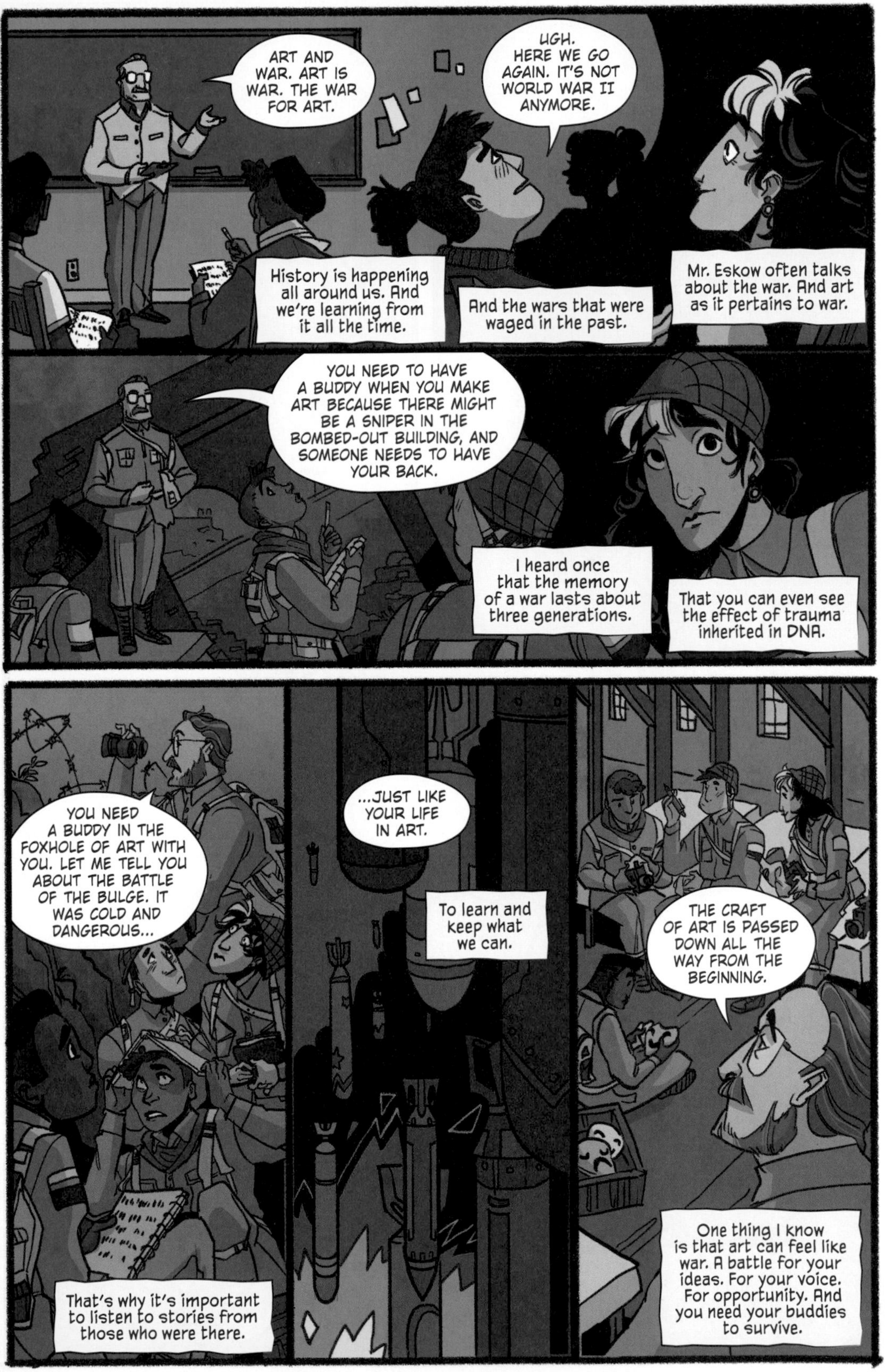
ART AND WAR. ART IS WAR. THE WAR FOR ART.
UGH. HERE WE GO AGAIN. IT'S NOT WORLD WAR II ANYMORE.
History is happening all around us. And we're learning from it all the time.
And the wars that were waged in the past.
Mr. Eskow often talks about the war. And art as it pertains to war.
YOU NEED TO HAVE A BUDDY WHEN YOU MAKE ART BECAUSE THERE MIGHT BE A SNIPER IN THE BOMBED-OUT BUILDING, AND SOMEONE NEEDS TO HAVE YOUR BACK.
I heard once that the memory of a war lasts about three generations.
That you can even see the effect of trauma inherited in DNA.
YOU NEED A BUDDY IN THE FOXHOLE OF ART WITH YOU. LET ME TELL YOU ABOUT THE BATTLE OF THE BULGE. IT WAS COLD AND DANGEROUS...
That's why it's important to listen to stories from those who were there.
...JUST LIKE YOUR LIFE IN ART.
To learn and keep what we can.
THE CRAFT OF ART IS PASSED DOWN ALL THE WAY FROM THE BEGINNING.
One thing I know is that art can feel like war. A battle for your ideas. For your voice. For opportunity. And you need your buddies to survive.

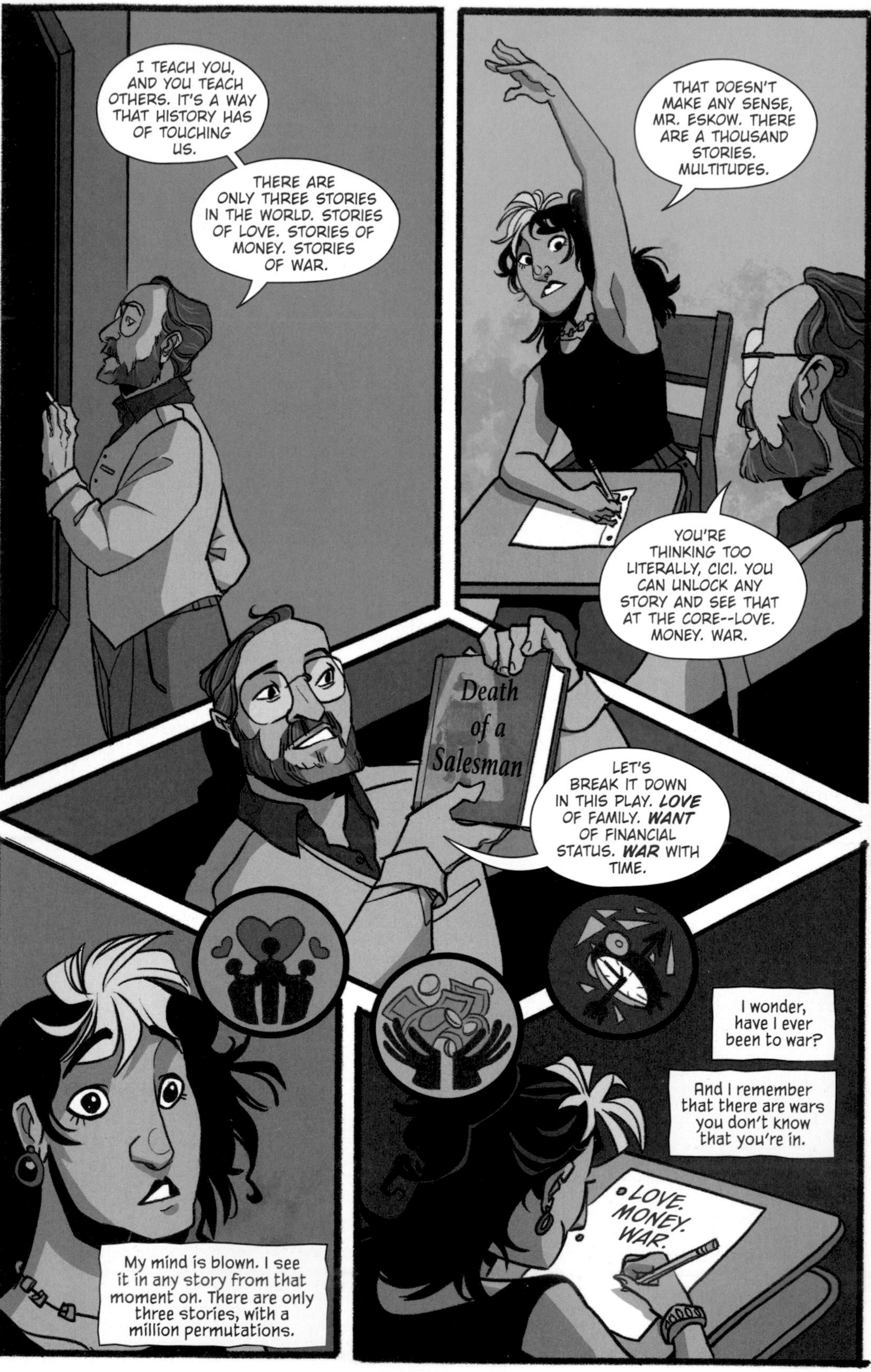
I TEACH YOU, AND YOU TEACH OTHERS. IT'S A WAY THAT HISTORY HAS OF TOUCHING US.
THERE ARE ONLY THREE STORIES IN THE WORLD. STORIES OF LOVE. STORIES OF MONEY. STORIES OF WAR.
THAT DOESN'T MAKE ANY SENSE, MR. ESKOW. THERE ARE A THOUSAND STORIES. MULTITUDES.
YOU'RE THINKING TOO LITERALLY, CICI. YOU CAN UNLOCK ANY STORY AND SEE THAT AT THE CORE--LOVE. MONEY. WAR.
Death of a Salesman
LET'S BREAK IT DOWN IN THIS PLAY. **LOVE** OF FAMILY. **WANT** OF FINANCIAL STATUS. **WAR** WITH TIME.
My mind is blown. I see it in any story from that moment on. There are only three stories, with a million permutations.
I wonder, have I ever been to war?
And I remember that there are wars you don't know that you're in.
LOVE. MONEY. WAR.

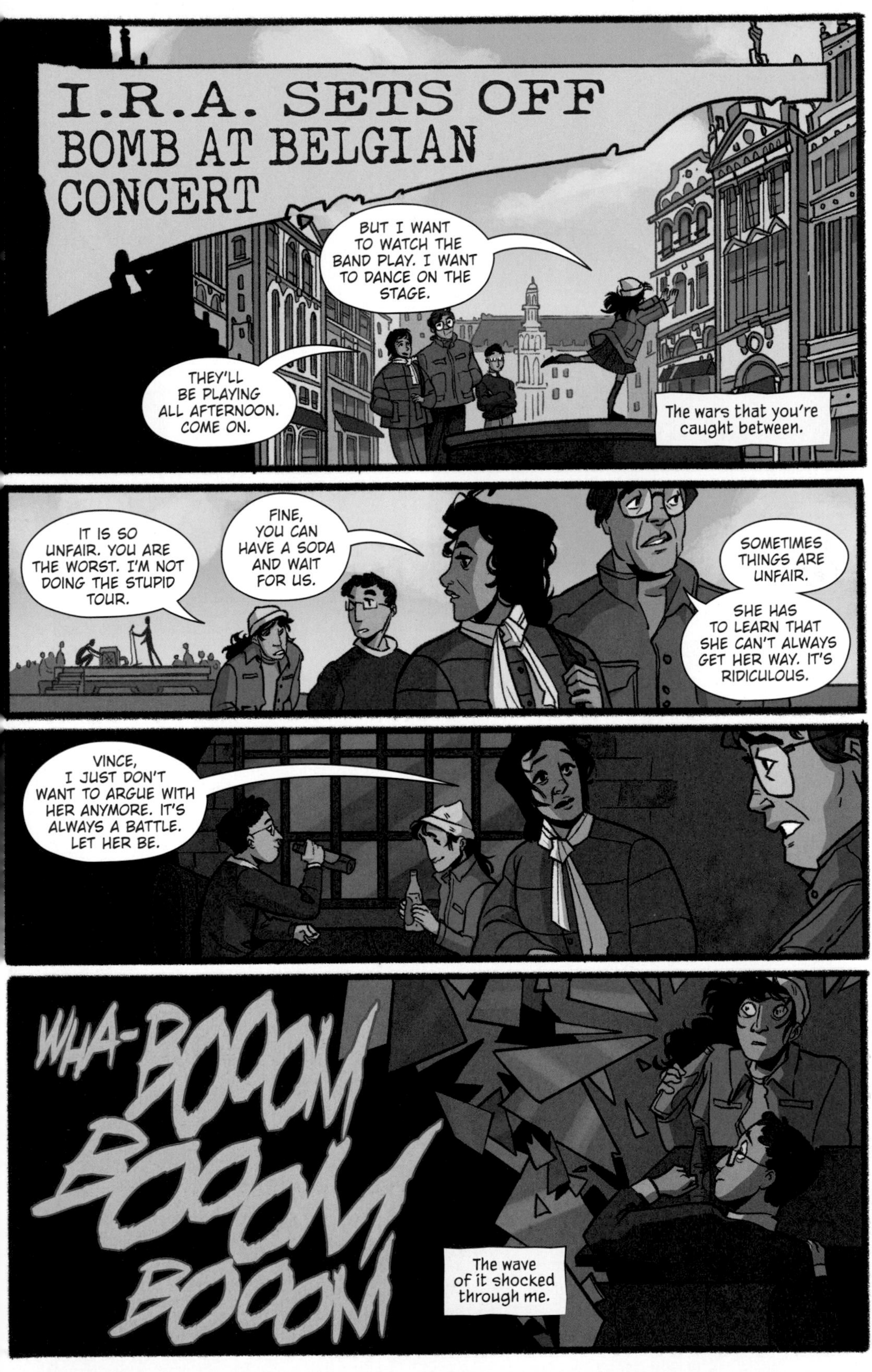
I.R.A. SETS OFF BOMB AT BELGIAN CONCERT
BUT I WANT TO WATCH THE BAND PLAY. I WANT TO DANCE ON THE STAGE.
THEY'LL BE PLAYING ALL AFTERNOON. COME ON.
The wars that you're caught between.
IT IS SO UNFAIR. YOU ARE THE WORST. I'M NOT DOING THE STUPID TOUR.
FINE, YOU CAN HAVE A SODA AND WAIT FOR US.
SOMETIMES THINGS ARE UNFAIR.
SHE HAS TO LEARN THAT SHE CAN'T ALWAYS GET HER WAY. IT'S RIDICULOUS.
VINCE, I JUST DON'T WANT TO ARGUE WITH HER ANYMORE. IT'S ALWAYS A BATTLE. LET HER BE.
WHA-BOOOM BOOOM BOOOM
The wave of it shocked through me.

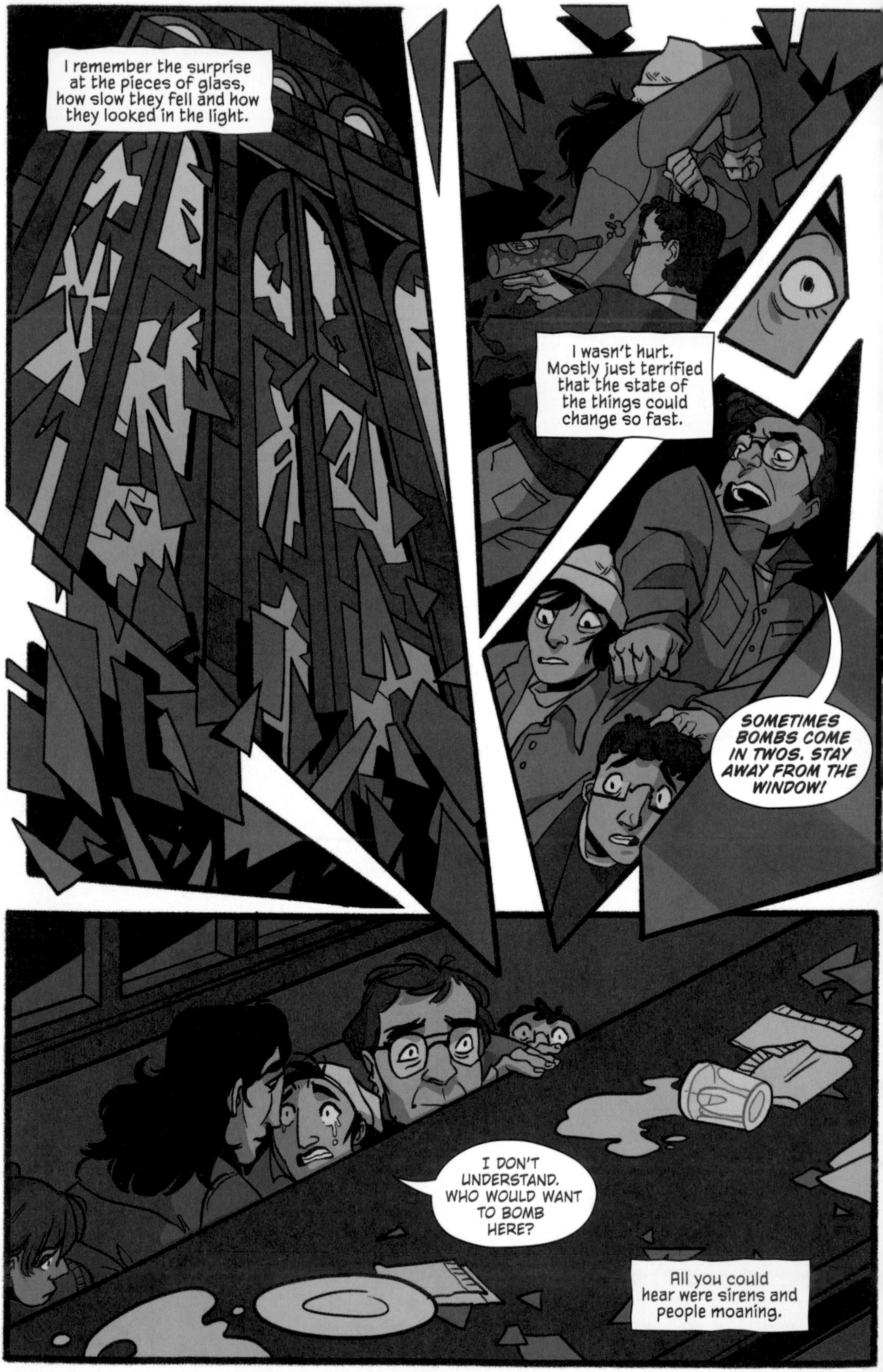

I remember the surprise at the pieces of glass, how slow they fell and how they looked in the light.
I wasn't hurt. Mostly just terrified that the state of the things could change so fast.
SOMETIMES BOMBS COME IN TWOS. STAY AWAY FROM THE WINDOW!
I DON'T UNDERSTAND. WHO WOULD WANT TO BOMB HERE?
All you could hear were sirens and people moaning.

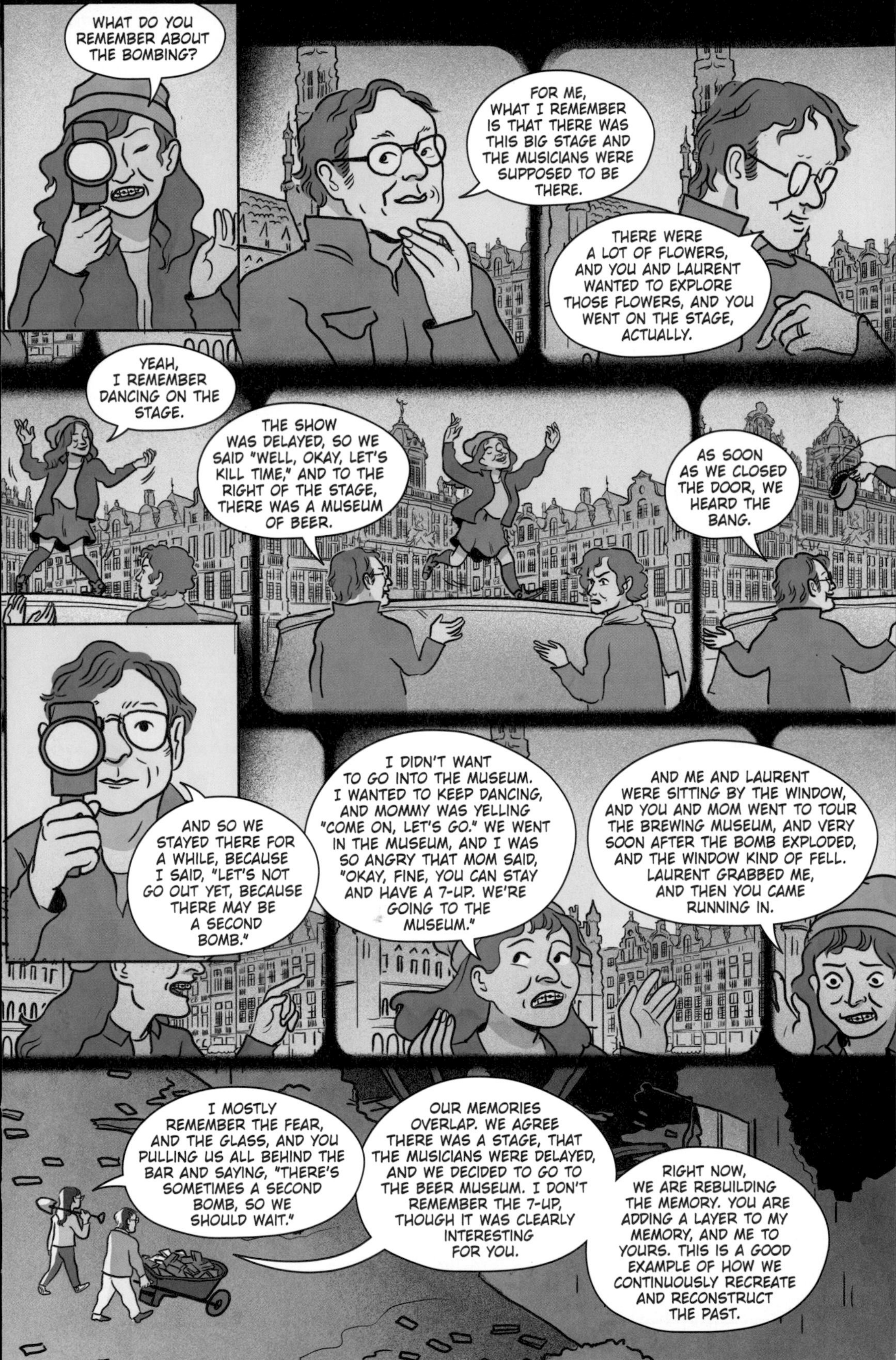
WHAT DO YOU REMEMBER ABOUT THE BOMBING?
FOR ME, WHAT I REMEMBER IS THAT THERE WAS THIS BIG STAGE AND THE MUSICIANS WERE SUPPOSED TO BE THERE.
THERE WERE A LOT OF FLOWERS, AND YOU AND LAURENT WANTED TO EXPLORE THOSE FLOWERS, AND YOU WENT ON THE STAGE, ACTUALLY.
YEAH, I REMEMBER DANCING ON THE STAGE.
THE SHOW WAS DELAYED, SO WE SAID "WELL, OKAY, LET'S KILL TIME," AND TO THE RIGHT OF THE STAGE, THERE WAS A MUSEUM OF BEER.
AS SOON AS WE CLOSED THE DOOR, WE HEARD THE BANG.
AND SO WE STAYED THERE FOR A WHILE, BECAUSE I SAID, "LET'S NOT GO OUT YET, BECAUSE THERE MAY BE A SECOND BOMB."
I DIDN'T WANT TO GO INTO THE MUSEUM. I WANTED TO KEEP DANCING, AND MOMMY WAS YELLING "COME ON, LET'S GO." WE WENT IN THE MUSEUM, AND I WAS SO ANGRY THAT MOM SAID, "OKAY, FINE, YOU CAN STAY AND HAVE A 7-UP. WE'RE GOING TO THE MUSEUM."
AND ME AND LAURENT WERE SITTING BY THE WINDOW, AND YOU AND MOM WENT TO TOUR THE BREWING MUSEUM, AND VERY SOON AFTER THE BOMB EXPLODED, AND THE WINDOW KIND OF FELL. LAURENT GRABBED ME, AND THEN YOU CAME RUNNING IN.
I MOSTLY REMEMBER THE FEAR, AND THE GLASS, AND YOU PULLING US ALL BEHIND THE BAR AND SAYING, "THERE'S SOMETIMES A SECOND BOMB, SO WE SHOULD WAIT."
OUR MEMORIES OVERLAP. WE AGREE THERE WAS A STAGE, THAT THE MUSICIANS WERE DELAYED, AND WE DECIDED TO GO TO THE BEER MUSEUM. I DON'T REMEMBER THE 7-UP, THOUGH IT WAS CLEARLY INTERESTING FOR YOU.
RIGHT NOW, WE ARE REBUILDING THE MEMORY. YOU ARE ADDING A LAYER TO MY MEMORY, AND ME TO YOURS. THIS IS A GOOD EXAMPLE OF HOW WE CONTINUOUSLY RECREATE AND RECONSTRUCT THE PAST.

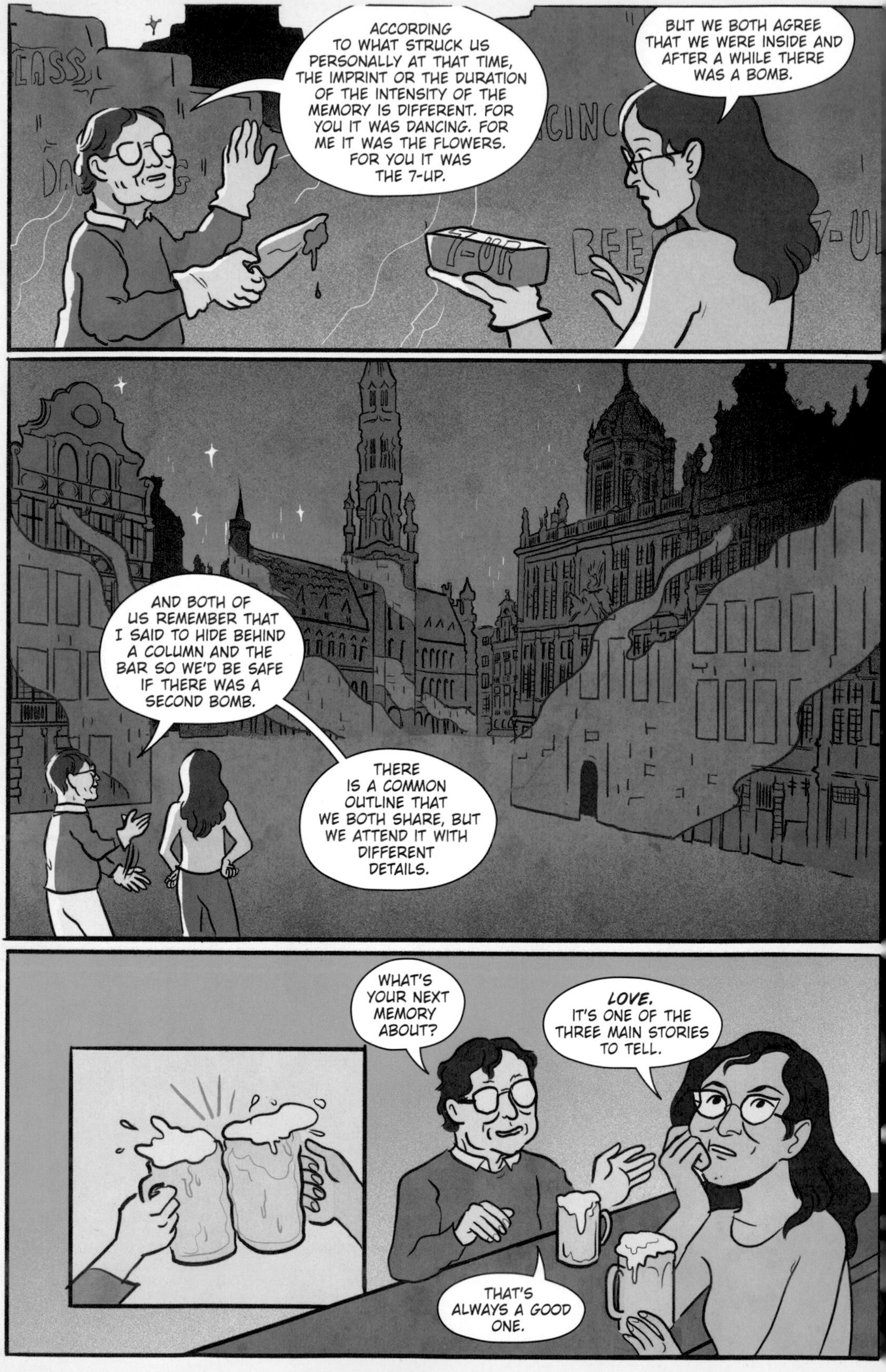

ACCORDING TO WHAT STRUCK US PERSONALLY AT THAT TIME, THE IMPRINT OR THE DURATION OF THE INTENSITY OF THE MEMORY IS DIFFERENT. FOR YOU IT WAS DANCING. FOR ME IT WAS THE FLOWERS. FOR YOU IT WAS THE 7-UP.
BUT WE BOTH AGREE THAT WE WERE INSIDE AND AFTER A WHILE THERE WAS A BOMB.
7-UP
AND BOTH OF US REMEMBER THAT I SAID TO HIDE BEHIND A COLUMN AND THE BAR SO WE'D BE SAFE IF THERE WAS A SECOND BOMB.
THERE IS A COMMON OUTLINE THAT WE BOTH SHARE, BUT WE ATTEND IT WITH DIFFERENT DETAILS.
WHAT'S YOUR NEXT MEMORY ABOUT?
LOVE. IT'S ONE OF THE THREE MAIN STORIES TO TELL.
THAT'S ALWAYS A GOOD ONE.

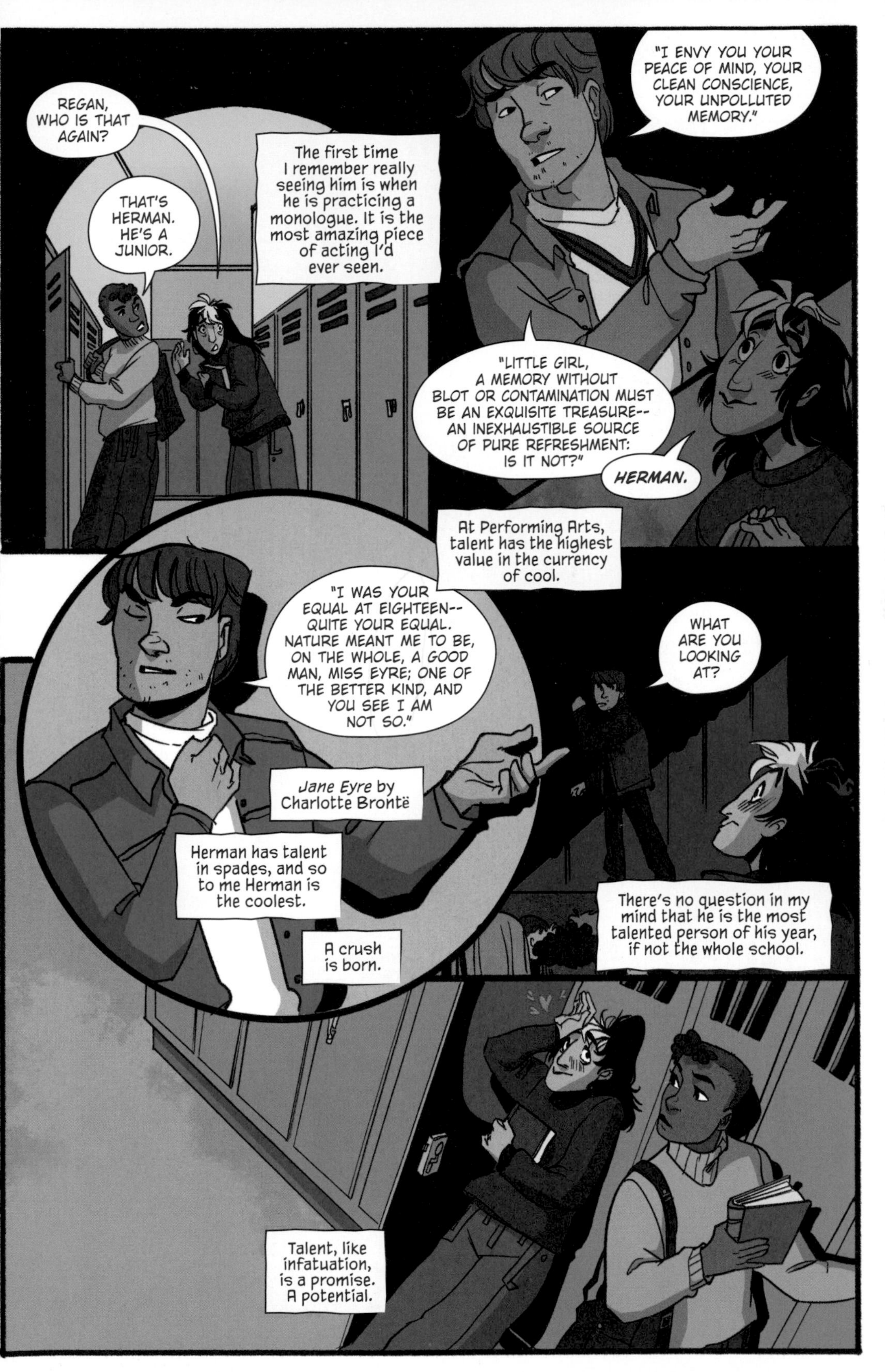
REGAN, WHO IS THAT AGAIN?
THAT'S HERMAN. HE'S A JUNIOR.
The first time I remember really seeing him is when he is practicing a monologue. It is the most amazing piece of acting I'd ever seen.
"I ENVY YOU YOUR PEACE OF MIND, YOUR CLEAN CONSCIENCE, YOUR UNPOLLUTED MEMORY."
"LITTLE GIRL, A MEMORY WITHOUT BLOT OR CONTAMINATION MUST BE AN EXQUISITE TREASURE-- AN INEXHAUSTIBLE SOURCE OF PURE REFRESHMENT: IS IT NOT?"
HERMAN.
At Performing Arts, talent has the highest value in the currency of cool.
"I WAS YOUR EQUAL AT EIGHTEEN-- QUITE YOUR EQUAL. NATURE MEANT ME TO BE, ON THE WHOLE, A GOOD MAN, MISS EYRE; ONE OF THE BETTER KIND, AND YOU SEE I AM NOT SO."
Jane Eyre by Charlotte Brontë
Herman has talent in spades, and so to me Herman is the coolest.
A crush is born.
WHAT ARE YOU LOOKING AT?
There's no question in my mind that he is the most talented person of his year, if not the whole school.
Talent, like infatuation, is a promise. A potential.

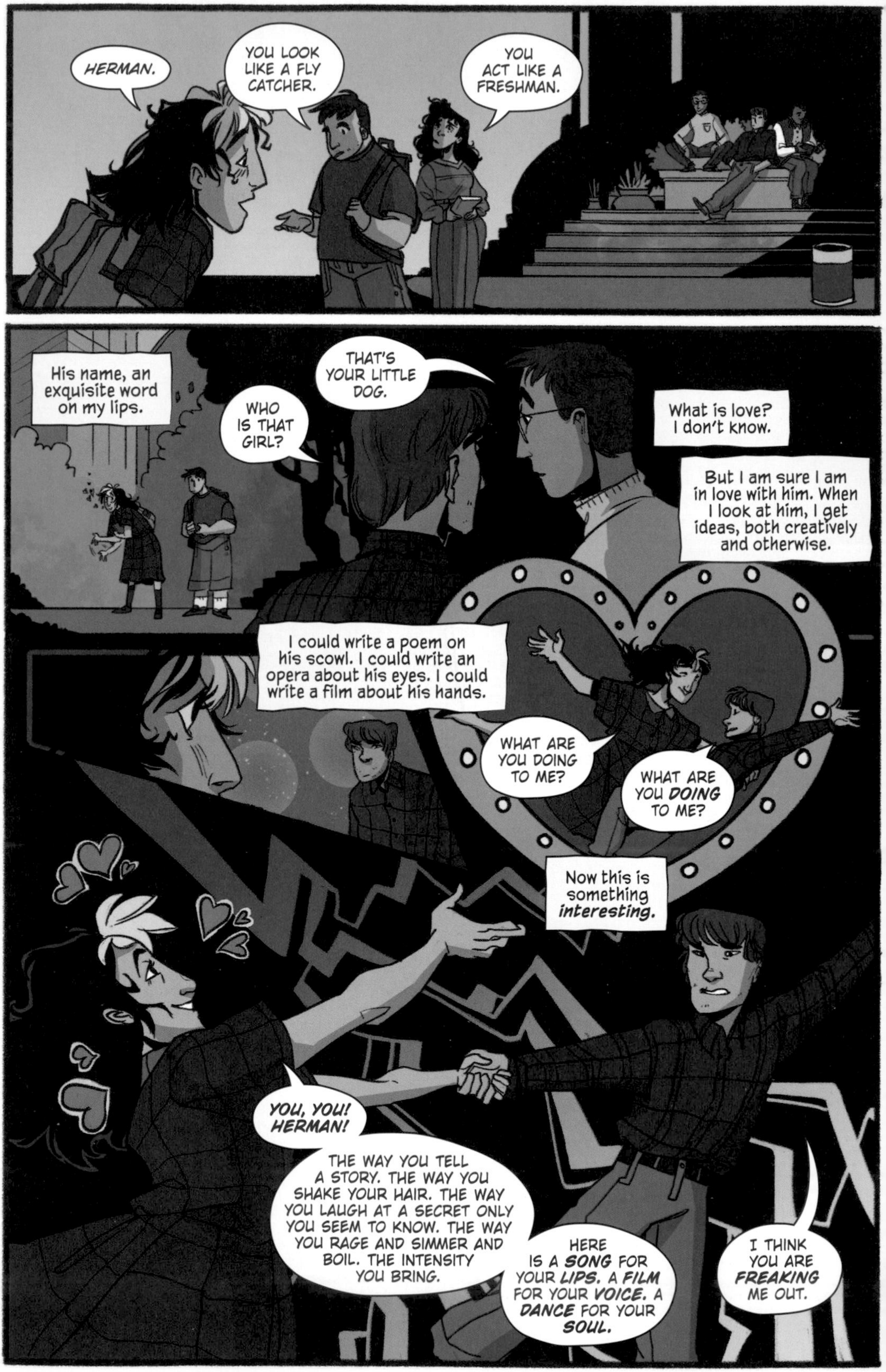

HERMAN.
YOU LOOK LIKE A FLY CATCHER.
YOU ACT LIKE A FRESHMAN.
His name, an exquisite word on my lips.
WHO IS THAT GIRL?
THAT'S YOUR LITTLE DOG.
What is love? I don't know.
But I am sure I am in love with him. When I look at him, I get ideas, both creatively and otherwise.
I could write a poem on his scowl. I could write an opera about his eyes. I could write a film about his hands.
WHAT ARE YOU DOING TO ME?
WHAT ARE YOU DOING TO ME?
Now this is something interesting.
YOU, YOU! HERMAN!
THE WAY YOU TELL A STORY. THE WAY YOU SHAKE YOUR HAIR. THE WAY YOU LAUGH AT A SECRET ONLY YOU SEEM TO KNOW. THE WAY YOU RAGE AND SIMMER AND BOIL. THE INTENSITY YOU BRING.
HERE IS A SONG FOR YOUR LIPS. A FILM FOR YOUR VOICE. A DANCE FOR YOUR SOUL.
I THINK YOU ARE FREAKING ME OUT.

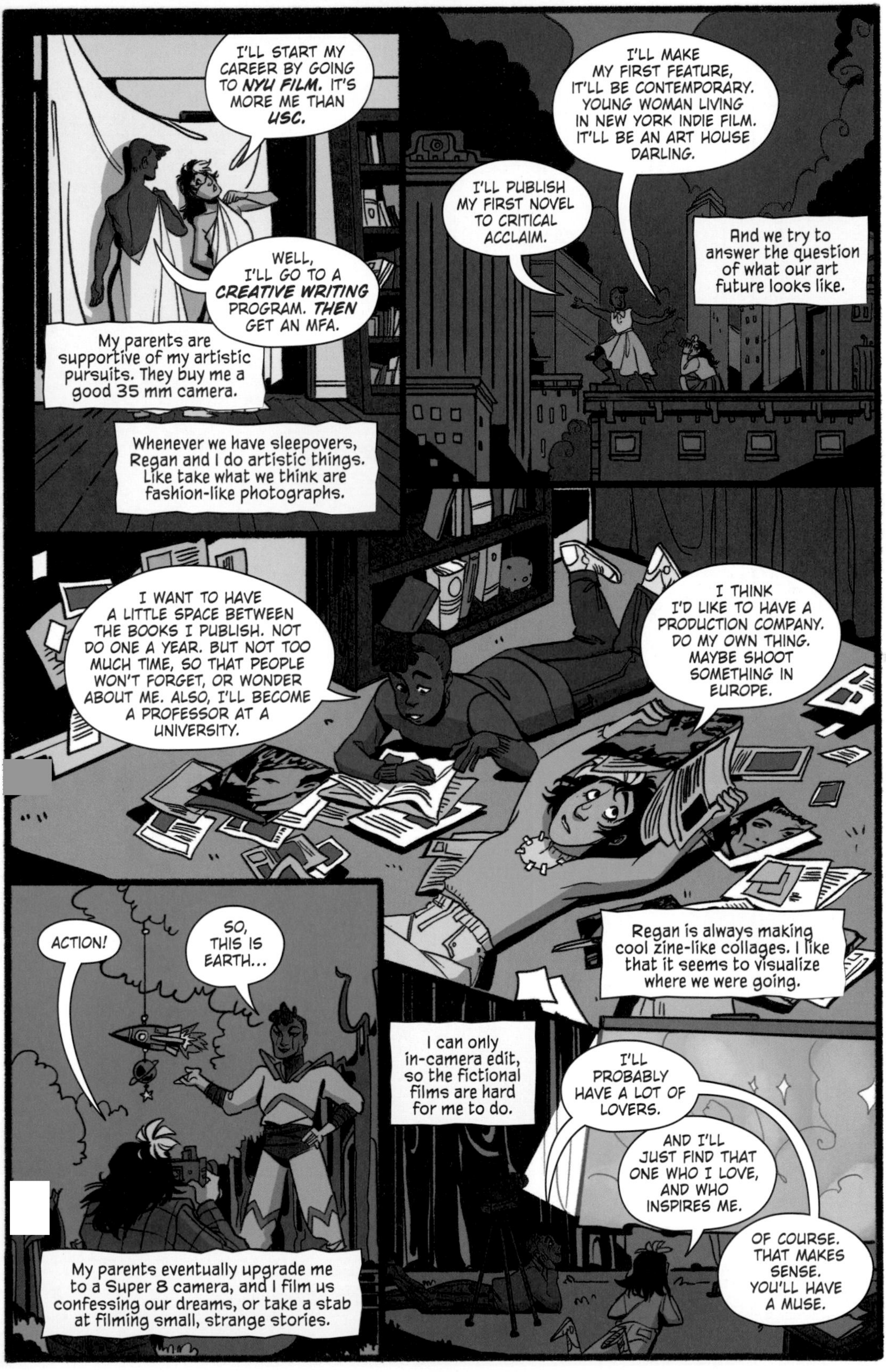
I'LL START MY CAREER BY GOING TO NYU FILM. IT'S MORE ME THAN USC.
WELL, I'LL GO TO A CREATIVE WRITING PROGRAM. THEN GET AN MFA.
My parents are supportive of my artistic pursuits. They buy me a good 35 mm camera.
Whenever we have sleepovers, Regan and I do artistic things. Like take what we think are fashion-like photographs.
I'LL MAKE MY FIRST FEATURE, IT'LL BE CONTEMPORARY. YOUNG WOMAN LIVING IN NEW YORK INDIE FILM. IT'LL BE AN ART HOUSE DARLING.
I'LL PUBLISH MY FIRST NOVEL TO CRITICAL ACCLAIM.
And we try to answer the question of what our art future looks like.
I WANT TO HAVE A LITTLE SPACE BETWEEN THE BOOKS I PUBLISH. NOT DO ONE A YEAR. BUT NOT TOO MUCH TIME, SO THAT PEOPLE WON'T FORGET, OR WONDER ABOUT ME. ALSO, I'LL BECOME A PROFESSOR AT A UNIVERSITY.
I THINK I'D LIKE TO HAVE A PRODUCTION COMPANY. DO MY OWN THING. MAYBE SHOOT SOMETHING IN EUROPE.
Regan is always making cool zine-like collages. I like that it seems to visualize where we were going.
ACTION!
SO, THIS IS EARTH...
My parents eventually upgrade me to a Super 8 camera, and I film us confessing our dreams, or take a stab at filming small, strange stories.
I can only in-camera edit, so the fictional films are hard for me to do.
I'LL PROBABLY HAVE A LOT OF LOVERS.
AND I'LL JUST FIND THAT ONE WHO I LOVE, AND WHO INSPIRES ME.
OF COURSE. THAT MAKES SENSE. YOU'LL HAVE A MUSE.

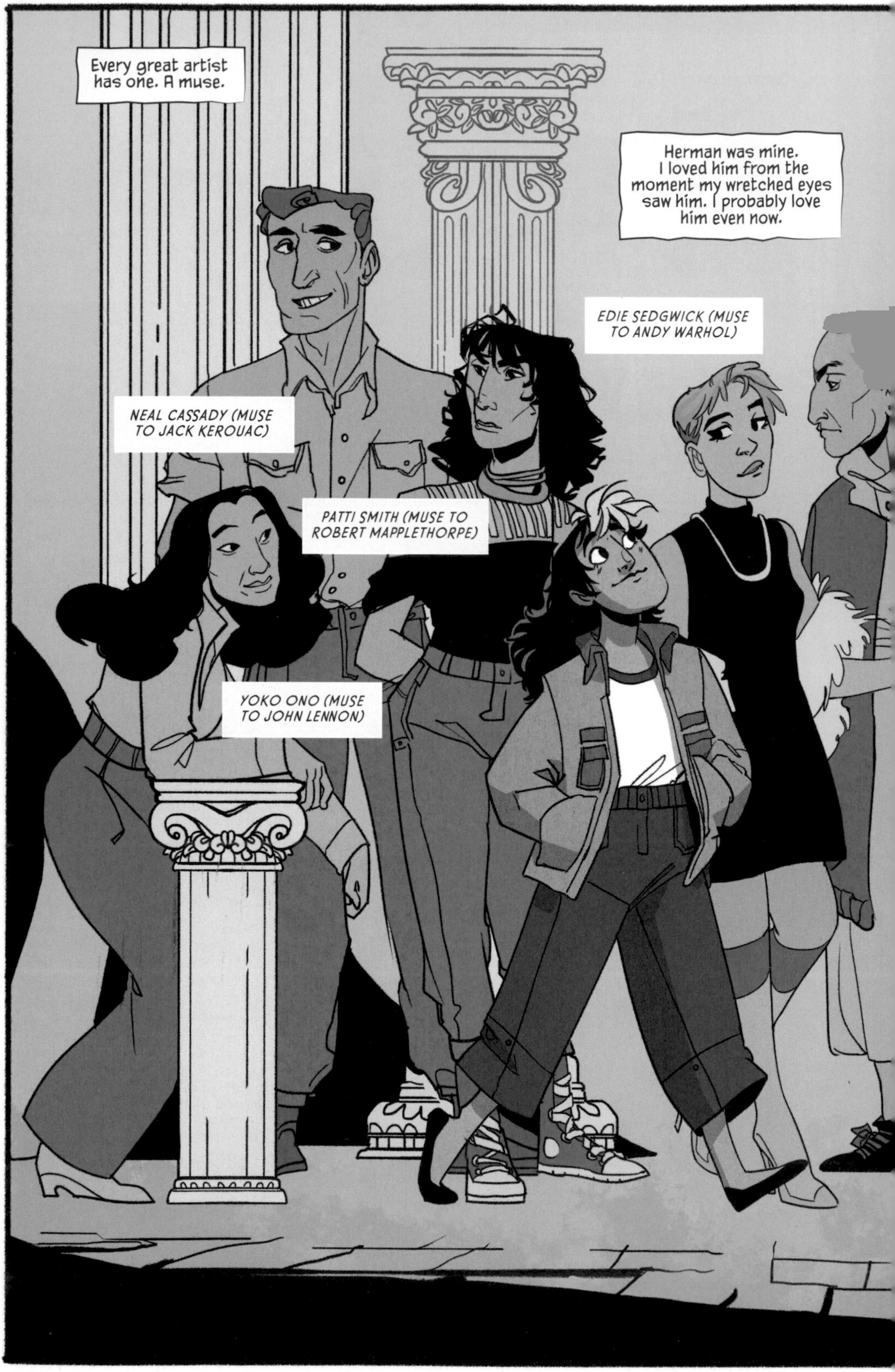
Every great artist has one. A muse.
Herman was mine. I loved him from the moment my wretched eyes saw him. I probably love him even now.
EDIE SEDGWICK (MUSE TO ANDY WARHOL)
NEAL CASSADY (MUSE TO JACK KEROUAC)
PATTI SMITH (MUSE TO ROBERT MAPPLETHORPE)
YOKO ONO (MUSE TO JOHN LENNON)

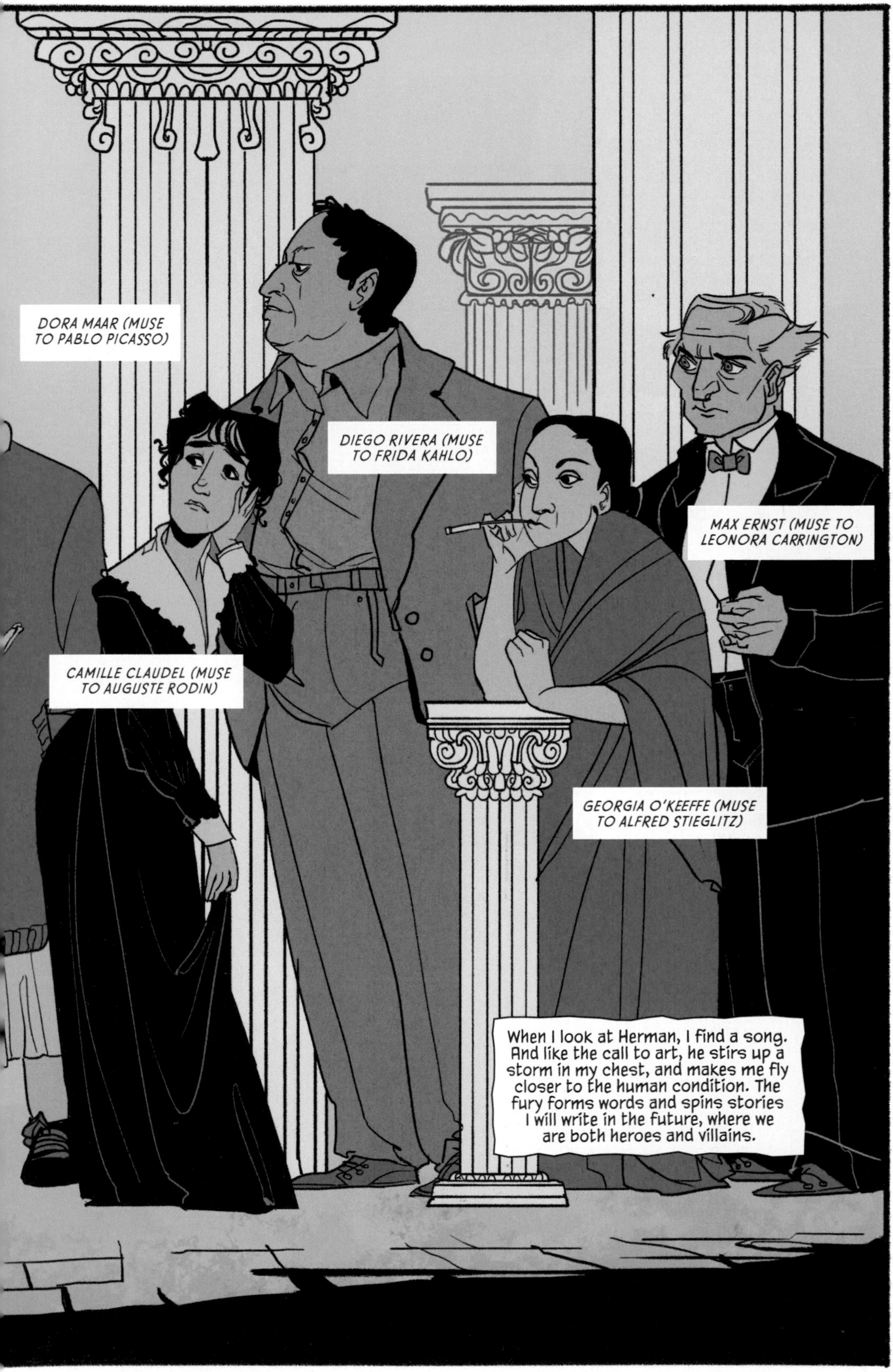
DORA MAAR (MUSE TO PABLO PICASSO)
DIEGO RIVERA (MUSE TO FRIDA KAHLO)
MAX ERNST (MUSE TO LEONORA CARRINGTON)
CAMILLE CLAUDEL (MUSE TO AUGUSTE RODIN)
GEORGIA O'KEEFFE (MUSE TO ALFRED STIEGLITZ)
When I look at Herman, I find a song. And like the call to art, he stirs up a storm in my chest, and makes me fly closer to the human condition. The fury forms words and spins stories I will write in the future, where we are both heroes and villains.

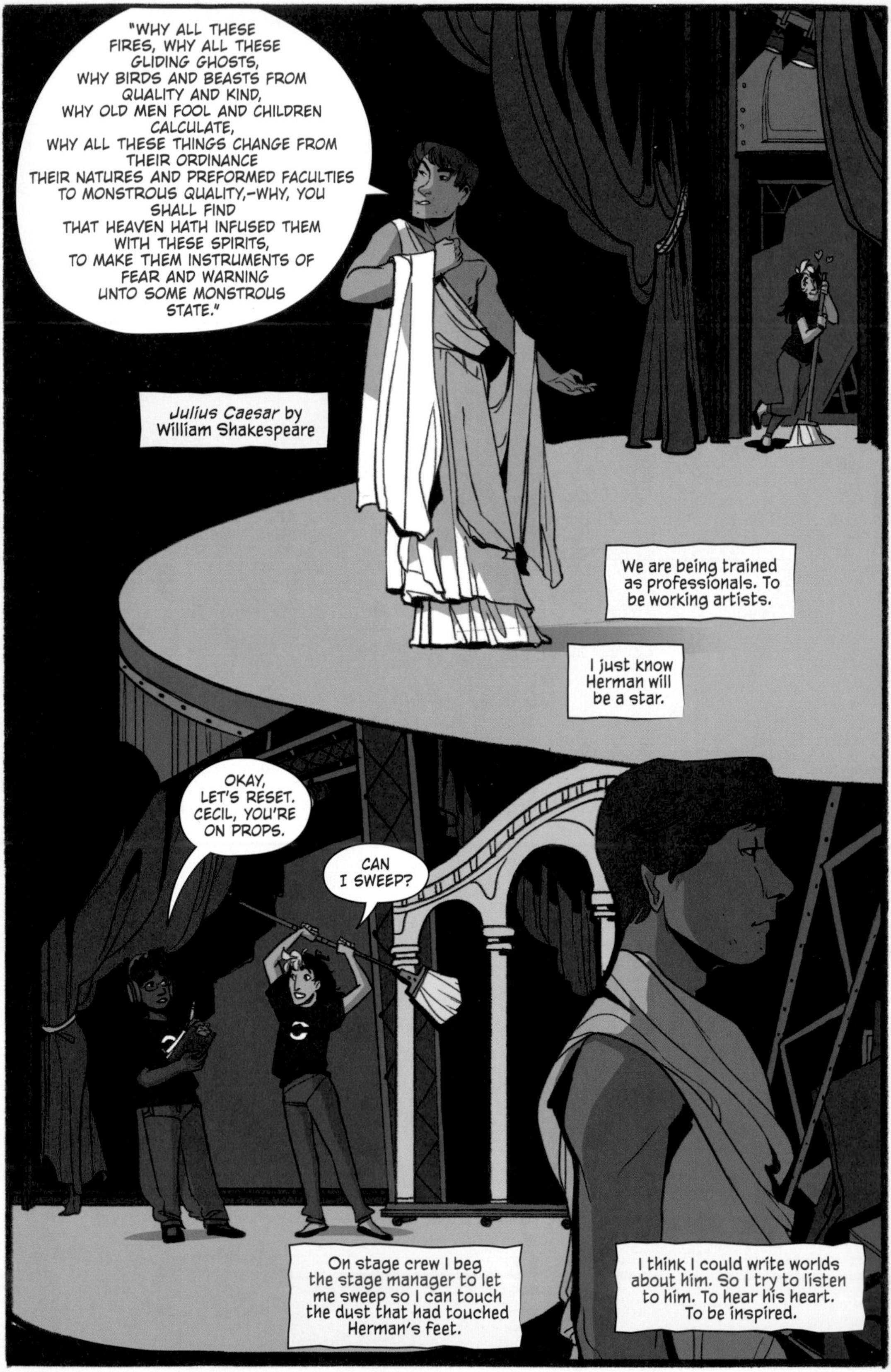
"WHY ALL THESE FIRES, WHY ALL THESE GLIDING GHOSTS, WHY BIRDS AND BEASTS FROM QUALITY AND KIND, WHY OLD MEN FOOL AND CHILDREN CALCULATE, WHY ALL THESE THINGS CHANGE FROM THEIR ORDINANCE THEIR NATURES AND PREFORMED FACULTIES TO MONSTROUS QUALITY,–WHY, YOU SHALL FIND THAT HEAVEN HATH INFUSED THEM WITH THESE SPIRITS, TO MAKE THEM INSTRUMENTS OF FEAR AND WARNING UNTO SOME MONSTROUS STATE."
Julius Caesar by William Shakespeare
We are being trained as professionals. To be working artists.
I just know Herman will be a star.
OKAY, LET'S RESET. CECIL, YOU'RE ON PROPS.
CAN I SWEEP?
On stage crew I beg the stage manager to let me sweep so I can touch the dust that had touched Herman's feet.
I think I could write worlds about him. So I try to listen to him. To hear his heart. To be inspired.

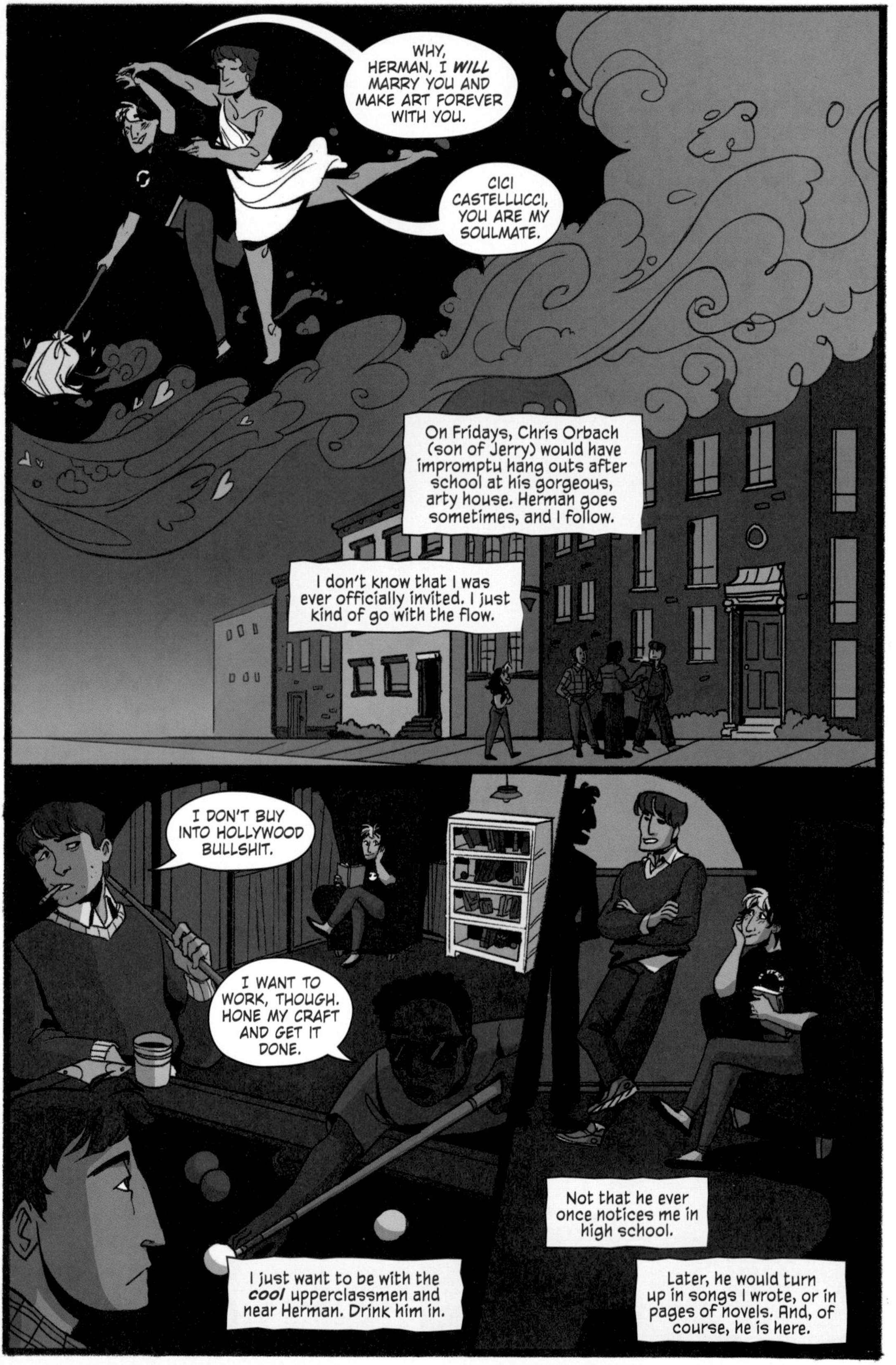

WHY, HERMAN, I *WILL* MARRY YOU AND MAKE ART FOREVER WITH YOU.
CICI CASTELLUCCI, YOU ARE MY SOULMATE.
On Fridays, Chris Orbach (son of Jerry) would have impromptu hang outs after school at his gorgeous, arty house. Herman goes sometimes, and I follow.
I don't know that I was ever officially invited. I just kind of go with the flow.
I DON'T BUY INTO HOLLYWOOD BULLSHIT.
I WANT TO WORK, THOUGH. HONE MY CRAFT AND GET IT DONE.
I just want to be with the *cool* upperclassmen and near Herman. Drink him in.
Not that he ever once notices me in high school.
Later, he would turn up in songs I wrote, or in pages of novels. And, of course, he is here.

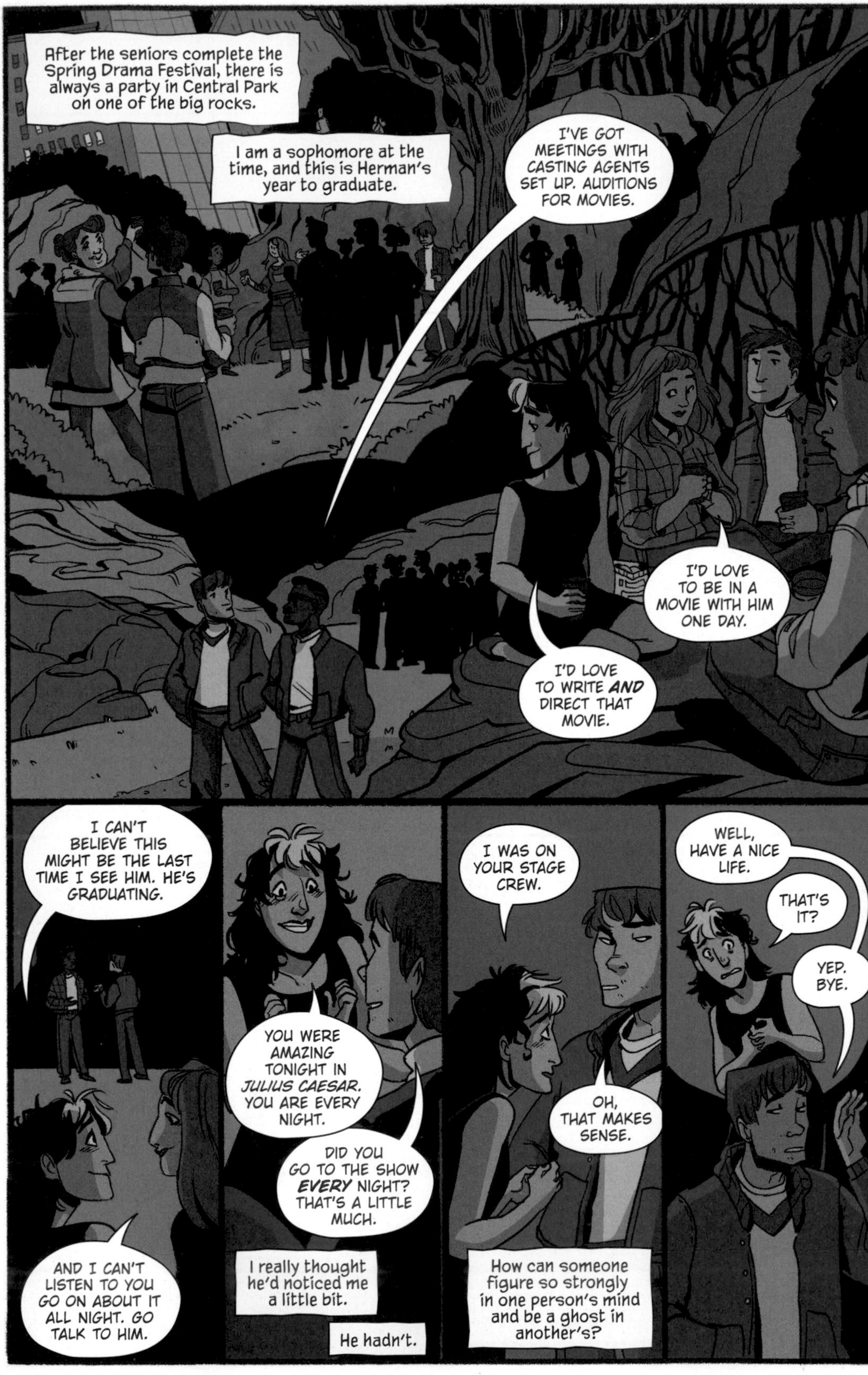
After the seniors complete the Spring Drama Festival, there is always a party in Central Park on one of the big rocks.
I am a sophomore at the time, and this is Herman's year to graduate.
I'VE GOT MEETINGS WITH CASTING AGENTS SET UP. AUDITIONS FOR MOVIES.
I'D LOVE TO BE IN A MOVIE WITH HIM ONE DAY.
I'D LOVE TO WRITE *AND* DIRECT THAT MOVIE.
I CAN'T BELIEVE THIS MIGHT BE THE LAST TIME I SEE HIM. HE'S GRADUATING.
AND I CAN'T LISTEN TO YOU GO ON ABOUT IT ALL NIGHT. GO TALK TO HIM.
YOU WERE AMAZING TONIGHT IN *JULIUS CAESAR.* YOU ARE EVERY NIGHT.
DID YOU GO TO THE SHOW *EVERY* NIGHT? THAT'S A LITTLE MUCH.
I really thought he'd noticed me a little bit.
He hadn't.
I WAS ON YOUR STAGE CREW.
OH, THAT MAKES SENSE.
How can someone figure so strongly in one person's mind and be a ghost in another's?
WELL, HAVE A NICE LIFE.
THAT'S IT?
YEP. BYE.

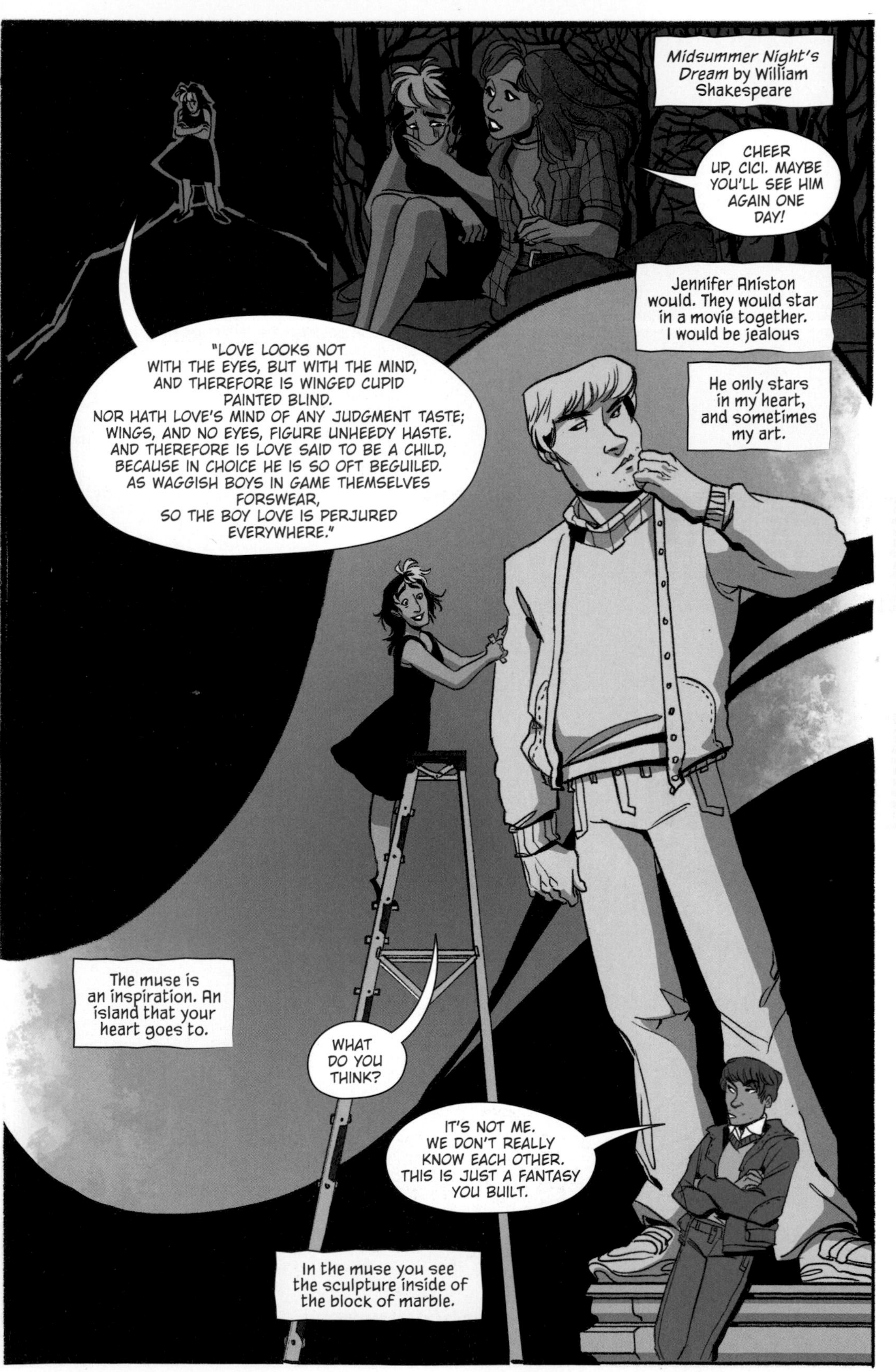

Midsummer Night's Dream by William Shakespeare
CHEER UP, CICI. MAYBE YOU'LL SEE HIM AGAIN ONE DAY!
Jennifer Aniston would. They would star in a movie together. I would be jealous
"LOVE LOOKS NOT WITH THE EYES, BUT WITH THE MIND, AND THEREFORE IS WINGED CUPID PAINTED BLIND. NOR HATH LOVE'S MIND OF ANY JUDGMENT TASTE; WINGS, AND NO EYES, FIGURE UNHEEDY HASTE. AND THEREFORE IS LOVE SAID TO BE A CHILD, BECAUSE IN CHOICE HE IS SO OFT BEGUILED. AS WAGGISH BOYS IN GAME THEMSELVES FORSWEAR, SO THE BOY LOVE IS PERJURED EVERYWHERE."
He only stars in my heart, and sometimes my art.
The muse is an inspiration. An island that your heart goes to.
WHAT DO YOU THINK?
IT'S NOT ME. WE DON'T REALLY KNOW EACH OTHER. THIS IS JUST A FANTASY YOU BUILT.
In the muse you see the sculpture inside of the block of marble.

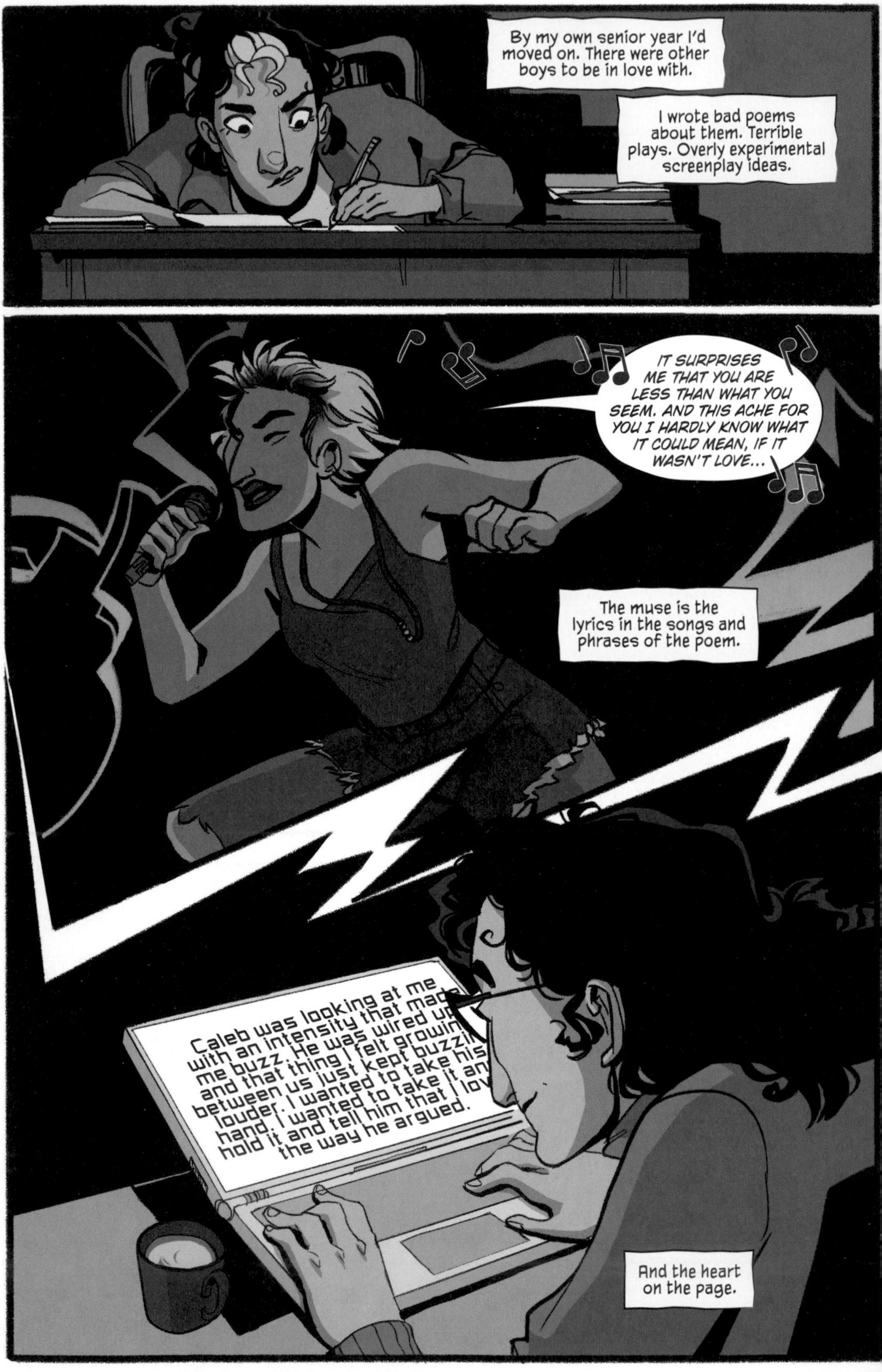

By my own senior year I'd moved on. There were other boys to be in love with.
I wrote bad poems about them. Terrible plays. Overly experimental screenplay ideas.
IT SURPRISES ME THAT YOU ARE LESS THAN WHAT YOU SEEM. AND THIS ACHE FOR YOU I HARDLY KNOW WHAT IT COULD MEAN, IF IT WASN'T LOVE...
The muse is the lyrics in the songs and phrases of the poem.
Caleb was looking at me
with an intensity that
me buzz. He was wired
and that thing I felt
between us just kept
louder. I wanted to take his
hand. I wanted to take it
hold it and tell him that I
the way he argued.
And the heart on the page.

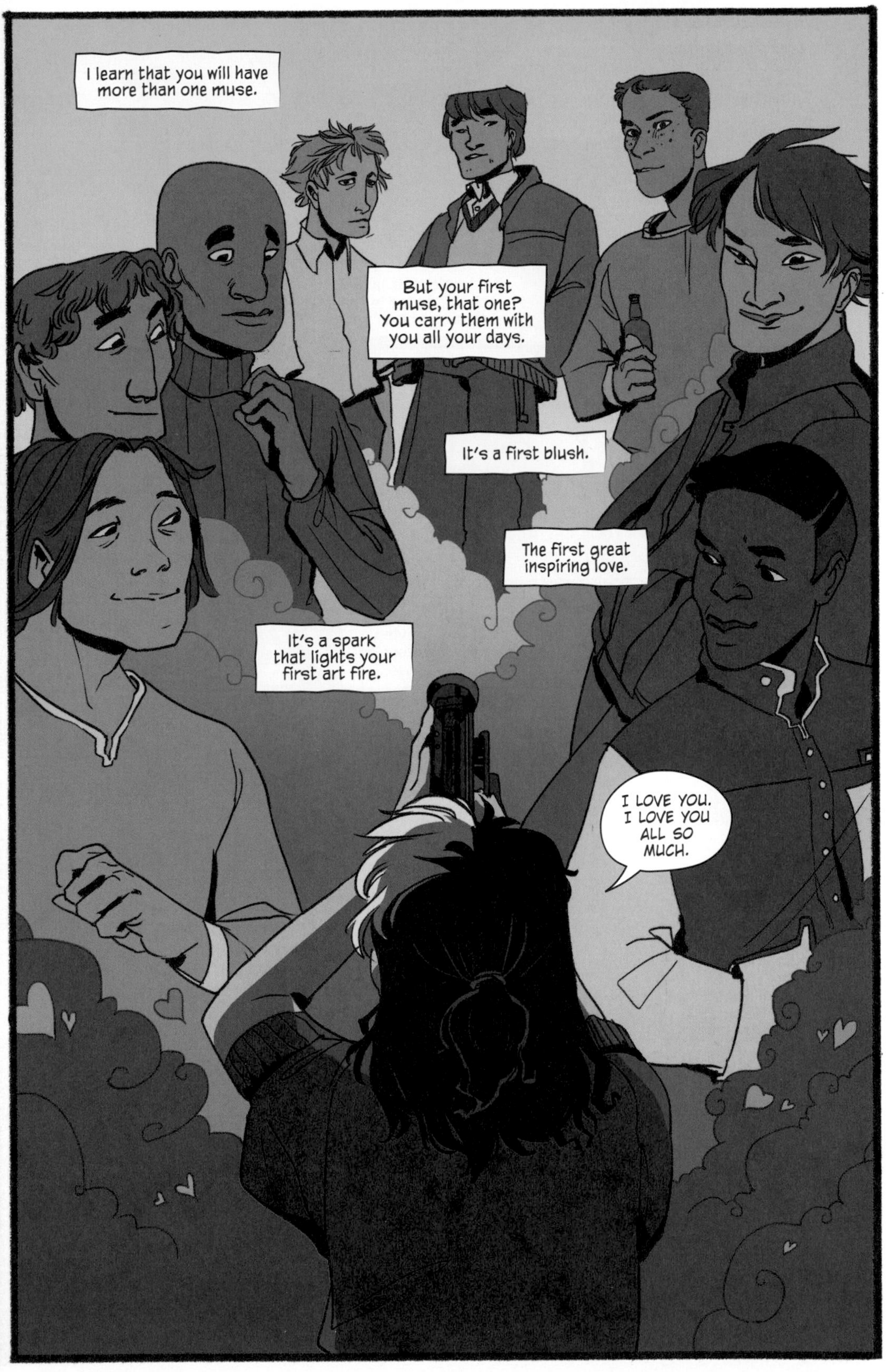
I learn that you will have more than one muse.
But your first muse, that one? You carry them with you all your days.
It's a first blush.
The first great inspiring love.
It's a spark that lights your first art fire.
I LOVE YOU. I LOVE YOU ALL SO MUCH.

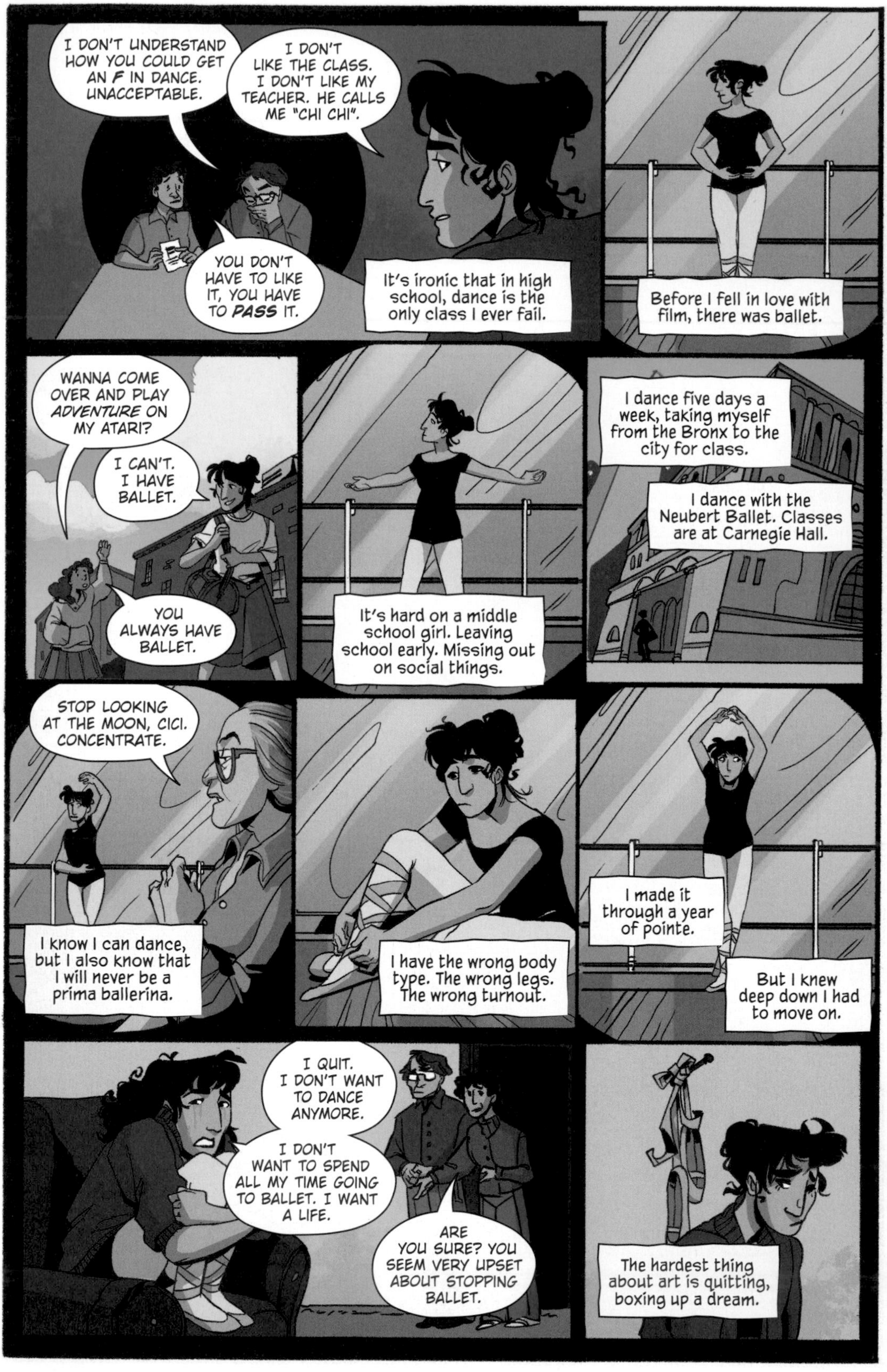
I DON'T UNDERSTAND HOW YOU COULD GET AN *F* IN DANCE. UNACCEPTABLE.
I DON'T LIKE THE CLASS. I DON'T LIKE MY TEACHER. HE CALLS ME "CHI CHI".
YOU DON'T HAVE TO LIKE IT, YOU HAVE TO ***PASS*** IT.
It's ironic that in high school, dance is the only class I ever fail.
Before I fell in love with film, there was ballet.
WANNA COME OVER AND PLAY *ADVENTURE* ON MY ATARI?
I CAN'T. I HAVE BALLET.
YOU ALWAYS HAVE BALLET.
It's hard on a middle school girl. Leaving school early. Missing out on social things.
I dance five days a week, taking myself from the Bronx to the city for class.
I dance with the Neubert Ballet. Classes are at Carnegie Hall.
STOP LOOKING AT THE MOON, CICI. CONCENTRATE.
I know I can dance, but I also know that I will never be a prima ballerina.
I have the wrong body type. The wrong legs. The wrong turnout.
I made it through a year of pointe.
But I knew deep down I had to move on.
I QUIT. I DON'T WANT TO DANCE ANYMORE.
I DON'T WANT TO SPEND ALL MY TIME GOING TO BALLET. I WANT A LIFE.
ARE YOU SURE? YOU SEEM VERY UPSET ABOUT STOPPING BALLET.
The hardest thing about art is quitting, boxing up a dream.

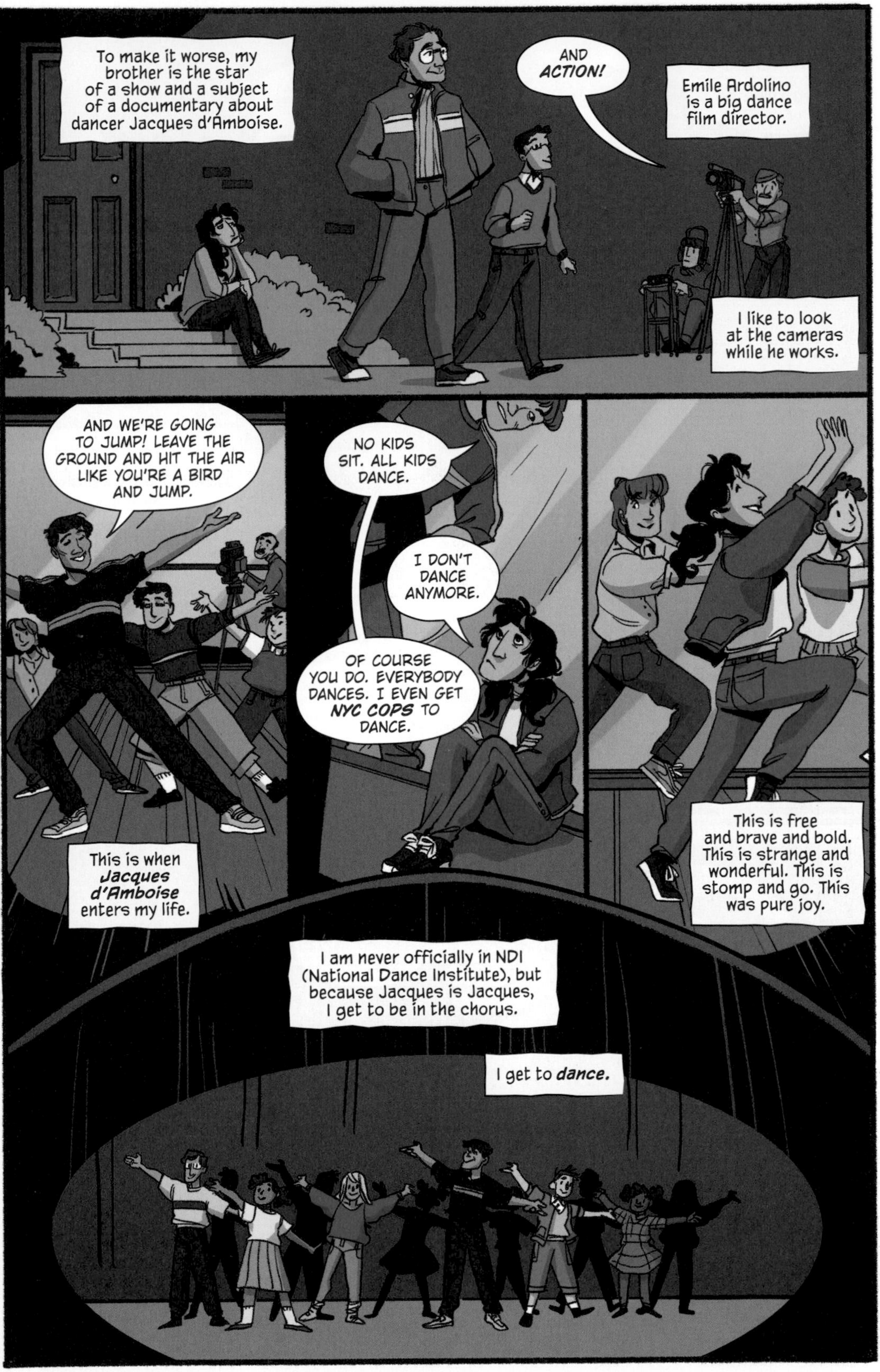
To make it worse, my brother is the star of a show and a subject of a documentary about dancer Jacques d'Amboise.
AND *ACTION!*
Emile Ardolino is a big dance film director.
I like to look at the cameras while he works.
AND WE'RE GOING TO JUMP! LEAVE THE GROUND AND HIT THE AIR LIKE YOU'RE A BIRD AND JUMP.
This is when ***Jacques d'Amboise*** enters my life.
NO KIDS SIT. ALL KIDS DANCE.
I DON'T DANCE ANYMORE.
OF COURSE YOU DO. EVERYBODY DANCES. I EVEN GET ***NYC COPS*** TO DANCE.
This is free and brave and bold. This is strange and wonderful. This is stomp and go. This was pure joy.
I am never officially in NDI (National Dance Institute), but because Jacques is Jacques, I get to be in the chorus.
I get to ***dance.***

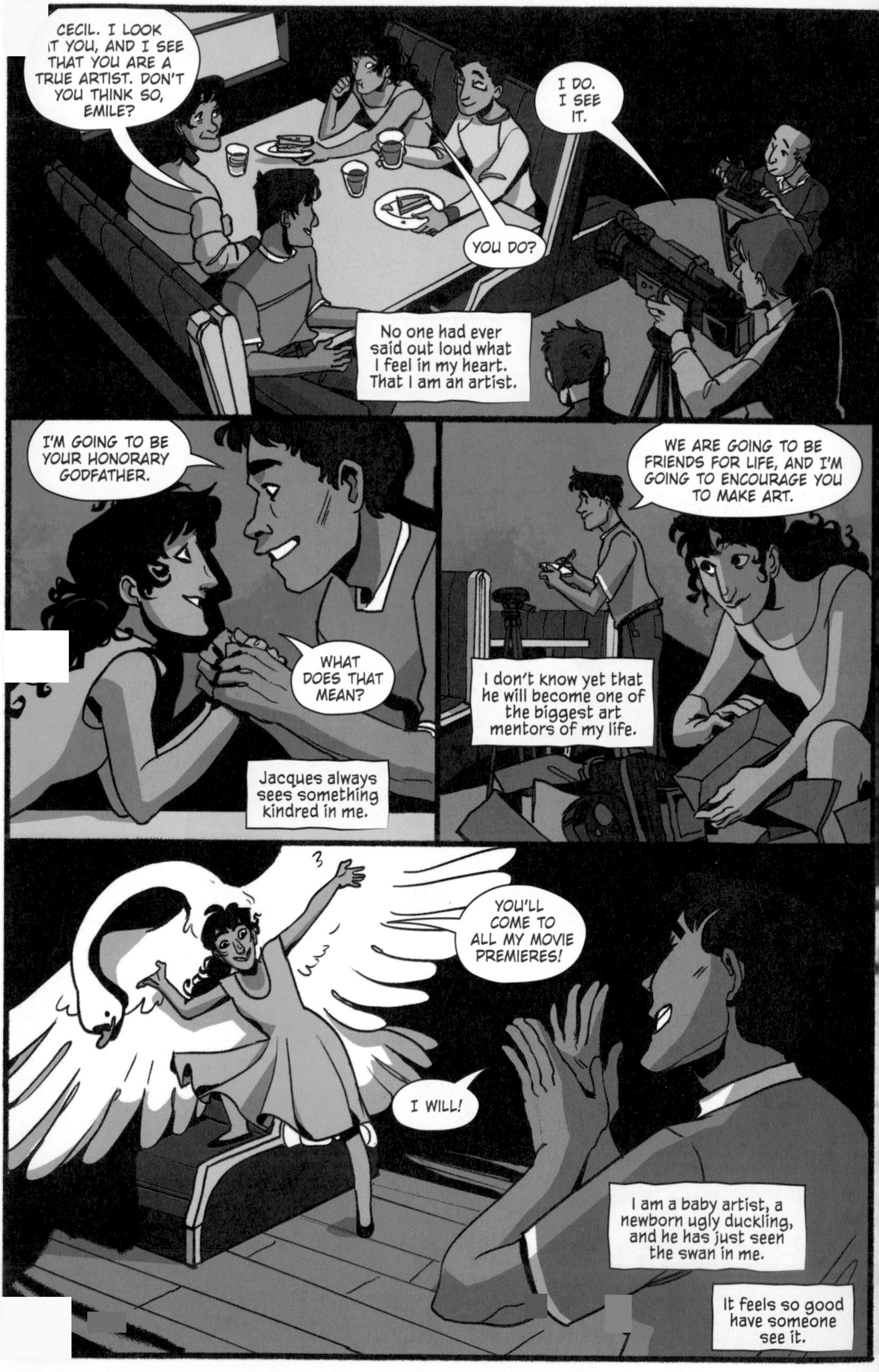

CECIL. I LOOK T YOU, AND I SEE THAT YOU ARE A TRUE ARTIST. DON'T YOU THINK SO, EMILE?
I DO. I SEE IT.
YOU DO?
No one had ever said out loud what I feel in my heart. That I am an artist.
I'M GOING TO BE YOUR HONORARY GODFATHER.
WHAT DOES THAT MEAN?
Jacques always sees something kindred in me.
WE ARE GOING TO BE FRIENDS FOR LIFE, AND I'M GOING TO ENCOURAGE YOU TO MAKE ART.
I don't know yet that he will become one of the biggest art mentors of my life.
YOU'LL COME TO ALL MY MOVIE PREMIERES!
I WILL!
I am a baby artist, a newborn ugly duckling, and he has just seen the swan in me.
It feels so good have someone see it.

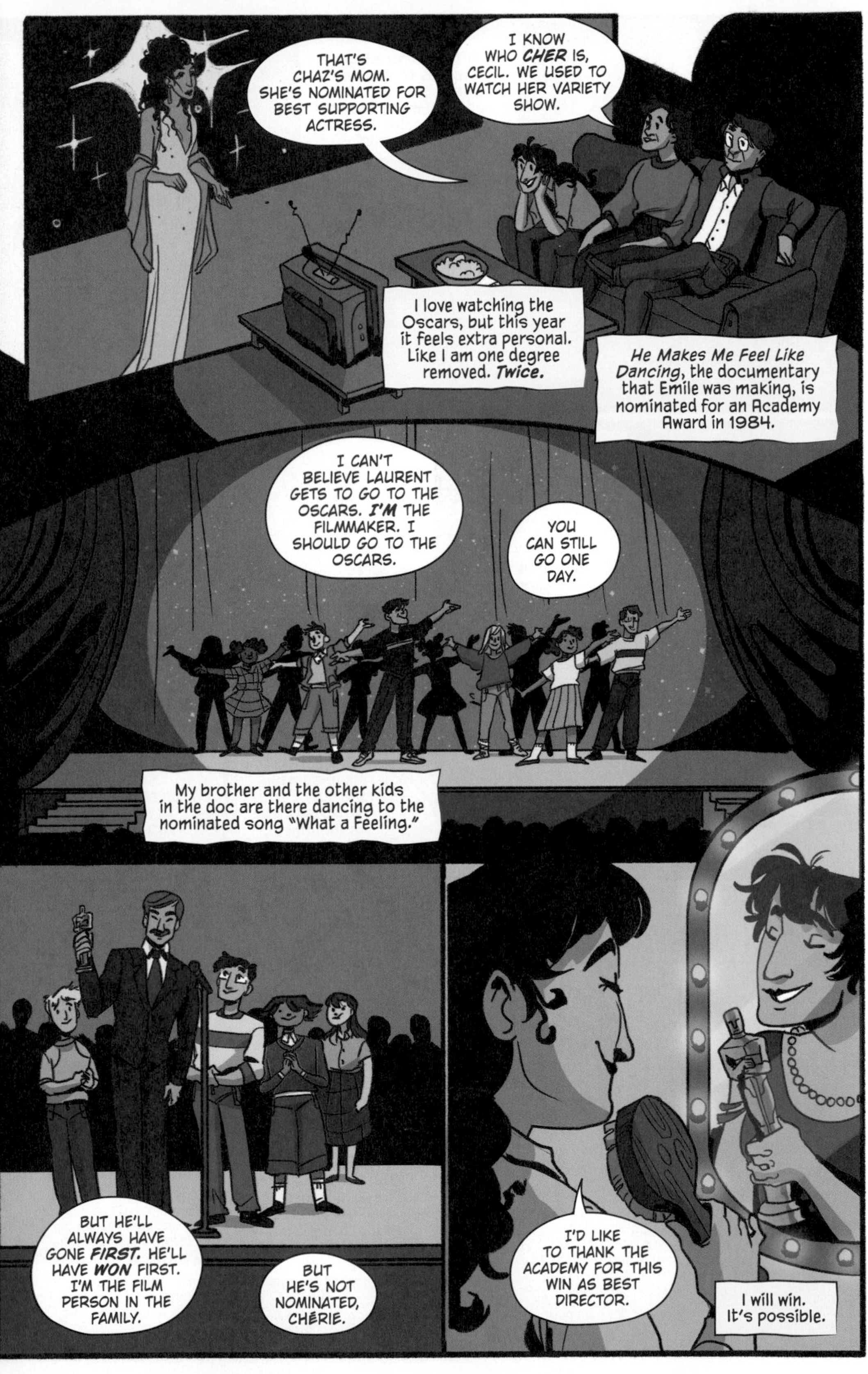
THAT'S CHAZ'S MOM. SHE'S NOMINATED FOR BEST SUPPORTING ACTRESS.
I KNOW WHO *CHER* IS, CECIL. WE USED TO WATCH HER VARIETY SHOW.
I love watching the Oscars, but this year it feels extra personal. Like I am one degree removed. *Twice.*
He Makes Me Feel Like Dancing, the documentary that Emile was making, is nominated for an Academy Award in 1984.
I CAN'T BELIEVE LAURENT GETS TO GO TO THE OSCARS. *I'M* THE FILMMAKER. I SHOULD GO TO THE OSCARS.
YOU CAN STILL GO ONE DAY.
My brother and the other kids in the doc are there dancing to the nominated song "What a Feeling."
BUT HE'LL ALWAYS HAVE GONE *FIRST.* HE'LL HAVE *WON* FIRST. I'M THE FILM PERSON IN THE FAMILY.
BUT HE'S NOT NOMINATED, CHÉRIE.
I'D LIKE TO THANK THE ACADEMY FOR THIS WIN AS BEST DIRECTOR.
I will win. It's possible.

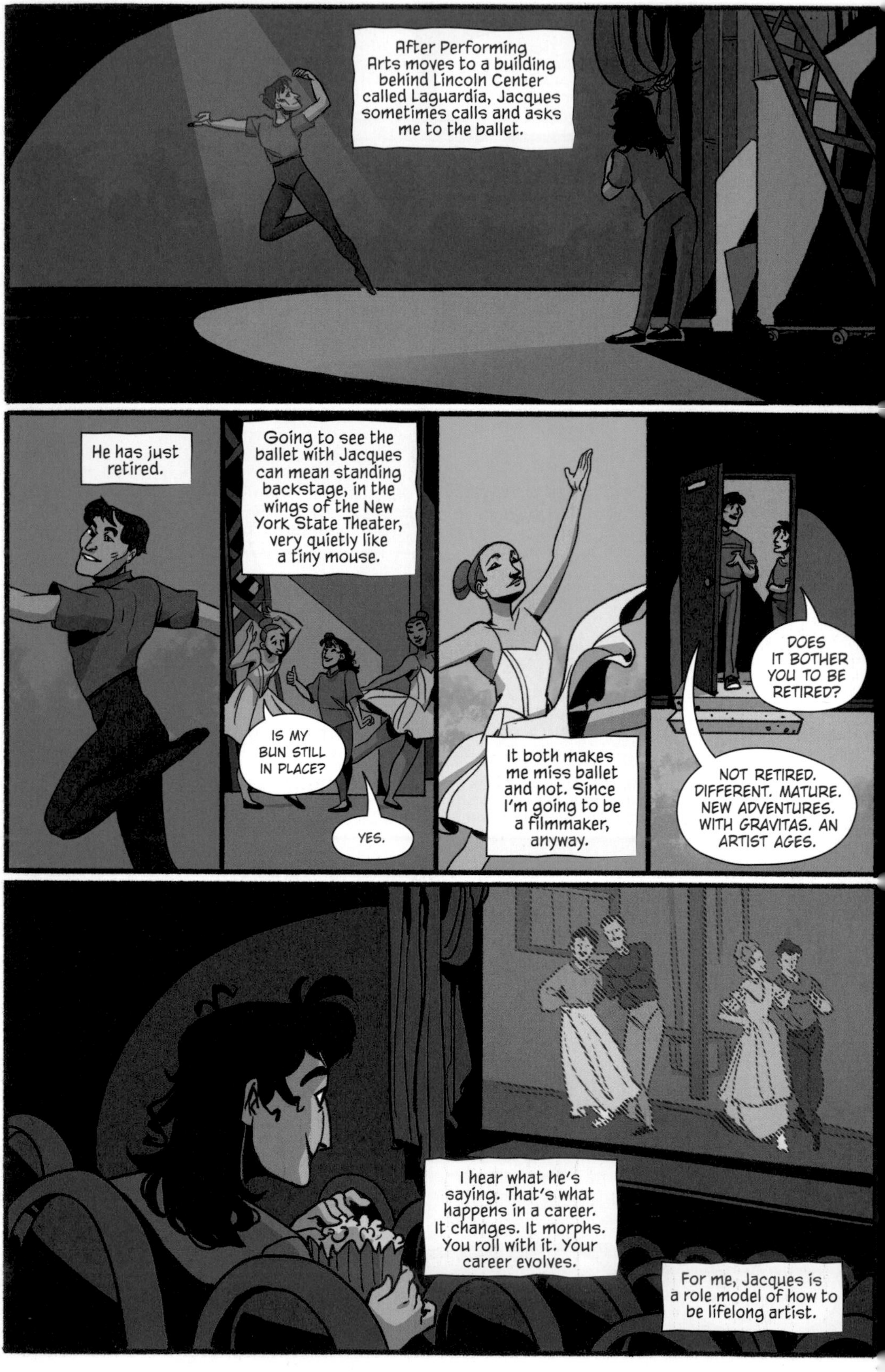
After Performing Arts moves to a building behind Lincoln Center called Laguardia, Jacques sometimes calls and asks me to the ballet.
He has just retired.
Going to see the ballet with Jacques can mean standing backstage, in the wings of the New York State Theater, very quietly like a tiny mouse.
IS MY BUN STILL IN PLACE?
YES.
It both makes me miss ballet and not. Since I'm going to be a filmmaker, anyway.
DOES IT BOTHER YOU TO BE RETIRED?
NOT RETIRED. DIFFERENT. MATURE. NEW ADVENTURES. WITH GRAVITAS. AN ARTIST AGES.
I hear what he's saying. That's what happens in a career. It changes. It morphs. You roll with it. Your career evolves.
For me, Jacques is a role model of how to be lifelong artist.

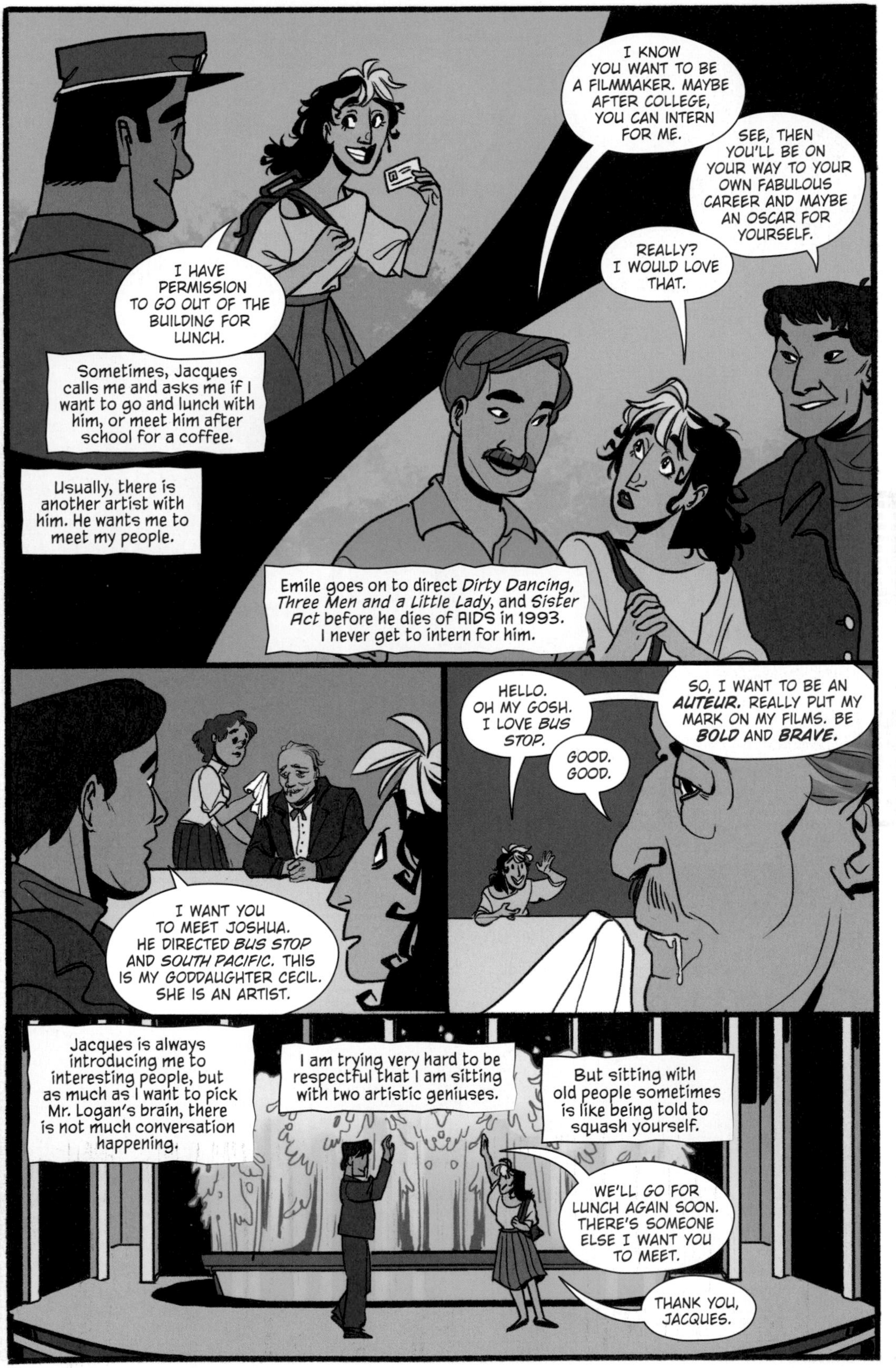
I HAVE PERMISSION TO GO OUT OF THE BUILDING FOR LUNCH.
Sometimes, Jacques calls me and asks me if I want to go and lunch with him, or meet him after school for a coffee.
Usually, there is another artist with him. He wants me to meet my people.
I KNOW YOU WANT TO BE A FILMMAKER. MAYBE AFTER COLLEGE, YOU CAN INTERN FOR ME.
SEE, THEN YOU'LL BE ON YOUR WAY TO YOUR OWN FABULOUS CAREER AND MAYBE AN OSCAR FOR YOURSELF.
REALLY? I WOULD LOVE THAT.
Emile goes on to direct *Dirty Dancing*, *Three Men and a Little Lady*, and *Sister Act* before he dies of AIDS in 1993. I never get to intern for him.
I WANT YOU TO MEET JOSHUA. HE DIRECTED *BUS STOP* AND *SOUTH PACIFIC*. THIS IS MY GODDAUGHTER CECIL. SHE IS AN ARTIST.
HELLO. OH MY GOSH. I LOVE *BUS STOP*.
GOOD. GOOD.
SO, I WANT TO BE AN ***AUTEUR.*** REALLY PUT MY MARK ON MY FILMS. BE **BOLD** AND ***BRAVE.***
Jacques is always introducing me to interesting people, but as much as I want to pick Mr. Logan's brain, there is not much conversation happening.
I am trying very hard to be respectful that I am sitting with two artistic geniuses.
But sitting with old people sometimes is like being told to squash yourself.
WE'LL GO FOR LUNCH AGAIN SOON. THERE'S SOMEONE ELSE I WANT YOU TO MEET.
THANK YOU, JACQUES.

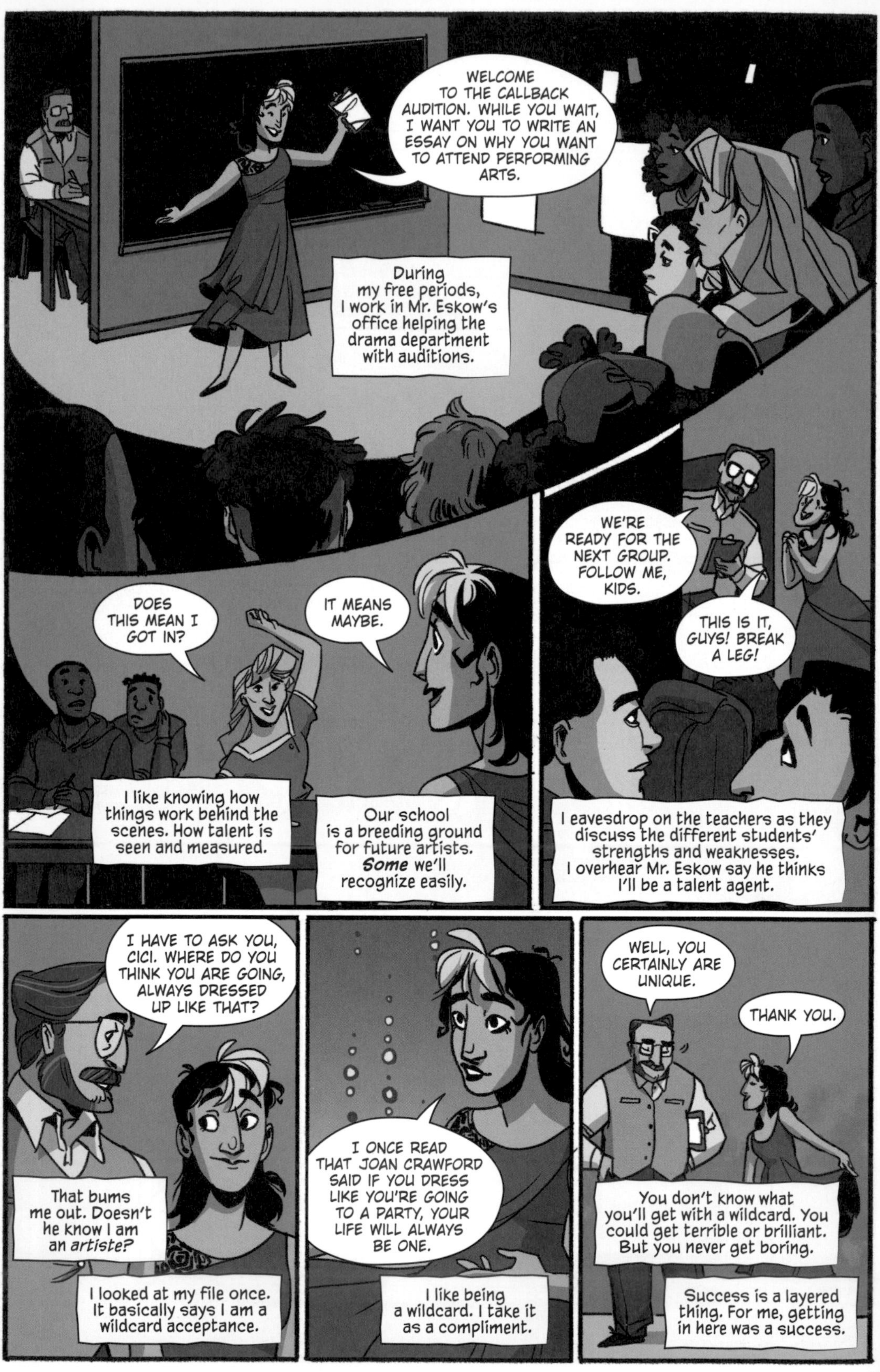
WELCOME TO THE CALLBACK AUDITION. WHILE YOU WAIT, I WANT YOU TO WRITE AN ESSAY ON WHY YOU WANT TO ATTEND PERFORMING ARTS.
During my free periods, I work in Mr. Eskow's office helping the drama department with auditions.
DOES THIS MEAN I GOT IN?
IT MEANS MAYBE.
I like knowing how things work behind the scenes. How talent is seen and measured.
Our school is a breeding ground for future artists. *Some* we'll recognize easily.
WE'RE READY FOR THE NEXT GROUP. FOLLOW ME, KIDS.
THIS IS IT, GUYS! BREAK A LEG!
I eavesdrop on the teachers as they discuss the different students' strengths and weaknesses. I overhear Mr. Eskow say he thinks I'll be a talent agent.
I HAVE TO ASK YOU, CICI. WHERE DO YOU THINK YOU ARE GOING, ALWAYS DRESSED UP LIKE THAT?
That bums me out. Doesn't he know I am an *artiste*?
I looked at my file once. It basically says I am a wildcard acceptance.
I ONCE READ THAT JOAN CRAWFORD SAID IF YOU DRESS LIKE YOU'RE GOING TO A PARTY, YOUR LIFE WILL ALWAYS BE ONE.
I like being a wildcard. I take it as a compliment.
WELL, YOU CERTAINLY ARE UNIQUE.
THANK YOU.
You don't know what you'll get with a wildcard. You could get terrible or brilliant. But you never get boring.
Success is a layered thing. For me, getting in here was a success.

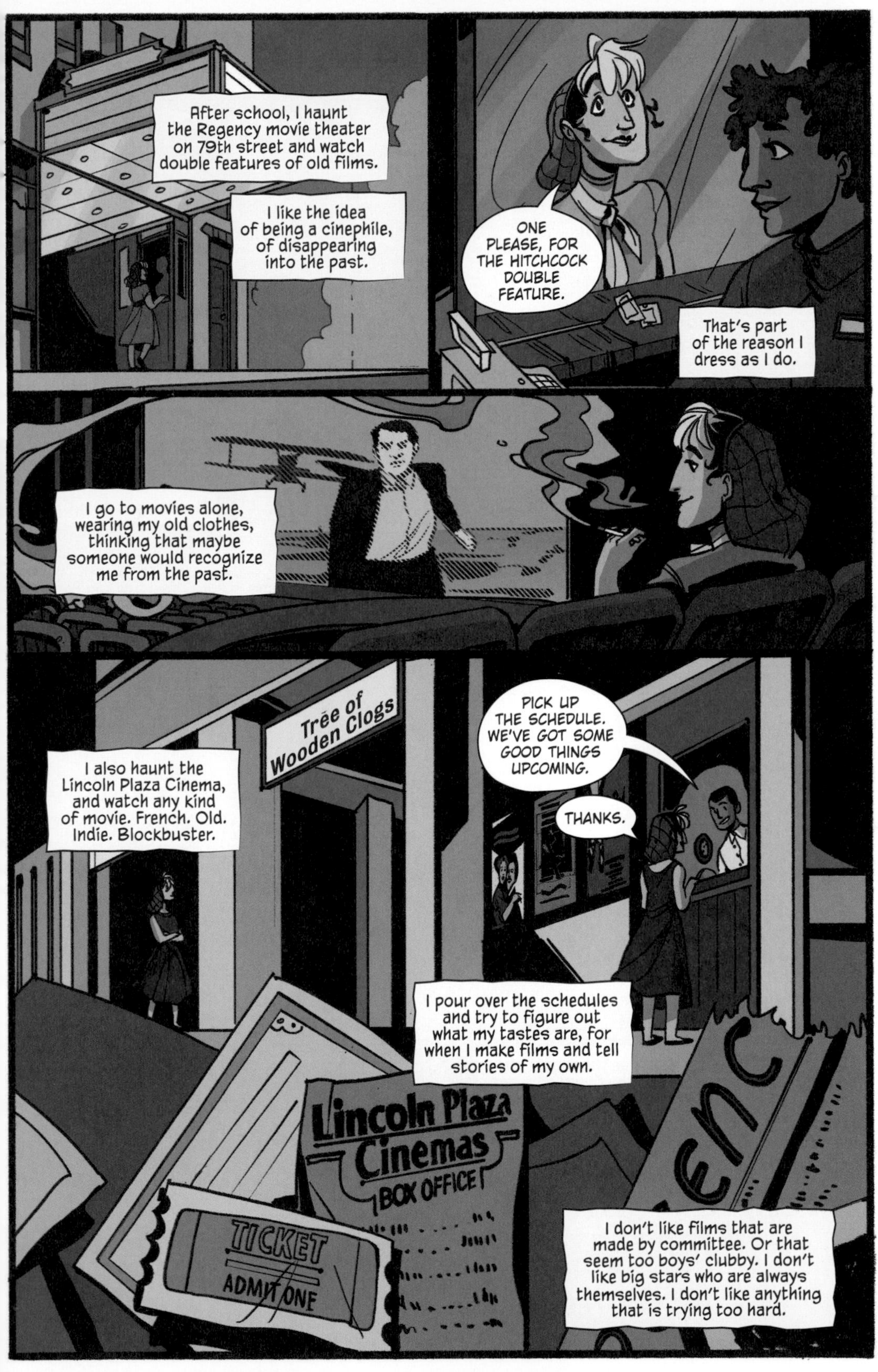
After school, I haunt the Regency movie theater on 79th street and watch double features of old films.
I like the idea of being a cinephile, of disappearing into the past.
ONE PLEASE, FOR THE HITCHCOCK DOUBLE FEATURE.
That's part of the reason I dress as I do.
I go to movies alone, wearing my old clothes, thinking that maybe someone would recognize me from the past.
Trēe of Wooden Clogs
I also haunt the Lincoln Plaza Cinema, and watch any kind of movie. French. Old. Indie. Blockbuster.
PICK UP THE SCHEDULE. WE'VE GOT SOME GOOD THINGS UPCOMING.
THANKS.
I pour over the schedules and try to figure out what my tastes are, for when I make films and tell stories of my own.
Lincoln Plaza Cinemas
BOX OFFICE
TICKET
ADMIT ONE
I don't like films that are made by committee. Or that seem too boys' clubby. I don't like big stars who are always themselves. I don't like anything that is trying too hard.

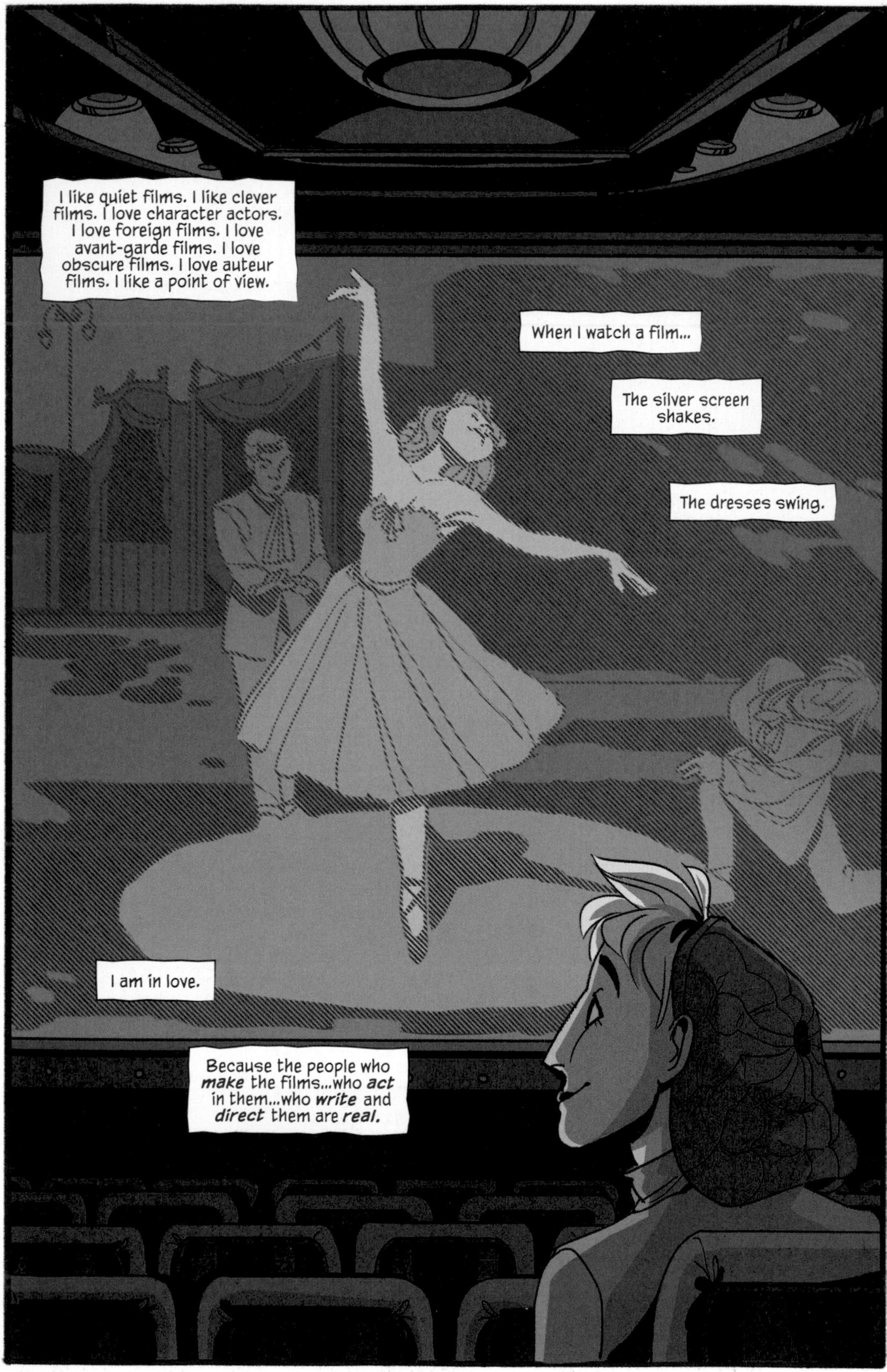
I like quiet films. I like clever films. I love character actors. I love foreign films. I love avant-garde films. I love obscure films. I love auteur films. I like a point of view.
When I watch a film...
The silver screen shakes.
The dresses swing.
I am in love.
Because the people who *make* the films...who *act* in them...who *write* and *direct* them are *real.*

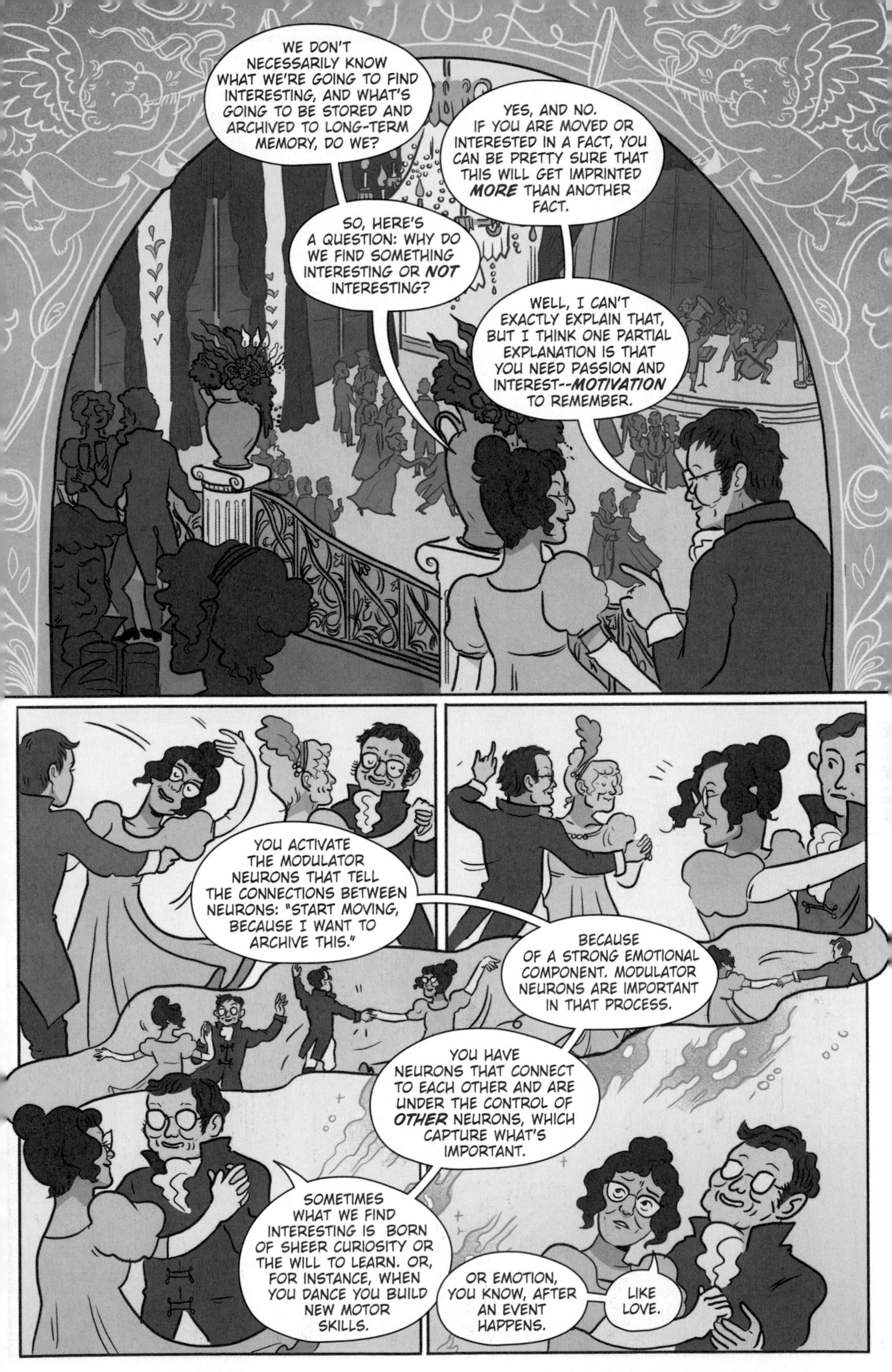
WE DON'T NECESSARILY KNOW WHAT WE'RE GOING TO FIND INTERESTING, AND WHAT'S GOING TO BE STORED AND ARCHIVED TO LONG-TERM MEMORY, DO WE?
YES, AND NO. IF YOU ARE MOVED OR INTERESTED IN A FACT, YOU CAN BE PRETTY SURE THAT THIS WILL GET IMPRINTED ***MORE*** THAN ANOTHER FACT.
SO, HERE'S A QUESTION: WHY DO WE FIND SOMETHING INTERESTING OR ***NOT*** INTERESTING?
WELL, I CAN'T EXACTLY EXPLAIN THAT, BUT I THINK ONE PARTIAL EXPLANATION IS THAT YOU NEED PASSION AND INTEREST--***MOTIVATION*** TO REMEMBER.
YOU ACTIVATE THE MODULATOR NEURONS THAT TELL THE CONNECTIONS BETWEEN NEURONS: "START MOVING, BECAUSE I WANT TO ARCHIVE THIS."
BECAUSE OF A STRONG EMOTIONAL COMPONENT. MODULATOR NEURONS ARE IMPORTANT IN THAT PROCESS.
YOU HAVE NEURONS THAT CONNECT TO EACH OTHER AND ARE UNDER THE CONTROL OF ***OTHER*** NEURONS, WHICH CAPTURE WHAT'S IMPORTANT.
SOMETIMES WHAT WE FIND INTERESTING IS BORN OF SHEER CURIOSITY OR THE WILL TO LEARN. OR, FOR INSTANCE, WHEN YOU DANCE YOU BUILD NEW MOTOR SKILLS.
OR EMOTION, YOU KNOW, AFTER AN EVENT HAPPENS.
LIKE LOVE.

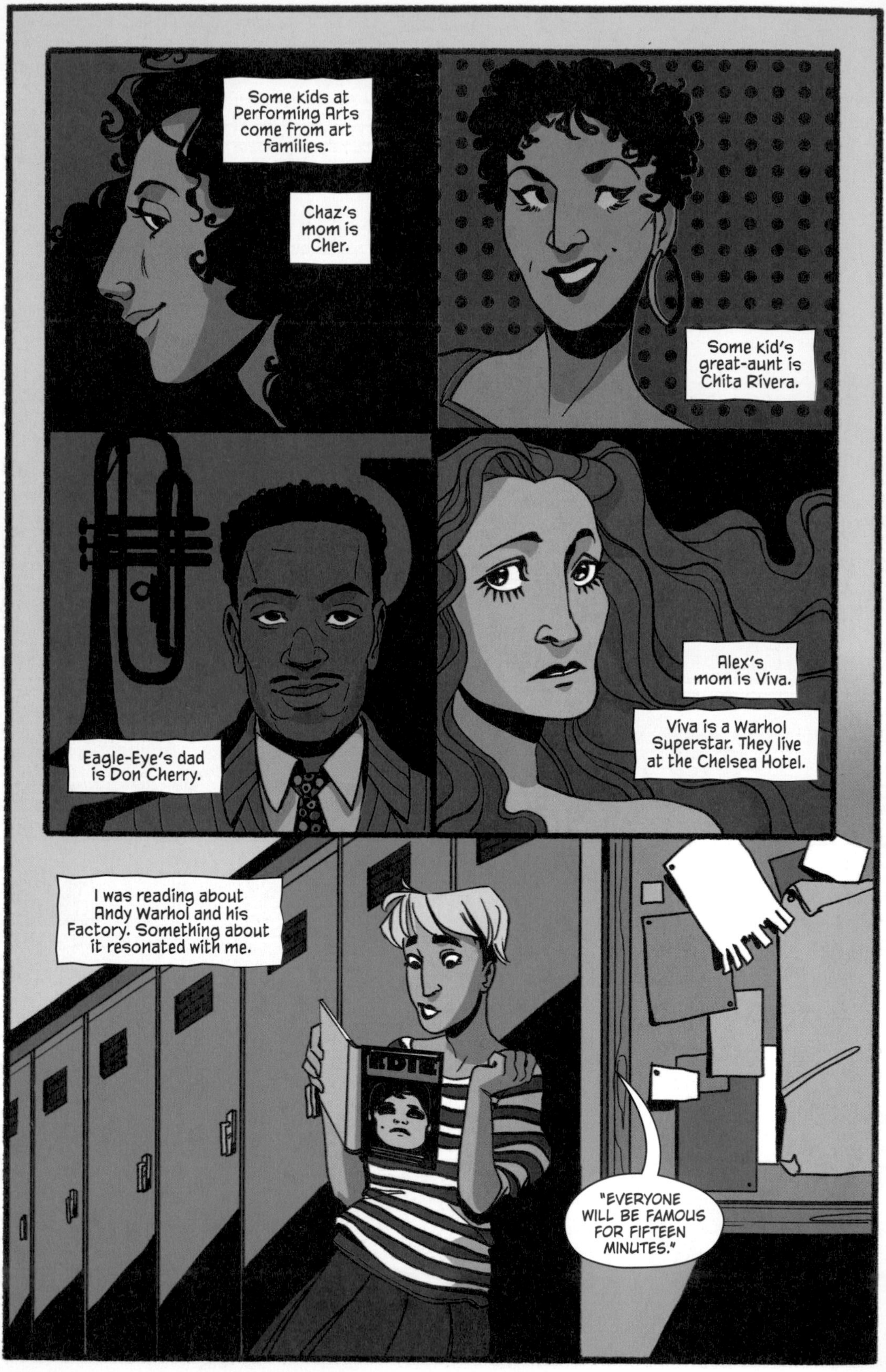

Some kids at Performing Arts come from art families.
Chaz's mom is Cher.
Some kid's great-aunt is Chita Rivera.
Eagle-Eye's dad is Don Cherry.
Alex's mom is Viva.
Viva is a Warhol Superstar. They live at the Chelsea Hotel.
I was reading about Andy Warhol and his Factory. Something about it resonated with me.
"EVERYONE WILL BE FAMOUS FOR FIFTEEN MINUTES."

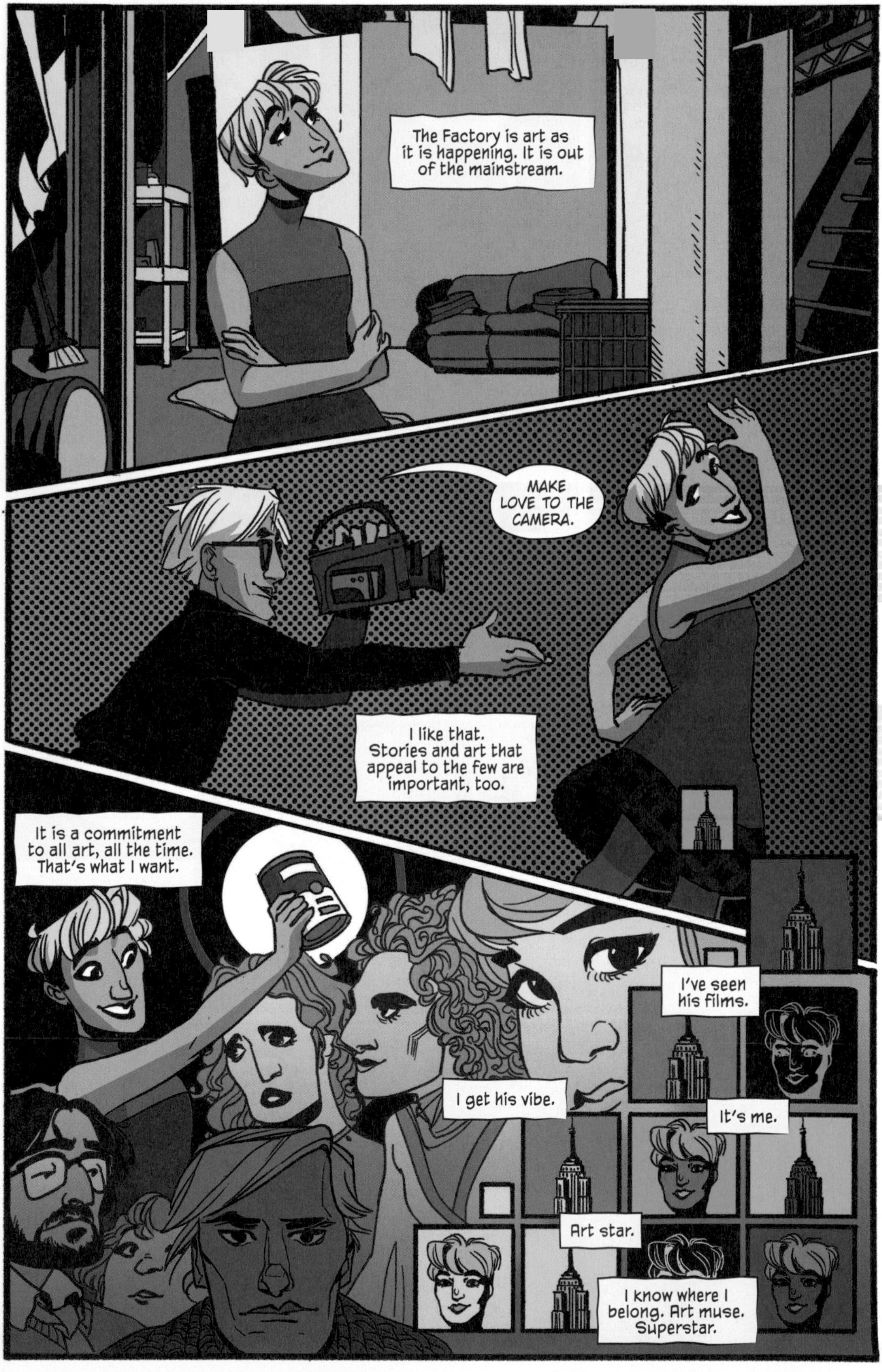

The Factory is art as it is happening. It is out of the mainstream.
MAKE LOVE TO THE CAMERA.
I like that. Stories and art that appeal to the few are important, too.
It is a commitment to all art, all the time. That's what I want.
I've seen his films.
I get his vibe.
It's me.
Art star.
I know where I belong. Art muse. Superstar.

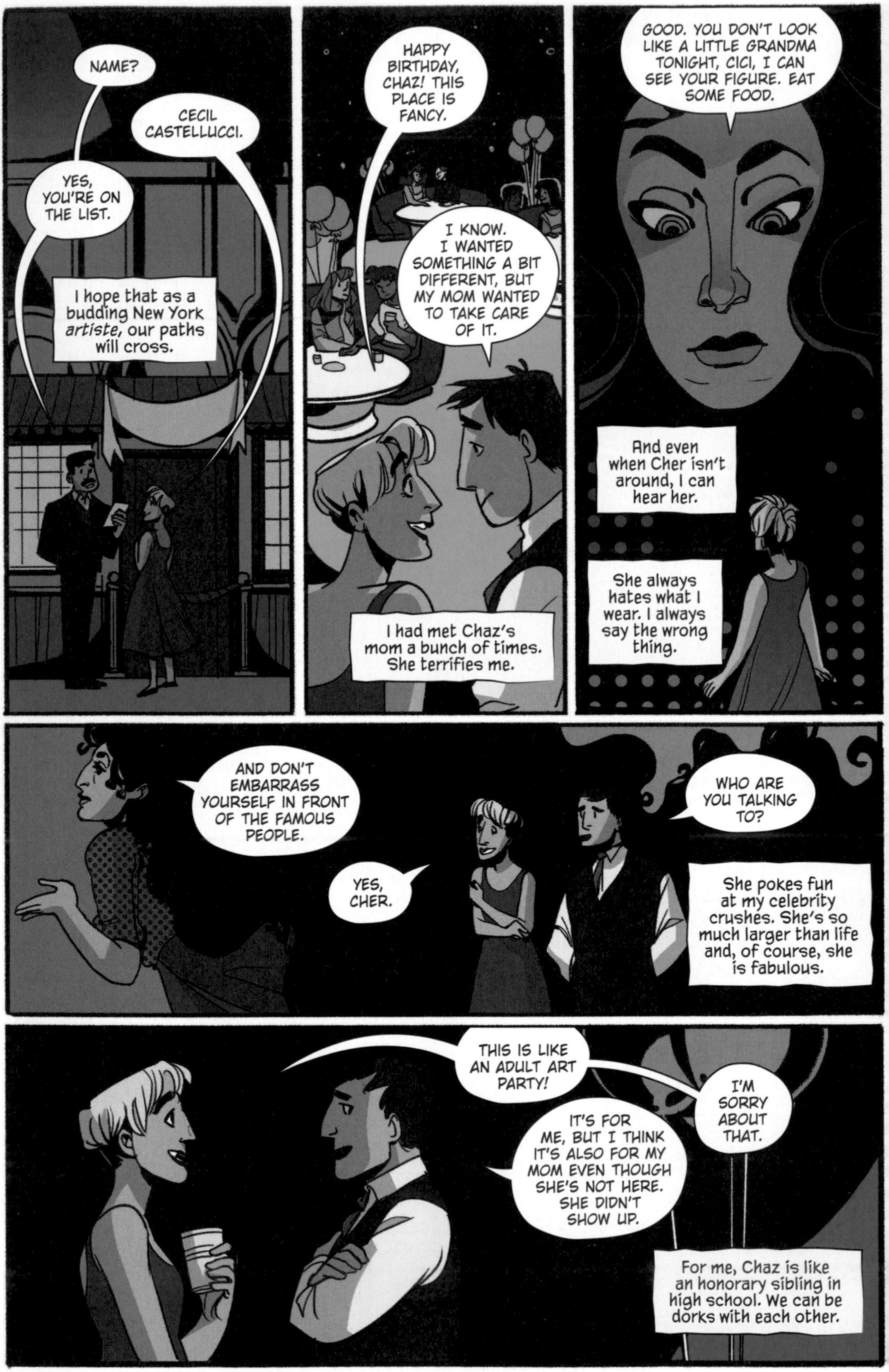
NAME?
CECIL CASTELLUCCI.
YES, YOU'RE ON THE LIST.
I hope that as a budding New York *artiste*, our paths will cross.
HAPPY BIRTHDAY, CHAZ! THIS PLACE IS FANCY.
I KNOW. I WANTED SOMETHING A BIT DIFFERENT, BUT MY MOM WANTED TO TAKE CARE OF IT.
I had met Chaz's mom a bunch of times. She terrifies me.
GOOD. YOU DON'T LOOK LIKE A LITTLE GRANDMA TONIGHT, CICI, I CAN SEE YOUR FIGURE. EAT SOME FOOD.
And even when Cher isn't around, I can hear her.
She always hates what I wear. I always say the wrong thing.
AND DON'T EMBARRASS YOURSELF IN FRONT OF THE FAMOUS PEOPLE.
YES, CHER.
WHO ARE YOU TALKING TO?
She pokes fun at my celebrity crushes. She's so much larger than life and, of course, she is fabulous.
THIS IS LIKE AN ADULT ART PARTY!
IT'S FOR ME, BUT I THINK IT'S ALSO FOR MY MOM EVEN THOUGH SHE'S NOT HERE. SHE DIDN'T SHOW UP.
I'M SORRY ABOUT THAT.
For me, Chaz is like an honorary sibling in high school. We can be dorks with each other.

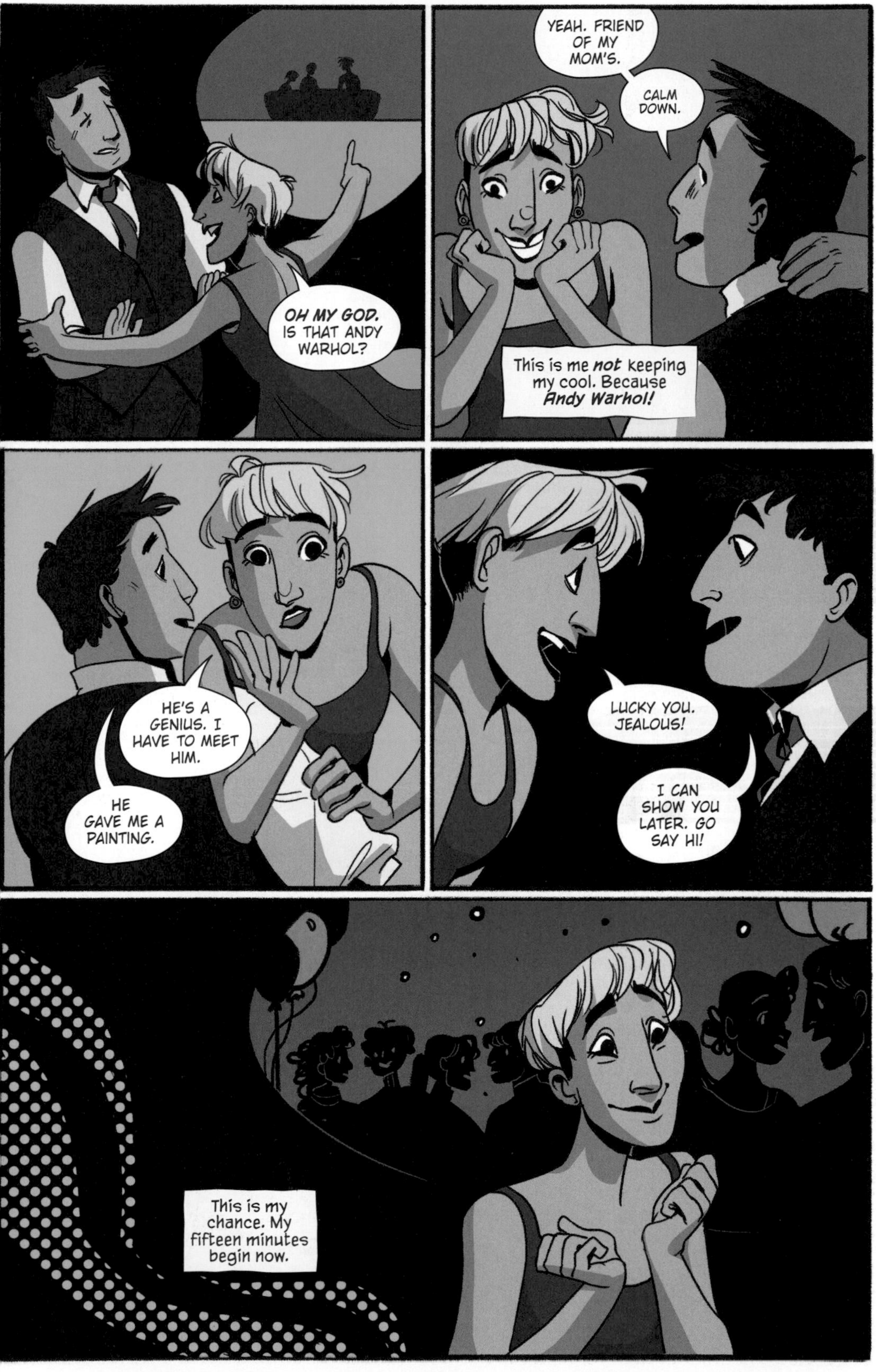
OH MY GOD. IS THAT ANDY WARHOL?
YEAH. FRIEND OF MY MOM'S.
CALM DOWN.
This is me not keeping my cool. Because Andy Warhol!
HE'S A GENIUS. I HAVE TO MEET HIM.
HE GAVE ME A PAINTING.
LUCKY YOU. JEALOUS!
I CAN SHOW YOU LATER. GO SAY HI!
This is my chance. My fifteen minutes begin now.

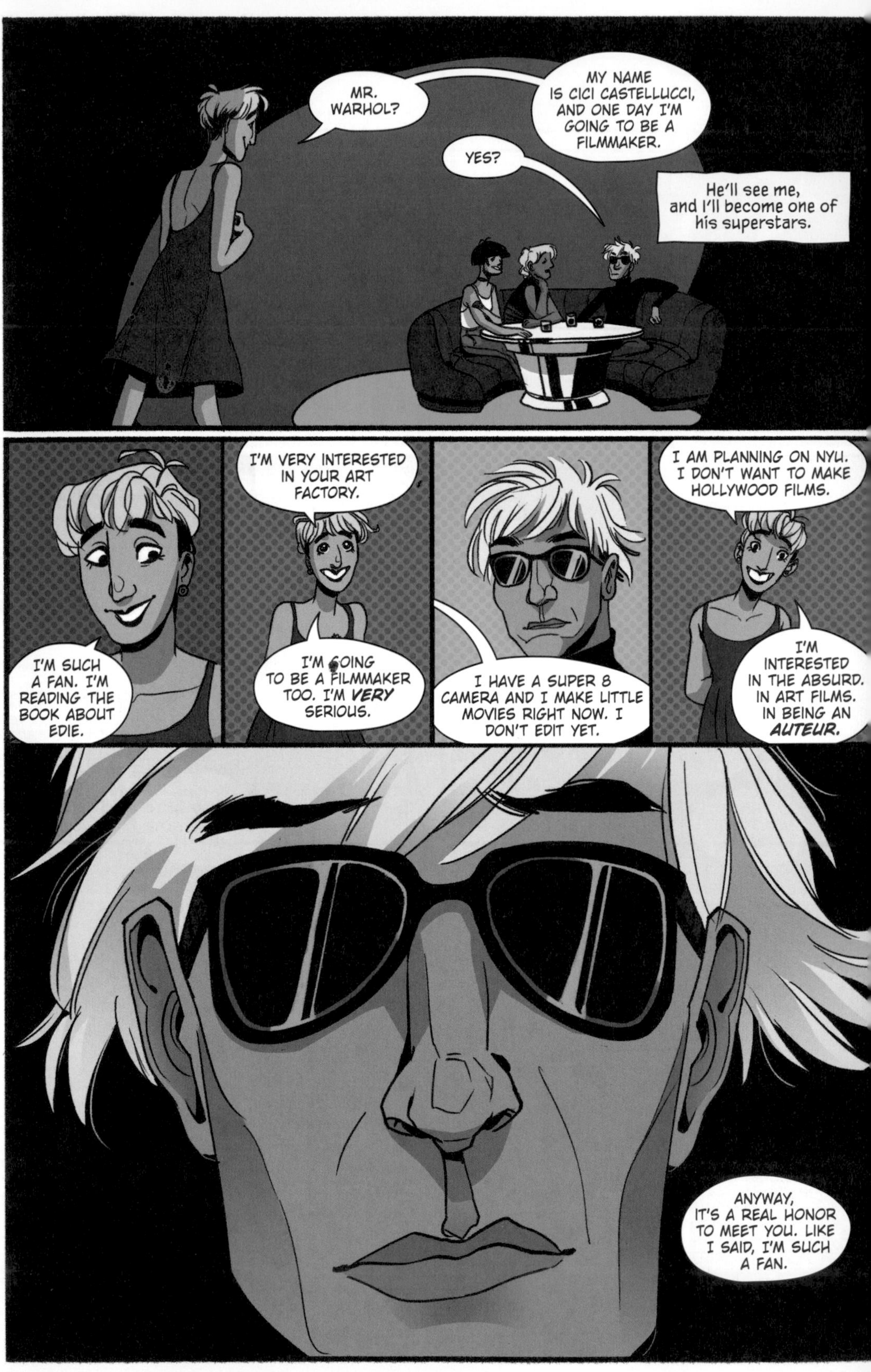
MR. WARHOL?
MY NAME IS CICI CASTELLUCCI, AND ONE DAY I'M GOING TO BE A FILMMAKER.
YES?
He'll see me, and I'll become one of his superstars.
I'M SUCH A FAN. I'M READING THE BOOK ABOUT EDIE.
I'M VERY INTERESTED IN YOUR ART FACTORY.
I'M GOING TO BE A FILMMAKER TOO. I'M VERY SERIOUS.
I HAVE A SUPER 8 CAMERA AND I MAKE LITTLE MOVIES RIGHT NOW. I DON'T EDIT YET.
I AM PLANNING ON NYU. I DON'T WANT TO MAKE HOLLYWOOD FILMS.
I'M INTERESTED IN THE ABSURD. IN ART FILMS. IN BEING AN AUTEUR.
ANYWAY, IT'S A REAL HONOR TO MEET YOU. LIKE I SAID, I'M SUCH A FAN.

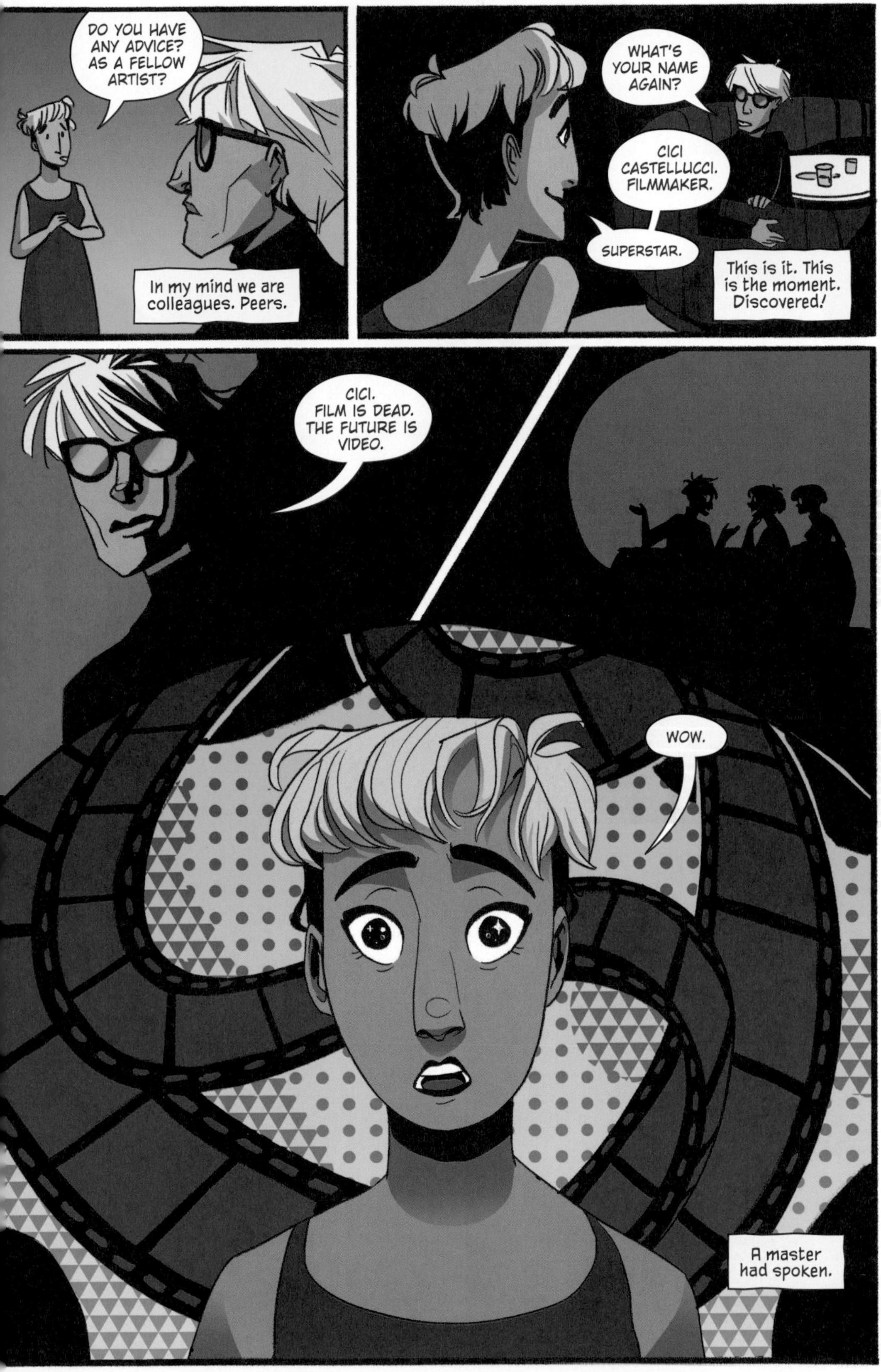
DO YOU HAVE ANY ADVICE? AS A FELLOW ARTIST?
In my mind we are colleagues. Peers.
WHAT'S YOUR NAME AGAIN?
CICI CASTELLUCCI. FILMMAKER.
SUPERSTAR.
This is it. This is the moment. Discovered!
CICI. FILM IS DEAD. THE FUTURE IS VIDEO.
WOW.
A master had spoken.

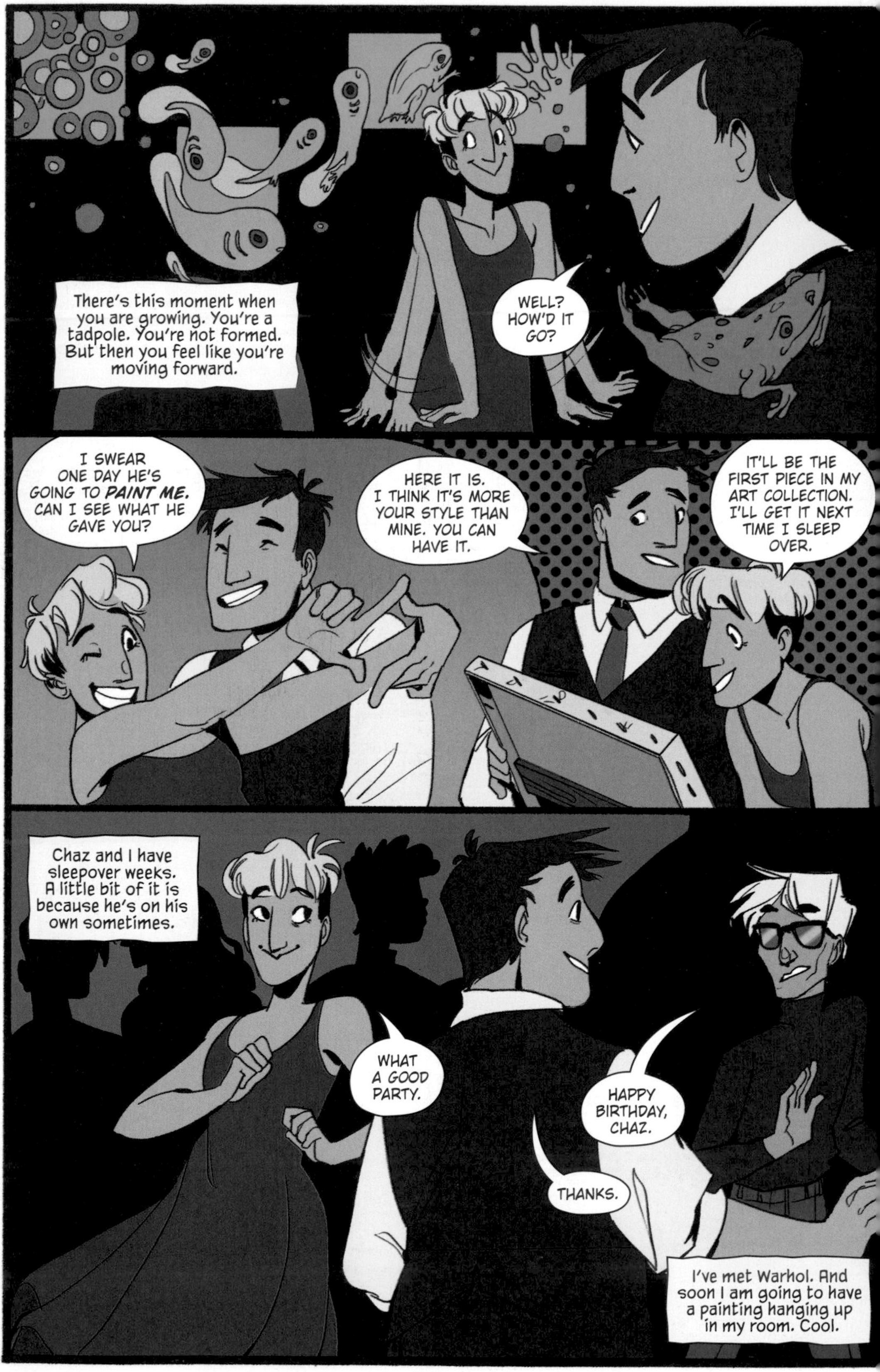
There's this moment when you are growing. You're a tadpole. You're not formed. But then you feel like you're moving forward.
WELL? HOW'D IT GO?
I SWEAR ONE DAY HE'S GOING TO PAINT ME. CAN I SEE WHAT HE GAVE YOU?
HERE IT IS. I THINK IT'S MORE YOUR STYLE THAN MINE. YOU CAN HAVE IT.
IT'LL BE THE FIRST PIECE IN MY ART COLLECTION. I'LL GET IT NEXT TIME I SLEEP OVER.
Chaz and I have sleepover weeks. A little bit of it is because he's on his own sometimes.
WHAT A GOOD PARTY.
HAPPY BIRTHDAY, CHAZ.
THANKS.
I've met Warhol. And soon I am going to have a painting hanging up in my room. Cool.

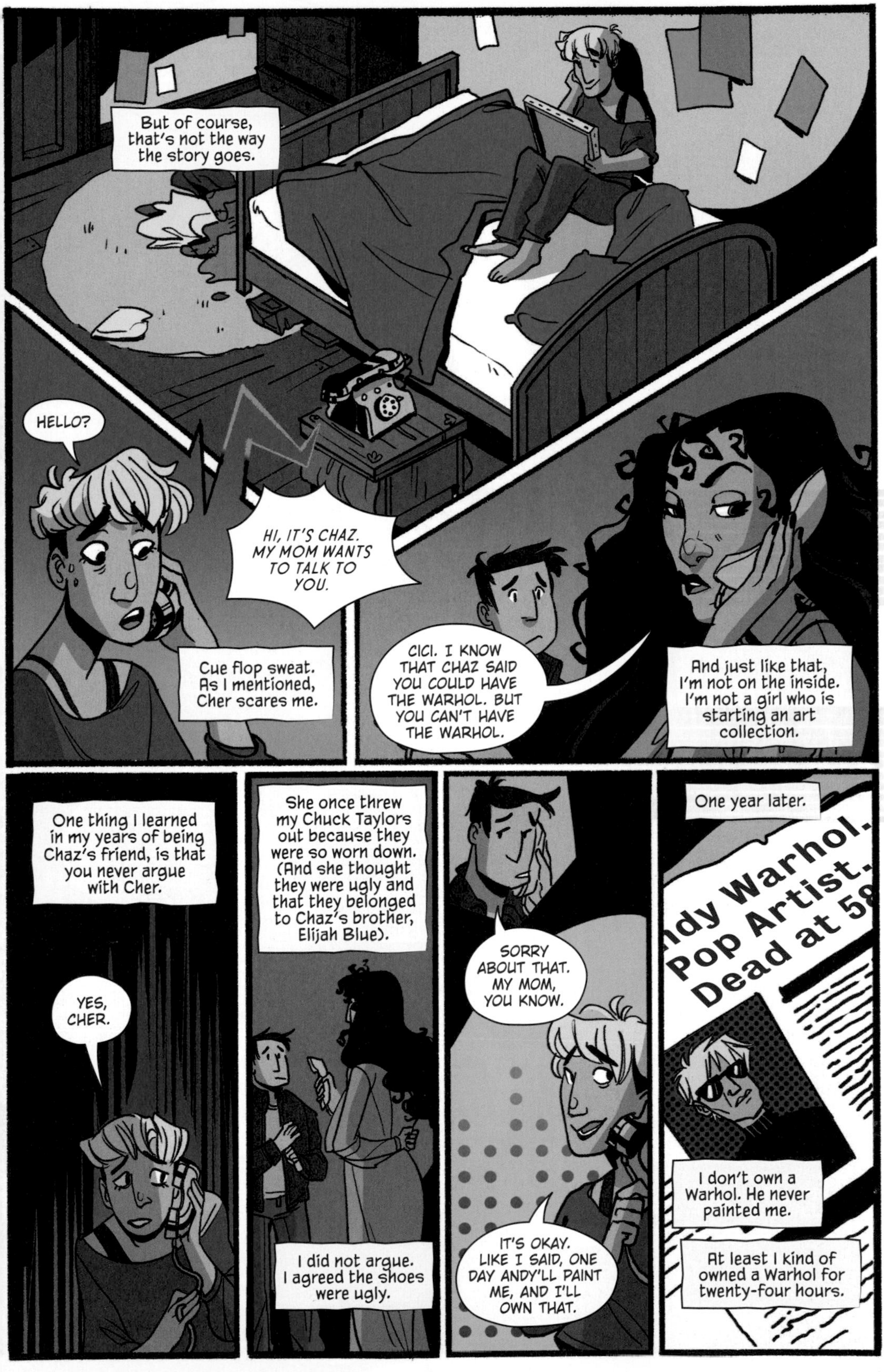

But of course, that's not the way the story goes.
HELLO?
HI, IT'S CHAZ. MY MOM WANTS TO TALK TO YOU.
Cue flop sweat. As I mentioned, Cher scares me.
CICI. I KNOW THAT CHAZ SAID YOU COULD HAVE THE WARHOL. BUT YOU CAN'T HAVE THE WARHOL.
And just like that, I'm not on the inside. I'm not a girl who is starting an art collection.
One thing I learned in my years of being Chaz's friend, is that you never argue with Cher.
YES, CHER.
She once threw my Chuck Taylors out because they were so worn down. (And she thought they were ugly and that they belonged to Chaz's brother, Elijah Blue).
I did not argue. I agreed the shoes were ugly.
SORRY ABOUT THAT. MY MOM, YOU KNOW.
IT'S OKAY. LIKE I SAID, ONE DAY ANDY'LL PAINT ME, AND I'LL OWN THAT.
One year later.
ndy Warhol. Pop Artist. Dead at 58
I don't own a Warhol. He never painted me.
At least I kind of owned a Warhol for twenty-four hours.

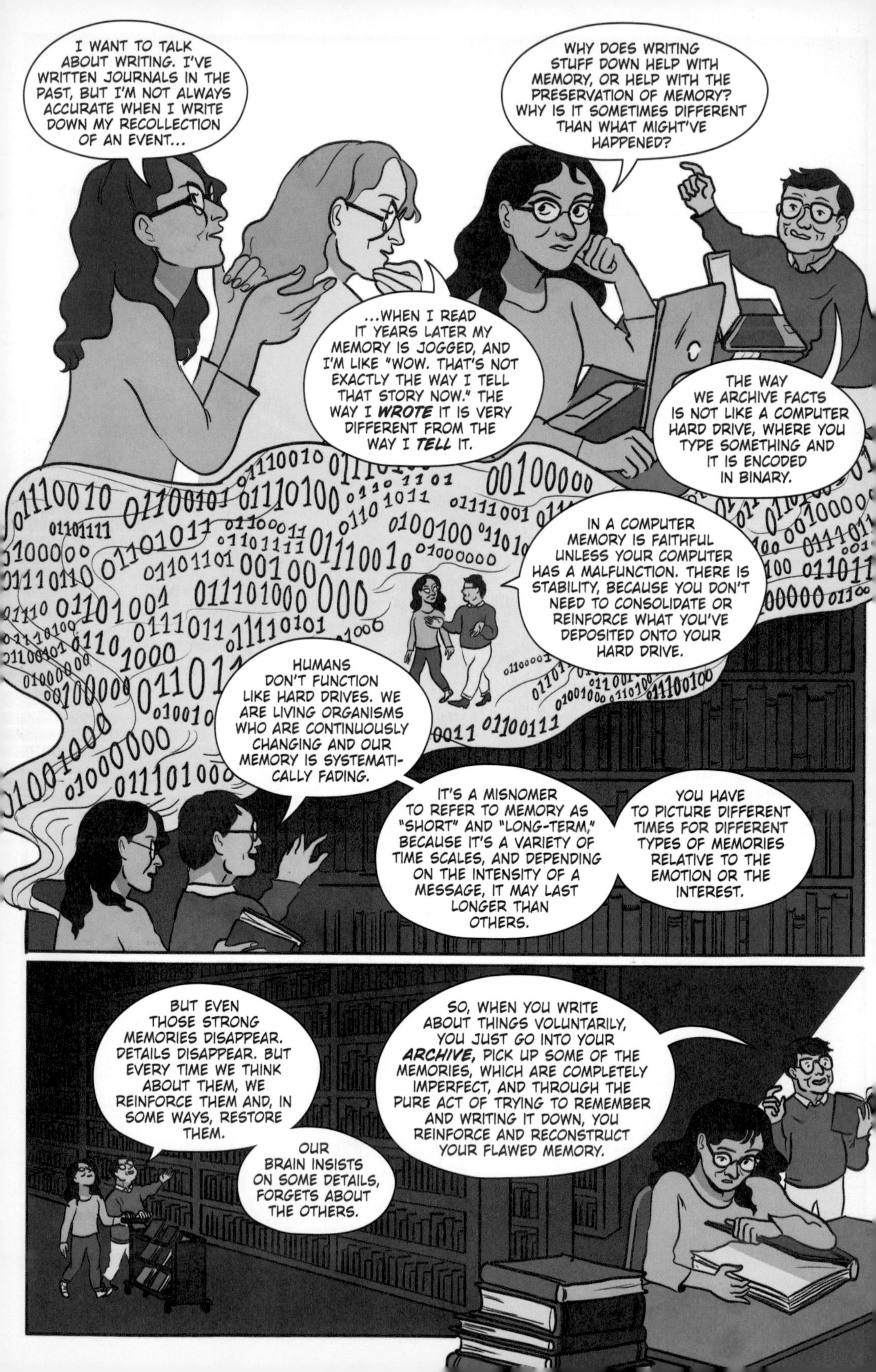
I WANT TO TALK ABOUT WRITING. I'VE WRITTEN JOURNALS IN THE PAST, BUT I'M NOT ALWAYS ACCURATE WHEN I WRITE DOWN MY RECOLLECTION OF AN EVENT...
...WHEN I READ IT YEARS LATER MY MEMORY IS JOGGED, AND I'M LIKE "WOW. THAT'S NOT EXACTLY THE WAY I TELL THAT STORY NOW." THE WAY I **WROTE** IT IS VERY DIFFERENT FROM THE WAY I **TELL** IT.
WHY DOES WRITING STUFF DOWN HELP WITH MEMORY, OR HELP WITH THE PRESERVATION OF MEMORY? WHY IS IT SOMETIMES DIFFERENT THAN WHAT MIGHT'VE HAPPENED?
THE WAY WE ARCHIVE FACTS IS NOT LIKE A COMPUTER HARD DRIVE, WHERE YOU TYPE SOMETHING AND IT IS ENCODED IN BINARY.
IN A COMPUTER MEMORY IS FAITHFUL UNLESS YOUR COMPUTER HAS A MALFUNCTION. THERE IS STABILITY, BECAUSE YOU DON'T NEED TO CONSOLIDATE OR REINFORCE WHAT YOU'VE DEPOSITED ONTO YOUR HARD DRIVE.
HUMANS DON'T FUNCTION LIKE HARD DRIVES. WE ARE LIVING ORGANISMS WHO ARE CONTINUOUSLY CHANGING AND OUR MEMORY IS SYSTEMATICALLY FADING.
IT'S A MISNOMER TO REFER TO MEMORY AS "SHORT" AND "LONG-TERM," BECAUSE IT'S A VARIETY OF TIME SCALES, AND DEPENDING ON THE INTENSITY OF A MESSAGE, IT MAY LAST LONGER THAN OTHERS.
YOU HAVE TO PICTURE DIFFERENT TIMES FOR DIFFERENT TYPES OF MEMORIES RELATIVE TO THE EMOTION OR THE INTEREST.
BUT EVEN THOSE STRONG MEMORIES DISAPPEAR. DETAILS DISAPPEAR. BUT EVERY TIME WE THINK ABOUT THEM, WE REINFORCE THEM AND, IN SOME WAYS, RESTORE THEM.
OUR BRAIN INSISTS ON SOME DETAILS, FORGETS ABOUT THE OTHERS.
SO, WHEN YOU WRITE ABOUT THINGS VOLUNTARILY, YOU JUST GO INTO YOUR **ARCHIVE,** PICK UP SOME OF THE MEMORIES, WHICH ARE COMPLETELY IMPERFECT, AND THROUGH THE PURE ACT OF TRYING TO REMEMBER AND WRITING IT DOWN, YOU REINFORCE AND RECONSTRUCT YOUR FLAWED MEMORY.

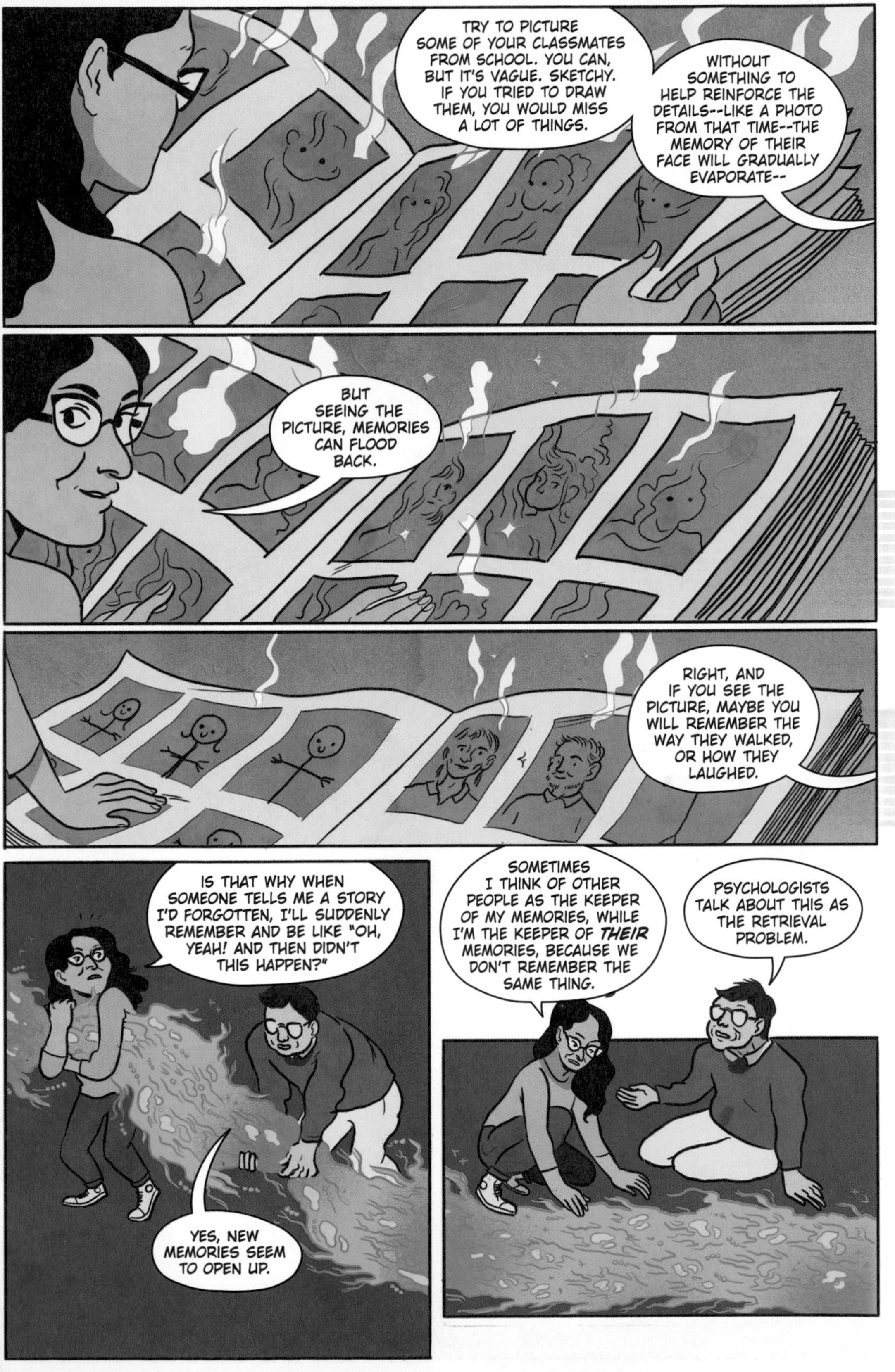
TRY TO PICTURE SOME OF YOUR CLASSMATES FROM SCHOOL. YOU CAN, BUT IT'S VAGUE. SKETCHY. IF YOU TRIED TO DRAW THEM, YOU WOULD MISS A LOT OF THINGS.
WITHOUT SOMETHING TO HELP REINFORCE THE DETAILS--LIKE A PHOTO FROM THAT TIME--THE MEMORY OF THEIR FACE WILL GRADUALLY EVAPORATE--
BUT SEEING THE PICTURE, MEMORIES CAN FLOOD BACK.
RIGHT, AND IF YOU SEE THE PICTURE, MAYBE YOU WILL REMEMBER THE WAY THEY WALKED, OR HOW THEY LAUGHED.
IS THAT WHY WHEN SOMEONE TELLS ME A STORY I'D FORGOTTEN, I'LL SUDDENLY REMEMBER AND BE LIKE "OH, YEAH! AND THEN DIDN'T THIS HAPPEN?"
YES, NEW MEMORIES SEEM TO OPEN UP.
SOMETIMES I THINK OF OTHER PEOPLE AS THE KEEPER OF MY MEMORIES, WHILE I'M THE KEEPER OF *THEIR* MEMORIES, BECAUSE WE DON'T REMEMBER THE SAME THING.
PSYCHOLOGISTS TALK ABOUT THIS AS THE RETRIEVAL PROBLEM.

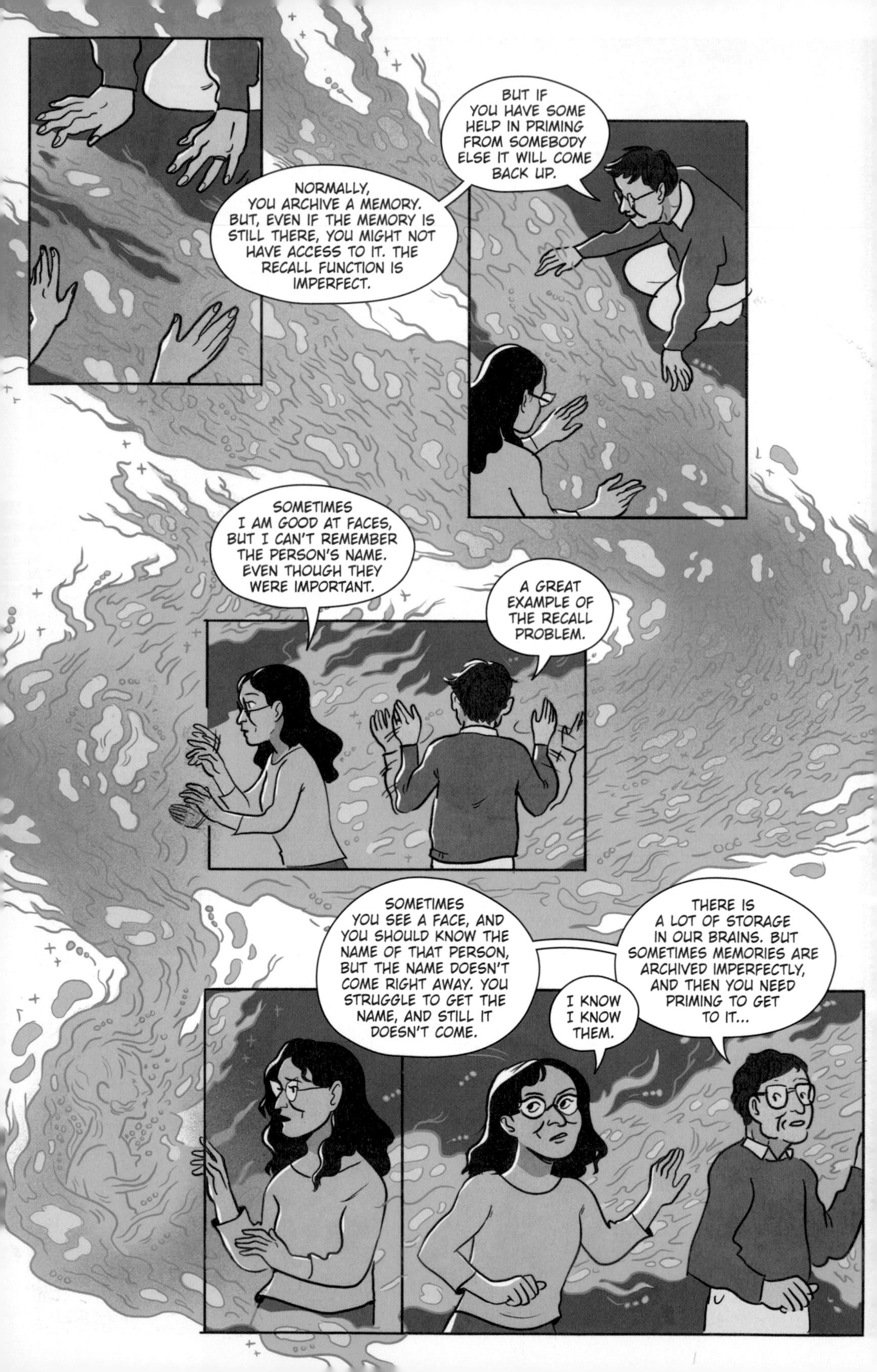
NORMALLY, YOU ARCHIVE A MEMORY. BUT, EVEN IF THE MEMORY IS STILL THERE, YOU MIGHT NOT HAVE ACCESS TO IT. THE RECALL FUNCTION IS IMPERFECT.
BUT IF YOU HAVE SOME HELP IN PRIMING FROM SOMEBODY ELSE IT WILL COME BACK UP.
SOMETIMES I AM GOOD AT FACES, BUT I CAN'T REMEMBER THE PERSON'S NAME. EVEN THOUGH THEY WERE IMPORTANT.
A GREAT EXAMPLE OF THE RECALL PROBLEM.
SOMETIMES YOU SEE A FACE, AND YOU SHOULD KNOW THE NAME OF THAT PERSON, BUT THE NAME DOESN'T COME RIGHT AWAY. YOU STRUGGLE TO GET THE NAME, AND STILL IT DOESN'T COME.
THERE IS A LOT OF STORAGE IN OUR BRAINS. BUT SOMETIMES MEMORIES ARE ARCHIVED IMPERFECTLY, AND THEN YOU NEED PRIMING TO GET TO IT...
I KNOW I KNOW THEM.

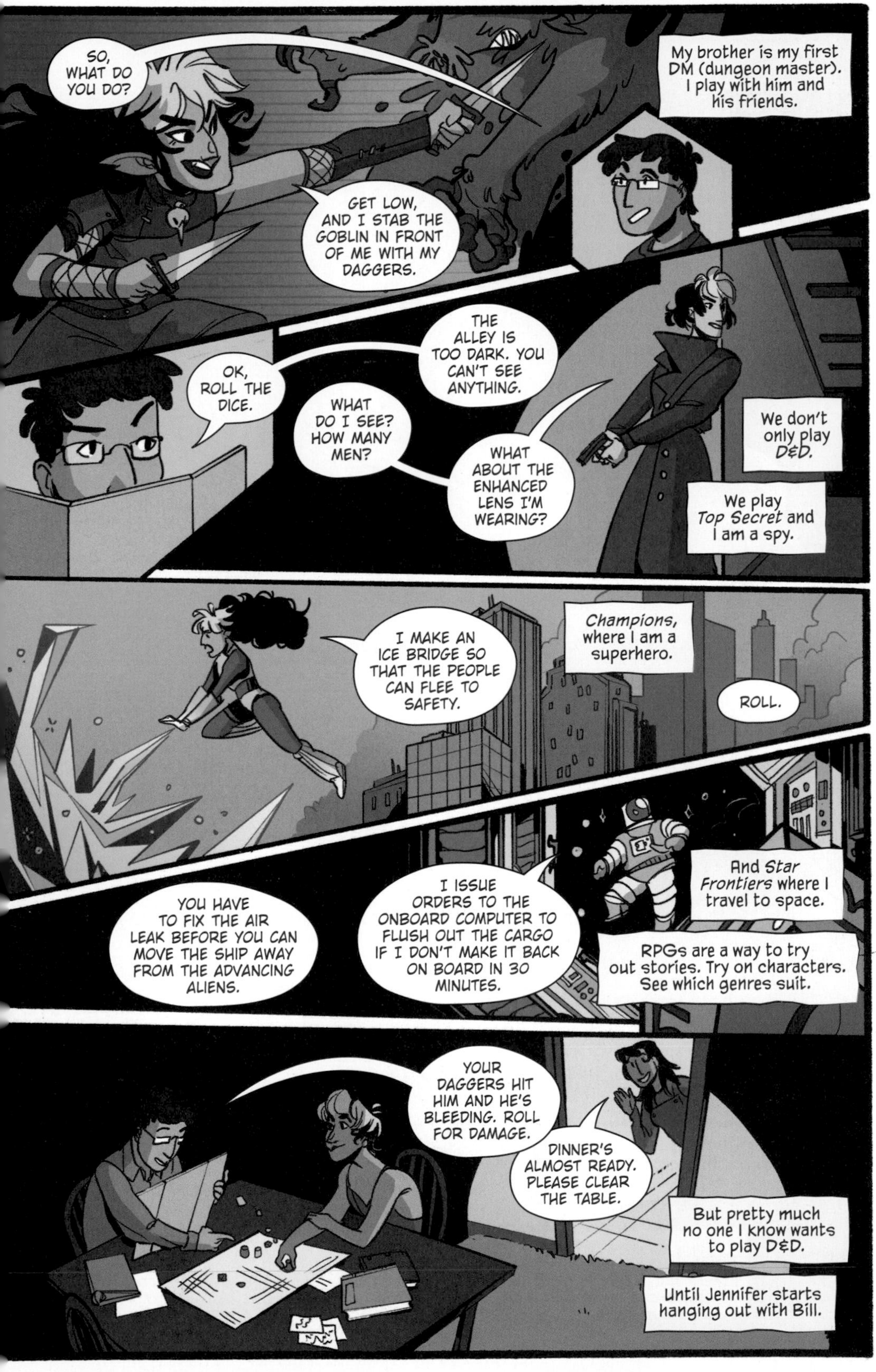
SO, WHAT DO YOU DO?
My brother is my first DM (dungeon master). I play with him and his friends.
GET LOW, AND I STAB THE GOBLIN IN FRONT OF ME WITH MY DAGGERS.
OK, ROLL THE DICE.
THE ALLEY IS TOO DARK. YOU CAN'T SEE ANYTHING.
WHAT DO I SEE? HOW MANY MEN?
WHAT ABOUT THE ENHANCED LENS I'M WEARING?
We don't only play *D&D*.
We play *Top Secret* and I am a spy.
I MAKE AN ICE BRIDGE SO THAT THE PEOPLE CAN FLEE TO SAFETY.
Champions, where I am a superhero.
ROLL.
YOU HAVE TO FIX THE AIR LEAK BEFORE YOU CAN MOVE THE SHIP AWAY FROM THE ADVANCING ALIENS.
I ISSUE ORDERS TO THE ONBOARD COMPUTER TO FLUSH OUT THE CARGO IF I DON'T MAKE IT BACK ON BOARD IN 30 MINUTES.
And *Star Frontiers* where I travel to space.
RPGs are a way to try out stories. Try on characters. See which genres suit.
YOUR DAGGERS HIT HIM AND HE'S BLEEDING. ROLL FOR DAMAGE.
DINNER'S ALMOST READY. PLEASE CLEAR THE TABLE.
But pretty much no one I know wants to play D&D.
Until Jennifer starts hanging out with Bill.

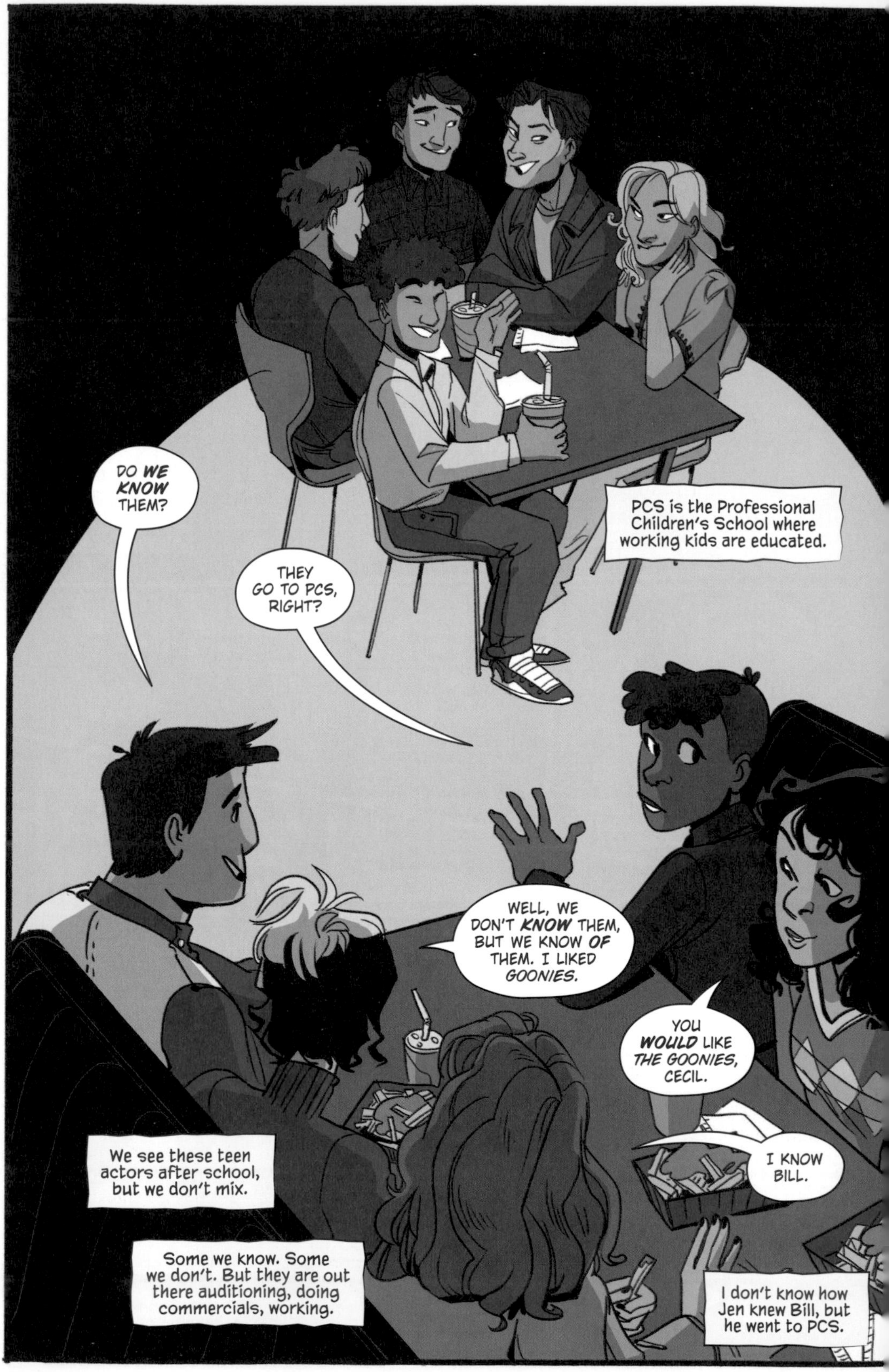

DO **WE** ***KNOW*** THEM?
THEY GO TO PCS, RIGHT?
PCS is the Professional Children's School where working kids are educated.
WELL, WE DON'T ***KNOW*** THEM, BUT WE KNOW ***OF*** THEM. I LIKED *GOONIES*.
YOU ***WOULD*** LIKE *THE GOONIES*, CECIL.
I KNOW BILL.
We see these teen actors after school, but we don't mix.
Some we know. Some we don't. But they are out there auditioning, doing commercials, working.
I don't know how Jen knew Bill, but he went to PCS.

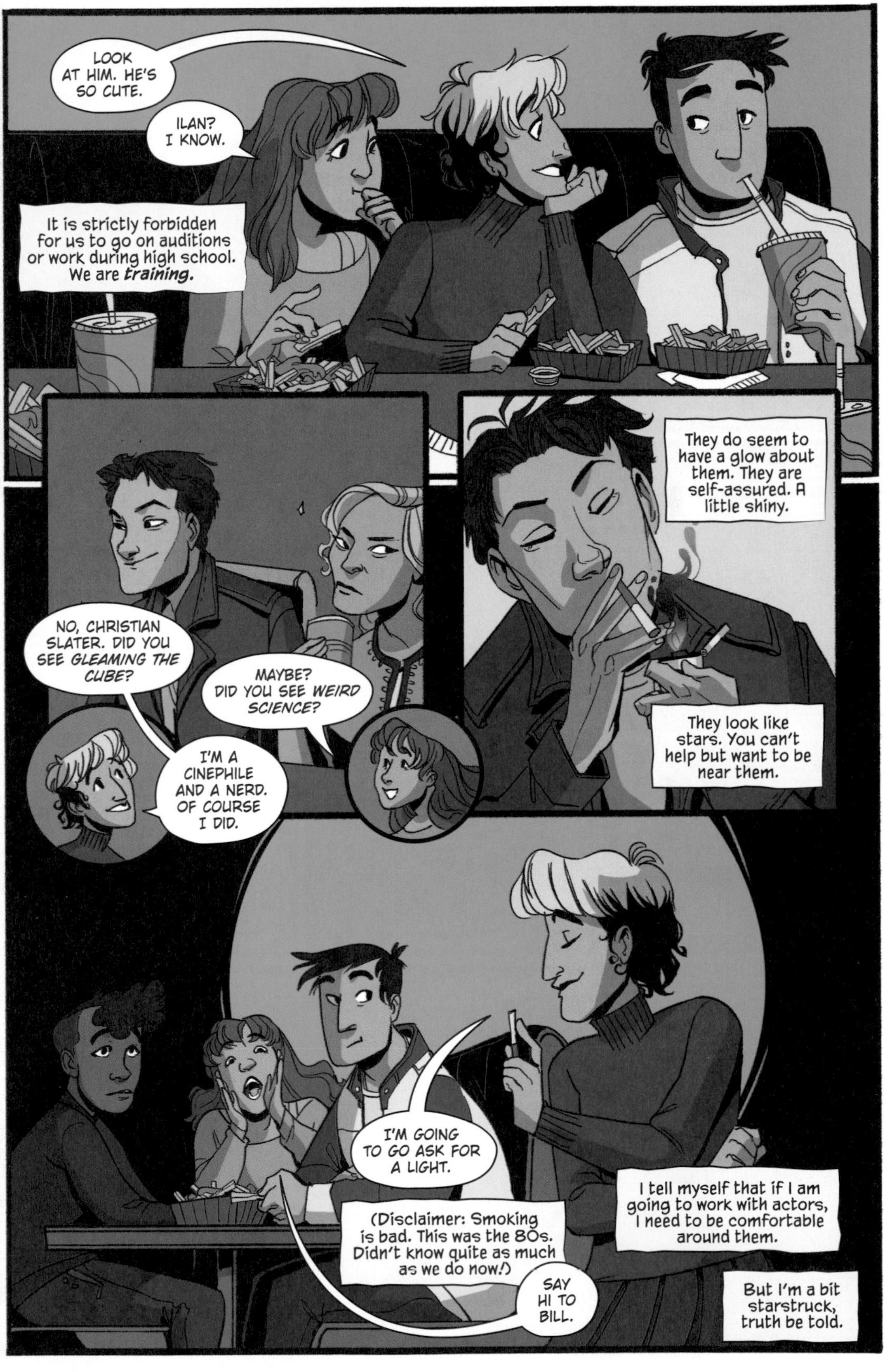
LOOK AT HIM. HE'S SO CUTE.
ILAN? I KNOW.
It is strictly forbidden for us to go on auditions or work during high school. We are *training.*
NO, CHRISTIAN SLATER. DID YOU SEE *GLEAMING THE CUBE?*
MAYBE? DID YOU SEE *WEIRD SCIENCE?*
I'M A CINEPHILE AND A NERD. OF COURSE I DID.
They do seem to have a glow about them. They are self-assured. A little shiny.
They look like stars. You can't help but want to be near them.
I'M GOING TO GO ASK FOR A LIGHT.
(Disclaimer: Smoking is bad. This was the 80s. Didn't know quite as much as we do now!)
SAY HI TO BILL.
I tell myself that if I am going to work with actors, I need to be comfortable around them.
But I'm a bit starstruck, truth be told.

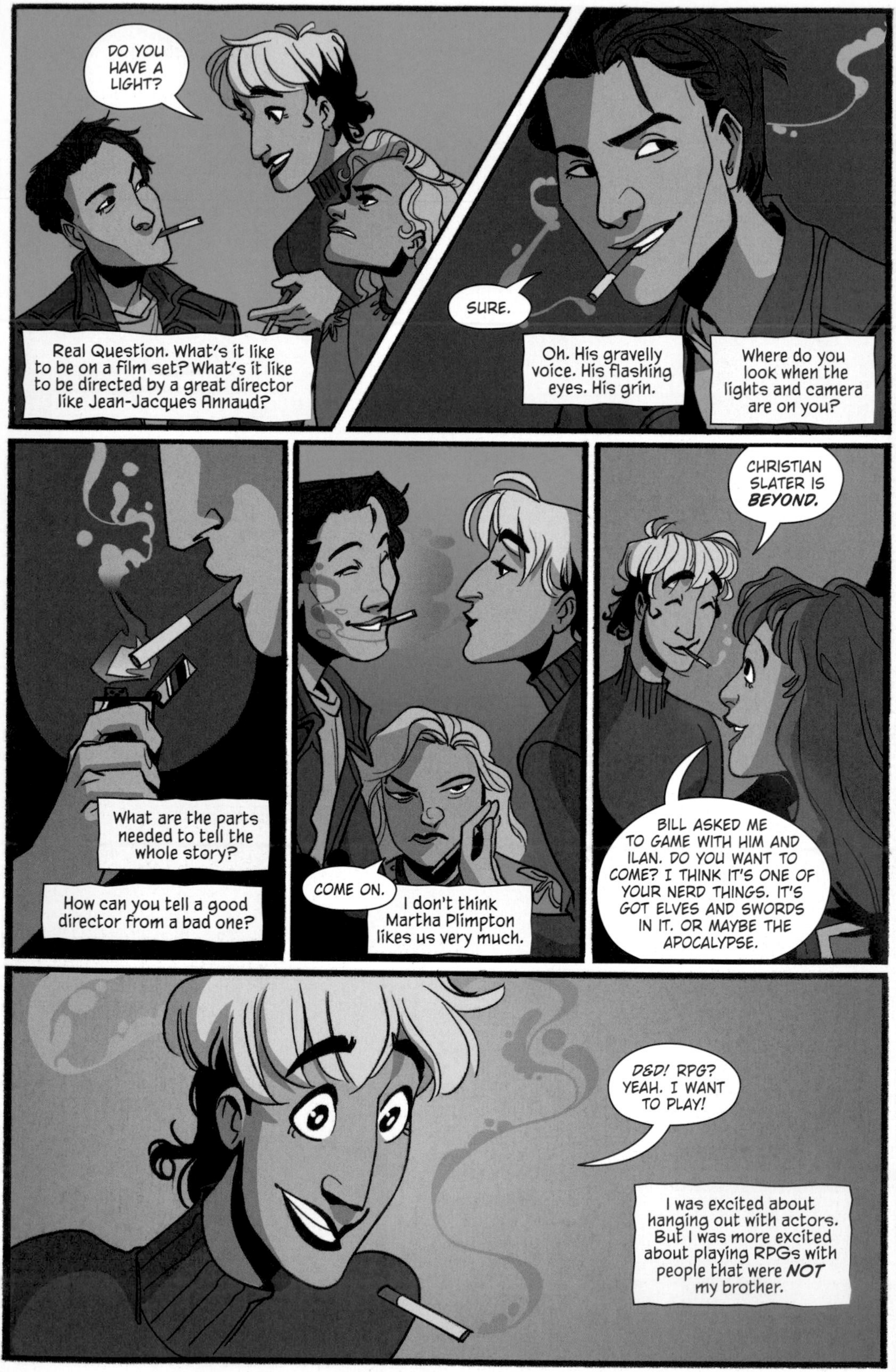
DO YOU HAVE A LIGHT?
Real Question. What's it like to be on a film set? What's it like to be directed by a great director like Jean-Jacques Annaud?
SURE.
Oh. His gravelly voice. His flashing eyes. His grin.
Where do you look when the lights and camera are on you?
What are the parts needed to tell the whole story?
How can you tell a good director from a bad one?
COME ON.
I don't think Martha Plimpton likes us very much.
CHRISTIAN SLATER IS *BEYOND.*
BILL ASKED ME TO GAME WITH HIM AND ILAN. DO YOU WANT TO COME? I THINK IT'S ONE OF YOUR NERD THINGS. IT'S GOT ELVES AND SWORDS IN IT. OR MAYBE THE APOCALYPSE.
D&D! RPG? YEAH. I WANT TO PLAY!
I was excited about hanging out with actors. But I was more excited about playing RPGs with people that were *NOT* my brother.

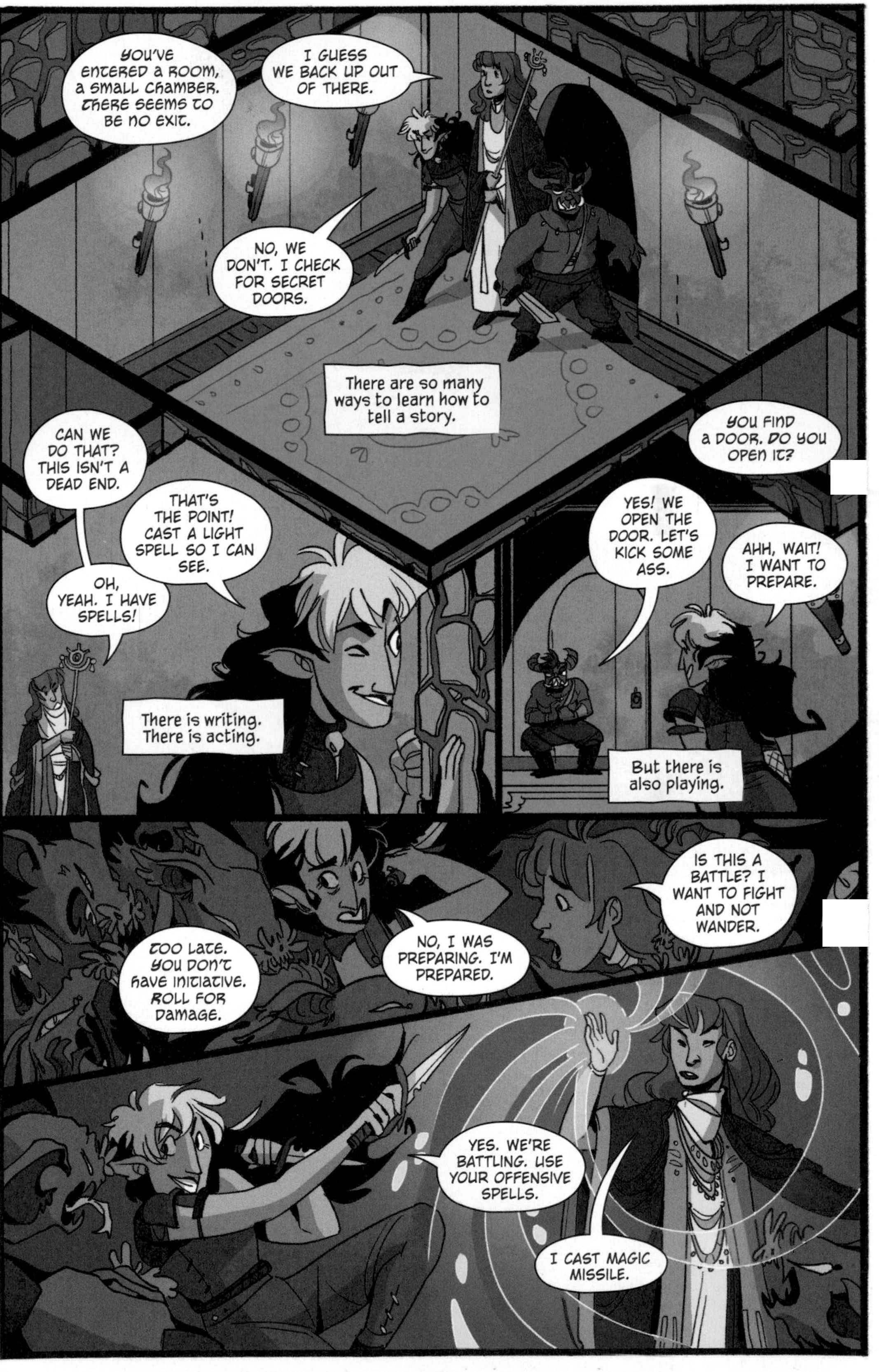

YOU'VE ENTERED A ROOM, A SMALL CHAMBER. THERE SEEMS TO BE NO EXIT.
I GUESS WE BACK UP OUT OF THERE.
NO, WE DON'T. I CHECK FOR SECRET DOORS.
There are so many ways to learn how to tell a story.
CAN WE DO THAT? THIS ISN'T A DEAD END.
THAT'S THE POINT! CAST A LIGHT SPELL SO I CAN SEE.
OH, YEAH. I HAVE SPELLS!
There is writing. There is acting.
YOU FIND A DOOR. DO YOU OPEN IT?
YES! WE OPEN THE DOOR. LET'S KICK SOME ASS.
AHH, WAIT! I WANT TO PREPARE.
But there is also playing.
TOO LATE. YOU DON'T HAVE INITIATIVE. ROLL FOR DAMAGE.
NO, I WAS PREPARING. I'M PREPARED.
IS THIS A BATTLE? I WANT TO FIGHT AND NOT WANDER.
YES. WE'RE BATTLING. USE YOUR OFFENSIVE SPELLS.
I CAST MAGIC MISSILE.

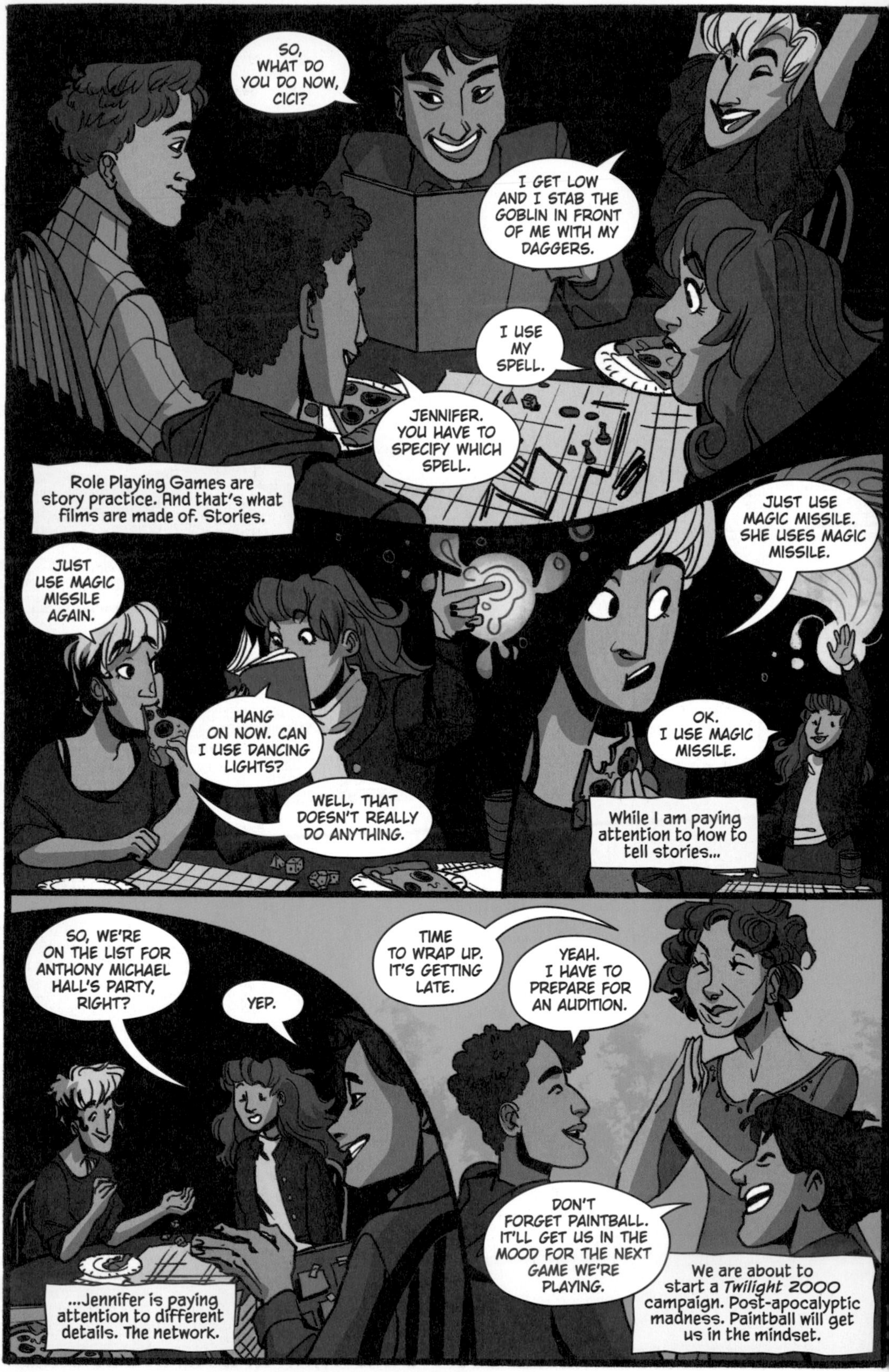
SO, WHAT DO YOU DO NOW, CICI?
I GET LOW AND I STAB THE GOBLIN IN FRONT OF ME WITH MY DAGGERS.
I USE MY SPELL.
JENNIFER. YOU HAVE TO SPECIFY WHICH SPELL.
Role Playing Games are story practice. And that's what films are made of. Stories.
JUST USE MAGIC MISSILE. SHE USES MAGIC MISSILE.
JUST USE MAGIC MISSILE AGAIN.
HANG ON NOW. CAN I USE DANCING LIGHTS?
WELL, THAT DOESN'T REALLY DO ANYTHING.
OK. I USE MAGIC MISSILE.
While I am paying attention to how to tell stories...
SO, WE'RE ON THE LIST FOR ANTHONY MICHAEL HALL'S PARTY, RIGHT?
YEP.
TIME TO WRAP UP. IT'S GETTING LATE.
YEAH. I HAVE TO PREPARE FOR AN AUDITION.
DON'T FORGET PAINTBALL. IT'LL GET US IN THE MOOD FOR THE NEXT GAME WE'RE PLAYING.
...Jennifer is paying attention to different details. The network.
We are about to start a *Twilight 2000* campaign. Post-apocalyptic madness. Paintball will get us in the mindset.

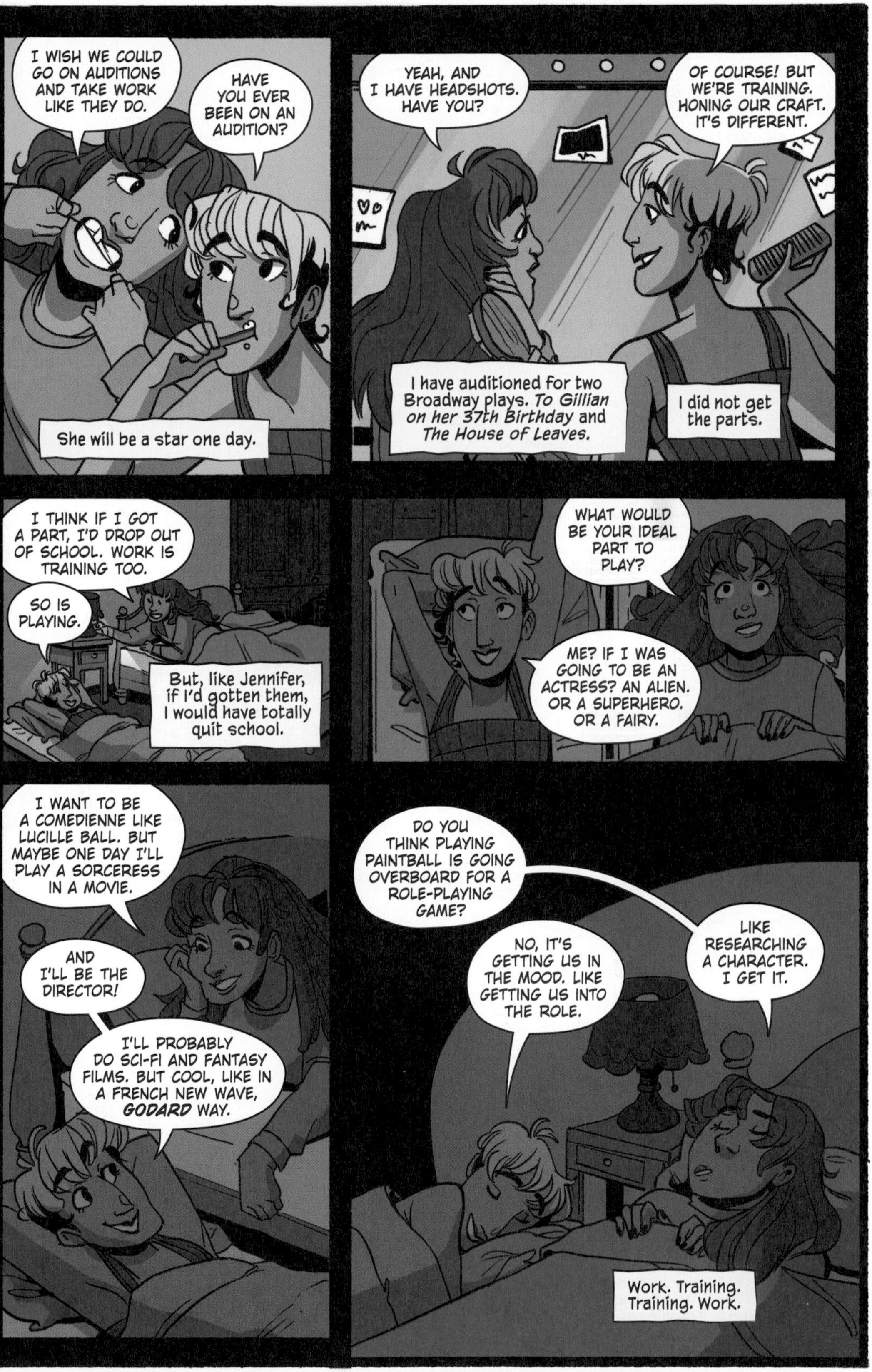
I WISH WE COULD GO ON AUDITIONS AND TAKE WORK LIKE THEY DO.
HAVE YOU EVER BEEN ON AN AUDITION?
She will be a star one day.
YEAH, AND I HAVE HEADSHOTS. HAVE YOU?
OF COURSE! BUT WE'RE TRAINING. HONING OUR CRAFT. IT'S DIFFERENT.
I have auditioned for two Broadway plays. *To Gillian on her 37th Birthday* and *The House of Leaves.*
I did not get the parts.
I THINK IF I GOT A PART, I'D DROP OUT OF SCHOOL. WORK IS TRAINING TOO.
SO IS PLAYING.
But, like Jennifer, if I'd gotten them, I would have totally quit school.
WHAT WOULD BE YOUR IDEAL PART TO PLAY?
ME? IF I WAS GOING TO BE AN ACTRESS? AN ALIEN. OR A SUPERHERO. OR A FAIRY.
I WANT TO BE A COMEDIENNE LIKE LUCILLE BALL. BUT MAYBE ONE DAY I'LL PLAY A SORCERESS IN A MOVIE.
AND I'LL BE THE DIRECTOR!
I'LL PROBABLY DO SCI-FI AND FANTASY FILMS. BUT COOL, LIKE IN A FRENCH NEW WAVE, **GODARD** WAY.
DO YOU THINK PLAYING PAINTBALL IS GOING OVERBOARD FOR A ROLE-PLAYING GAME?
NO, IT'S GETTING US IN THE MOOD. LIKE GETTING US INTO THE ROLE.
LIKE RESEARCHING A CHARACTER. I GET IT.
Work. Training. Training. Work.

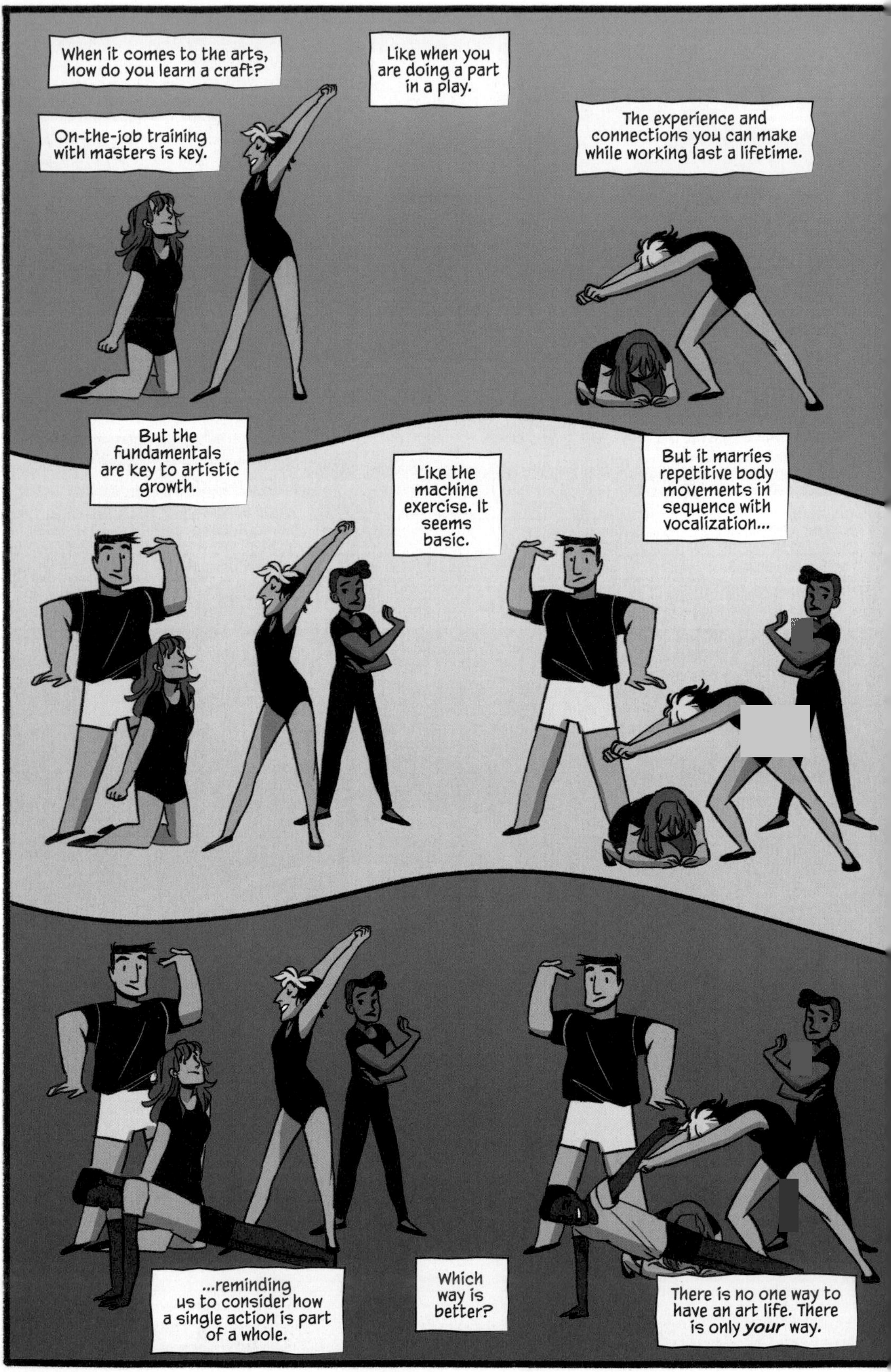
When it comes to the arts, how do you learn a craft?
On-the-job training with masters is key.
Like when you are doing a part in a play.
The experience and connections you can make while working last a lifetime.
But the fundamentals are key to artistic growth.
Like the machine exercise. It seems basic.
But it marries repetitive body movements in sequence with vocalization...
...reminding us to consider how a single action is part of a whole.
Which way is better?
There is no one way to have an art life. There is only *your* way.

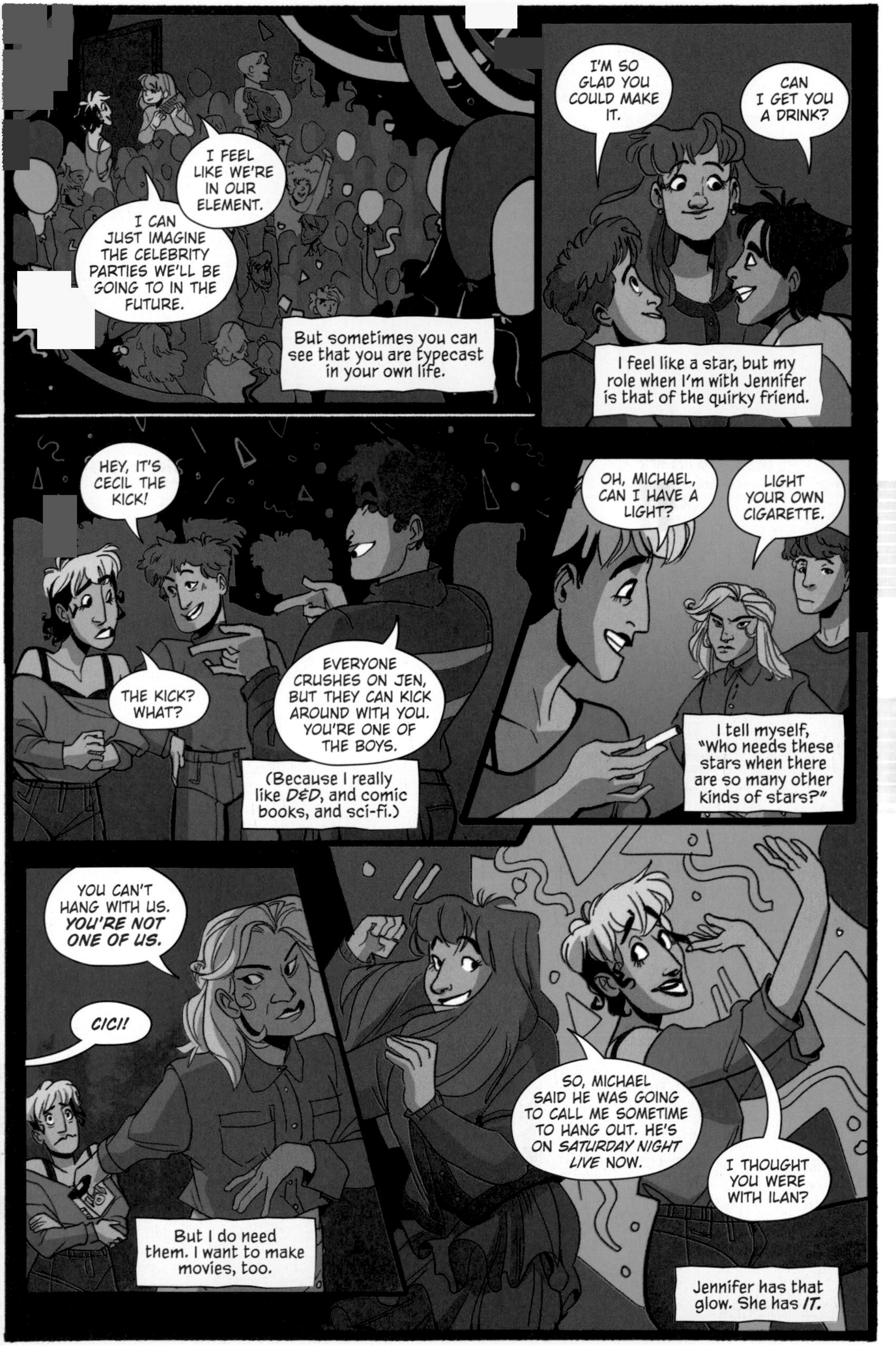
I FEEL LIKE WE'RE IN OUR ELEMENT.
I CAN JUST IMAGINE THE CELEBRITY PARTIES WE'LL BE GOING TO IN THE FUTURE.
But sometimes you can see that you are typecast in your own life.
I'M SO GLAD YOU COULD MAKE IT.
CAN I GET YOU A DRINK?
I feel like a star, but my role when I'm with Jennifer is that of the quirky friend.
HEY, IT'S CECIL THE KICK!
THE KICK? WHAT?
EVERYONE CRUSHES ON JEN, BUT THEY CAN KICK AROUND WITH YOU. YOU'RE ONE OF THE BOYS.
(Because I really like *D&D*, and comic books, and sci-fi.)
OH, MICHAEL, CAN I HAVE A LIGHT?
LIGHT YOUR OWN CIGARETTE.
I tell myself, "Who needs these stars when there are so many other kinds of stars?"
YOU CAN'T HANG WITH US. ***YOU'RE NOT ONE OF US.***
CICI!
But I do need them. I want to make movies, too.
SO, MICHAEL SAID HE WAS GOING TO CALL ME SOMETIME TO HANG OUT. HE'S ON *SATURDAY NIGHT LIVE* NOW.
I THOUGHT YOU WERE WITH ILAN?
Jennifer has that glow. She has ***IT.***

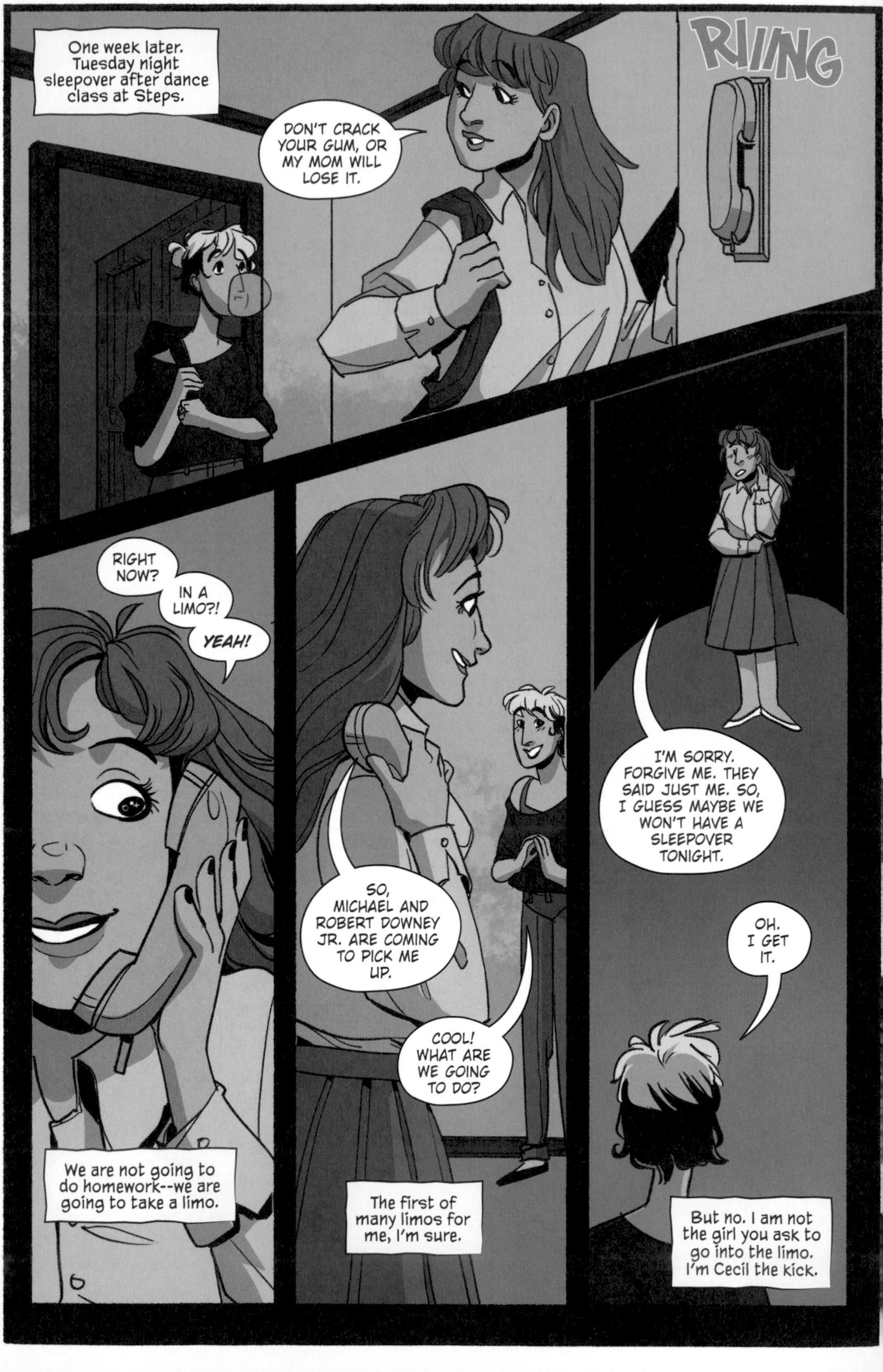
One week later. Tuesday night sleepover after dance class at Steps.
DON'T CRACK YOUR GUM, OR MY MOM WILL LOSE IT.
RIIING
RIGHT NOW?
IN A LIMO?!
YEAH!
We are not going to do homework--we are going to take a limo.
SO, MICHAEL AND ROBERT DOWNEY JR. ARE COMING TO PICK ME UP.
COOL! WHAT ARE WE GOING TO DO?
The first of many limos for me, I'm sure.
I'M SORRY. FORGIVE ME. THEY SAID JUST ME. SO, I GUESS MAYBE WE WON'T HAVE A SLEEPOVER TONIGHT.
OH. I GET IT.
But no. I am not the girl you ask to go into the limo. I'm Cecil the kick.

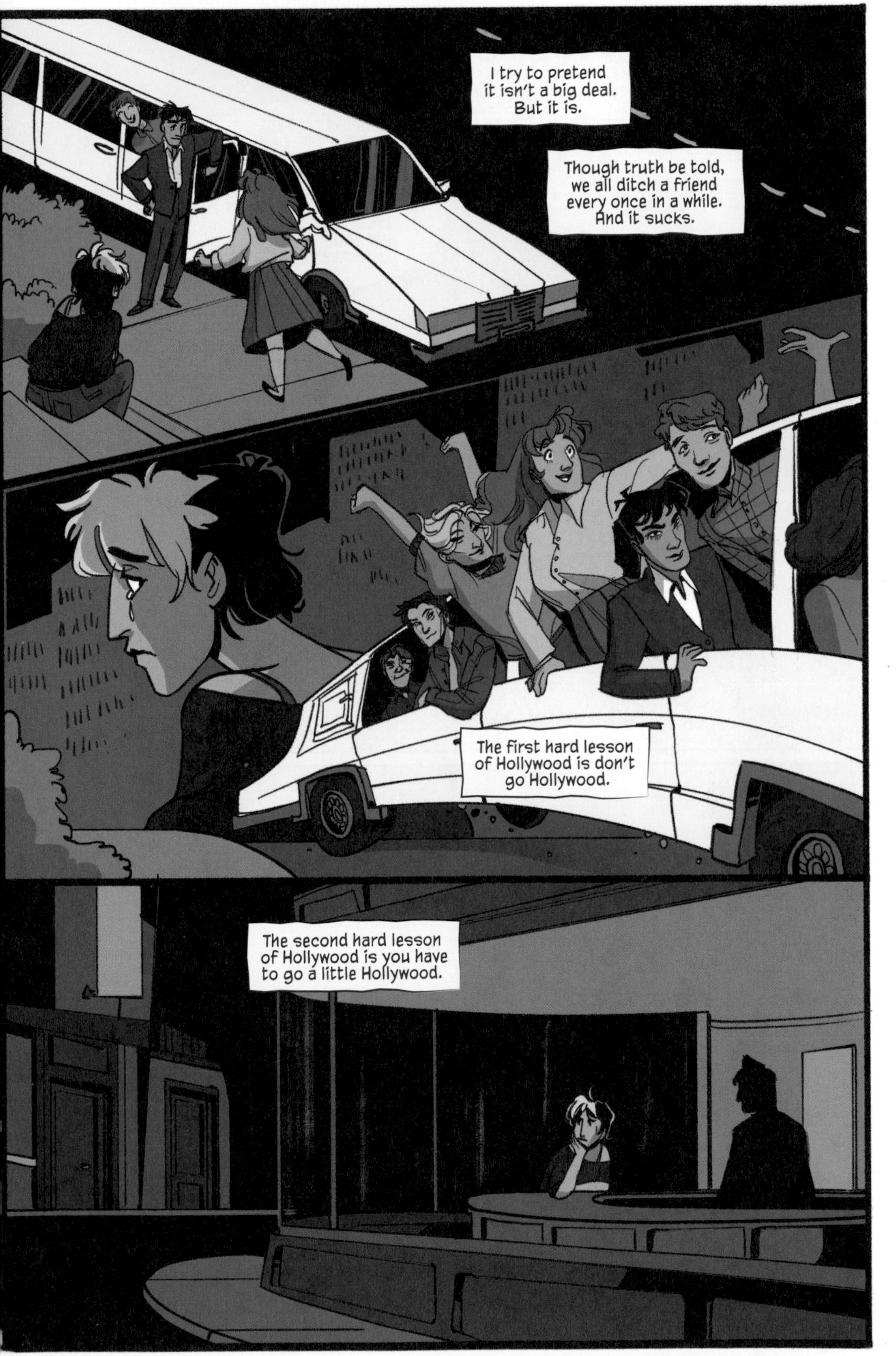

I try to pretend it isn't a big deal. But it is.
Though truth be told, we all ditch a friend every once in a while. And it sucks.
The first hard lesson of Hollywood is don't go Hollywood.
The second hard lesson of Hollywood is you have to go a little Hollywood.

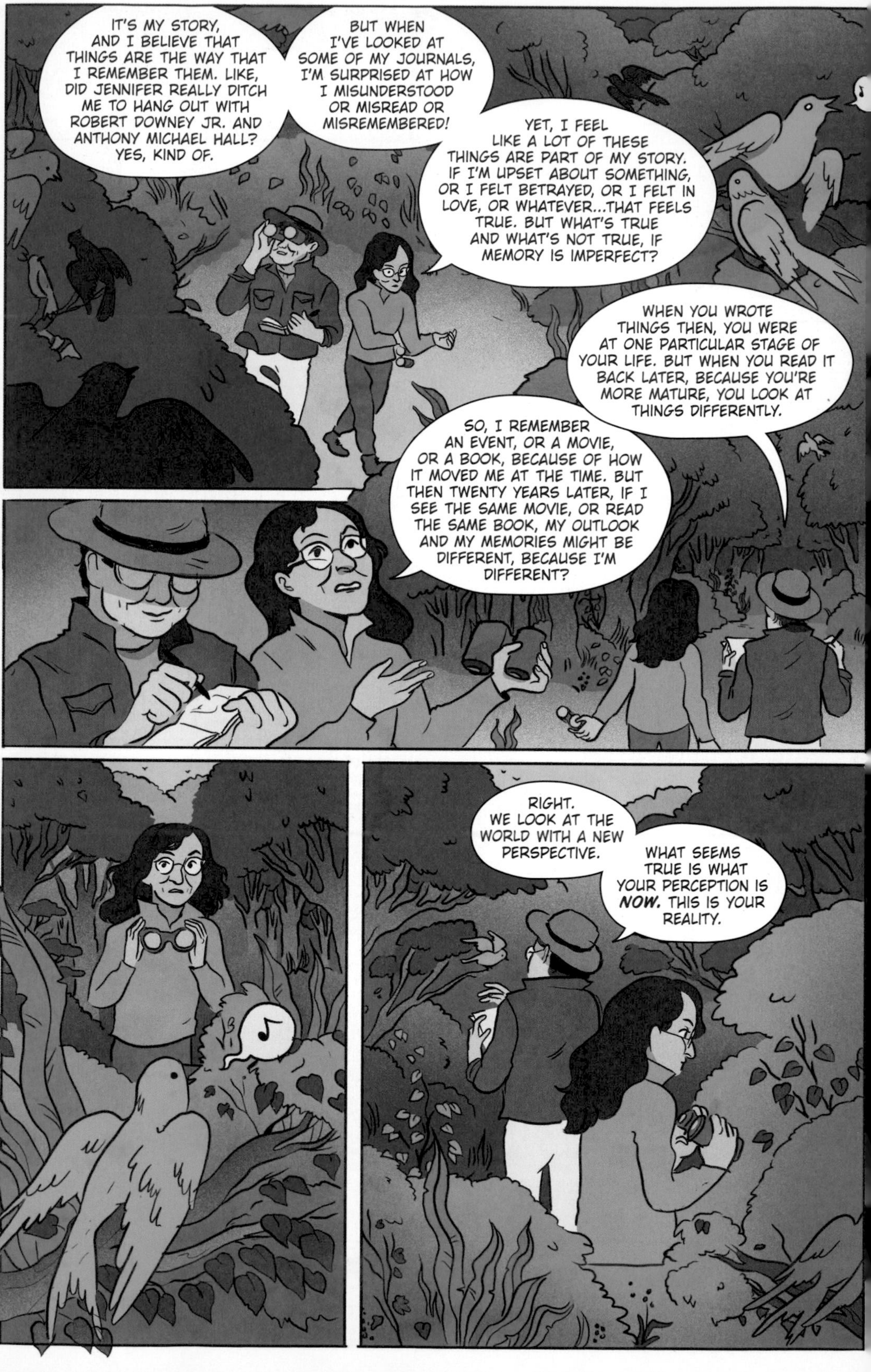
IT'S MY STORY, AND I BELIEVE THAT THINGS ARE THE WAY THAT I REMEMBER THEM. LIKE, DID JENNIFER REALLY DITCH ME TO HANG OUT WITH ROBERT DOWNEY JR. AND ANTHONY MICHAEL HALL? YES, KIND OF.
BUT WHEN I'VE LOOKED AT SOME OF MY JOURNALS, I'M SURPRISED AT HOW I MISUNDERSTOOD OR MISREAD OR MISREMEMBERED!
YET, I FEEL LIKE A LOT OF THESE THINGS ARE PART OF MY STORY. IF I'M UPSET ABOUT SOMETHING, OR I FELT BETRAYED, OR I FELT IN LOVE, OR WHATEVER...THAT FEELS TRUE. BUT WHAT'S TRUE AND WHAT'S NOT TRUE, IF MEMORY IS IMPERFECT?
WHEN YOU WROTE THINGS THEN, YOU WERE AT ONE PARTICULAR STAGE OF YOUR LIFE. BUT WHEN YOU READ IT BACK LATER, BECAUSE YOU'RE MORE MATURE, YOU LOOK AT THINGS DIFFERENTLY.
SO, I REMEMBER AN EVENT, OR A MOVIE, OR A BOOK, BECAUSE OF HOW IT MOVED ME AT THE TIME. BUT THEN TWENTY YEARS LATER, IF I SEE THE SAME MOVIE, OR READ THE SAME BOOK, MY OUTLOOK AND MY MEMORIES MIGHT BE DIFFERENT, BECAUSE I'M DIFFERENT?
RIGHT. WE LOOK AT THE WORLD WITH A NEW PERSPECTIVE.
WHAT SEEMS TRUE IS WHAT YOUR PERCEPTION IS **NOW.** THIS IS YOUR REALITY.

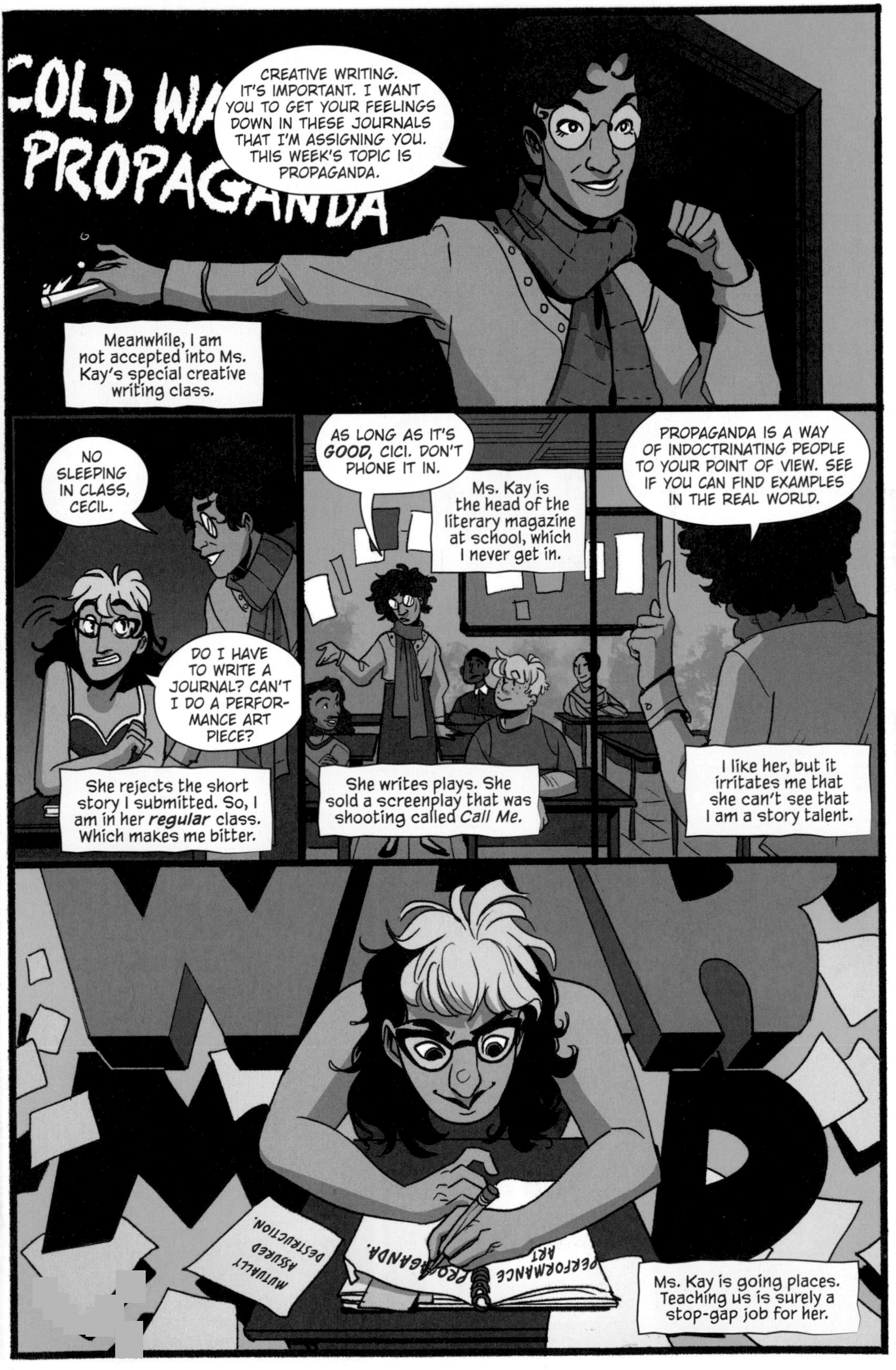
COLD WAR PROPAGANDA
CREATIVE WRITING. IT'S IMPORTANT. I WANT YOU TO GET YOUR FEELINGS DOWN IN THESE JOURNALS THAT I'M ASSIGNING YOU. THIS WEEK'S TOPIC IS PROPAGANDA.
Meanwhile, I am not accepted into Ms. Kay's special creative writing class.
NO SLEEPING IN CLASS, CECIL.
DO I HAVE TO WRITE A JOURNAL? CAN'T I DO A PERFORMANCE ART PIECE?
She rejects the short story I submitted. So, I am in her *regular* class. Which makes me bitter.
AS LONG AS IT'S *GOOD*, CICI. DON'T PHONE IT IN.
Ms. Kay is the head of the literary magazine at school, which I never get in.
She writes plays. She sold a screenplay that was shooting called *Call Me.*
PROPAGANDA IS A WAY OF INDOCTRINATING PEOPLE TO YOUR POINT OF VIEW. SEE IF YOU CAN FIND EXAMPLES IN THE REAL WORLD.
I like her, but it irritates me that she can't see that I am a story talent.
MUTUALLY ASSURED DESTRUCTION.
PERFORMANCE ART
PROPAGANDA.
Ms. Kay is going places. Teaching us is surely a stop-gap job for her.

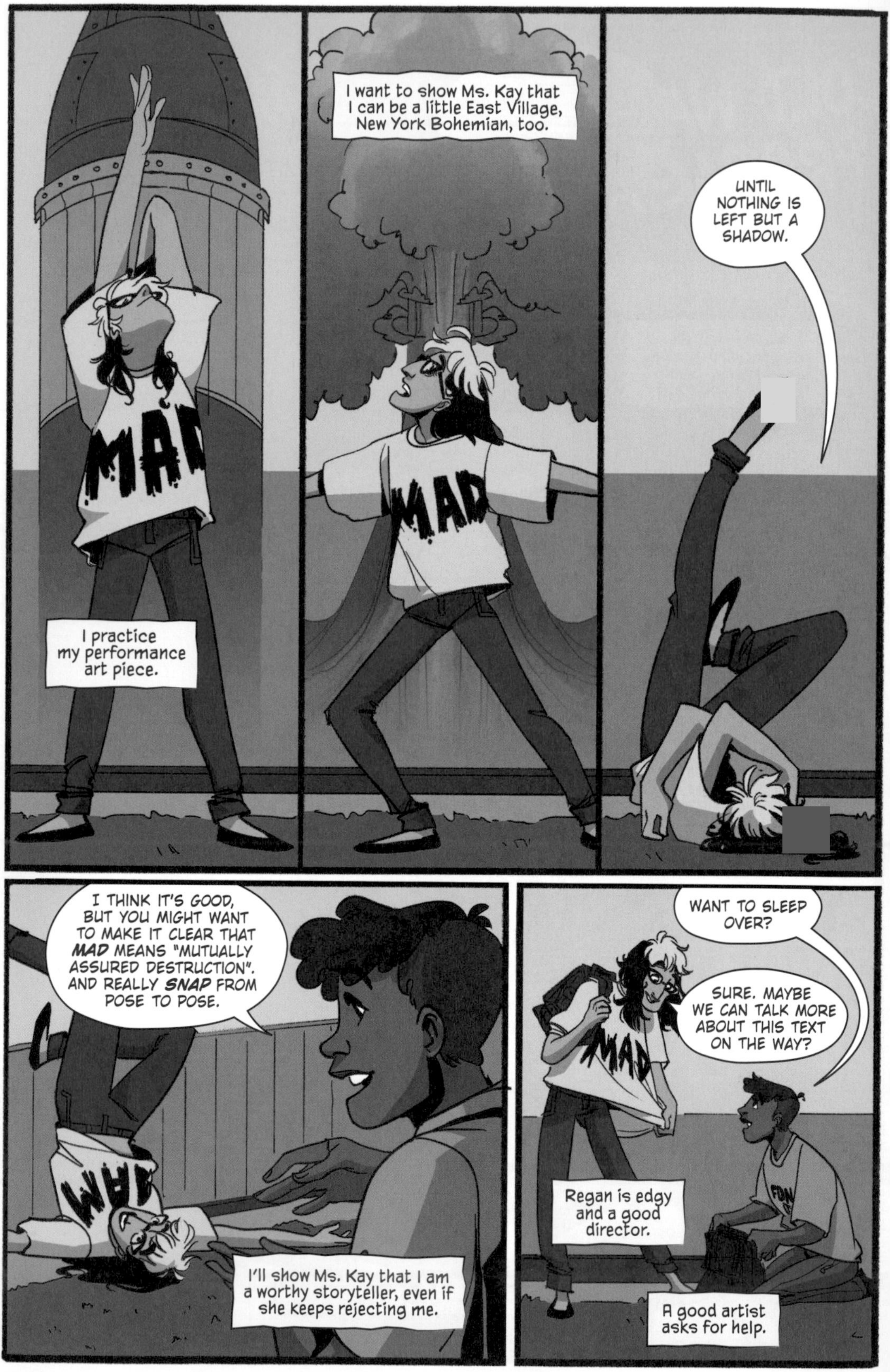
I practice my performance art piece.
I want to show Ms. Kay that I can be a little East Village, New York Bohemian, too.
UNTIL NOTHING IS LEFT BUT A SHADOW.
I THINK IT'S GOOD, BUT YOU MIGHT WANT TO MAKE IT CLEAR THAT MAD MEANS "MUTUALLY ASSURED DESTRUCTION". AND REALLY SNAP FROM POSE TO POSE.
I'll show Ms. Kay that I am a worthy storyteller, even if she keeps rejecting me.
WANT TO SLEEP OVER?
SURE. MAYBE WE CAN TALK MORE ABOUT THIS TEXT ON THE WAY?
Regan is edgy and a good director.
A good artist asks for help.

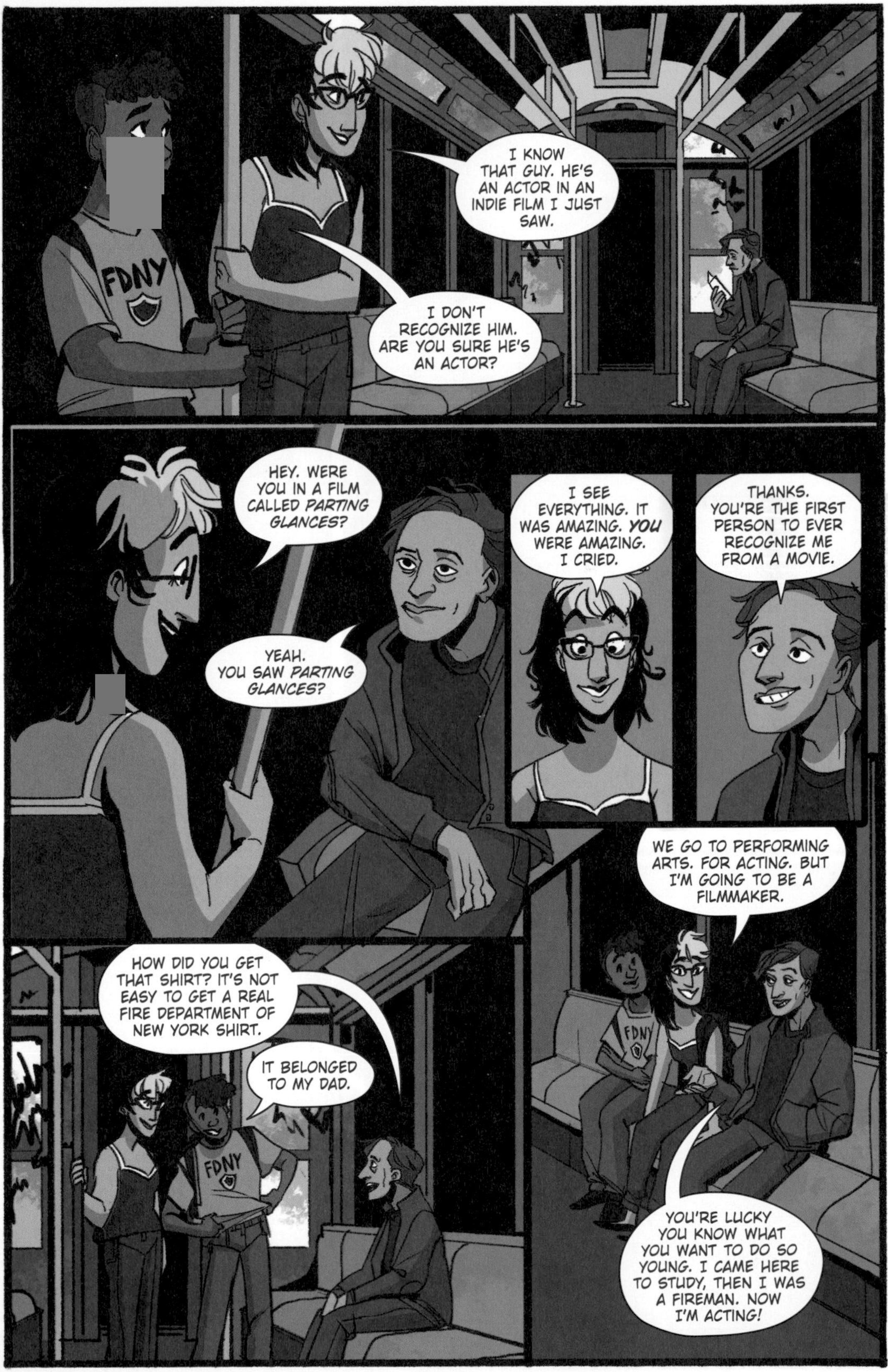
I KNOW THAT GUY. HE'S AN ACTOR IN AN INDIE FILM I JUST SAW.
I DON'T RECOGNIZE HIM. ARE YOU SURE HE'S AN ACTOR?
HEY. WERE YOU IN A FILM CALLED *PARTING GLANCES?*
YEAH. YOU SAW *PARTING GLANCES?*
I SEE EVERYTHING. IT WAS AMAZING. ***YOU*** WERE AMAZING. I CRIED.
THANKS. YOU'RE THE FIRST PERSON TO EVER RECOGNIZE ME FROM A MOVIE.
WE GO TO PERFORMING ARTS. FOR ACTING. BUT I'M GOING TO BE A FILMMAKER.
YOU'RE LUCKY YOU KNOW WHAT YOU WANT TO DO SO YOUNG. I CAME HERE TO STUDY, THEN I WAS A FIREMAN. NOW I'M ACTING!
HOW DID YOU GET THAT SHIRT? IT'S NOT EASY TO GET A REAL FIRE DEPARTMENT OF NEW YORK SHIRT.
IT BELONGED TO MY DAD.

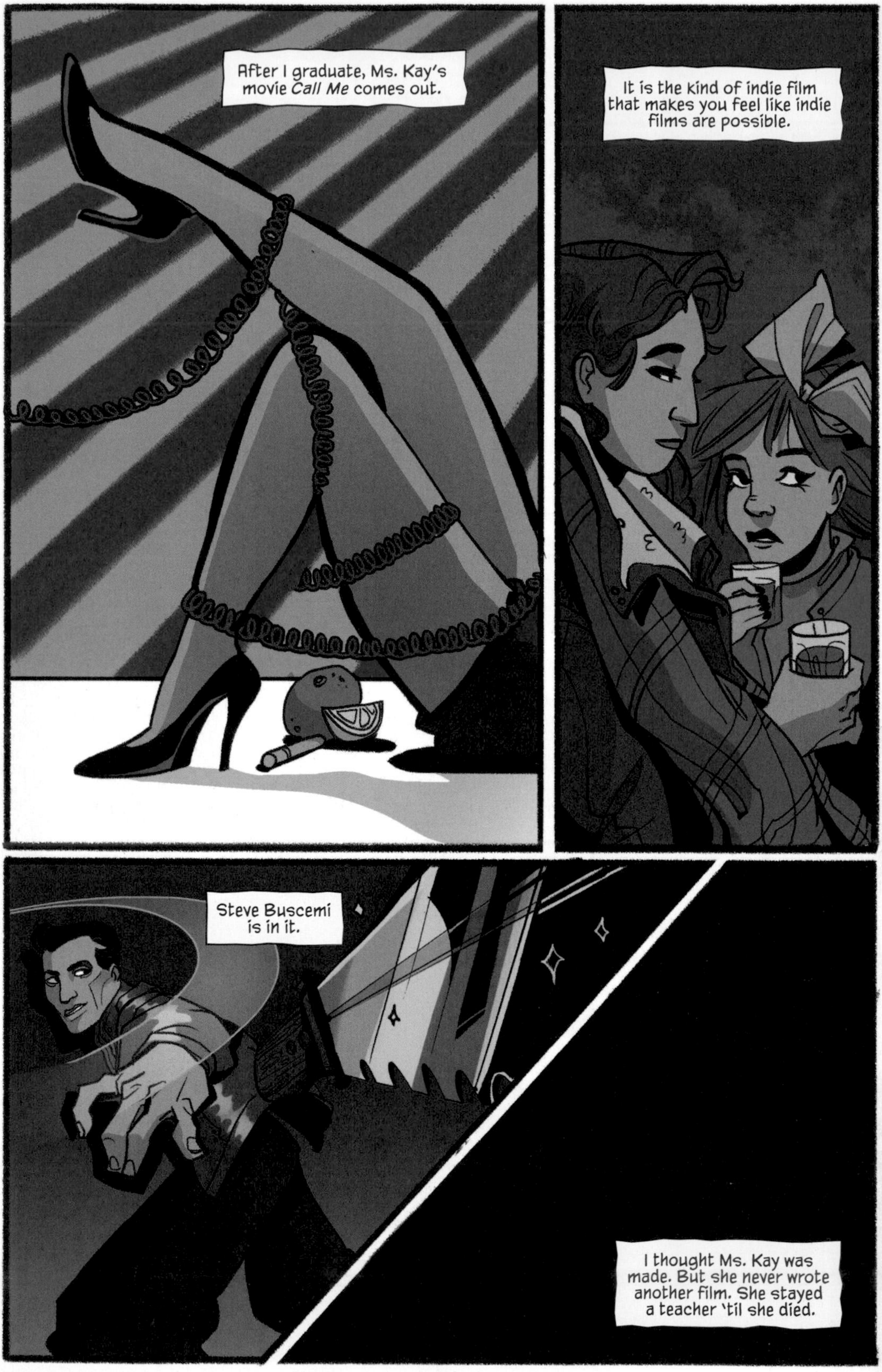
After I graduate, Ms. Kay's movie *Call Me* comes out.
It is the kind of indie film that makes you feel like indie films are possible.
Steve Buscemi is in it.
I thought Ms. Kay was made. But she never wrote another film. She stayed a teacher 'til she died.

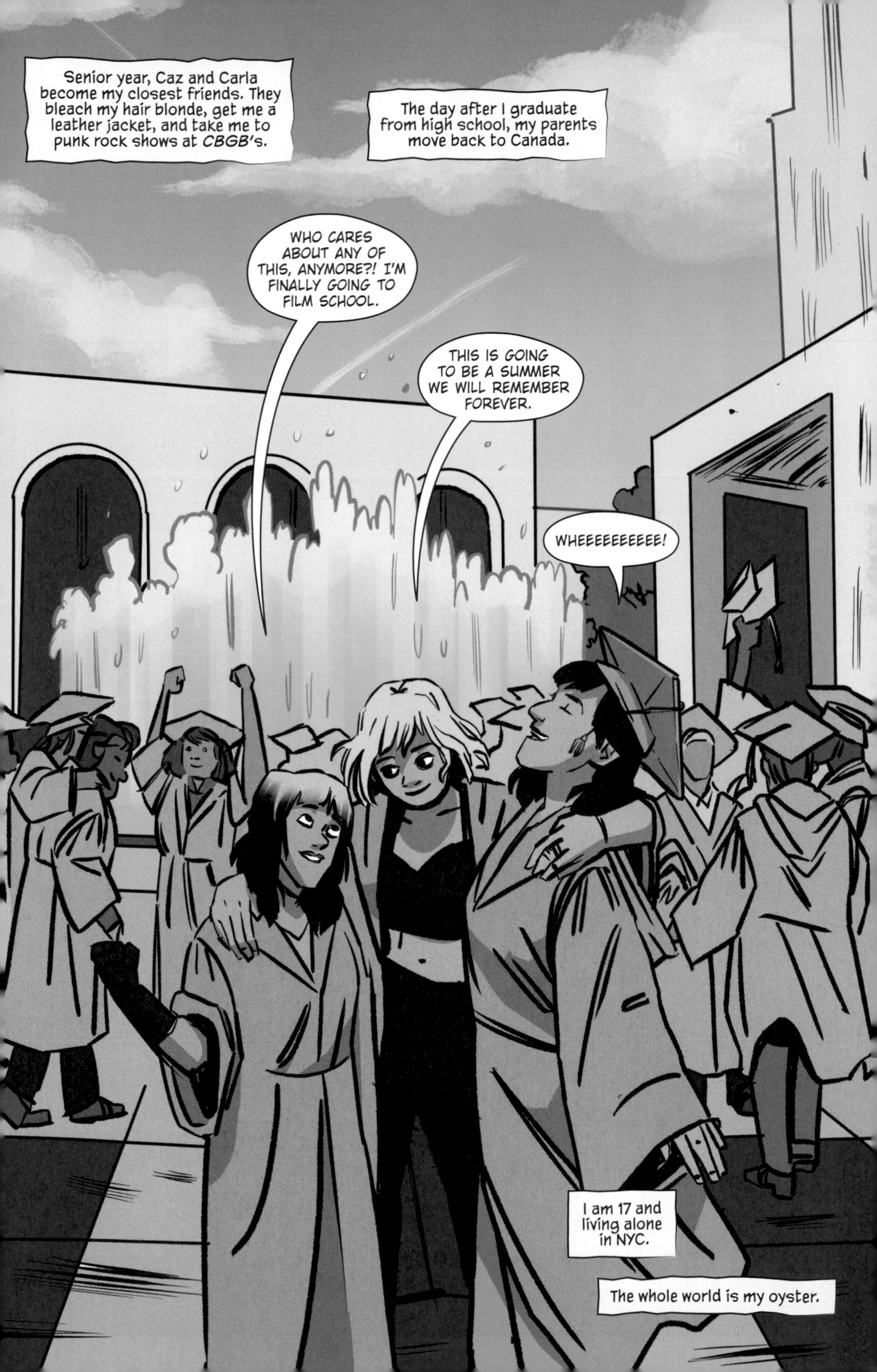
Senior year, Caz and Carla become my closest friends. They bleach my hair blonde, get me a leather jacket, and take me to punk rock shows at *CBGB's*.
The day after I graduate from high school, my parents move back to Canada.
WHO CARES ABOUT ANY OF THIS, ANYMORE?! I'M FINALLY GOING TO FILM SCHOOL.
THIS IS GOING TO BE A SUMMER WE WILL REMEMBER FOREVER.
WHEEEEEEEEEE!
I am 17 and living alone in NYC.
The whole world is my oyster.

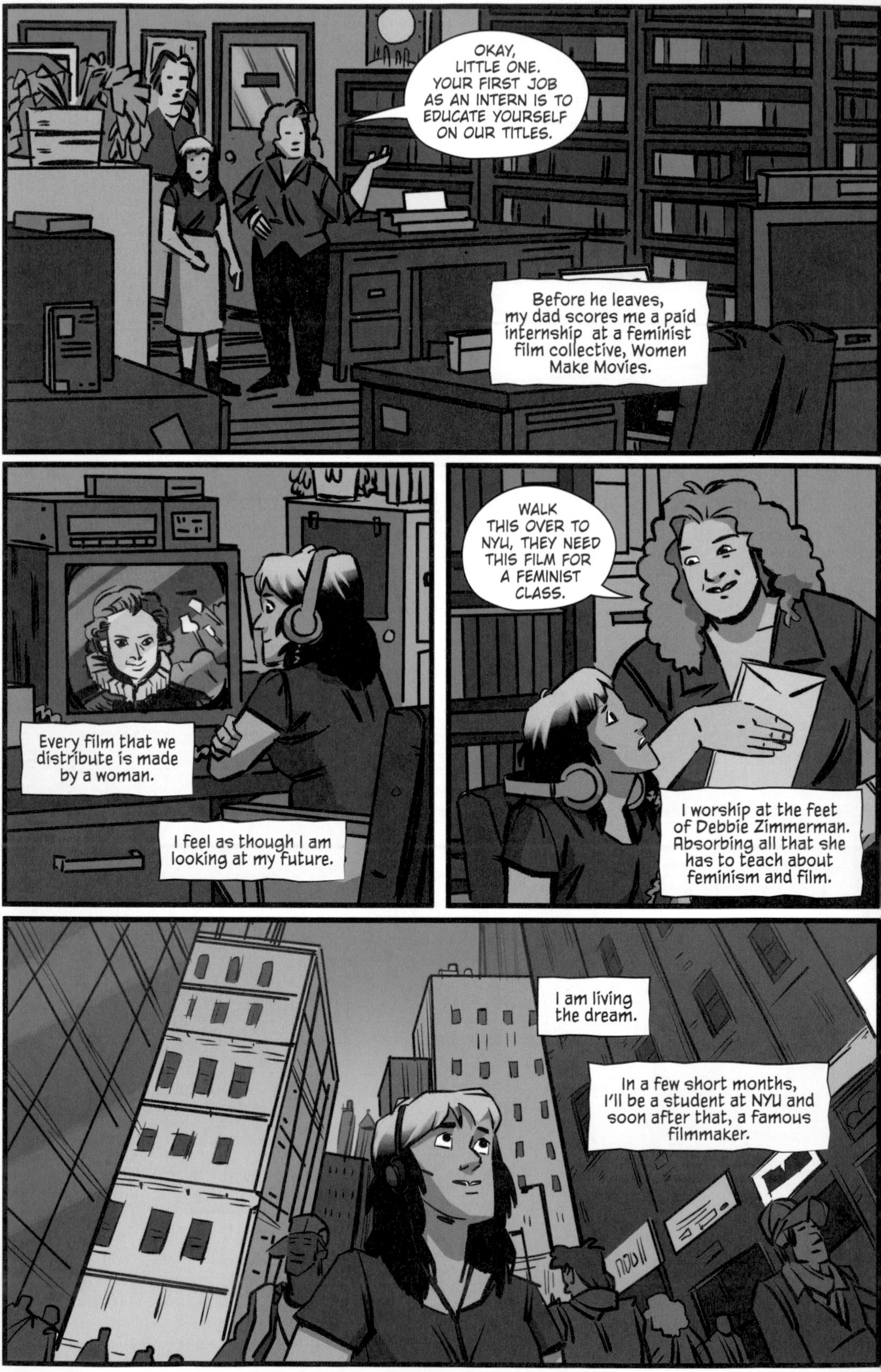
OKAY, LITTLE ONE. YOUR FIRST JOB AS AN INTERN IS TO EDUCATE YOURSELF ON OUR TITLES.
Before he leaves, my dad scores me a paid internship at a feminist film collective, Women Make Movies.
Every film that we distribute is made by a woman.
I feel as though I am looking at my future.
WALK THIS OVER TO NYU, THEY NEED THIS FILM FOR A FEMINIST CLASS.
I worship at the feet of Debbie Zimmerman. Absorbing all that she has to teach about feminism and film.
I am living the dream.
In a few short months, I'll be a student at NYU and soon after that, a famous filmmaker.

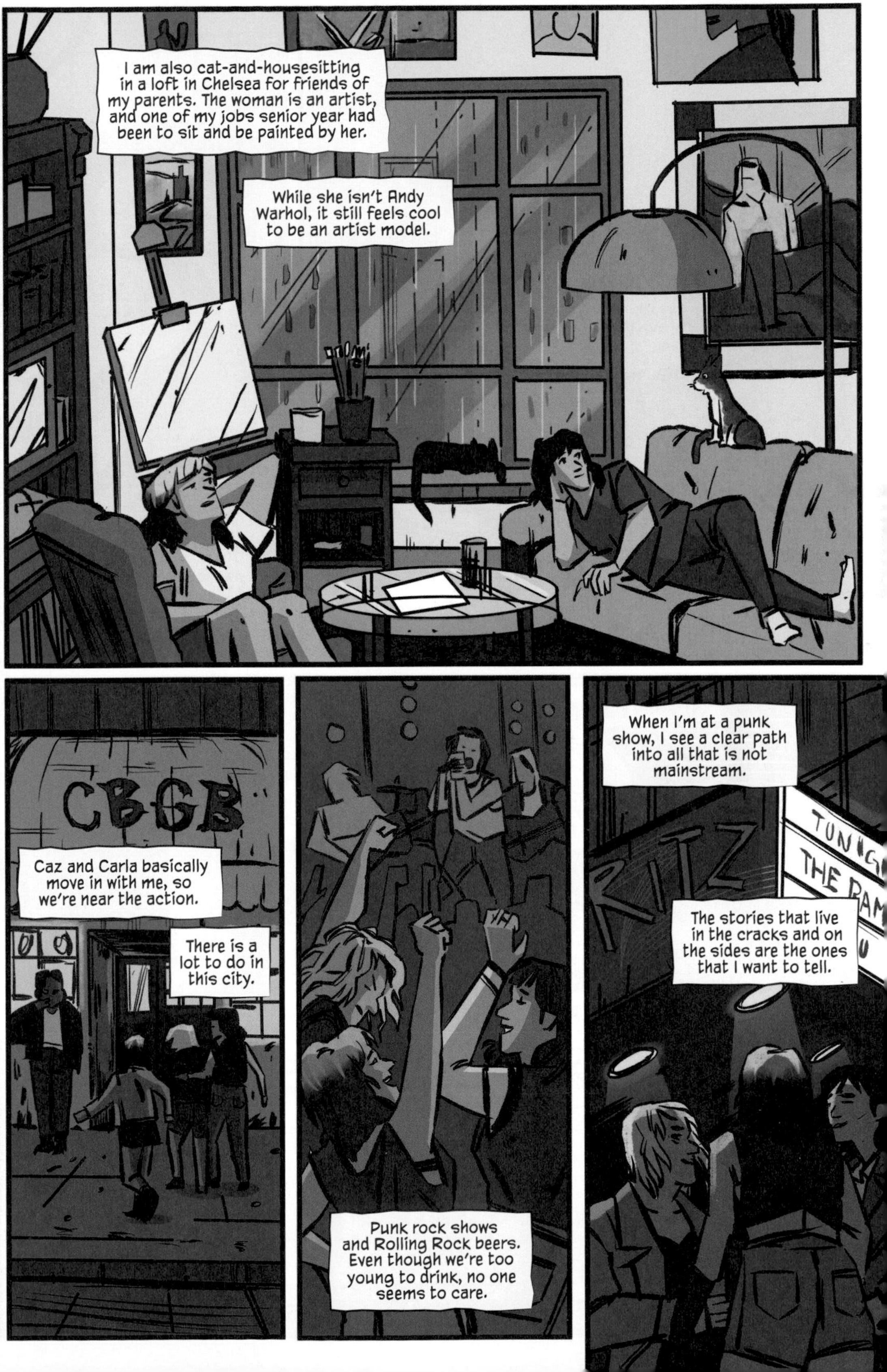
I am also cat-and-housesitting in a loft in Chelsea for friends of my parents. The woman is an artist, and one of my jobs senior year had been to sit and be painted by her.
While she isn't Andy Warhol, it still feels cool to be an artist model.
CBGB
Caz and Carla basically move in with me, so we're near the action.
There is a lot to do in this city.
Punk rock shows and Rolling Rock beers. Even though we're too young to drink, no one seems to care.
When I'm at a punk show, I see a clear path into all that is not mainstream.
RITZ
The stories that live in the cracks and on the sides are the ones that I want to tell.

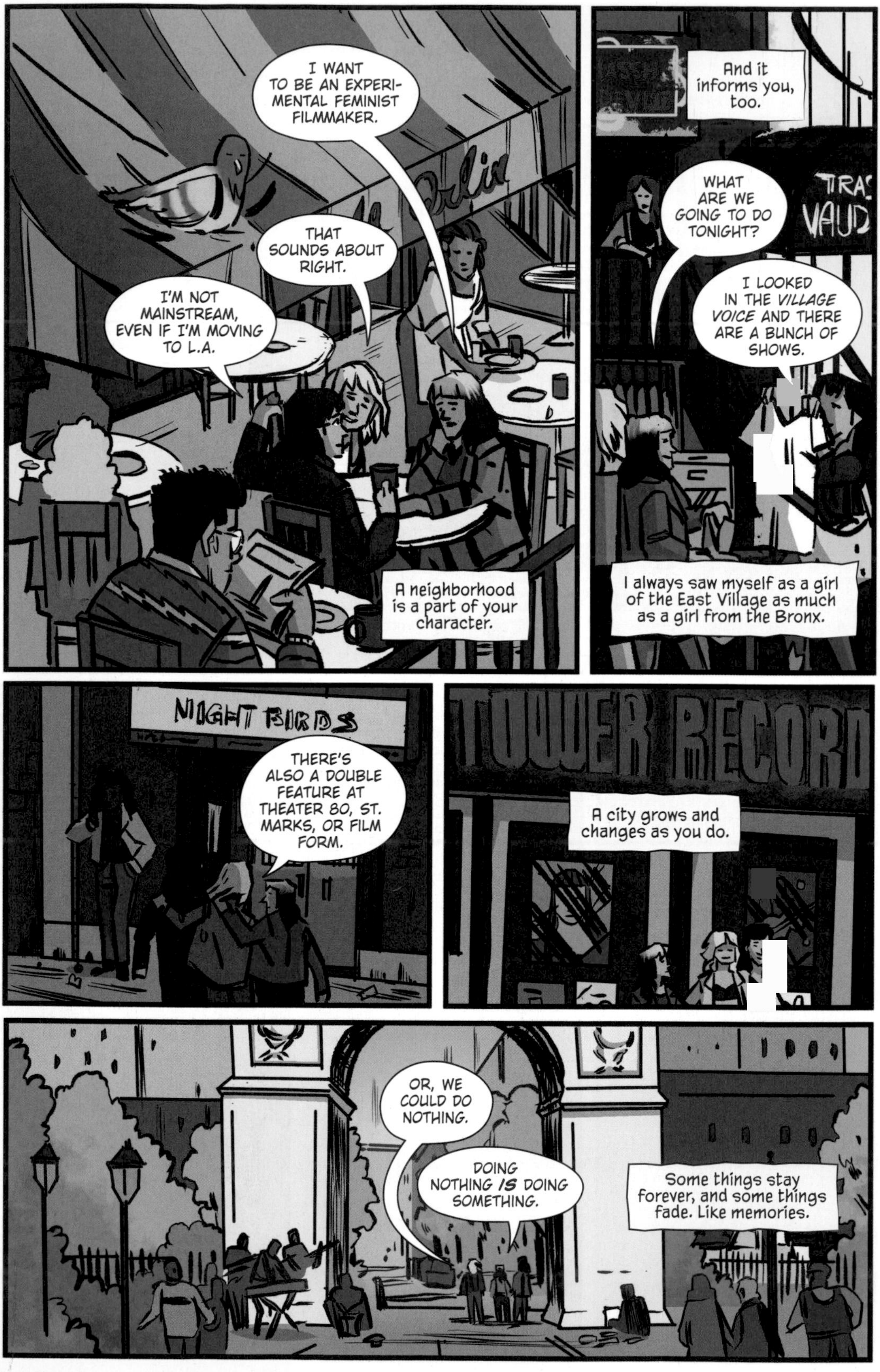
I WANT TO BE AN EXPERIMENTAL FEMINIST FILMMAKER.
THAT SOUNDS ABOUT RIGHT.
I'M NOT MAINSTREAM, EVEN IF I'M MOVING TO L.A.
A neighborhood is a part of your character.
And it informs you, too.
TRAS
VAUD
WHAT ARE WE GOING TO DO TONIGHT?
I LOOKED IN THE *VILLAGE VOICE* AND THERE ARE A BUNCH OF SHOWS.
I always saw myself as a girl of the East Village as much as a girl from the Bronx.
NIGHT BIRDS
THERE'S ALSO A DOUBLE FEATURE AT THEATER 80, ST. MARKS, OR FILM FORM.
TOWER RECORD
A city grows and changes as you do.
OR, WE COULD DO NOTHING.
DOING NOTHING *IS* DOING SOMETHING.
Some things stay forever, and some things fade. Like memories.

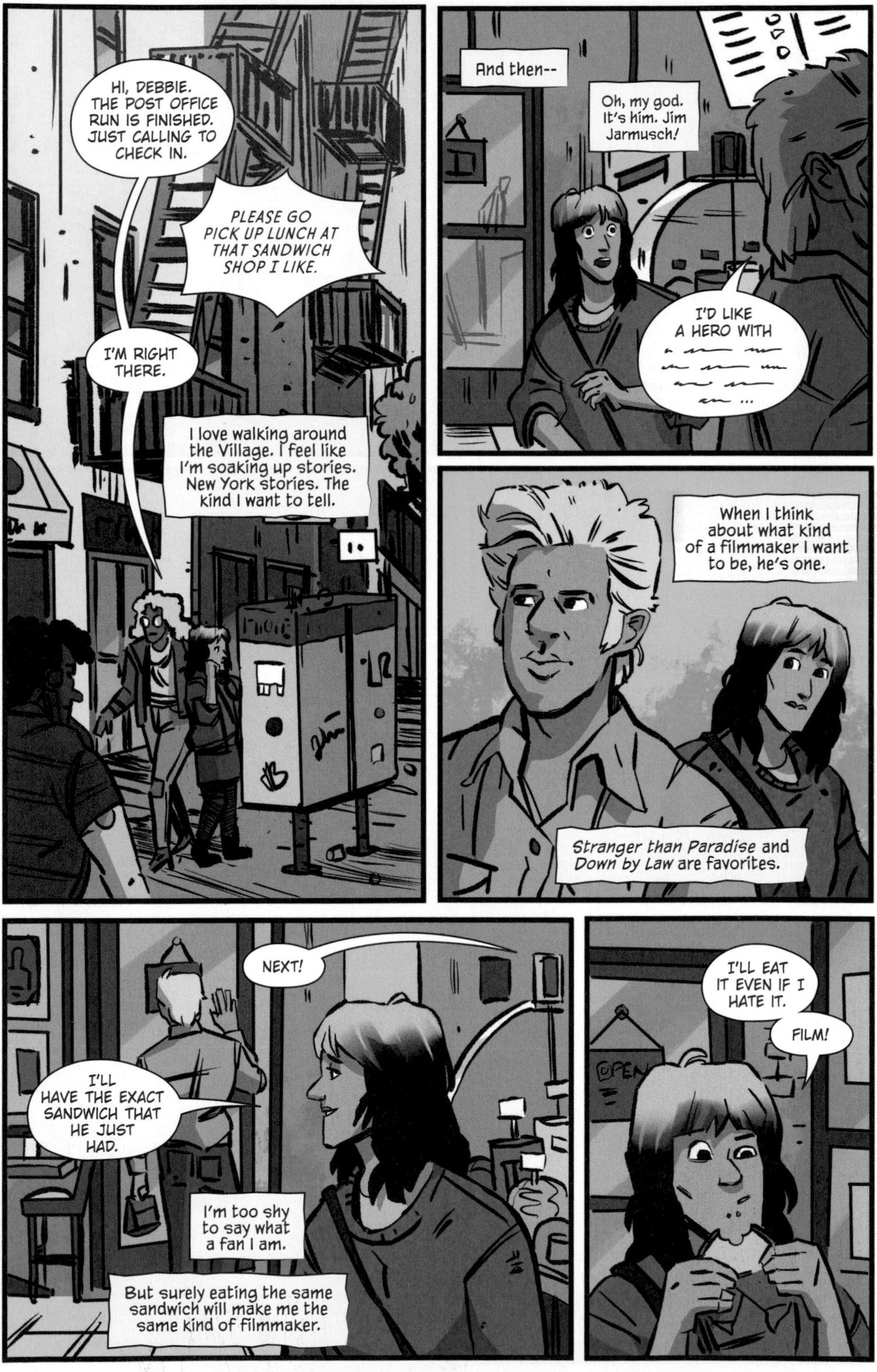
HI, DEBBIE. THE POST OFFICE RUN IS FINISHED. JUST CALLING TO CHECK IN.
PLEASE GO PICK UP LUNCH AT THAT SANDWICH SHOP I LIKE.
I'M RIGHT THERE.
I love walking around the Village. I feel like I'm soaking up stories. New York stories. The kind I want to tell.
And then--
Oh, my god. It's him. Jim Jarmusch!
I'D LIKE A HERO WITH ...
When I think about what kind of a filmmaker I want to be, he's one.
Stranger than Paradise and *Down by Law* are favorites.
NEXT!
I'LL HAVE THE EXACT SANDWICH THAT HE JUST HAD.
I'm too shy to say what a fan I am.
But surely eating the same sandwich will make me the same kind of filmmaker.
I'LL EAT IT EVEN IF I HATE IT.
FILM!

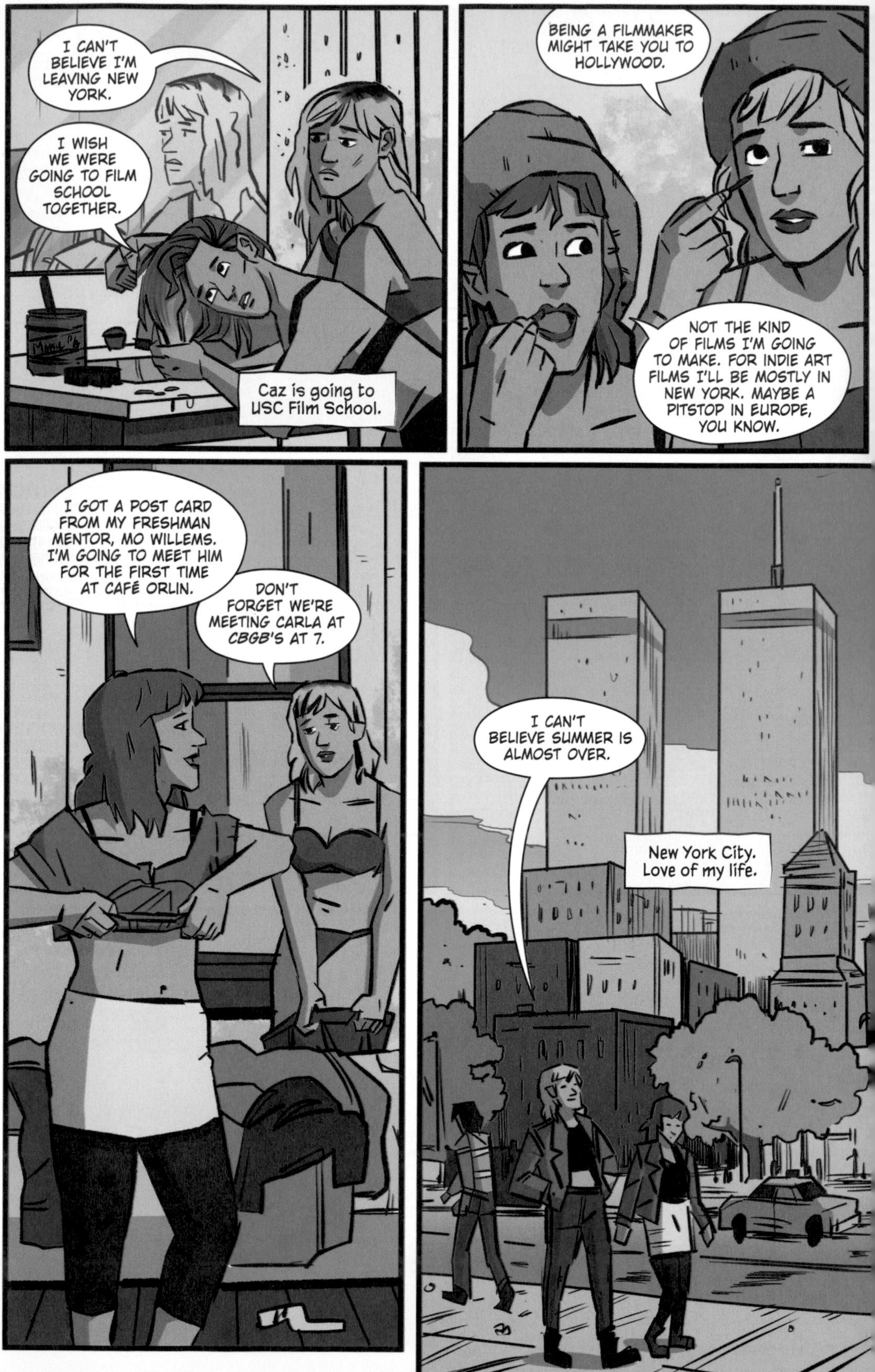
I CAN'T BELIEVE I'M LEAVING NEW YORK.
I WISH WE WERE GOING TO FILM SCHOOL TOGETHER.
Caz is going to USC Film School.
BEING A FILMMAKER MIGHT TAKE YOU TO HOLLYWOOD.
NOT THE KIND OF FILMS I'M GOING TO MAKE. FOR INDIE ART FILMS I'LL BE MOSTLY IN NEW YORK. MAYBE A PITSTOP IN EUROPE, YOU KNOW.
I GOT A POST CARD FROM MY FRESHMAN MENTOR, MO WILLEMS. I'M GOING TO MEET HIM FOR THE FIRST TIME AT CAFÉ ORLIN.
DON'T FORGET WE'RE MEETING CARLA AT CBGB'S AT 7.
I CAN'T BELIEVE SUMMER IS ALMOST OVER.
New York City. Love of my life.

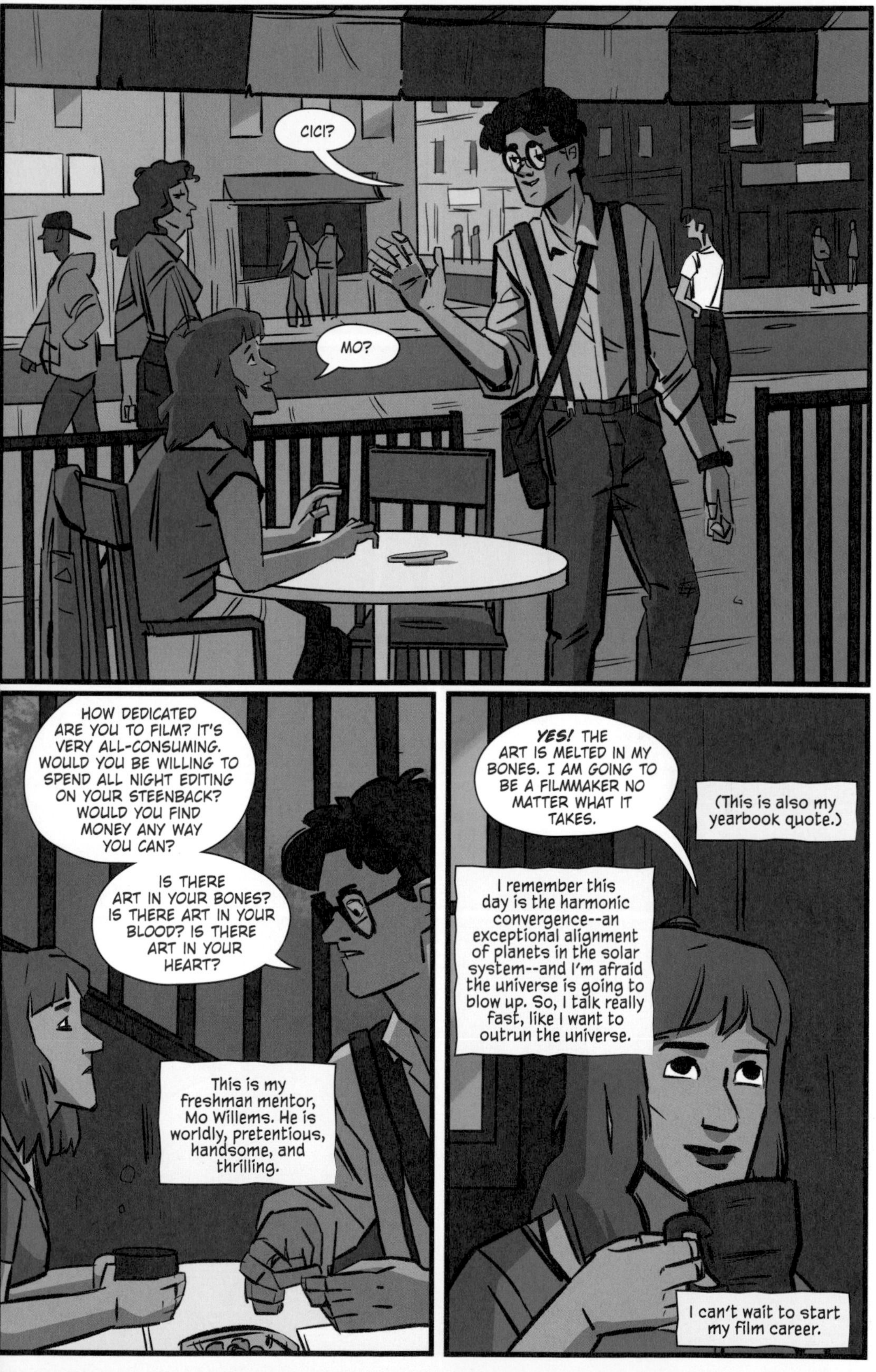
CICI?
MO?
HOW DEDICATED ARE YOU TO FILM? IT'S VERY ALL-CONSUMING. WOULD YOU BE WILLING TO SPEND ALL NIGHT EDITING ON YOUR STEENBACK? WOULD YOU FIND MONEY ANY WAY YOU CAN?
IS THERE ART IN YOUR BONES? IS THERE ART IN YOUR BLOOD? IS THERE ART IN YOUR HEART?
This is my freshman mentor, Mo Willems. He is worldly, pretentious, handsome, and thrilling.
YES! THE ART IS MELTED IN MY BONES. I AM GOING TO BE A FILMMAKER NO MATTER WHAT IT TAKES.
(This is also my yearbook quote.)
I remember this day is the harmonic convergence--an exceptional alignment of planets in the solar system--and I'm afraid the universe is going to blow up. So, I talk really fast, like I want to outrun the universe.
I can't wait to start my film career.

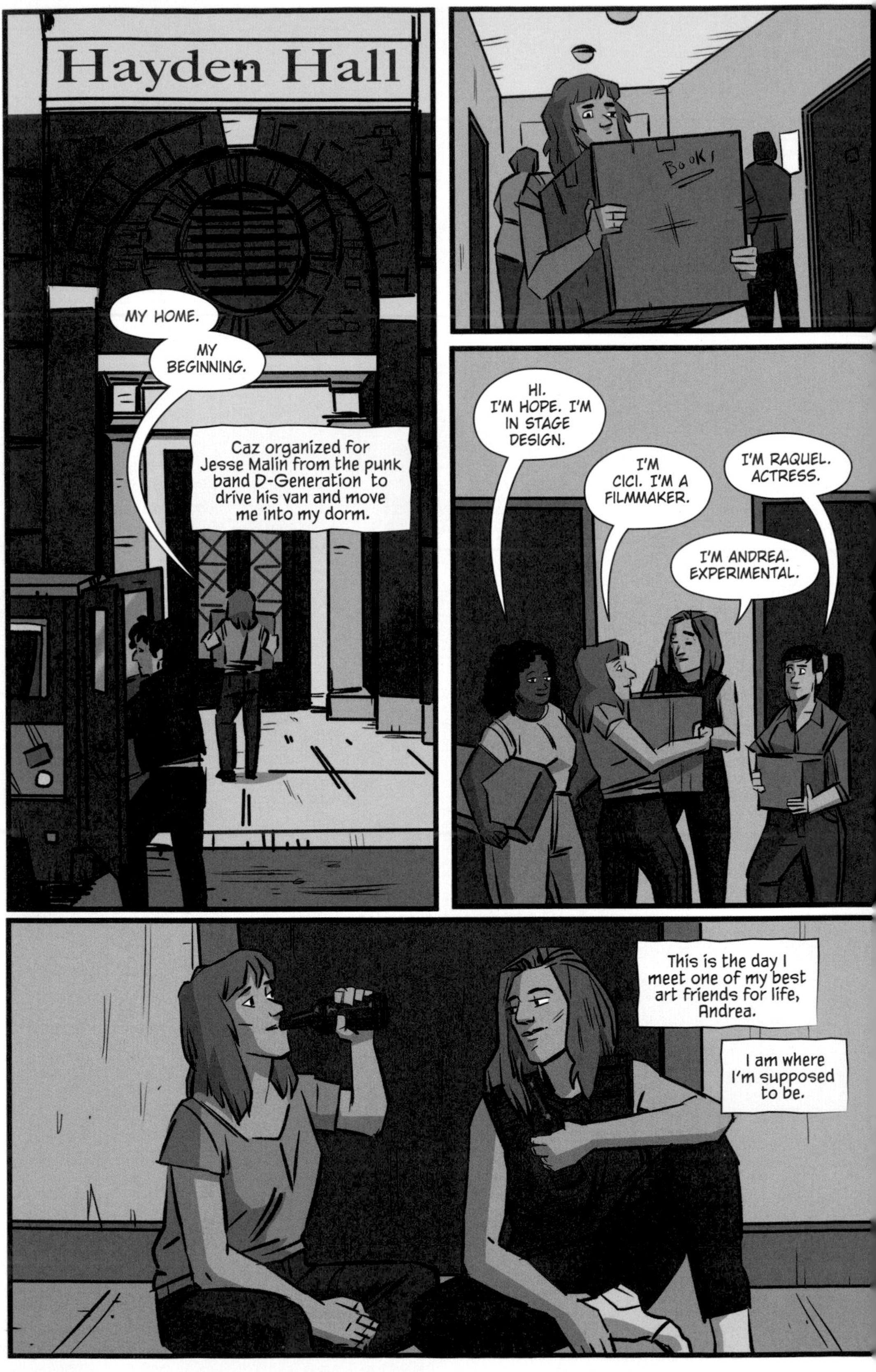
Hayden Hall
MY HOME.
MY BEGINNING.
Caz organized for Jesse Malin from the punk band D-Generation to drive his van and move me into my dorm.
BOOKS
HI. I'M HOPE. I'M IN STAGE DESIGN.
I'M CICI. I'M A FILMMAKER.
I'M RAQUEL. ACTRESS.
I'M ANDREA. EXPERIMENTAL.
This is the day I meet one of my best art friends for life, Andrea.
I am where I'm supposed to be.

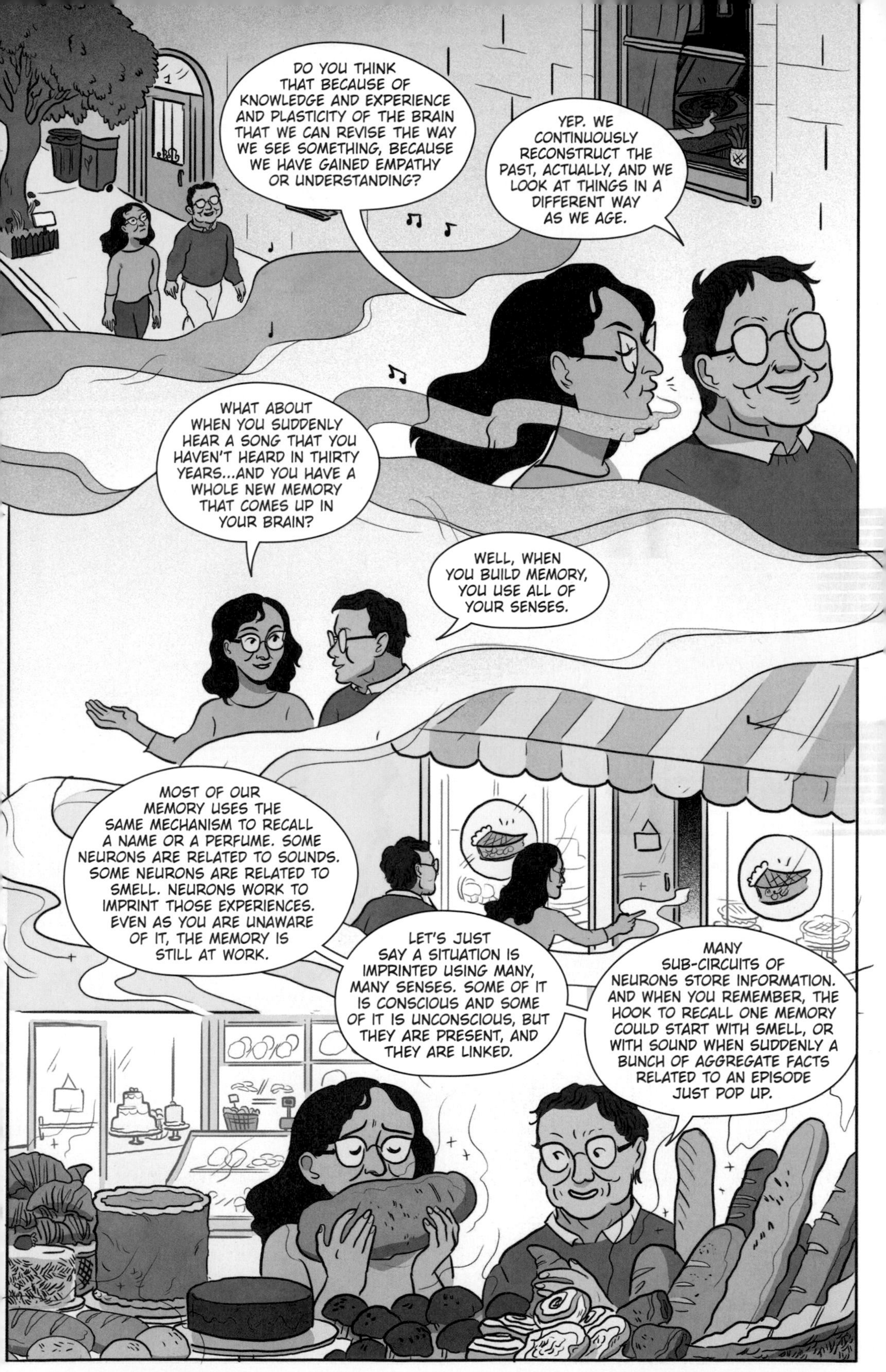
DO YOU THINK THAT BECAUSE OF KNOWLEDGE AND EXPERIENCE AND PLASTICITY OF THE BRAIN THAT WE CAN REVISE THE WAY WE SEE SOMETHING, BECAUSE WE HAVE GAINED EMPATHY OR UNDERSTANDING?
YEP. WE CONTINUOUSLY RECONSTRUCT THE PAST, ACTUALLY, AND WE LOOK AT THINGS IN A DIFFERENT WAY AS WE AGE.
WHAT ABOUT WHEN YOU SUDDENLY HEAR A SONG THAT YOU HAVEN'T HEARD IN THIRTY YEARS...AND YOU HAVE A WHOLE NEW MEMORY THAT COMES UP IN YOUR BRAIN?
WELL, WHEN YOU BUILD MEMORY, YOU USE ALL OF YOUR SENSES.
MOST OF OUR MEMORY USES THE SAME MECHANISM TO RECALL A NAME OR A PERFUME. SOME NEURONS ARE RELATED TO SOUNDS. SOME NEURONS ARE RELATED TO SMELL. NEURONS WORK TO IMPRINT THOSE EXPERIENCES. EVEN AS YOU ARE UNAWARE OF IT, THE MEMORY IS STILL AT WORK.
LET'S JUST SAY A SITUATION IS IMPRINTED USING MANY, MANY SENSES. SOME OF IT IS CONSCIOUS AND SOME OF IT IS UNCONSCIOUS, BUT THEY ARE PRESENT, AND THEY ARE LINKED.
MANY SUB-CIRCUITS OF NEURONS STORE INFORMATION. AND WHEN YOU REMEMBER, THE HOOK TO RECALL ONE MEMORY COULD START WITH SMELL, OR WITH SOUND WHEN SUDDENLY A BUNCH OF AGGREGATE FACTS RELATED TO AN EPISODE JUST POP UP.

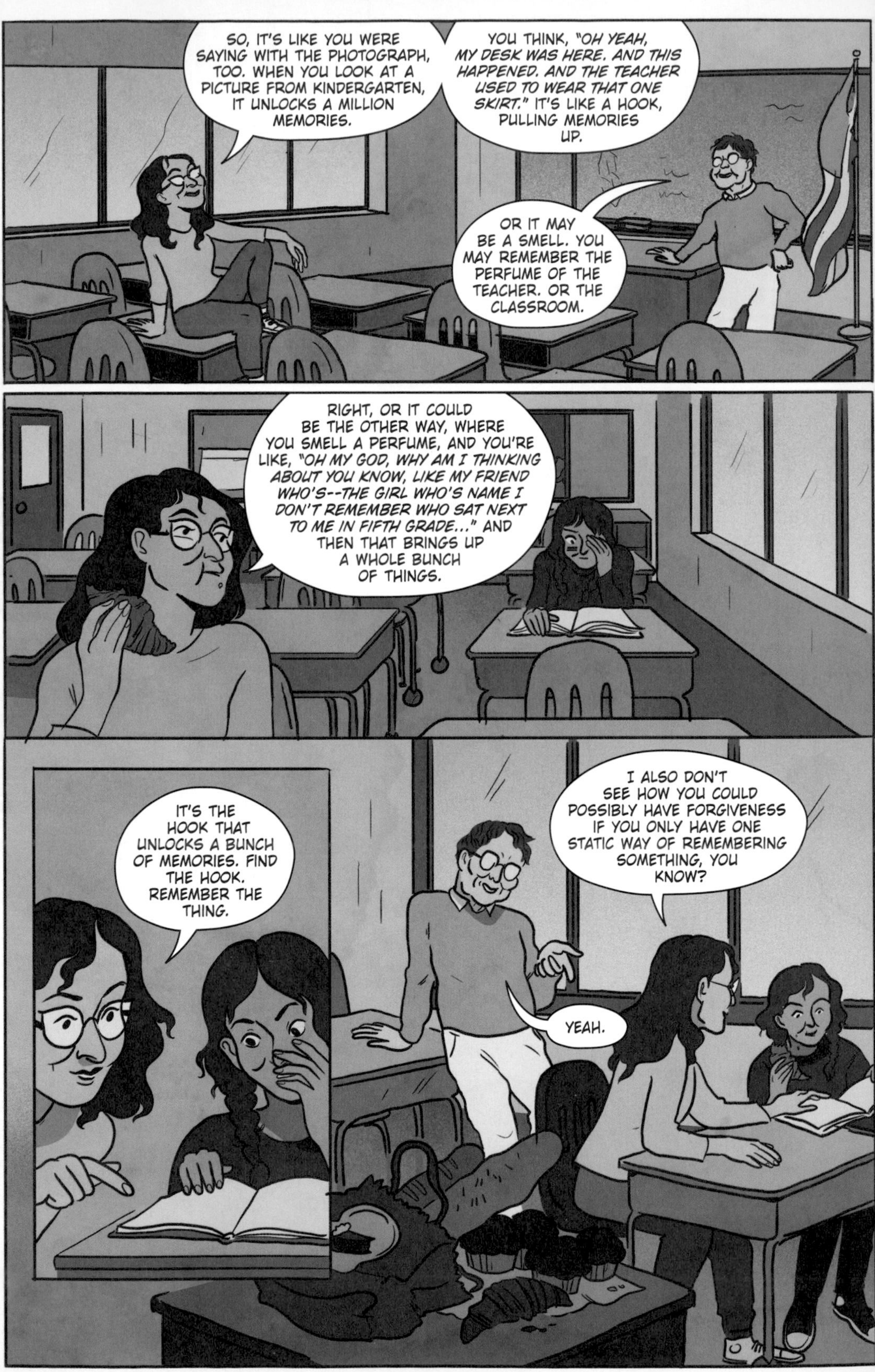
SO, IT'S LIKE YOU WERE SAYING WITH THE PHOTOGRAPH, TOO. WHEN YOU LOOK AT A PICTURE FROM KINDERGARTEN, IT UNLOCKS A MILLION MEMORIES.
YOU THINK, *"OH YEAH, MY DESK WAS HERE. AND THIS HAPPENED. AND THE TEACHER USED TO WEAR THAT ONE SKIRT."* IT'S LIKE A HOOK, PULLING MEMORIES UP.
OR IT MAY BE A SMELL. YOU MAY REMEMBER THE PERFUME OF THE TEACHER. OR THE CLASSROOM.
RIGHT, OR IT COULD BE THE OTHER WAY, WHERE YOU SMELL A PERFUME, AND YOU'RE LIKE, *"OH MY GOD, WHY AM I THINKING ABOUT YOU KNOW, LIKE MY FRIEND WHO'S--THE GIRL WHO'S NAME I DON'T REMEMBER WHO SAT NEXT TO ME IN FIFTH GRADE..."* AND THEN THAT BRINGS UP A WHOLE BUNCH OF THINGS.
IT'S THE HOOK THAT UNLOCKS A BUNCH OF MEMORIES. FIND THE HOOK. REMEMBER THE THING.
I ALSO DON'T SEE HOW YOU COULD POSSIBLY HAVE FORGIVENESS IF YOU ONLY HAVE ONE STATIC WAY OF REMEMBERING SOMETHING, YOU KNOW?
YEAH.

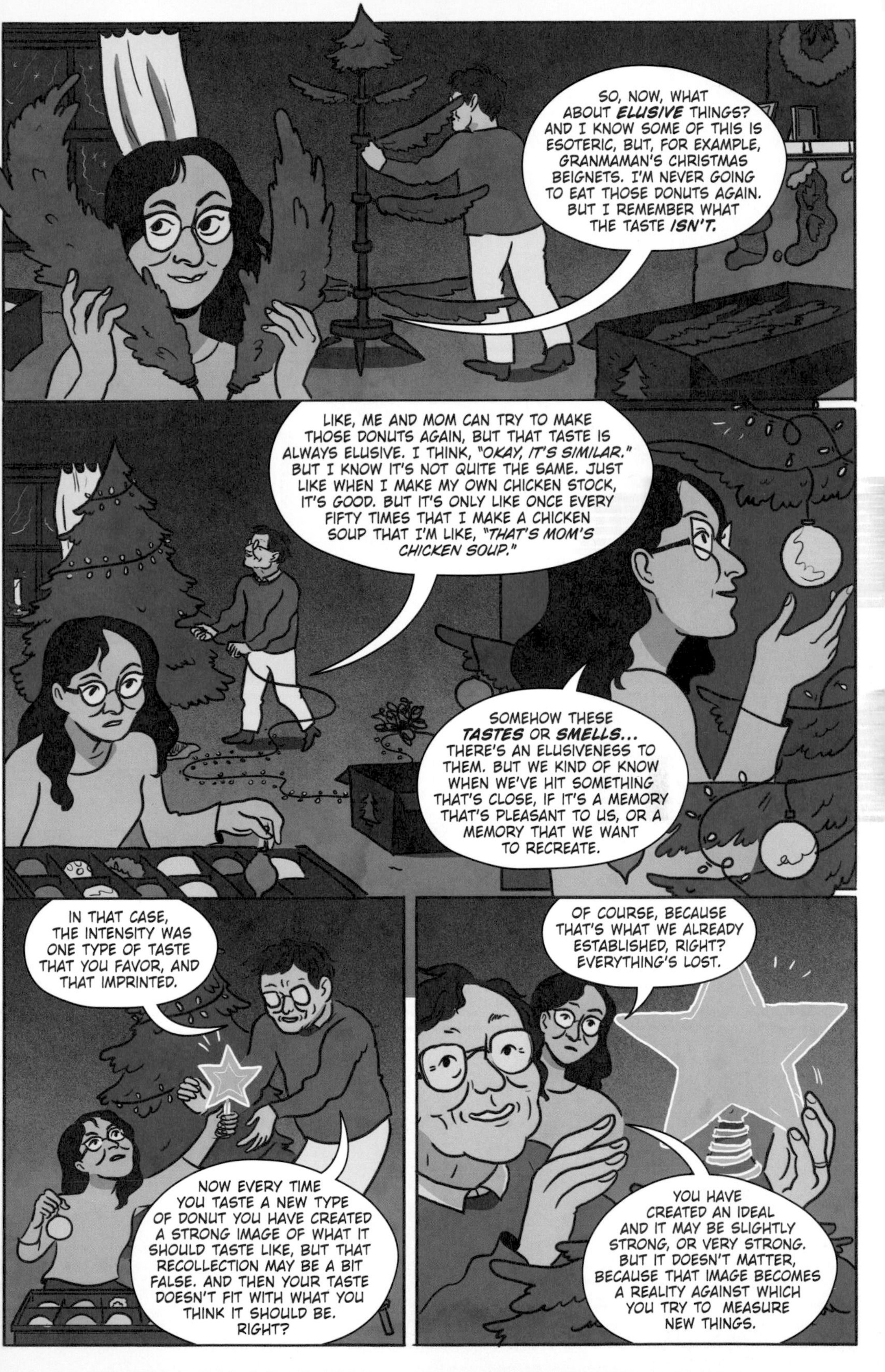
SO, NOW, WHAT ABOUT ELUSIVE THINGS? AND I KNOW SOME OF THIS IS ESOTERIC, BUT, FOR EXAMPLE, GRANMAMAN'S CHRISTMAS BEIGNETS. I'M NEVER GOING TO EAT THOSE DONUTS AGAIN. BUT I REMEMBER WHAT THE TASTE ISN'T.
LIKE, ME AND MOM CAN TRY TO MAKE THOSE DONUTS AGAIN, BUT THAT TASTE IS ALWAYS ELUSIVE. I THINK, "OKAY, IT'S SIMILAR." BUT I KNOW IT'S NOT QUITE THE SAME. JUST LIKE WHEN I MAKE MY OWN CHICKEN STOCK, IT'S GOOD. BUT IT'S ONLY LIKE ONCE EVERY FIFTY TIMES THAT I MAKE A CHICKEN SOUP THAT I'M LIKE, "THAT'S MOM'S CHICKEN SOUP."
SOMEHOW THESE TASTES OR SMELLS... THERE'S AN ELUSIVENESS TO THEM. BUT WE KIND OF KNOW WHEN WE'VE HIT SOMETHING THAT'S CLOSE, IF IT'S A MEMORY THAT'S PLEASANT TO US, OR A MEMORY THAT WE WANT TO RECREATE.
IN THAT CASE, THE INTENSITY WAS ONE TYPE OF TASTE THAT YOU FAVOR, AND THAT IMPRINTED.
NOW EVERY TIME YOU TASTE A NEW TYPE OF DONUT YOU HAVE CREATED A STRONG IMAGE OF WHAT IT SHOULD TASTE LIKE, BUT THAT RECOLLECTION MAY BE A BIT FALSE. AND THEN YOUR TASTE DOESN'T FIT WITH WHAT YOU THINK IT SHOULD BE. RIGHT?
OF COURSE, BECAUSE THAT'S WHAT WE ALREADY ESTABLISHED, RIGHT? EVERYTHING'S LOST.
YOU HAVE CREATED AN IDEAL AND IT MAY BE SLIGHTLY STRONG, OR VERY STRONG. BUT IT DOESN'T MATTER, BECAUSE THAT IMAGE BECOMES A REALITY AGAINST WHICH YOU TRY TO MEASURE NEW THINGS.

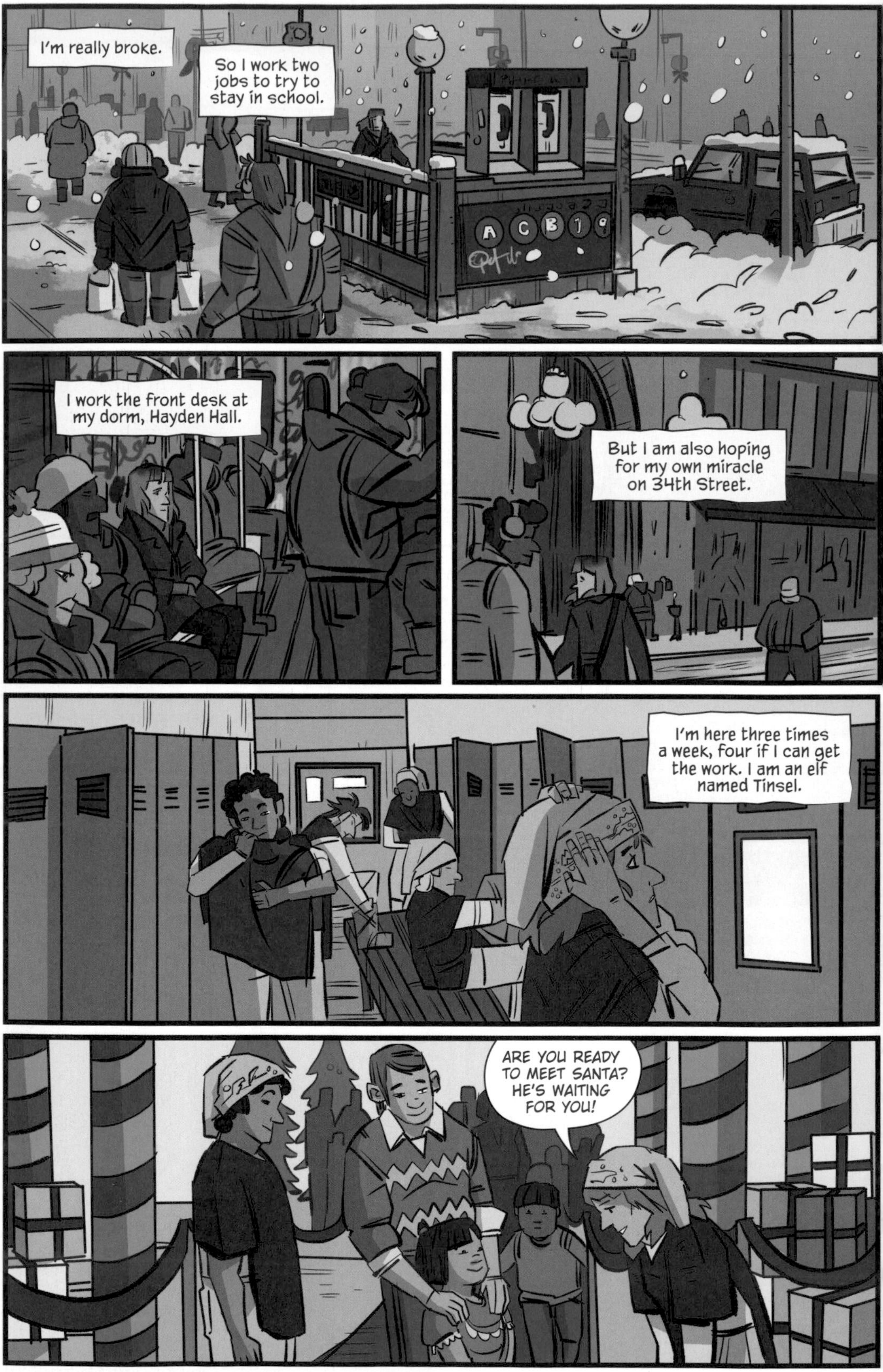
I'm really broke.
So I work two jobs to try to stay in school.
A C B 1 9
I work the front desk at my dorm, Hayden Hall.
But I am also hoping for my own miracle on 34th Street.
I'm here three times a week, four if I can get the work. I am an elf named Tinsel.
ARE YOU READY TO MEET SANTA? HE'S WAITING FOR YOU!

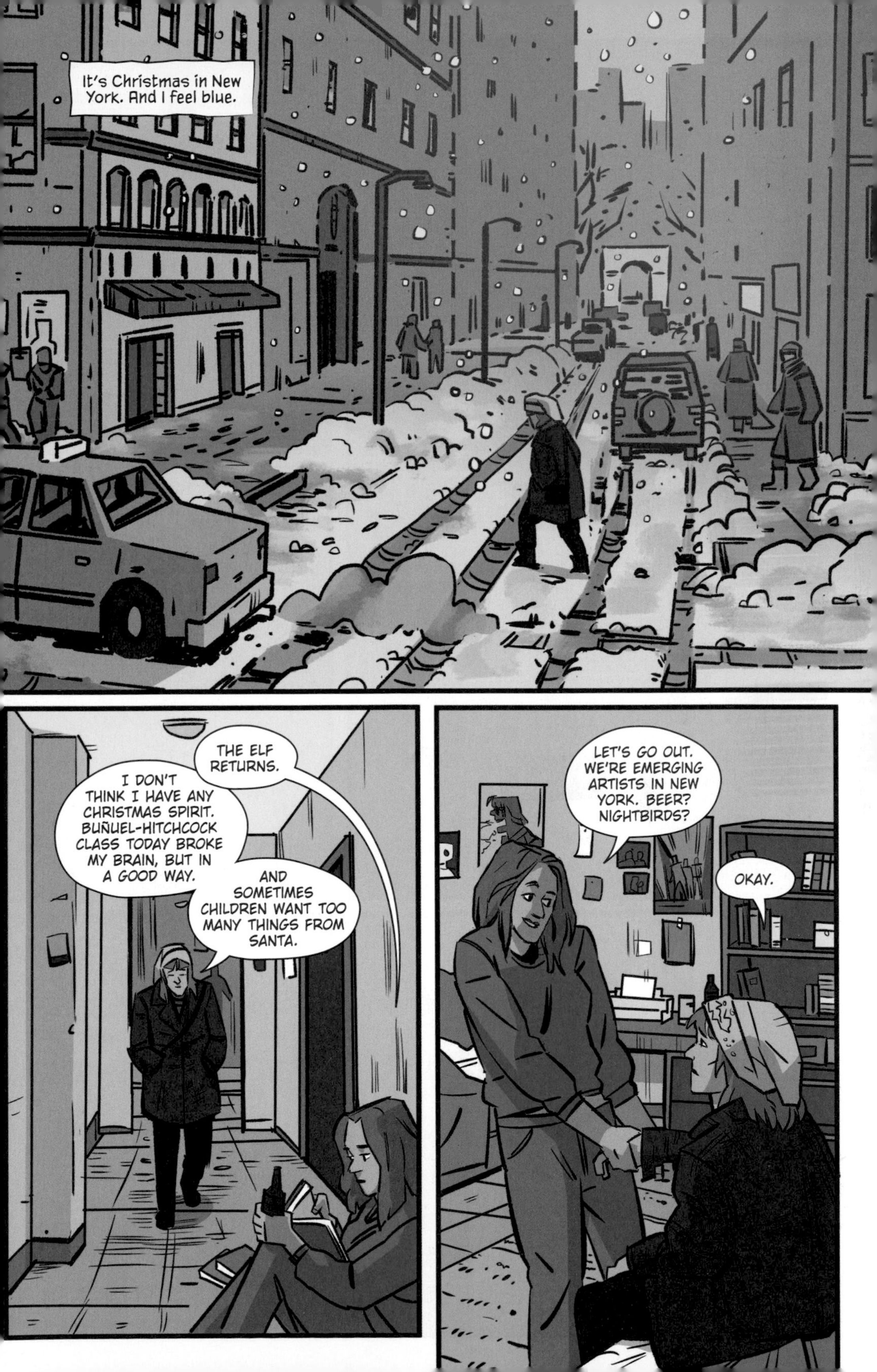
It's Christmas in New York. And I feel blue.
I DON'T THINK I HAVE ANY CHRISTMAS SPIRIT. BUÑUEL-HITCHCOCK CLASS TODAY BROKE MY BRAIN, BUT IN A GOOD WAY.
THE ELF RETURNS.
AND SOMETIMES CHILDREN WANT TOO MANY THINGS FROM SANTA.
LET'S GO OUT. WE'RE EMERGING ARTISTS IN NEW YORK. BEER? NIGHTBIRDS?
OKAY.

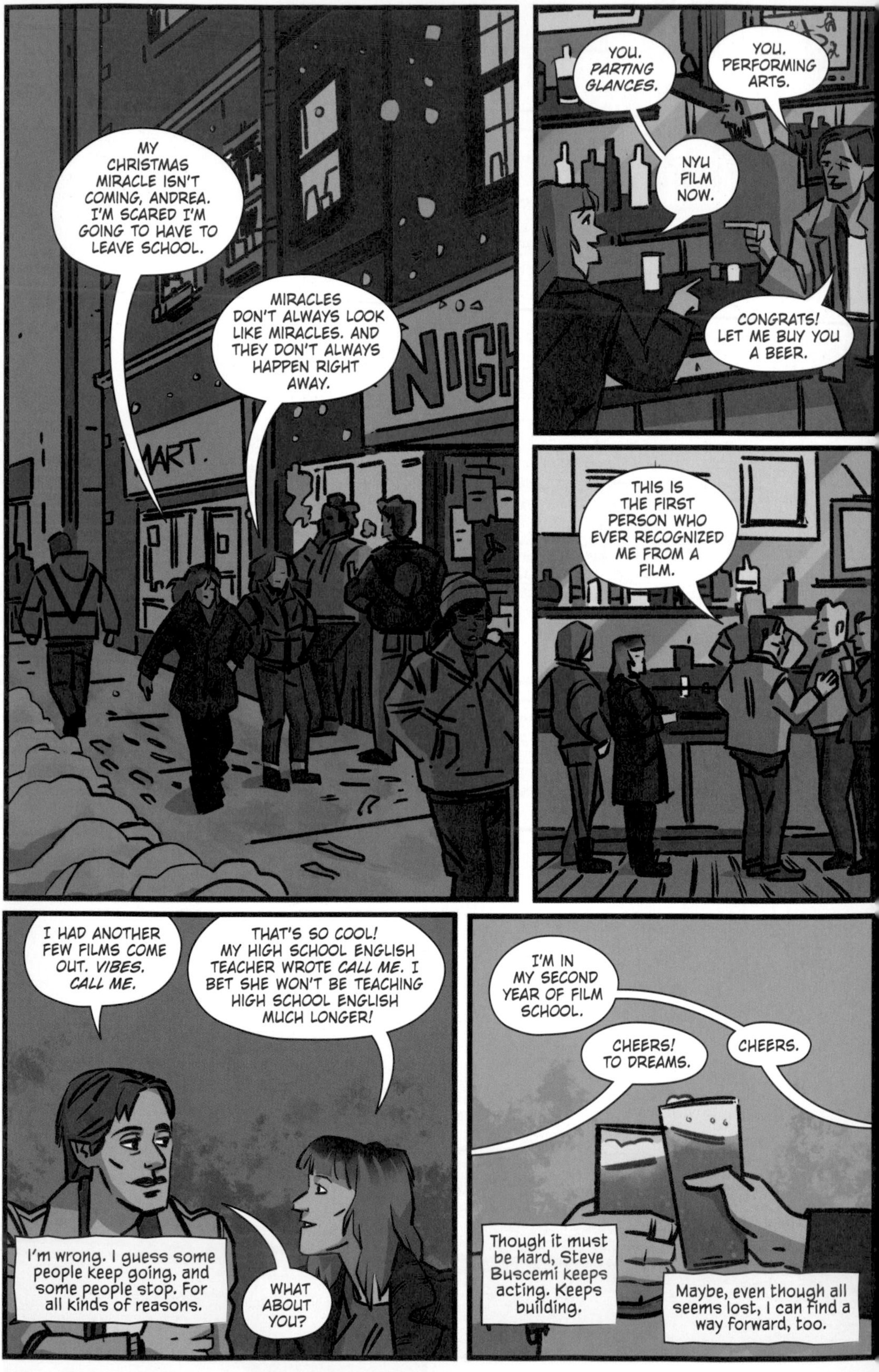
MY CHRISTMAS MIRACLE ISN'T COMING, ANDREA. I'M SCARED I'M GOING TO HAVE TO LEAVE SCHOOL.
MIRACLES DON'T ALWAYS LOOK LIKE MIRACLES. AND THEY DON'T ALWAYS HAPPEN RIGHT AWAY.
NIGH
MART.
YOU. *PARTING GLANCES.*
YOU. PERFORMING ARTS.
NYU FILM NOW.
CONGRATS! LET ME BUY YOU A BEER.
THIS IS THE FIRST PERSON WHO EVER RECOGNIZED ME FROM A FILM.
I HAD ANOTHER FEW FILMS COME OUT. *VIBES. CALL ME.*
THAT'S SO COOL! MY HIGH SCHOOL ENGLISH TEACHER WROTE *CALL ME*. I BET SHE WON'T BE TEACHING HIGH SCHOOL ENGLISH MUCH LONGER!
I'm wrong. I guess some people keep going, and some people stop. For all kinds of reasons.
WHAT ABOUT YOU?
I'M IN MY SECOND YEAR OF FILM SCHOOL.
CHEERS! TO DREAMS.
CHEERS.
Though it must be hard, Steve Buscemi keeps acting. Keeps building.
Maybe, even though all seems lost, I can find a way forward, too.

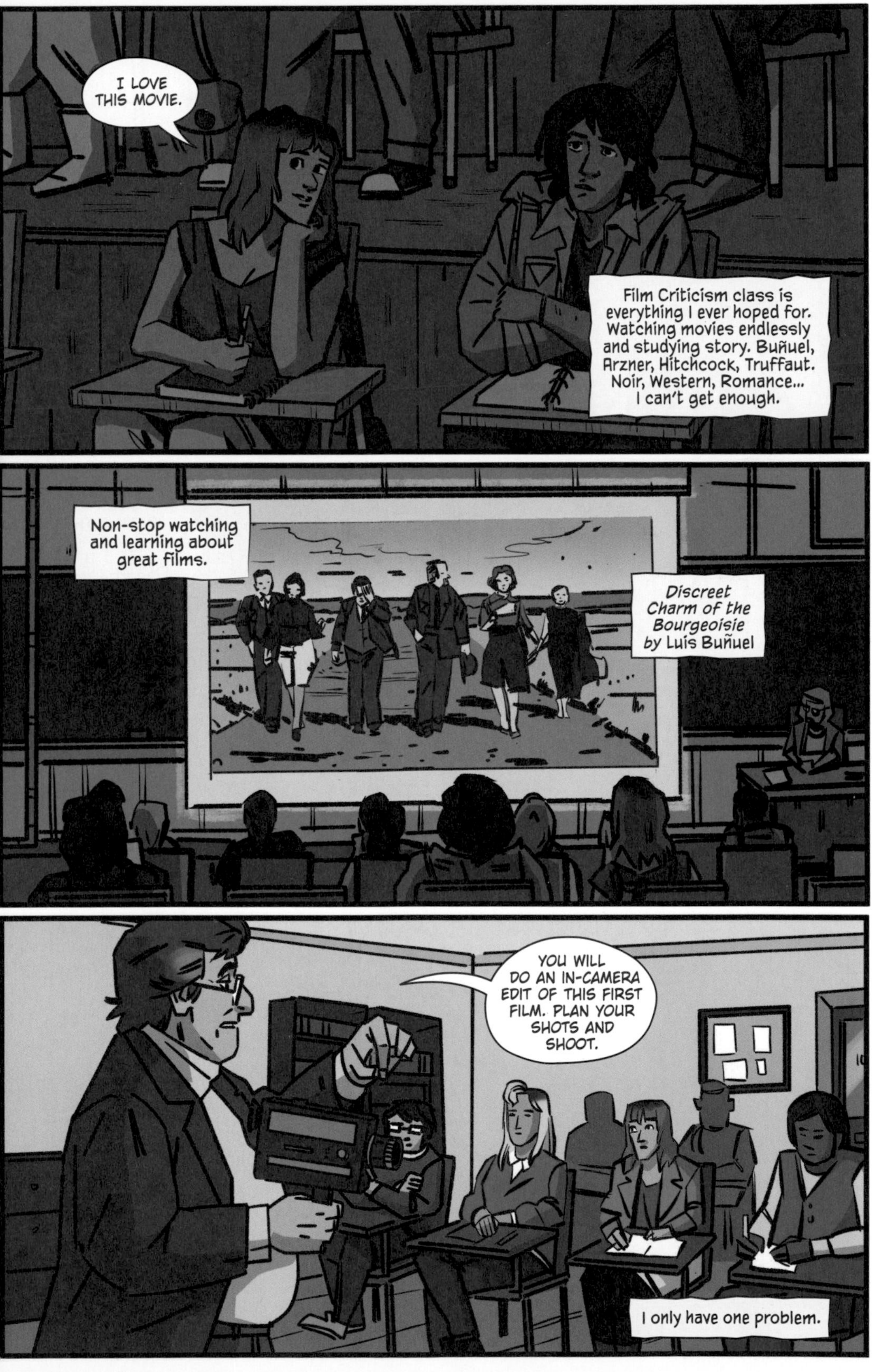
I LOVE THIS MOVIE.
Film Criticism class is everything I ever hoped for. Watching movies endlessly and studying story. Buñuel, Arzner, Hitchcock, Truffaut. Noir, Western, Romance... I can't get enough.
Non-stop watching and learning about great films.
Discreet Charm of the Bourgeoisie by Luis Buñuel
YOU WILL DO AN IN-CAMERA EDIT OF THIS FIRST FILM. PLAN YOUR SHOTS AND SHOOT.
I only have one problem.

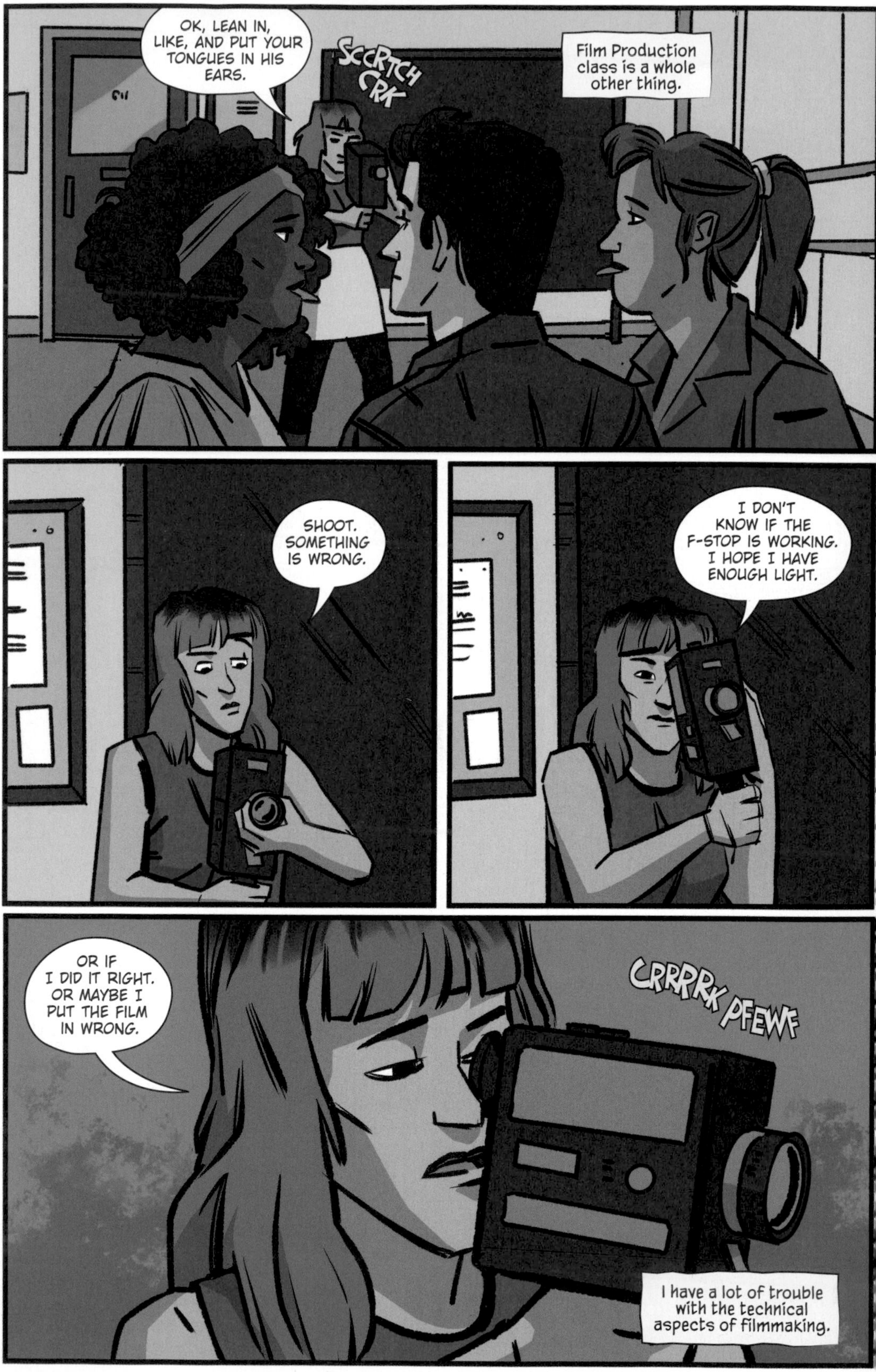
OK, LEAN IN, LIKE, AND PUT YOUR TONGUES IN HIS EARS.
SCCRTCH CRK
Film Production class is a whole other thing.
SHOOT. SOMETHING IS WRONG.
I DON'T KNOW IF THE F-STOP IS WORKING. I HOPE I HAVE ENOUGH LIGHT.
OR IF I DID IT RIGHT. OR MAYBE I PUT THE FILM IN WRONG.
CRRRRK PFEWF
I have a lot of trouble with the technical aspects of filmmaking.

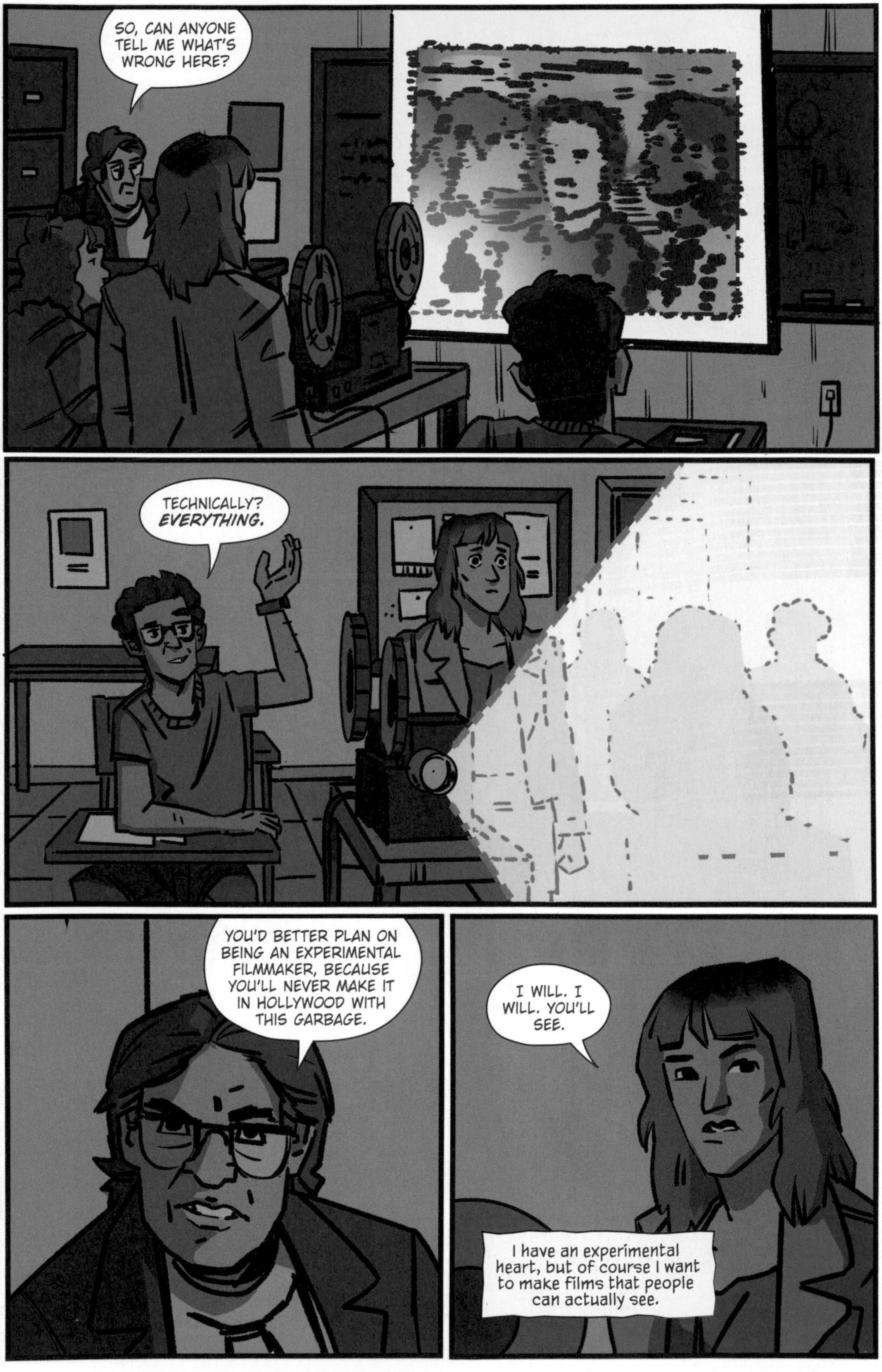
SO, CAN ANYONE TELL ME WHAT'S WRONG HERE?
TECHNICALLY? *EVERYTHING.*
YOU'D BETTER PLAN ON BEING AN EXPERIMENTAL FILMMAKER, BECAUSE YOU'LL NEVER MAKE IT IN HOLLYWOOD WITH THIS GARBAGE.
I WILL. I WILL. YOU'LL SEE.
I have an experimental heart, but of course I want to make films that people can actually see.

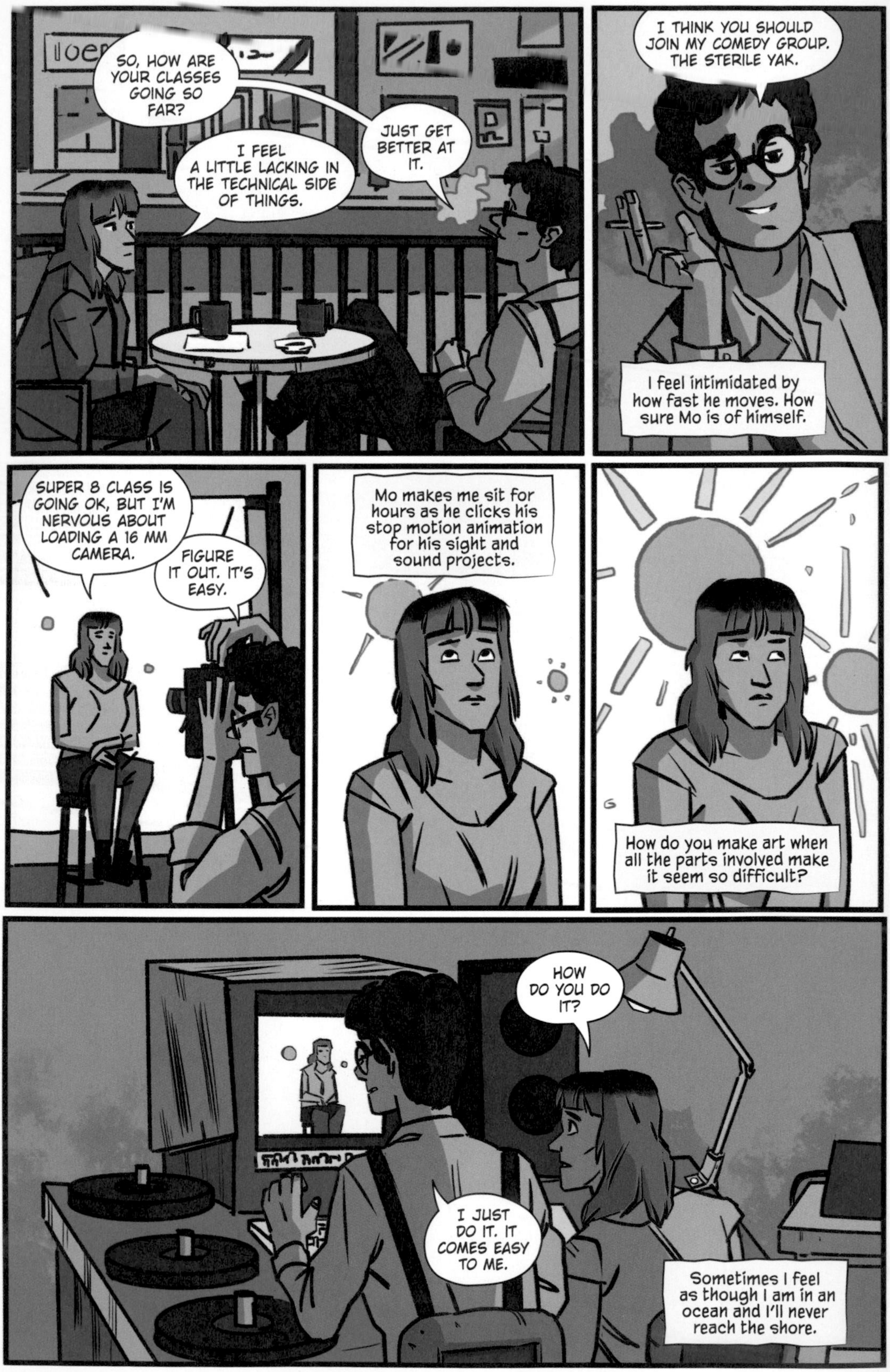
SO, HOW ARE YOUR CLASSES GOING SO FAR?
I FEEL A LITTLE LACKING IN THE TECHNICAL SIDE OF THINGS.
JUST GET BETTER AT IT.
I THINK YOU SHOULD JOIN MY COMEDY GROUP. THE STERILE YAK.
I feel intimidated by how fast he moves. How sure Mo is of himself.
SUPER 8 CLASS IS GOING OK, BUT I'M NERVOUS ABOUT LOADING A 16 MM CAMERA.
FIGURE IT OUT. IT'S EASY.
Mo makes me sit for hours as he clicks his stop motion animation for his sight and sound projects.
How do you make art when all the parts involved make it seem so difficult?
HOW DO YOU DO IT?
I JUST DO IT. IT COMES EASY TO ME.
Sometimes I feel as though I am in an ocean and I'll never reach the shore.

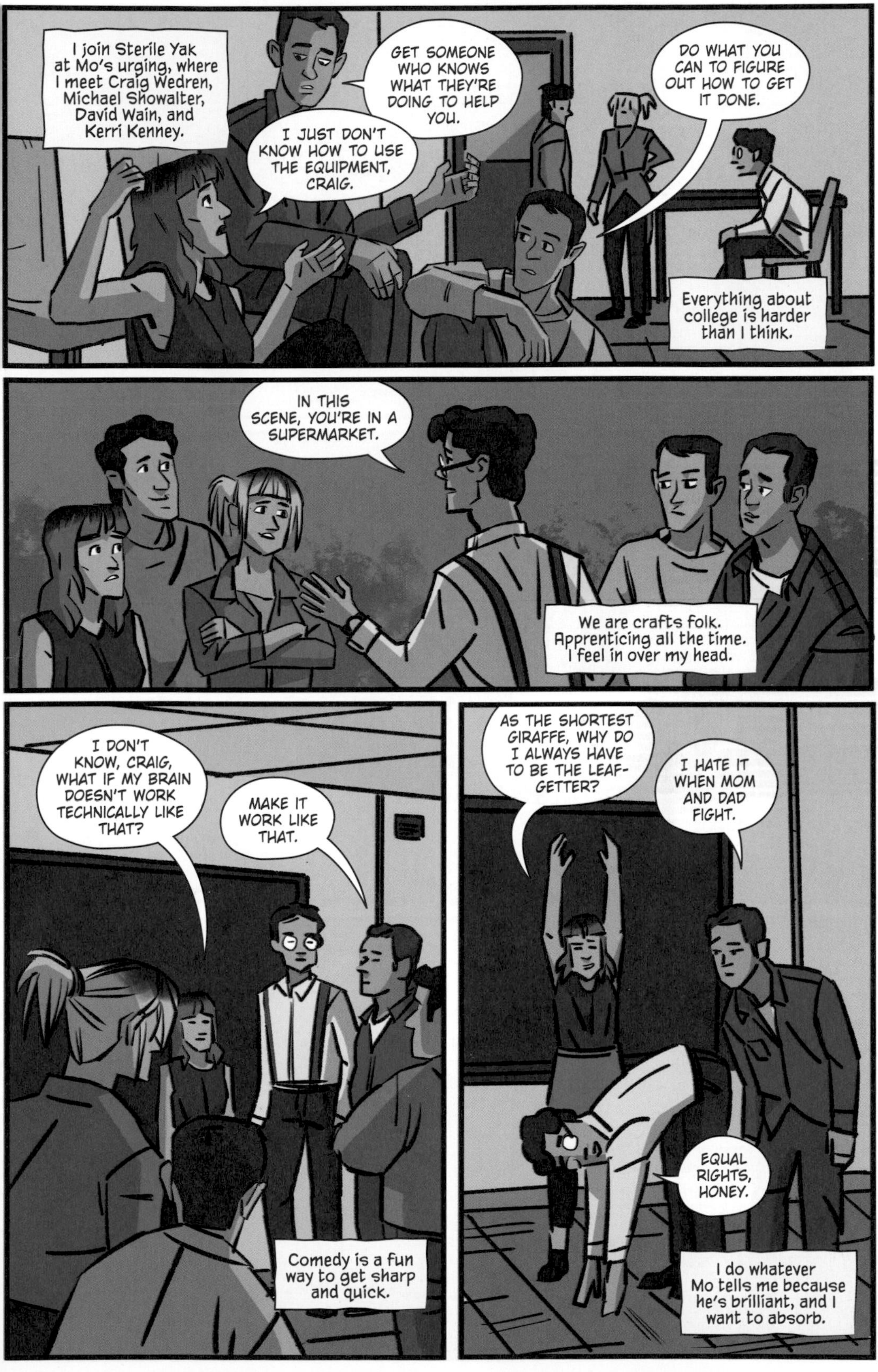
I join Sterile Yak at Mo's urging, where I meet Craig Wedren, Michael Showalter, David Wain, and Kerri Kenney.
I JUST DON'T KNOW HOW TO USE THE EQUIPMENT, CRAIG.
GET SOMEONE WHO KNOWS WHAT THEY'RE DOING TO HELP YOU.
DO WHAT YOU CAN TO FIGURE OUT HOW TO GET IT DONE.
Everything about college is harder than I think.
IN THIS SCENE, YOU'RE IN A SUPERMARKET.
We are crafts folk. Apprenticing all the time. I feel in over my head.
I DON'T KNOW, CRAIG, WHAT IF MY BRAIN DOESN'T WORK TECHNICALLY LIKE THAT?
MAKE IT WORK LIKE THAT.
Comedy is a fun way to get sharp and quick.
AS THE SHORTEST GIRAFFE, WHY DO I ALWAYS HAVE TO BE THE LEAF-GETTER?
I HATE IT WHEN MOM AND DAD FIGHT.
EQUAL RIGHTS, HONEY.
I do whatever Mo tells me because he's brilliant, and I want to absorb.

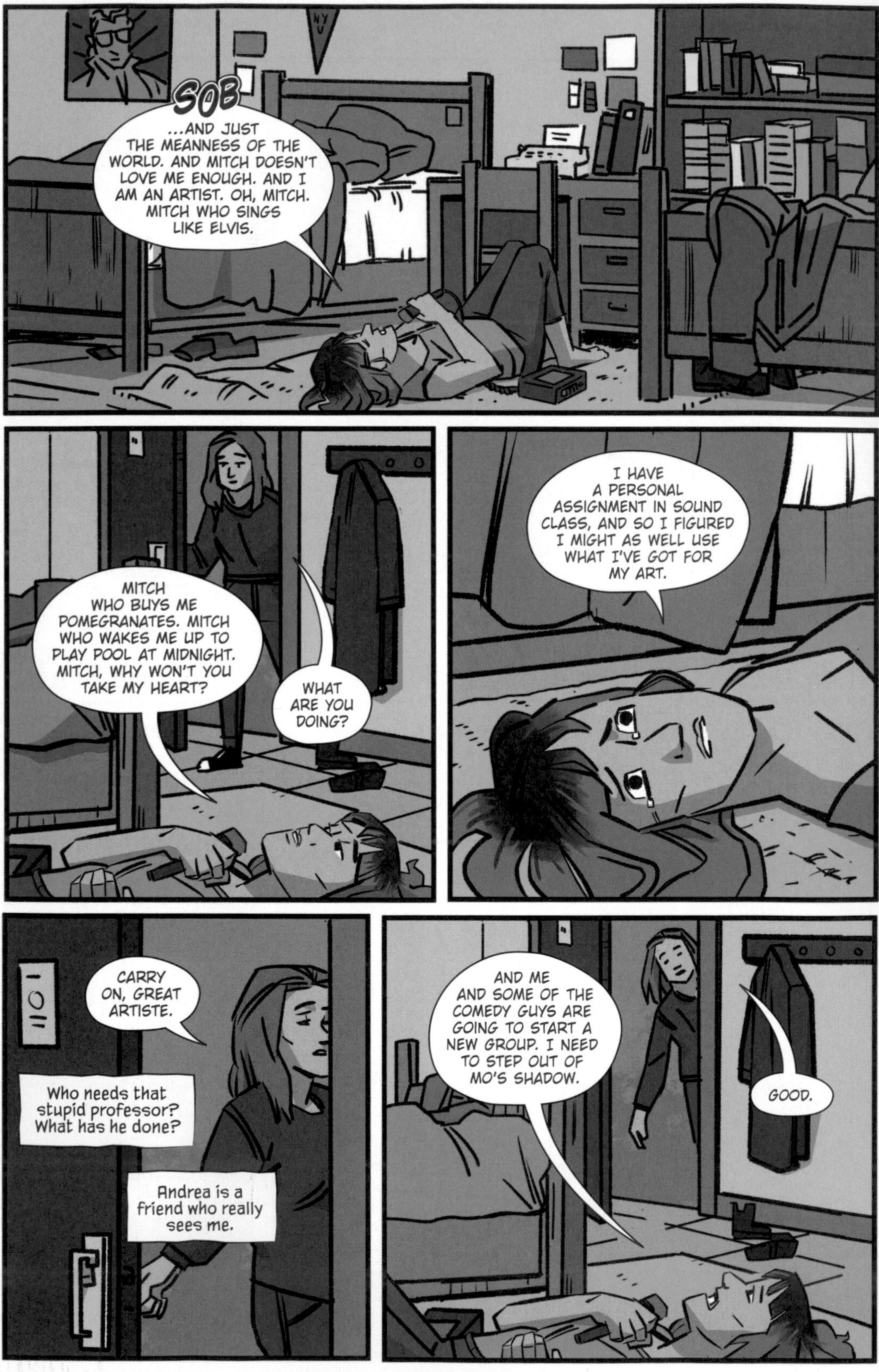
SOB
...AND JUST THE MEANNESS OF THE WORLD. AND MITCH DOESN'T LOVE ME ENOUGH. AND I AM AN ARTIST. OH, MITCH. MITCH WHO SINGS LIKE ELVIS.
MITCH WHO BUYS ME POMEGRANATES. MITCH WHO WAKES ME UP TO PLAY POOL AT MIDNIGHT. MITCH, WHY WON'T YOU TAKE MY HEART?
WHAT ARE YOU DOING?
I HAVE A PERSONAL ASSIGNMENT IN SOUND CLASS, AND SO I FIGURED I MIGHT AS WELL USE WHAT I'VE GOT FOR MY ART.
CARRY ON, GREAT ARTISTE.
Who needs that stupid professor? What has he done?
Andrea is a friend who really sees me.
AND ME AND SOME OF THE COMEDY GUYS ARE GOING TO START A NEW GROUP. I NEED TO STEP OUT OF MO'S SHADOW.
GOOD.

I'm learning so much from Mo, but I also feel like I can't find my own voice. So, I leave Sterile Yak to start a new group with Todd Holoubek and David Wain.

WE'LL BE READY FOR YOU ALL IN A MOMENT.

AUDITION
TODAY
COMEDY!
ROVE!
TCA!
OOM 204

I can't wait to see what I learn from those who join: Kerri Kenney, Joe LoTruglio, Michael Ian Black, Ken Marino, Michael Showalter, and Ben Garant.

Forge your own path forward even when you don't fit in.

(Play and practice. Hone your skill. Find the perfect group to learn with.)

I'M SO EXCITED!

Bring great people together, even if you have to let them go.

Most of the new group goes on to form the sketch comedy TV show *The State* in 1993.

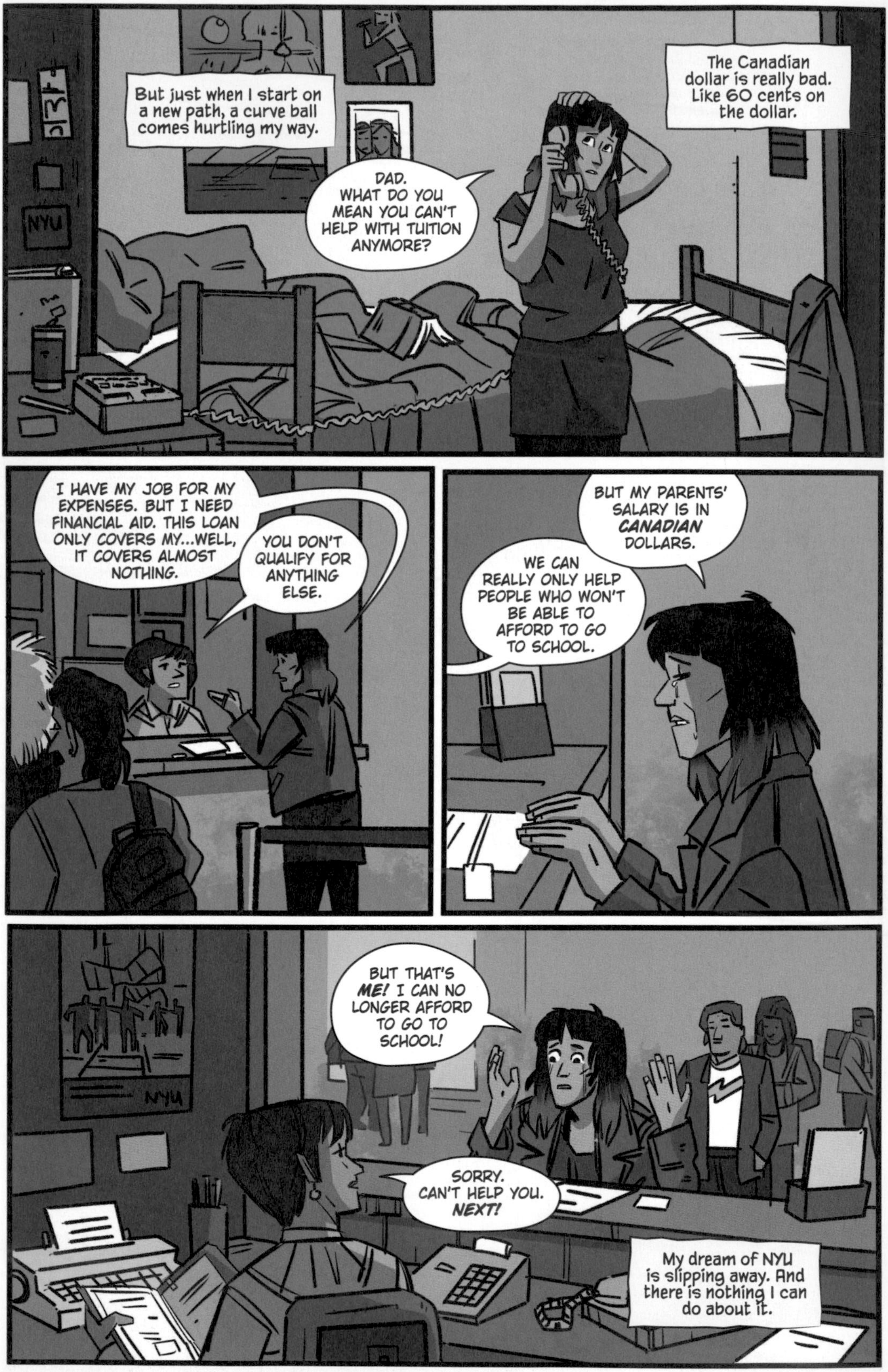
But just when I start on a new path, a curve ball comes hurtling my way.
The Canadian dollar is really bad. Like 60 cents on the dollar.
DAD. WHAT DO YOU MEAN YOU CAN'T HELP WITH TUITION ANYMORE?
I HAVE MY JOB FOR MY EXPENSES. BUT I NEED FINANCIAL AID. THIS LOAN ONLY COVERS MY...WELL, IT COVERS ALMOST NOTHING.
YOU DON'T QUALIFY FOR ANYTHING ELSE.
BUT MY PARENTS' SALARY IS IN CANADIAN DOLLARS.
WE CAN REALLY ONLY HELP PEOPLE WHO WON'T BE ABLE TO AFFORD TO GO TO SCHOOL.
BUT THAT'S ME! I CAN NO LONGER AFFORD TO GO TO SCHOOL!
SORRY. CAN'T HELP YOU. NEXT!
My dream of NYU is slipping away. And there is nothing I can do about it.

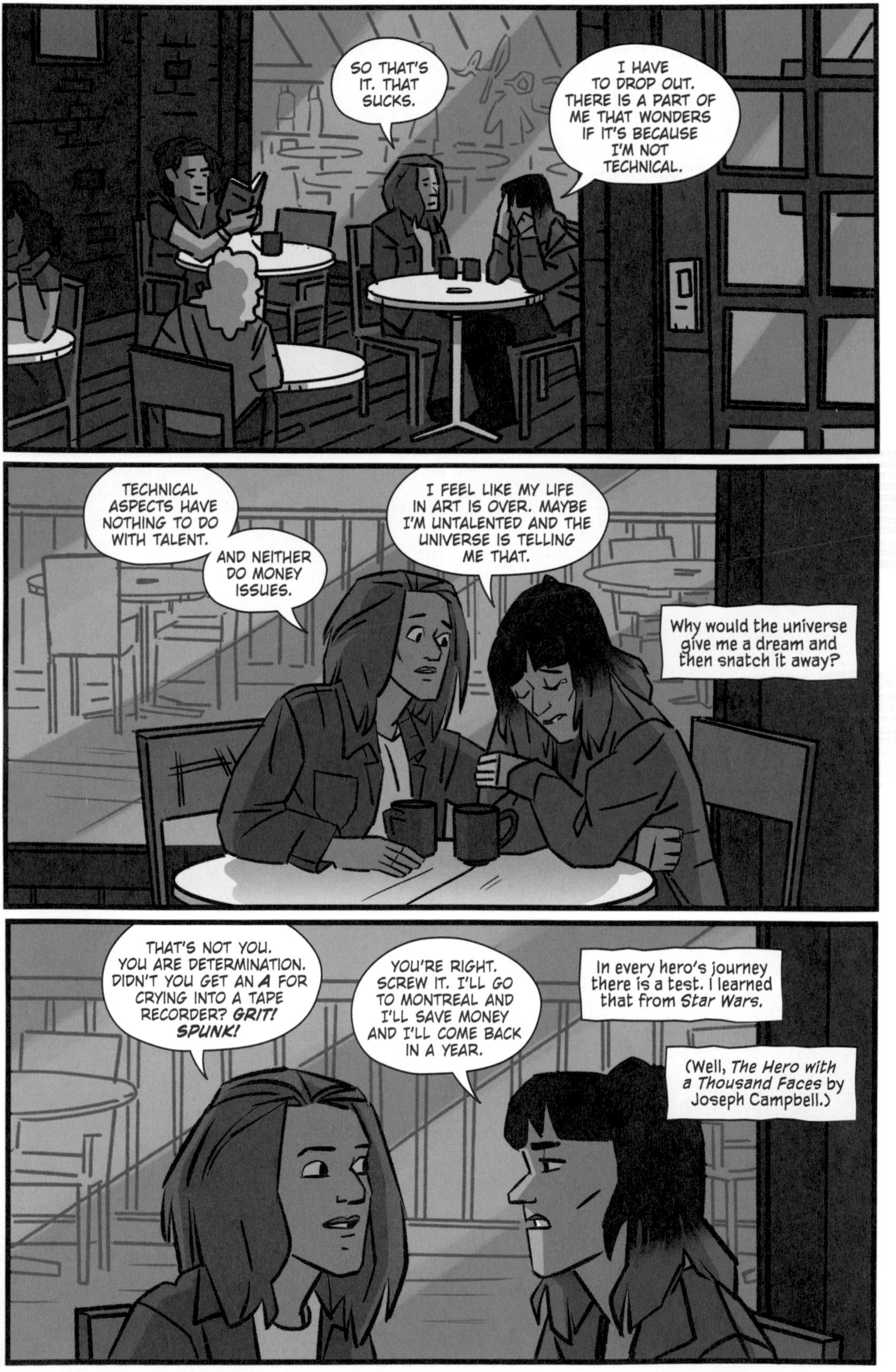
SO THAT'S IT. THAT SUCKS.
I HAVE TO DROP OUT. THERE IS A PART OF ME THAT WONDERS IF IT'S BECAUSE I'M NOT TECHNICAL.
TECHNICAL ASPECTS HAVE NOTHING TO DO WITH TALENT.
AND NEITHER DO MONEY ISSUES.
I FEEL LIKE MY LIFE IN ART IS OVER. MAYBE I'M UNTALENTED AND THE UNIVERSE IS TELLING ME THAT.
Why would the universe give me a dream and then snatch it away?
THAT'S NOT YOU. YOU ARE DETERMINATION. DIDN'T YOU GET AN *A* FOR CRYING INTO A TAPE RECORDER? ***GRIT! SPUNK!***
YOU'RE RIGHT. SCREW IT. I'LL GO TO MONTREAL AND I'LL SAVE MONEY AND I'LL COME BACK IN A YEAR.
In every hero's journey there is a test. I learned that from *Star Wars.*
(Well, *The Hero with a Thousand Faces* by Joseph Campbell.)

I have taken this road trip to Quebec a million times in my life to visit my grandmother and cousins. But this time, it feels like a most mournful voyage.

BIENVENUE - WELCOME
Dames Customs
Canada

BIENVENUE AU CANADA.

Like a dream is dying.

Like I'll never live in New York City again.

OH MY GOD. IS THAT A NOSE RING?

MOM! NOT IMPORTANT RIGHT NOW!

I'M GETTING OUT OF THIS JOKE OF A CITY AS FAST AS I CAN. YOU HAVE NOTHING TO OFFER ME.

They say that comedy is tragedy plus time.

This laugh will take eons.

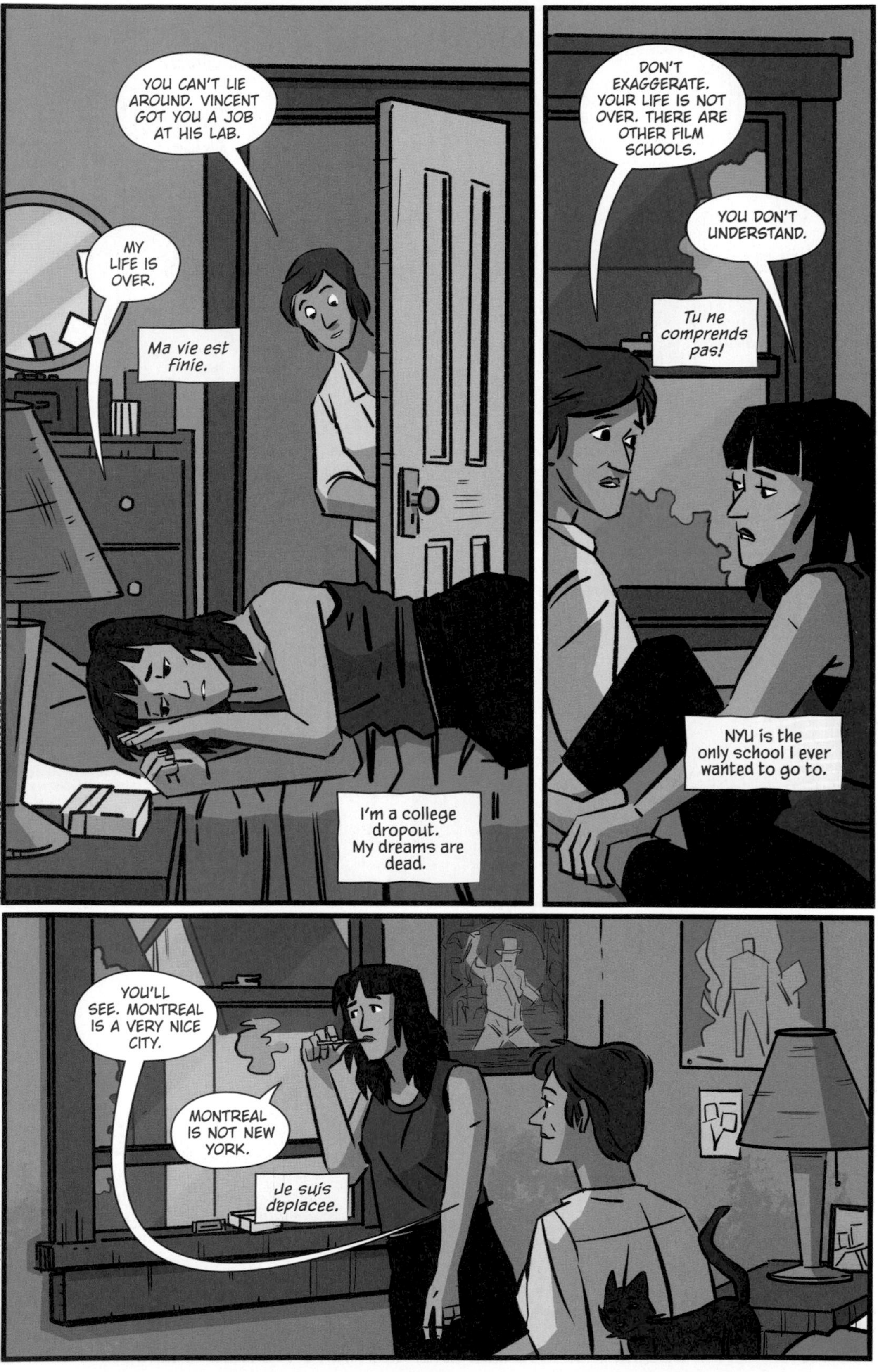
YOU CAN'T LIE AROUND. VINCENT GOT YOU A JOB AT HIS LAB.
MY LIFE IS OVER.
Ma vie est finie.
I'm a college dropout. My dreams are dead.
DON'T EXAGGERATE. YOUR LIFE IS NOT OVER. THERE ARE OTHER FILM SCHOOLS.
YOU DON'T UNDERSTAND.
Tu ne comprends pas!
NYU is the only school I ever wanted to go to.
YOU'LL SEE. MONTREAL IS A VERY NICE CITY.
MONTREAL IS NOT NEW YORK.
Je suis deplacee.

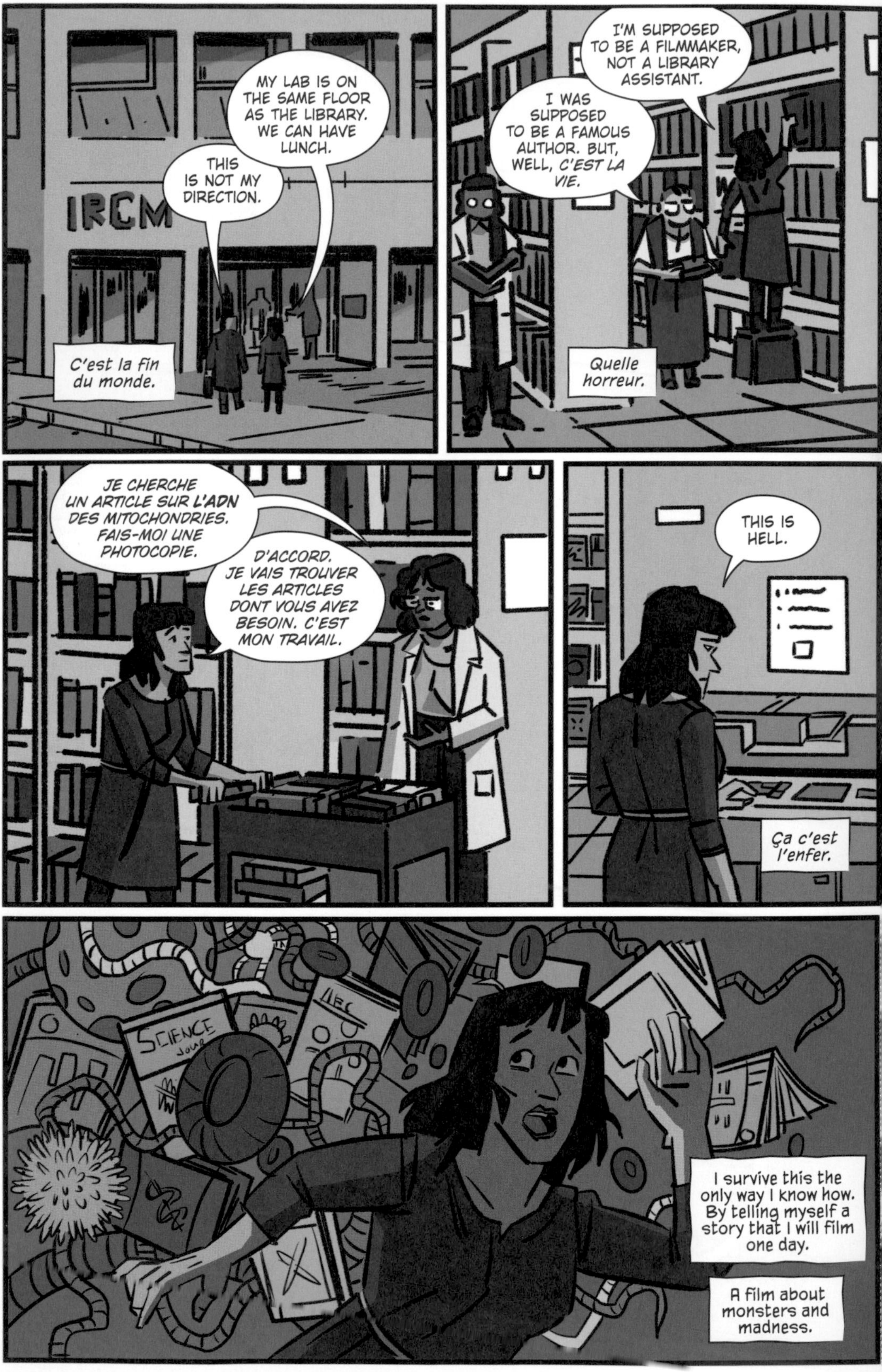
MY LAB IS ON THE SAME FLOOR AS THE LIBRARY. WE CAN HAVE LUNCH.
THIS IS NOT MY DIRECTION.
IRCM
C'est la fin du monde.
I'M SUPPOSED TO BE A FILMMAKER, NOT A LIBRARY ASSISTANT.
I WAS SUPPOSED TO BE A FAMOUS AUTHOR. BUT, WELL, C'EST LA VIE.
Quelle horreur.
JE CHERCHE UN ARTICLE SUR L'ADN DES MITOCHONDRIES. FAIS-MOI UNE PHOTOCOPIE.
D'ACCORD. JE VAIS TROUVER LES ARTICLES DONT VOUS AVEZ BESOIN. C'EST MON TRAVAIL.
THIS IS HELL.
Ça c'est l'enfer.
SCIENCE
I survive this the only way I know how. By telling myself a story that I will film one day.
A film about monsters and madness.

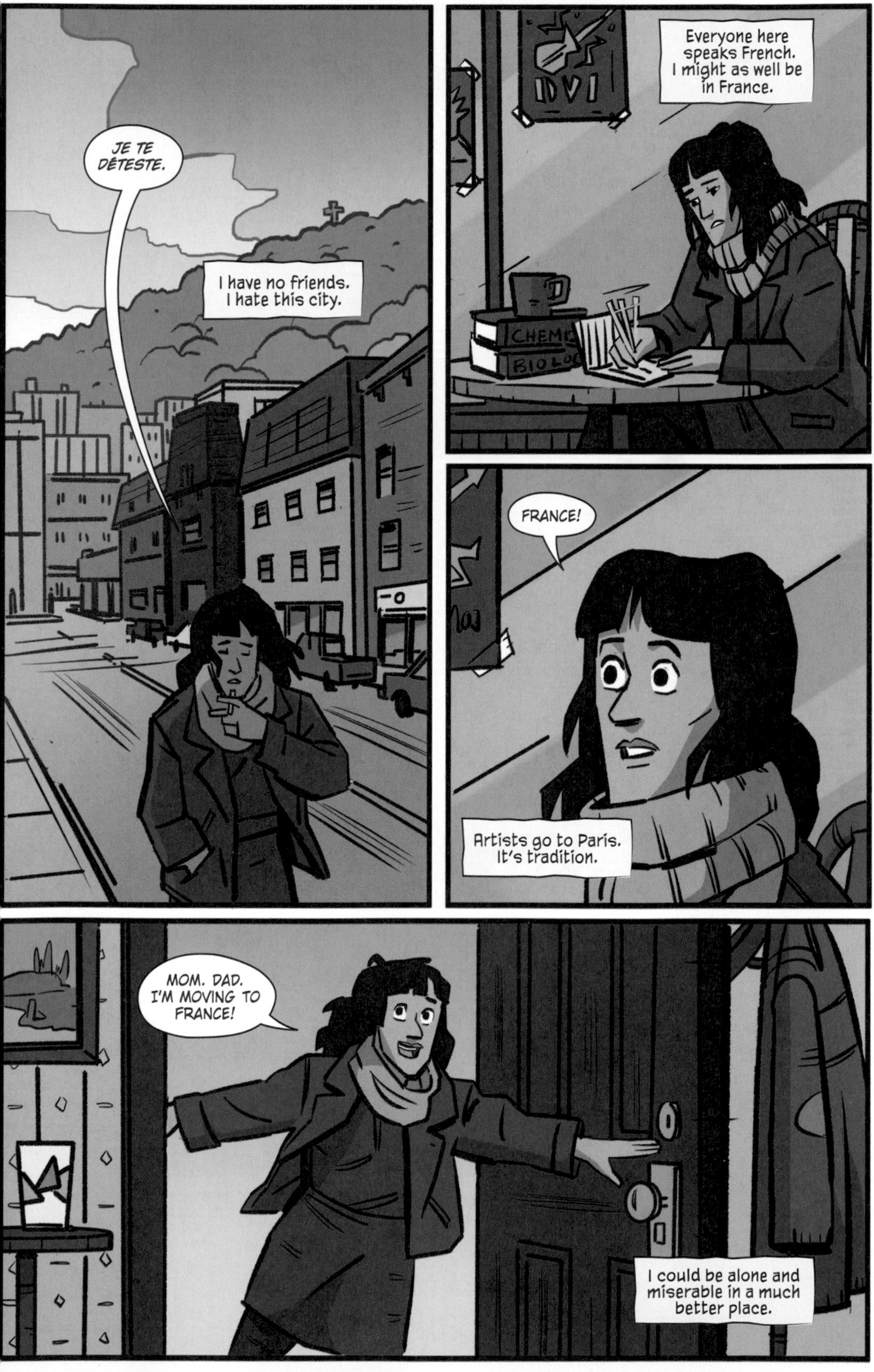
JE TE DÉTESTE.
I have no friends. I hate this city.
Everyone here speaks French. I might as well be in France.
CHEMI
BIOLO
FRANCE!
Artists go to Paris. It's tradition.
MOM. DAD. I'M MOVING TO FRANCE!
I could be alone and miserable in a much better place.

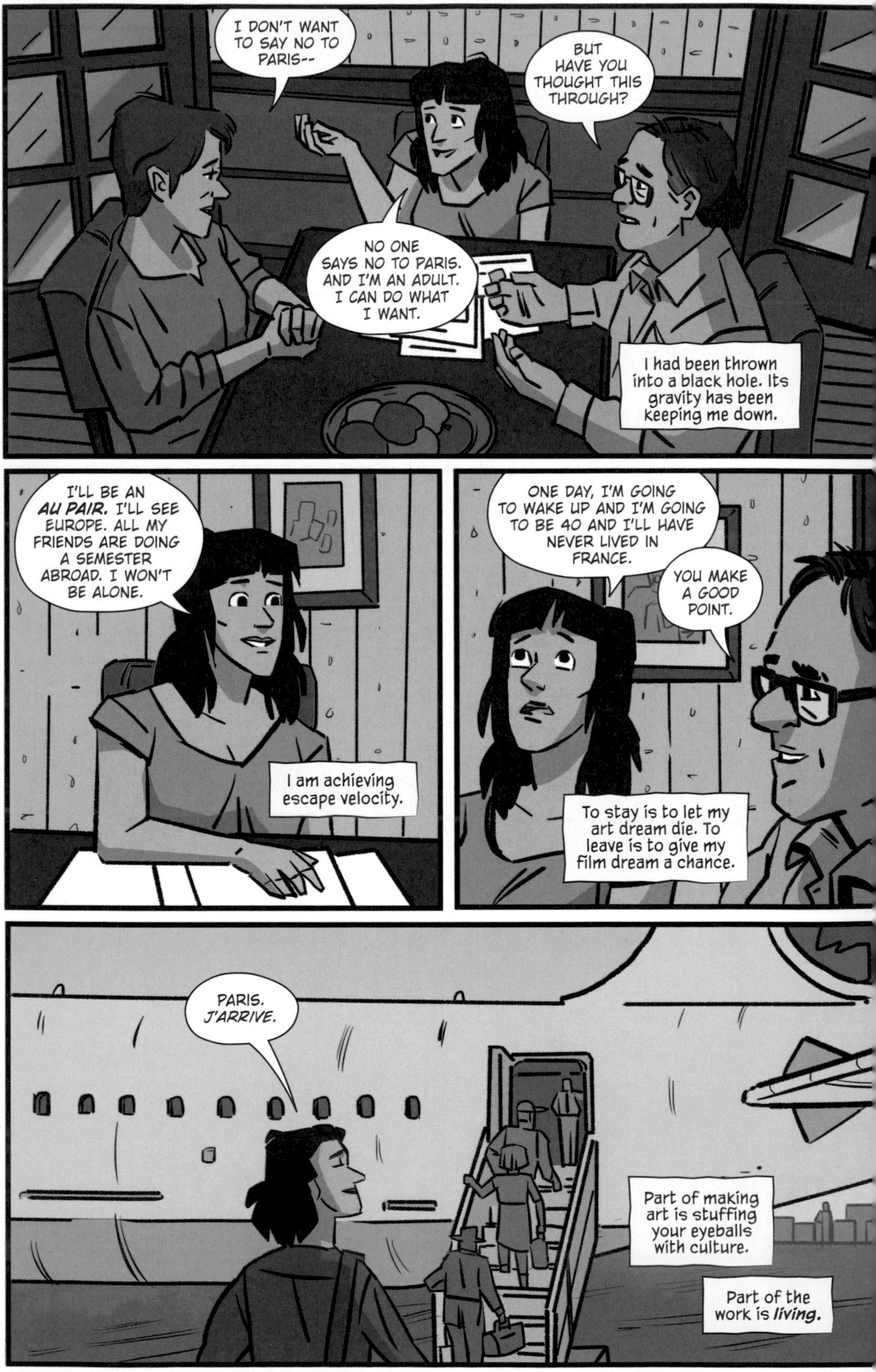
I DON'T WANT TO SAY NO TO PARIS--
BUT HAVE YOU THOUGHT THIS THROUGH?
NO ONE SAYS NO TO PARIS. AND I'M AN ADULT. I CAN DO WHAT I WANT.
I had been thrown into a black hole. Its gravity has been keeping me down.
I'LL BE AN ***AU PAIR.*** I'LL SEE EUROPE. ALL MY FRIENDS ARE DOING A SEMESTER ABROAD. I WON'T BE ALONE.
I am achieving escape velocity.
ONE DAY, I'M GOING TO WAKE UP AND I'M GOING TO BE 40 AND I'LL HAVE NEVER LIVED IN FRANCE.
YOU MAKE A GOOD POINT.
To stay is to let my art dream die. To leave is to give my film dream a chance.
PARIS. *J'ARRIVE.*
Part of making art is stuffing your eyeballs with culture.
Part of the work is ***living.***

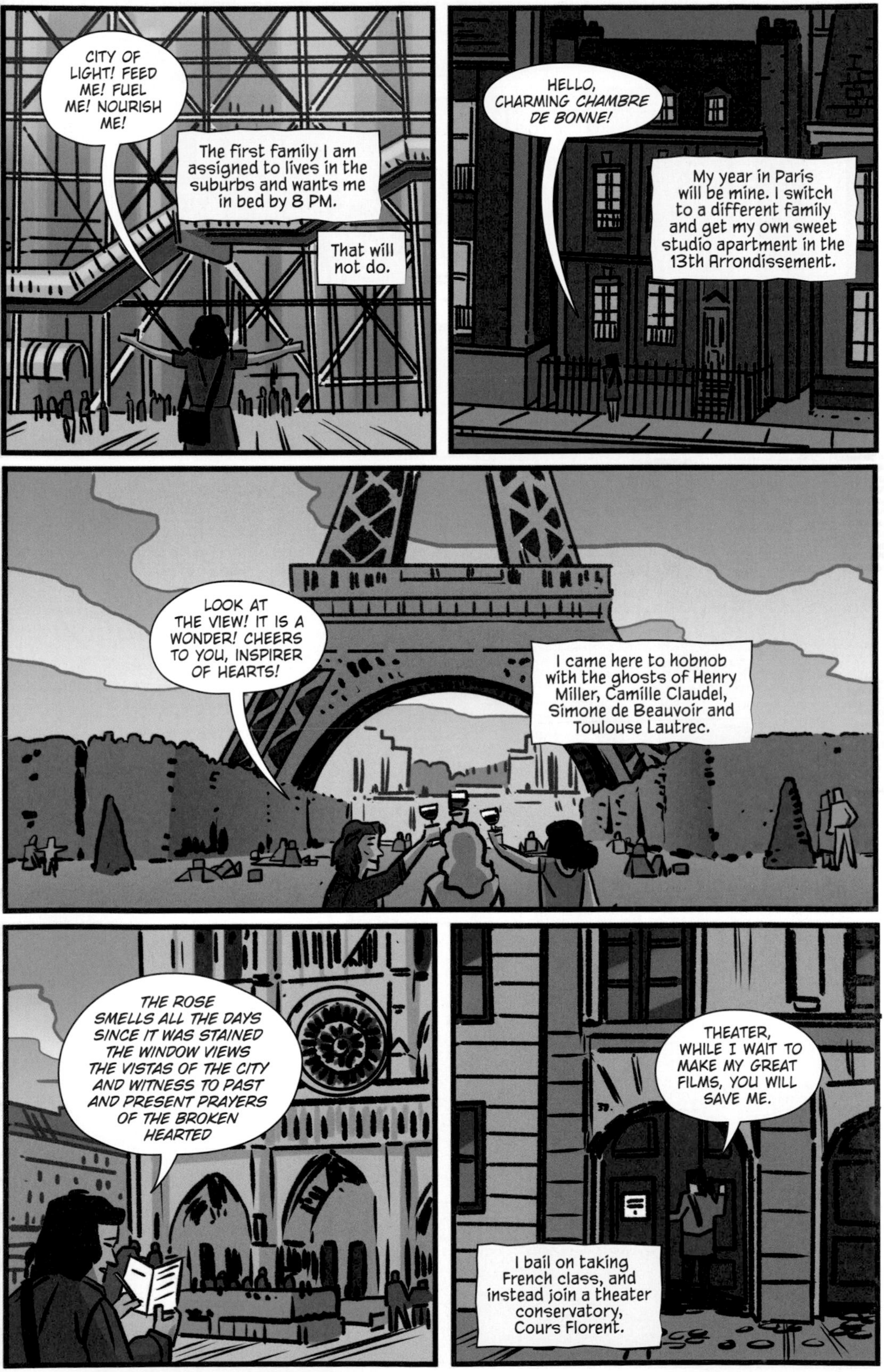
CITY OF LIGHT! FEED ME! FUEL ME! NOURISH ME!
The first family I am assigned to lives in the suburbs and wants me in bed by 8 PM.
That will not do.
HELLO, CHARMING *CHAMBRE DE BONNE!*
My year in Paris will be mine. I switch to a different family and get my own sweet studio apartment in the 13th Arrondissement.
LOOK AT THE VIEW! IT IS A WONDER! CHEERS TO YOU, INSPIRER OF HEARTS!
I came here to hobnob with the ghosts of Henry Miller, Camille Claudel, Simone de Beauvoir and Toulouse Lautrec.
THE ROSE SMELLS ALL THE DAYS SINCE IT WAS STAINED THE WINDOW VIEWS THE VISTAS OF THE CITY AND WITNESS TO PAST AND PRESENT PRAYERS OF THE BROKEN HEARTED
THEATER, WHILE I WAIT TO MAKE MY GREAT FILMS, YOU WILL SAVE ME.
I bail on taking French class, and instead join a theater conservatory, Cours Florent.

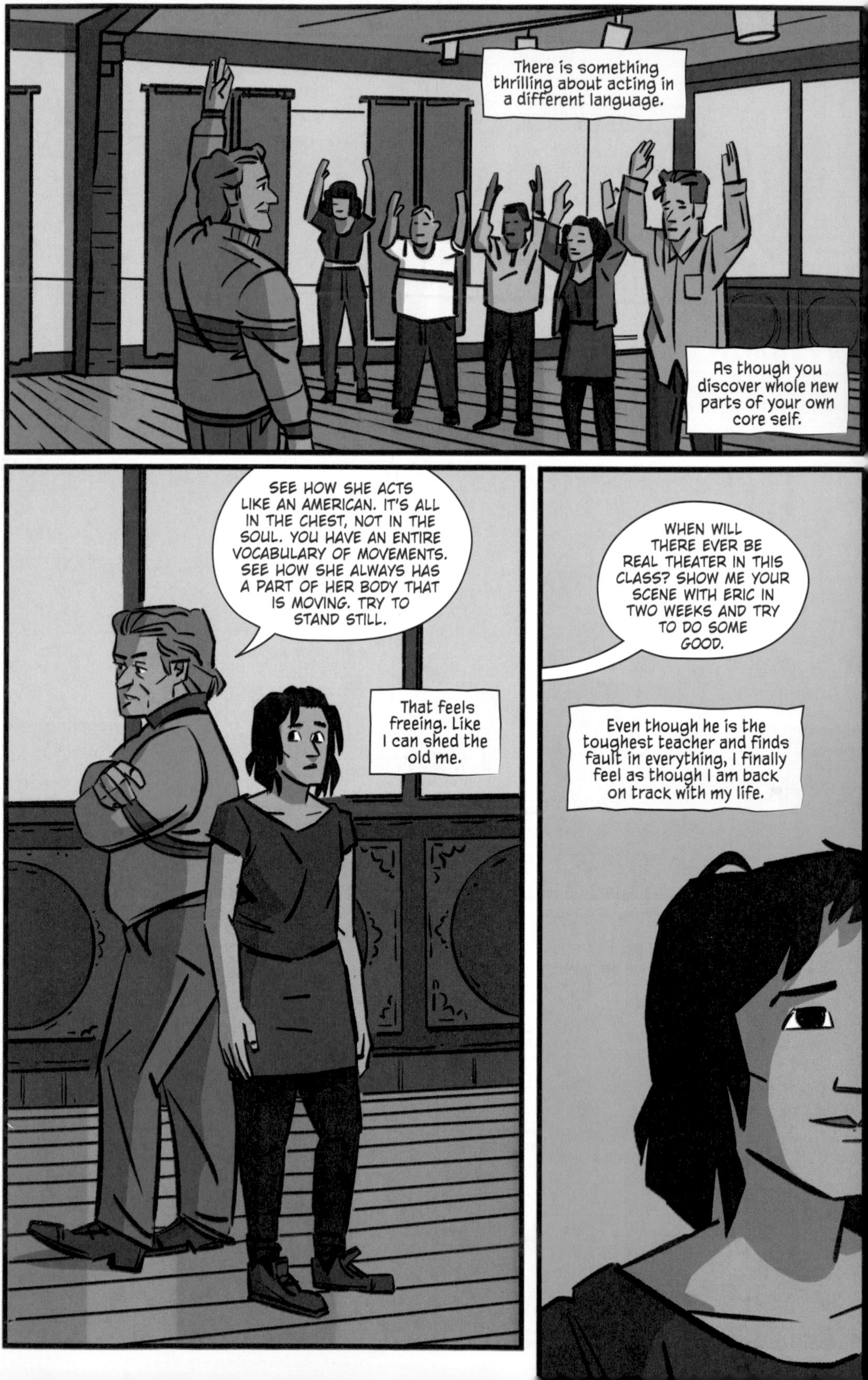
There is something thrilling about acting in a different language.
As though you discover whole new parts of your own core self.
SEE HOW SHE ACTS LIKE AN AMERICAN. IT'S ALL IN THE CHEST, NOT IN THE SOUL. YOU HAVE AN ENTIRE VOCABULARY OF MOVEMENTS. SEE HOW SHE ALWAYS HAS A PART OF HER BODY THAT IS MOVING. TRY TO STAND STILL.
That feels freeing. Like I can shed the old me.
WHEN WILL THERE EVER BE REAL THEATER IN THIS CLASS? SHOW ME YOUR SCENE WITH ERIC IN TWO WEEKS AND TRY TO DO SOME GOOD.
Even though he is the toughest teacher and finds fault in everything, I finally feel as though I am back on track with my life.

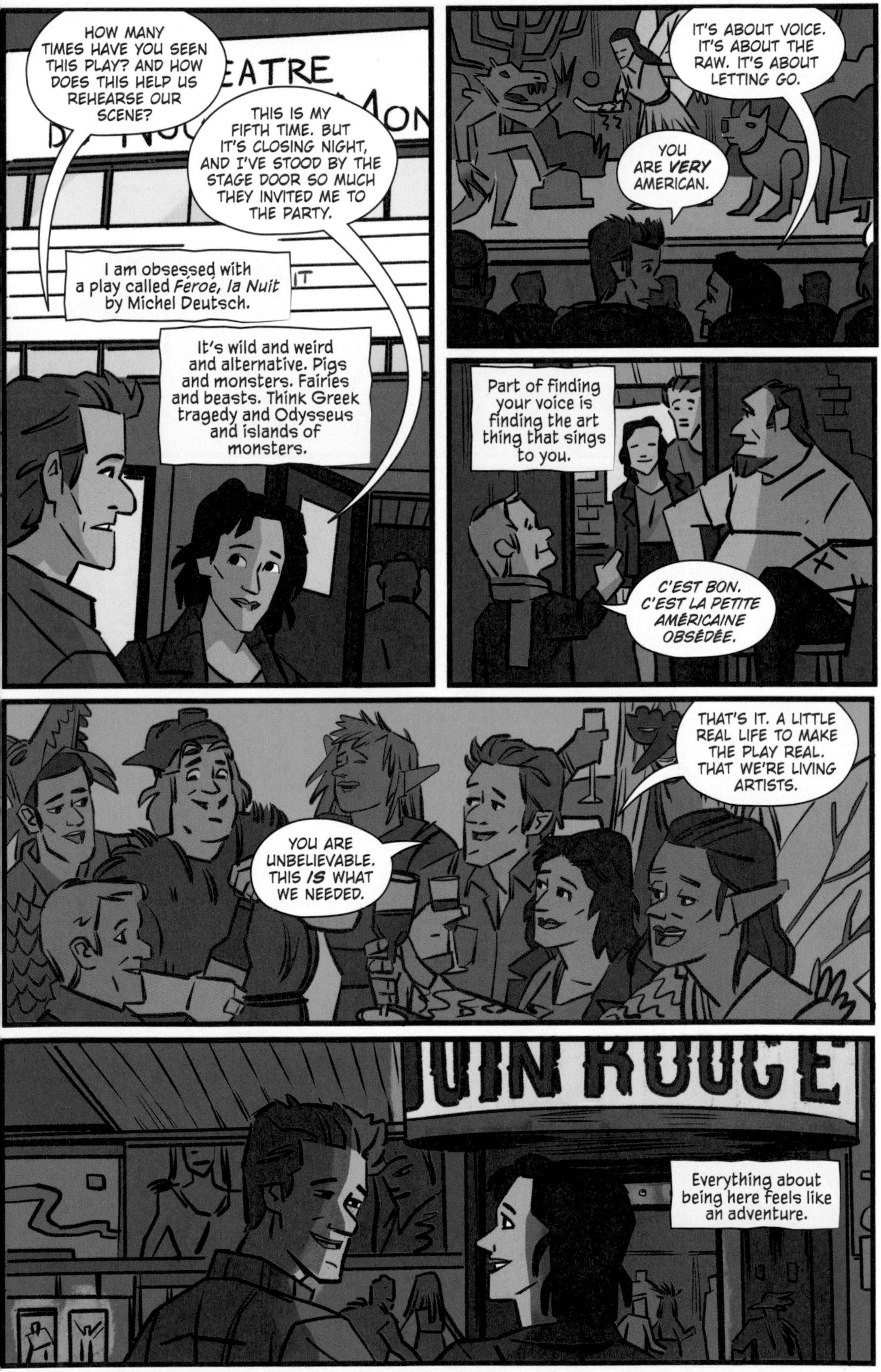
HOW MANY TIMES HAVE YOU SEEN THIS PLAY? AND HOW DOES THIS HELP US REHEARSE OUR SCENE?
THIS IS MY FIFTH TIME. BUT IT'S CLOSING NIGHT, AND I'VE STOOD BY THE STAGE DOOR SO MUCH THEY INVITED ME TO THE PARTY.
I am obsessed with a play called *Féroé, la Nuit* by Michel Deutsch.
It's wild and weird and alternative. Pigs and monsters. Fairies and beasts. Think Greek tragedy and Odysseus and islands of monsters.
IT'S ABOUT VOICE. IT'S ABOUT THE RAW. IT'S ABOUT LETTING GO.
YOU ARE ***VERY*** AMERICAN.
Part of finding your voice is finding the art thing that sings to you.
C'EST BON. C'EST LA PETITE AMÉRICAINE OBSÉDÉE.
THAT'S IT. A LITTLE REAL LIFE TO MAKE THE PLAY REAL. THAT WE'RE LIVING ARTISTS.
YOU ARE UNBELIEVABLE. THIS ***IS*** WHAT WE NEEDED.
UIN ROUGE
Everything about being here feels like an adventure.

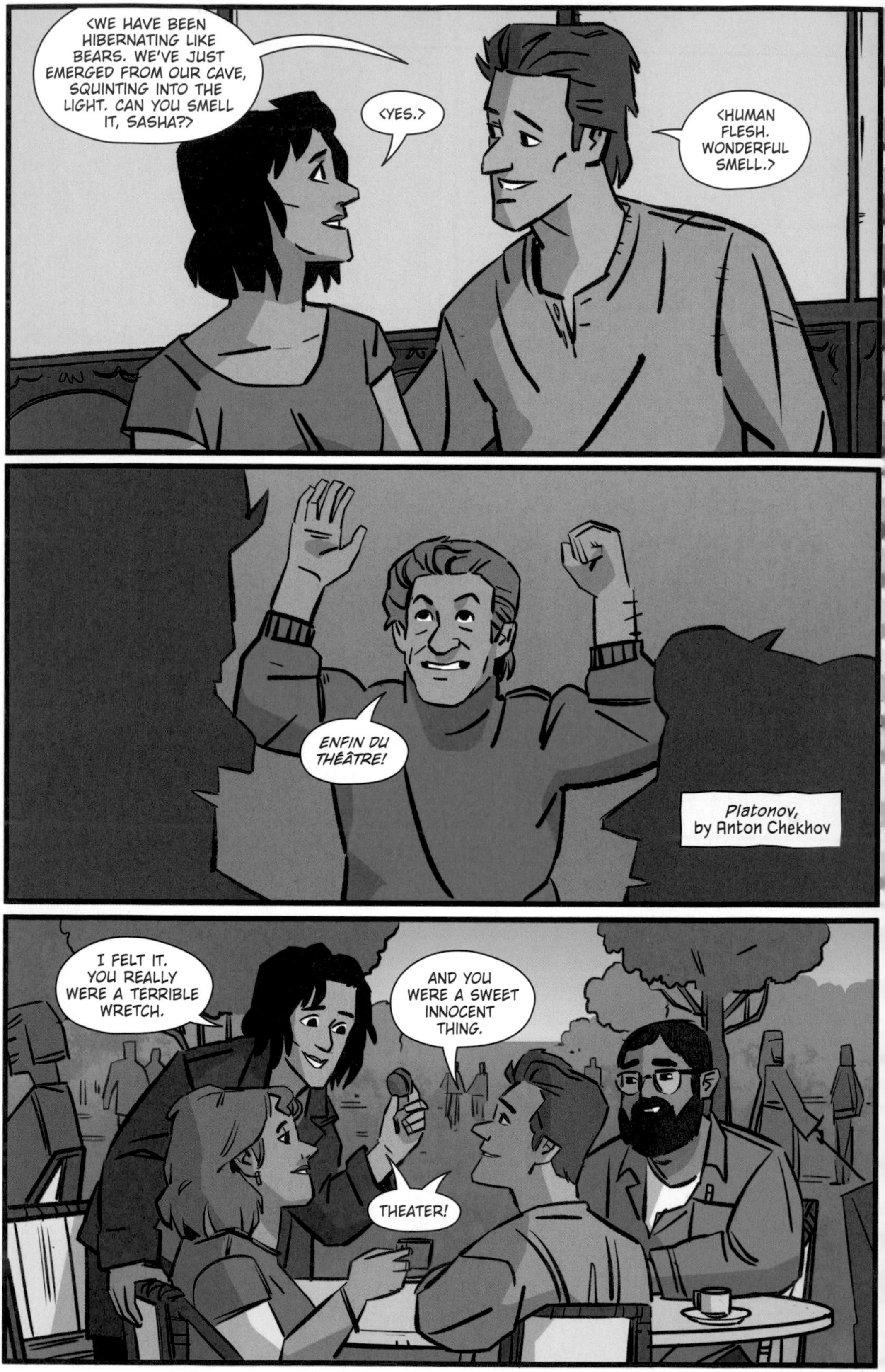
<WE HAVE BEEN HIBERNATING LIKE BEARS. WE'VE JUST EMERGED FROM OUR CAVE, SQUINTING INTO THE LIGHT. CAN YOU SMELL IT, SASHA?>
<YES.>
<HUMAN FLESH. WONDERFUL SMELL.>
ENFIN DU THÉÂTRE!
Platonov, by Anton Chekhov
I FELT IT. YOU REALLY WERE A TERRIBLE WRETCH.
AND YOU WERE A SWEET INNOCENT THING.
THEATER!

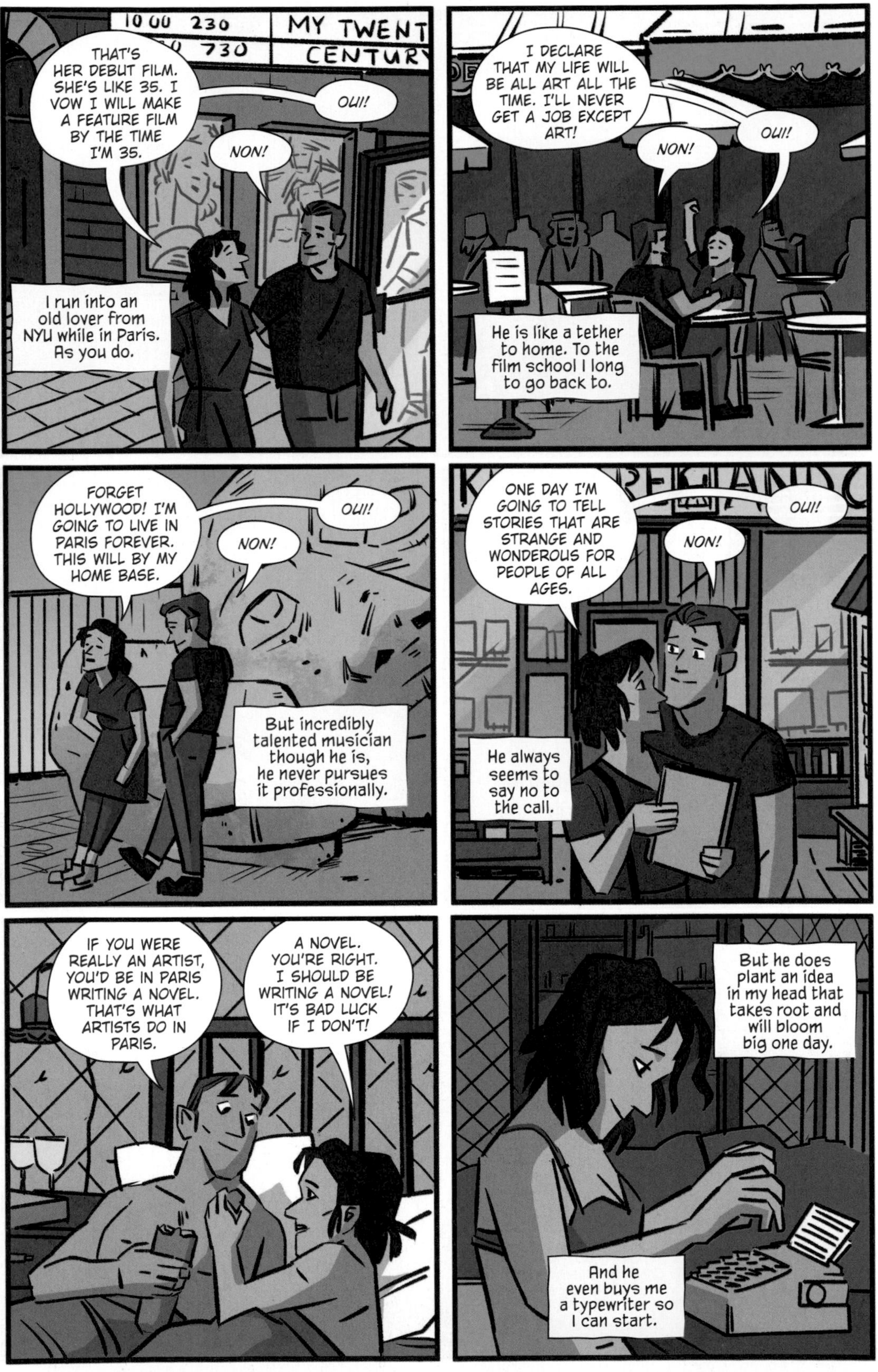

10 00 230
MY TWENT
CENTURY
THAT'S HER DEBUT FILM. SHE'S LIKE 35. I VOW I WILL MAKE A FEATURE FILM BY THE TIME I'M 35.
OUI!
NON!
I run into an old lover from NYU while in Paris. As you do.
I DECLARE THAT MY LIFE WILL BE ALL ART ALL THE TIME. I'LL NEVER GET A JOB EXCEPT ART!
OUI!
NON!
He is like a tether to home. To the film school I long to go back to.
FORGET HOLLYWOOD! I'M GOING TO LIVE IN PARIS FOREVER. THIS WILL BY MY HOME BASE.
OUI!
NON!
But incredibly talented musician though he is, he never pursues it professionally.
ONE DAY I'M GOING TO TELL STORIES THAT ARE STRANGE AND WONDEROUS FOR PEOPLE OF ALL AGES.
OUI!
NON!
He always seems to say no to the call.
IF YOU WERE REALLY AN ARTIST, YOU'D BE IN PARIS WRITING A NOVEL. THAT'S WHAT ARTISTS DO IN PARIS.
A NOVEL. YOU'RE RIGHT. I SHOULD BE WRITING A NOVEL! IT'S BAD LUCK IF I DON'T!
But he does plant an idea in my head that takes root and will bloom big one day.
And he even buys me a typewriter so I can start.

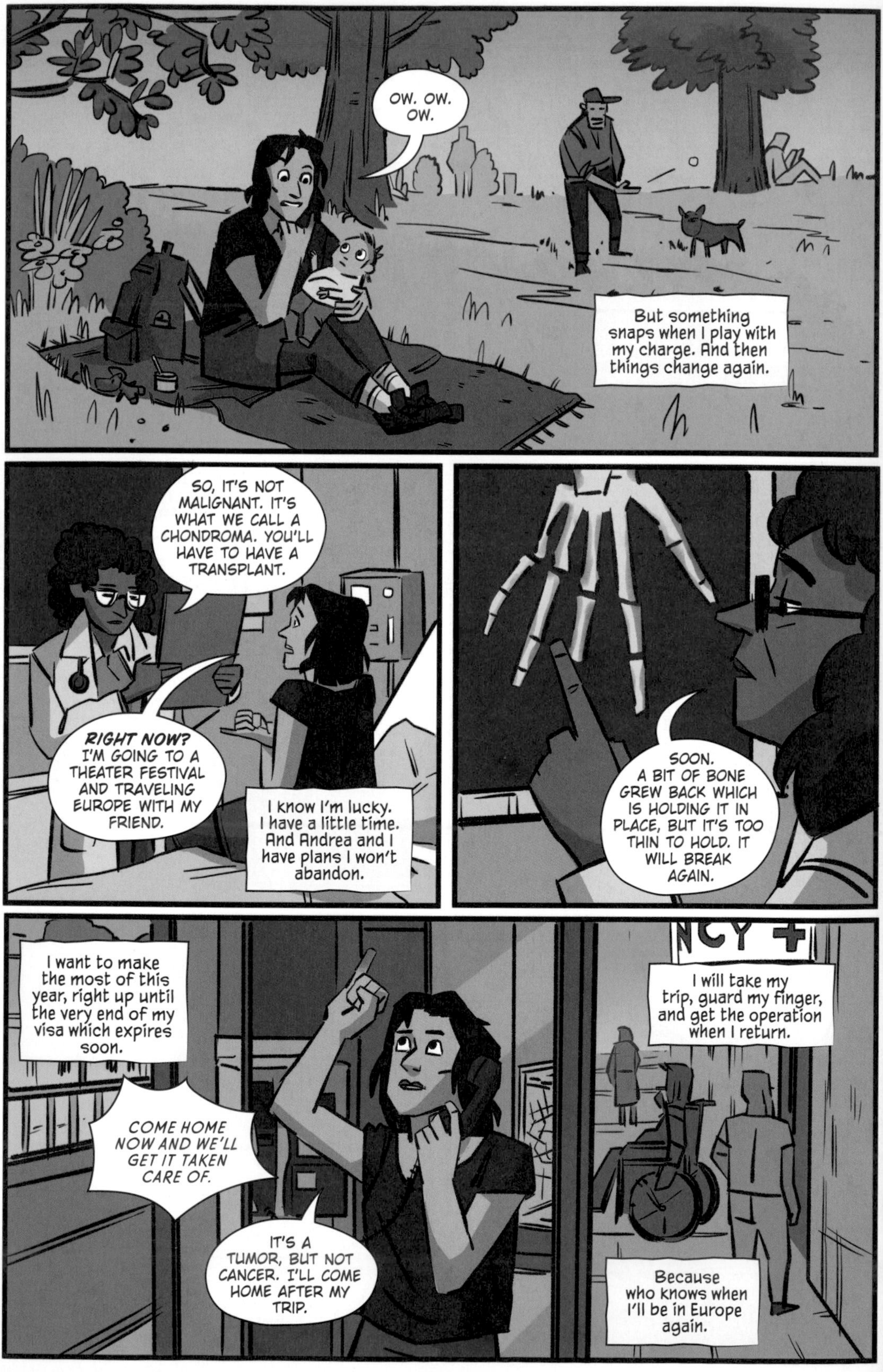

OW. OW. OW.
But something snaps when I play with my charge. And then things change again.
SO, IT'S NOT MALIGNANT. IT'S WHAT WE CALL A CHONDROMA. YOU'LL HAVE TO HAVE A TRANSPLANT.
RIGHT NOW? I'M GOING TO A THEATER FESTIVAL AND TRAVELING EUROPE WITH MY FRIEND.
I know I'm lucky. I have a little time. And Andrea and I have plans I won't abandon.
SOON. A BIT OF BONE GREW BACK WHICH IS HOLDING IT IN PLACE, BUT IT'S TOO THIN TO HOLD. IT WILL BREAK AGAIN.
I want to make the most of this year, right up until the very end of my visa which expires soon.
COME HOME NOW AND WE'LL GET IT TAKEN CARE OF.
IT'S A TUMOR, BUT NOT CANCER. I'LL COME HOME AFTER MY TRIP.
NCY
I will take my trip, guard my finger, and get the operation when I return.
Because who knows when I'll be in Europe again.

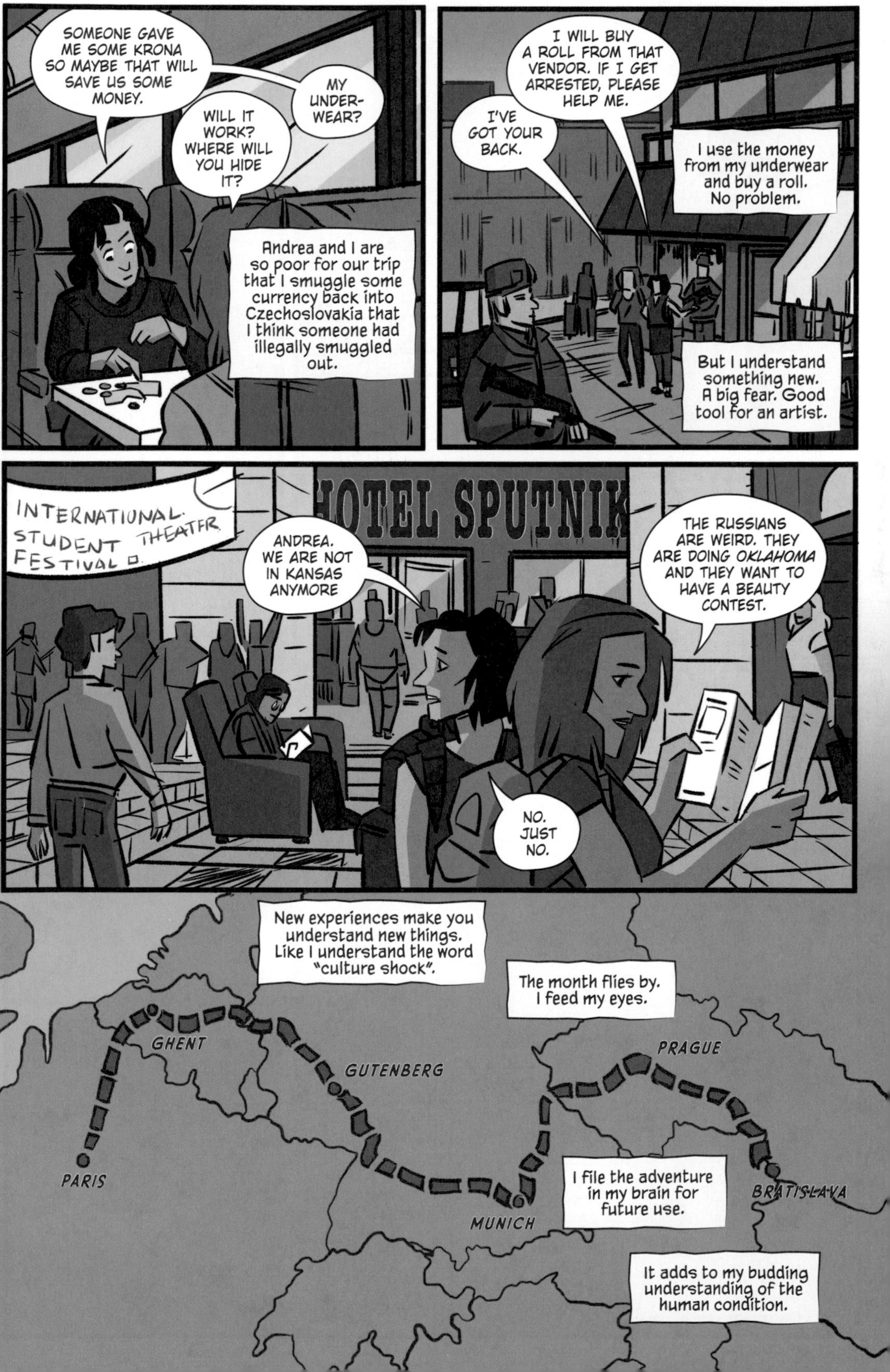
SOMEONE GAVE ME SOME KRONA SO MAYBE THAT WILL SAVE US SOME MONEY.
WILL IT WORK? WHERE WILL YOU HIDE IT?
MY UNDER-WEAR?
Andrea and I are so poor for our trip that I smuggle some currency back into Czechoslovakia that I think someone had illegally smuggled out.
I WILL BUY A ROLL FROM THAT VENDOR. IF I GET ARRESTED, PLEASE HELP ME.
I'VE GOT YOUR BACK.
I use the money from my underwear and buy a roll. No problem.
But I understand something new. A big fear. Good tool for an artist.
INTERNATIONAL STUDENT THEATER FESTIVAL
HOTEL SPUTNIK
ANDREA. WE ARE NOT IN KANSAS ANYMORE
THE RUSSIANS ARE WEIRD. THEY ARE DOING *OKLAHOMA* AND THEY WANT TO HAVE A BEAUTY CONTEST.
NO. JUST NO.
New experiences make you understand new things. Like I understand the word "culture shock".
The month flies by. I feed my eyes.
GHENT
GUTENBERG
PRAGUE
PARIS
MUNICH
BRATISLAVA
I file the adventure in my brain for future use.
It adds to my budding understanding of the human condition.

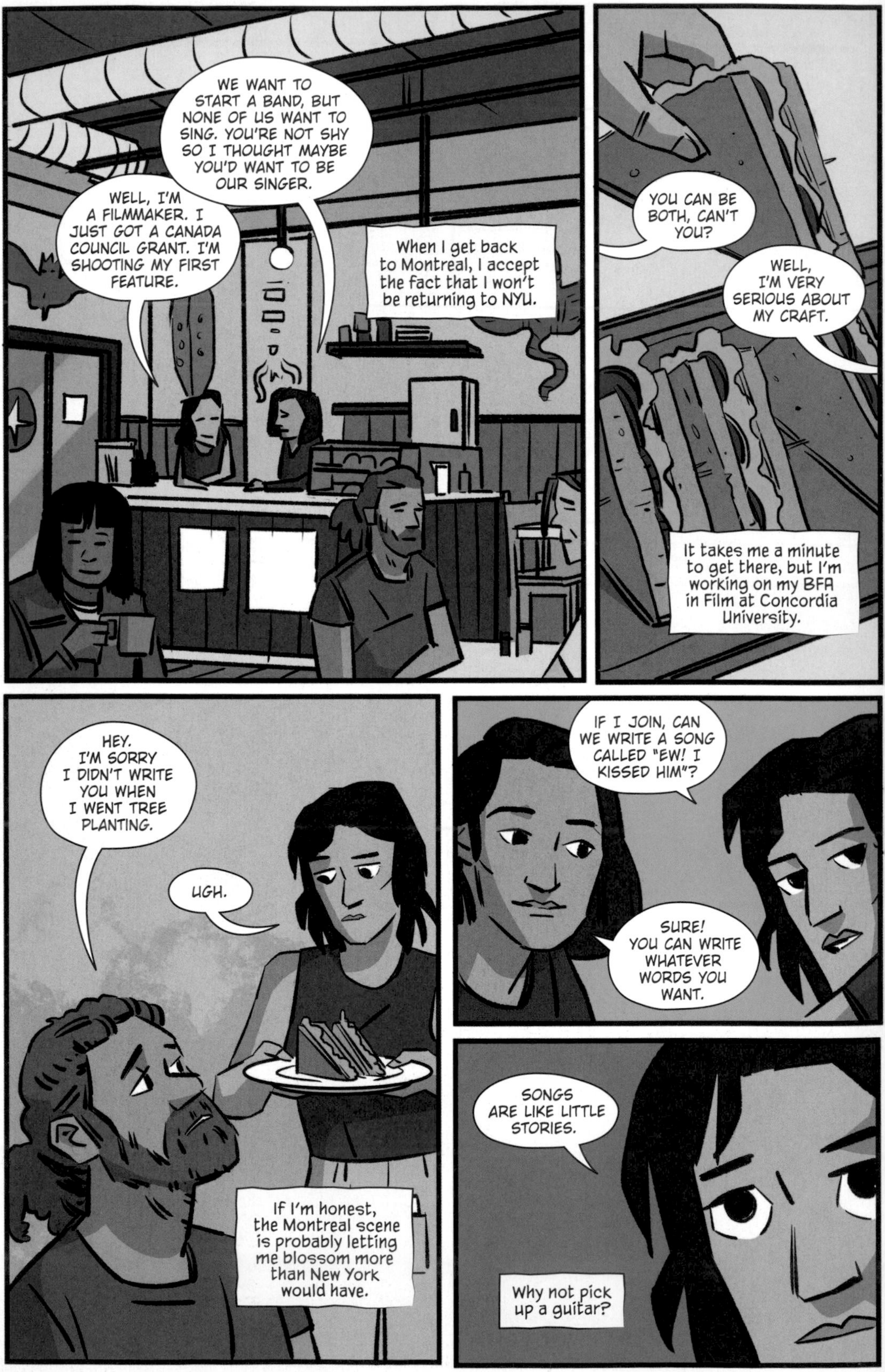

WE WANT TO START A BAND, BUT NONE OF US WANT TO SING. YOU'RE NOT SHY SO I THOUGHT MAYBE YOU'D WANT TO BE OUR SINGER.
WELL, I'M A FILMMAKER. I JUST GOT A CANADA COUNCIL GRANT. I'M SHOOTING MY FIRST FEATURE.
When I get back to Montreal, I accept the fact that I won't be returning to NYU.
YOU CAN BE BOTH, CAN'T YOU?
WELL, I'M VERY SERIOUS ABOUT MY CRAFT.
It takes me a minute to get there, but I'm working on my BFA in Film at Concordia University.
HEY. I'M SORRY I DIDN'T WRITE YOU WHEN I WENT TREE PLANTING.
UGH.
If I'm honest, the Montreal scene is probably letting me blossom more than New York would have.
IF I JOIN, CAN WE WRITE A SONG CALLED "EW! I KISSED HIM"?
SURE! YOU CAN WRITE WHATEVER WORDS YOU WANT.
SONGS ARE LIKE LITTLE STORIES.
Why not pick up a guitar?

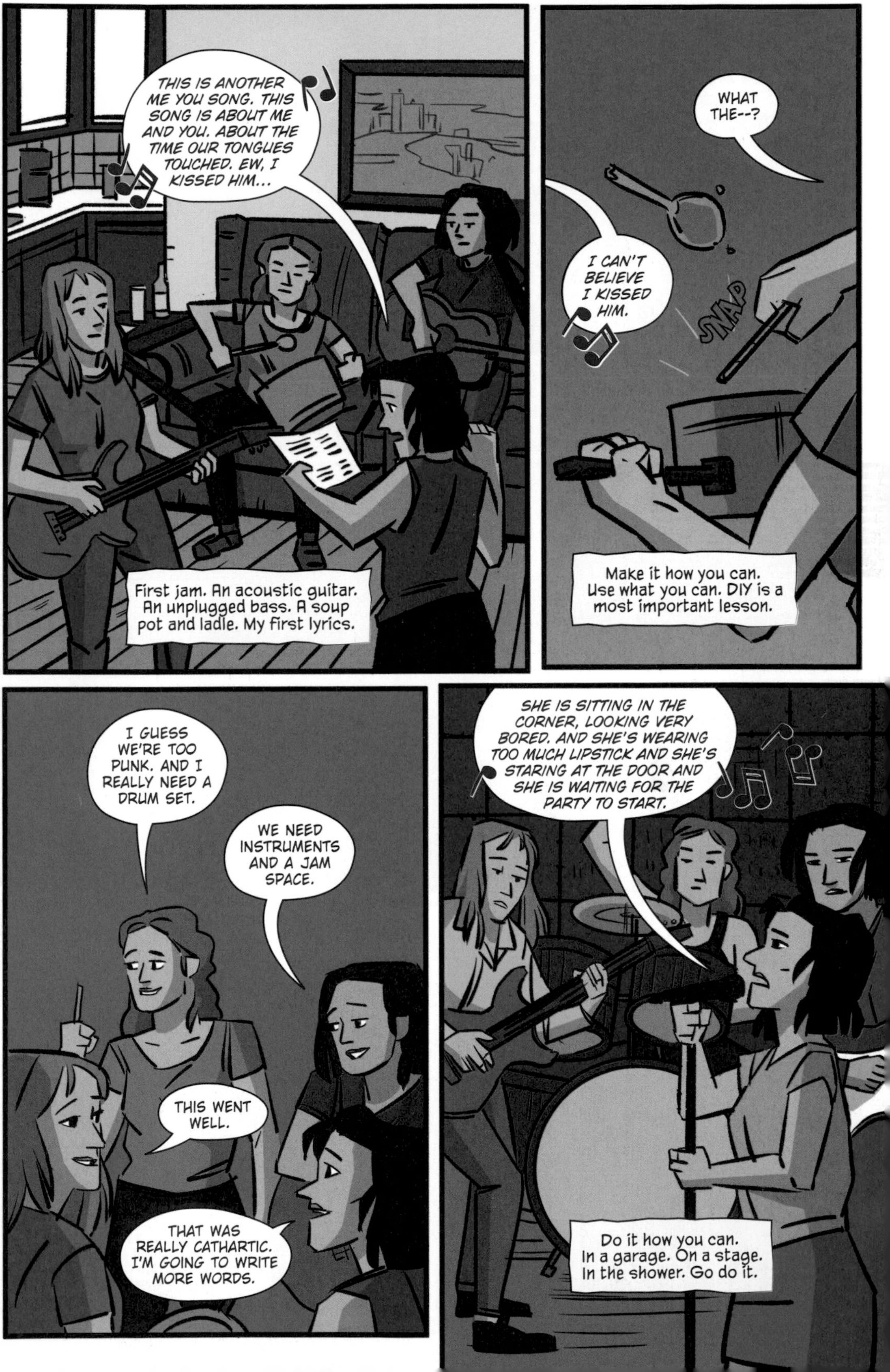
THIS IS ANOTHER ME YOU SONG. THIS SONG IS ABOUT ME AND YOU. ABOUT THE TIME OUR TONGUES TOUCHED. EW, I KISSED HIM...
First jam. An acoustic guitar. An unplugged bass. A soup pot and ladle. My first lyrics.
WHAT THE--?
I CAN'T BELIEVE I KISSED HIM.
SNAP
Make it how you can. Use what you can. DIY is a most important lesson.
I GUESS WE'RE TOO PUNK. AND I REALLY NEED A DRUM SET.
WE NEED INSTRUMENTS AND A JAM SPACE.
THIS WENT WELL.
THAT WAS REALLY CATHARTIC. I'M GOING TO WRITE MORE WORDS.
SHE IS SITTING IN THE CORNER, LOOKING VERY BORED. AND SHE'S WEARING TOO MUCH LIPSTICK AND SHE'S STARING AT THE DOOR AND SHE IS WAITING FOR THE PARTY TO START.
Do it how you can. In a garage. On a stage. In the shower. Go do it.

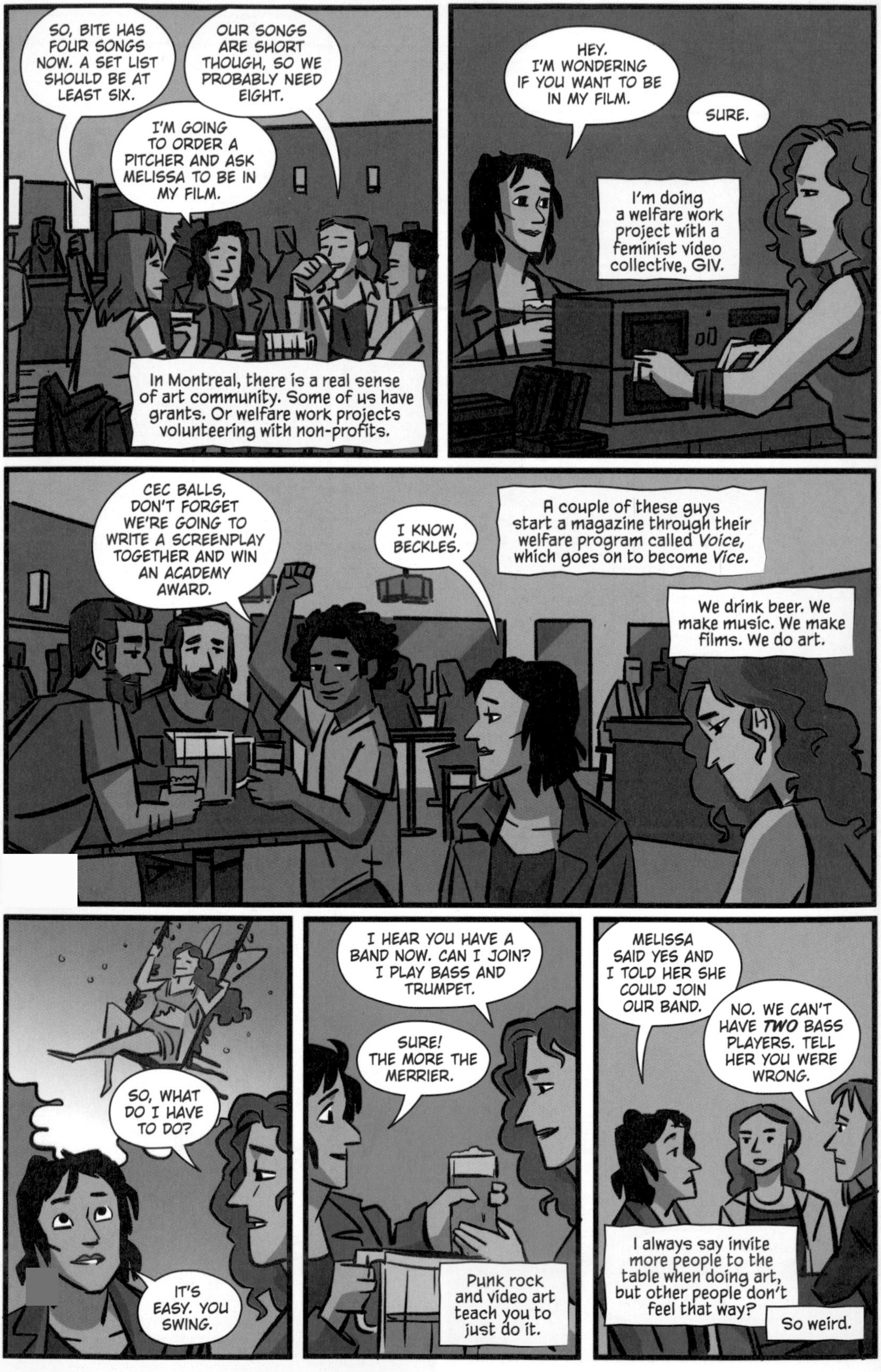
SO, BITE HAS FOUR SONGS NOW. A SET LIST SHOULD BE AT LEAST SIX.
OUR SONGS ARE SHORT THOUGH, SO WE PROBABLY NEED EIGHT.
I'M GOING TO ORDER A PITCHER AND ASK MELISSA TO BE IN MY FILM.
In Montreal, there is a real sense of art community. Some of us have grants. Or welfare work projects volunteering with non-profits.
HEY. I'M WONDERING IF YOU WANT TO BE IN MY FILM.
SURE.
I'm doing a welfare work project with a feminist video collective, GIV.
CEC BALLS, DON'T FORGET WE'RE GOING TO WRITE A SCREENPLAY TOGETHER AND WIN AN ACADEMY AWARD.
I KNOW, BECKLES.
A couple of these guys start a magazine through their welfare program called *Voice*, which goes on to become *Vice*.
We drink beer. We make music. We make films. We do art.
SO, WHAT DO I HAVE TO DO?
IT'S EASY. YOU SWING.
I HEAR YOU HAVE A BAND NOW. CAN I JOIN? I PLAY BASS AND TRUMPET.
SURE! THE MORE THE MERRIER.
Punk rock and video art teach you to just do it.
MELISSA SAID YES AND I TOLD HER SHE COULD JOIN OUR BAND.
NO. WE CAN'T HAVE **TWO** BASS PLAYERS. TELL HER YOU WERE WRONG.
I always say invite more people to the table when doing art, but other people don't feel that way?
So weird.

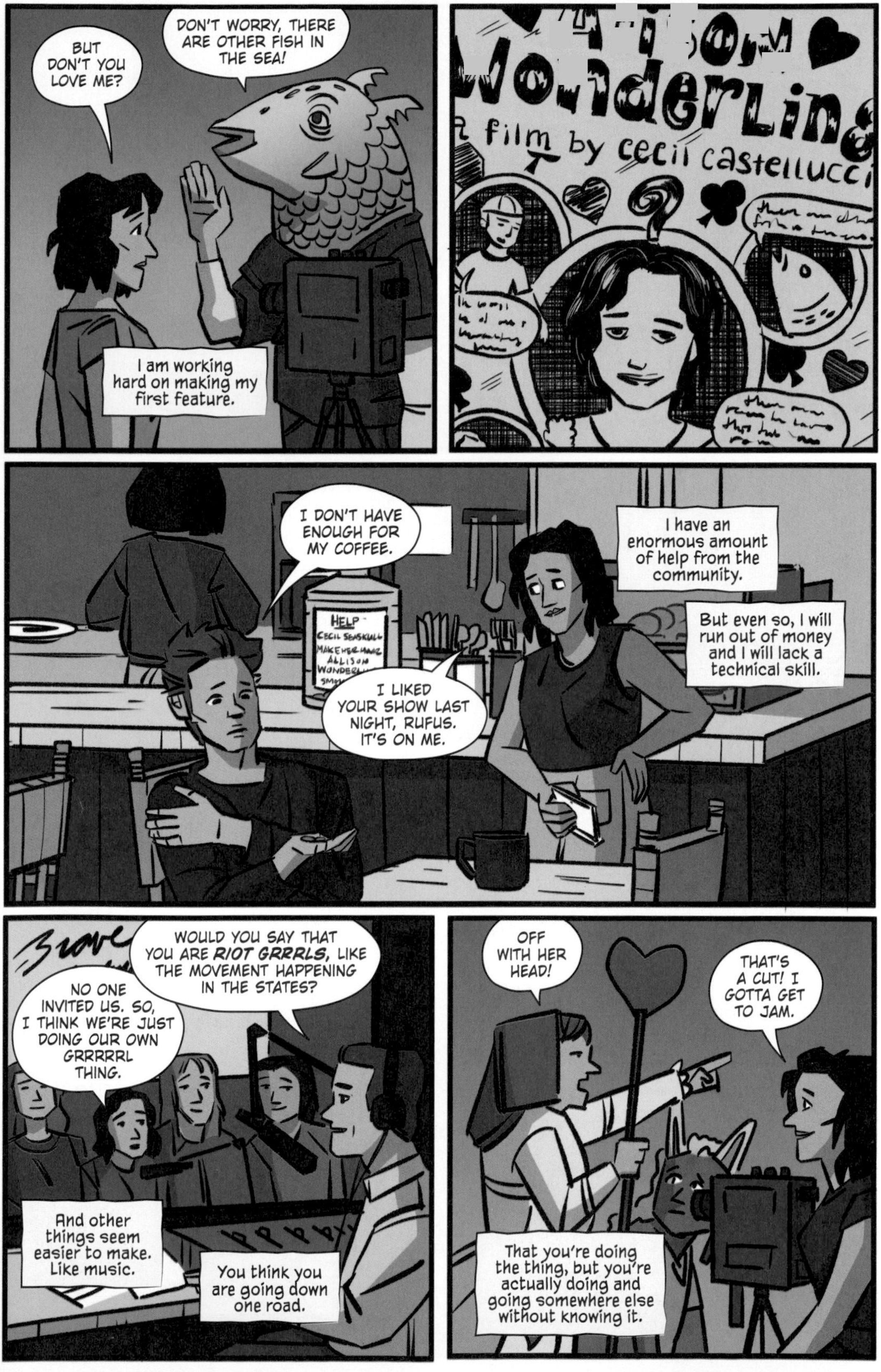
BUT DON'T YOU LOVE ME?
DON'T WORRY, THERE ARE OTHER FISH IN THE SEA!
I am working hard on making my first feature.
a film by cecil castellucci
I DON'T HAVE ENOUGH FOR MY COFFEE.
HELP
I have an enormous amount of help from the community.
But even so, I will run out of money and I will lack a technical skill.
I LIKED YOUR SHOW LAST NIGHT, RUFUS. IT'S ON ME.
WOULD YOU SAY THAT YOU ARE *RIOT GRRRLS,* LIKE THE MOVEMENT HAPPENING IN THE STATES?
NO ONE INVITED US. SO, I THINK WE'RE JUST DOING OUR OWN GRRRRRL THING.
And other things seem easier to make. Like music.
You think you are going down one road.
OFF WITH HER HEAD!
THAT'S A CUT! I GOTTA GET TO JAM.
That you're doing the thing, but you're actually doing and going somewhere else without knowing it.

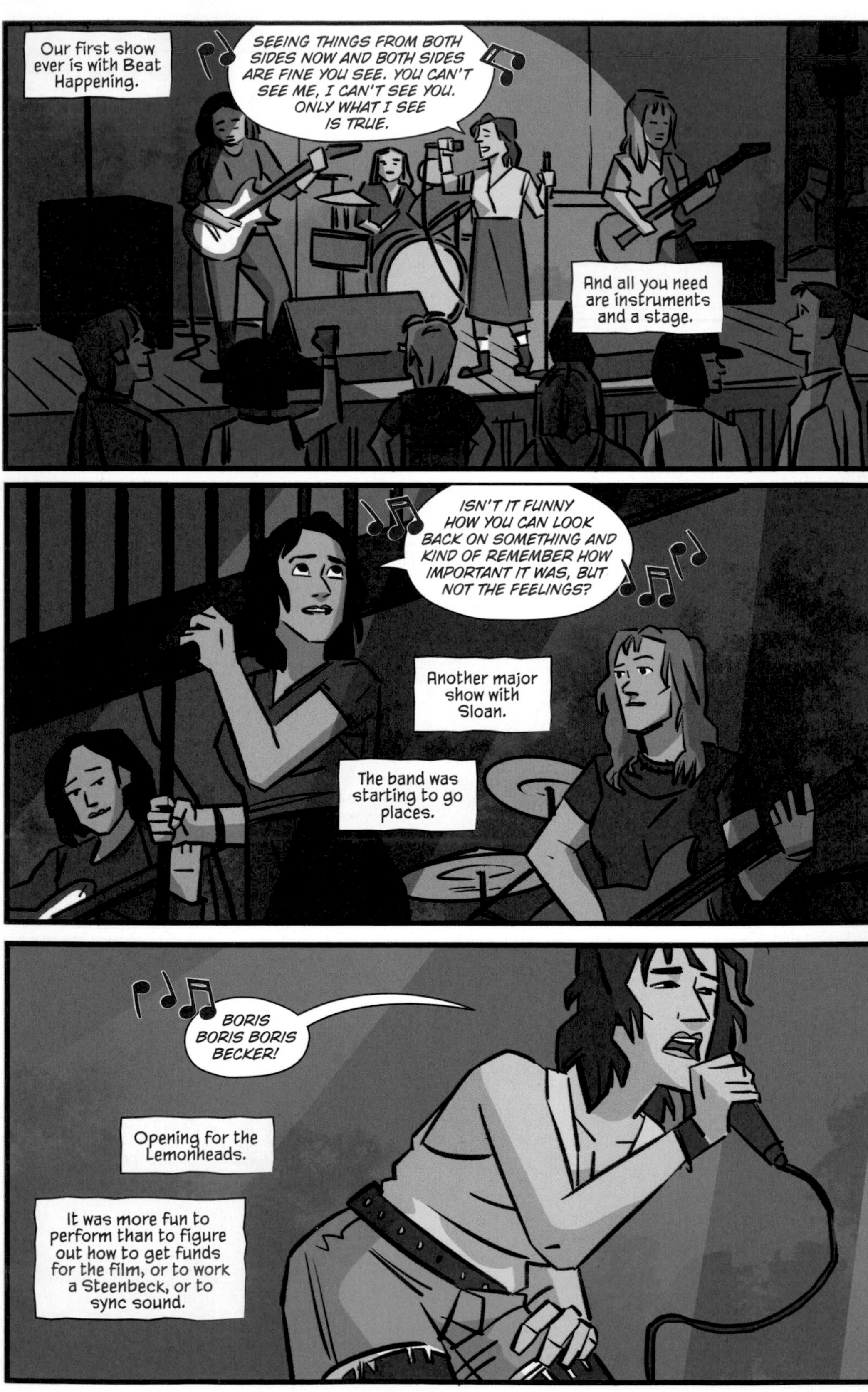
Our first show ever is with Beat Happening.
SEEING THINGS FROM BOTH SIDES NOW AND BOTH SIDES ARE FINE YOU SEE. YOU CAN'T SEE ME, I CAN'T SEE YOU. ONLY WHAT I SEE IS TRUE.
And all you need are instruments and a stage.
ISN'T IT FUNNY HOW YOU CAN LOOK BACK ON SOMETHING AND KIND OF REMEMBER HOW IMPORTANT IT WAS, BUT NOT THE FEELINGS?
Another major show with Sloan.
The band was starting to go places.
BORIS BORIS BORIS BECKER!
Opening for the Lemonheads.
It was more fun to perform than to figure out how to get funds for the film, or to work a Steenbeck, or to sync sound.

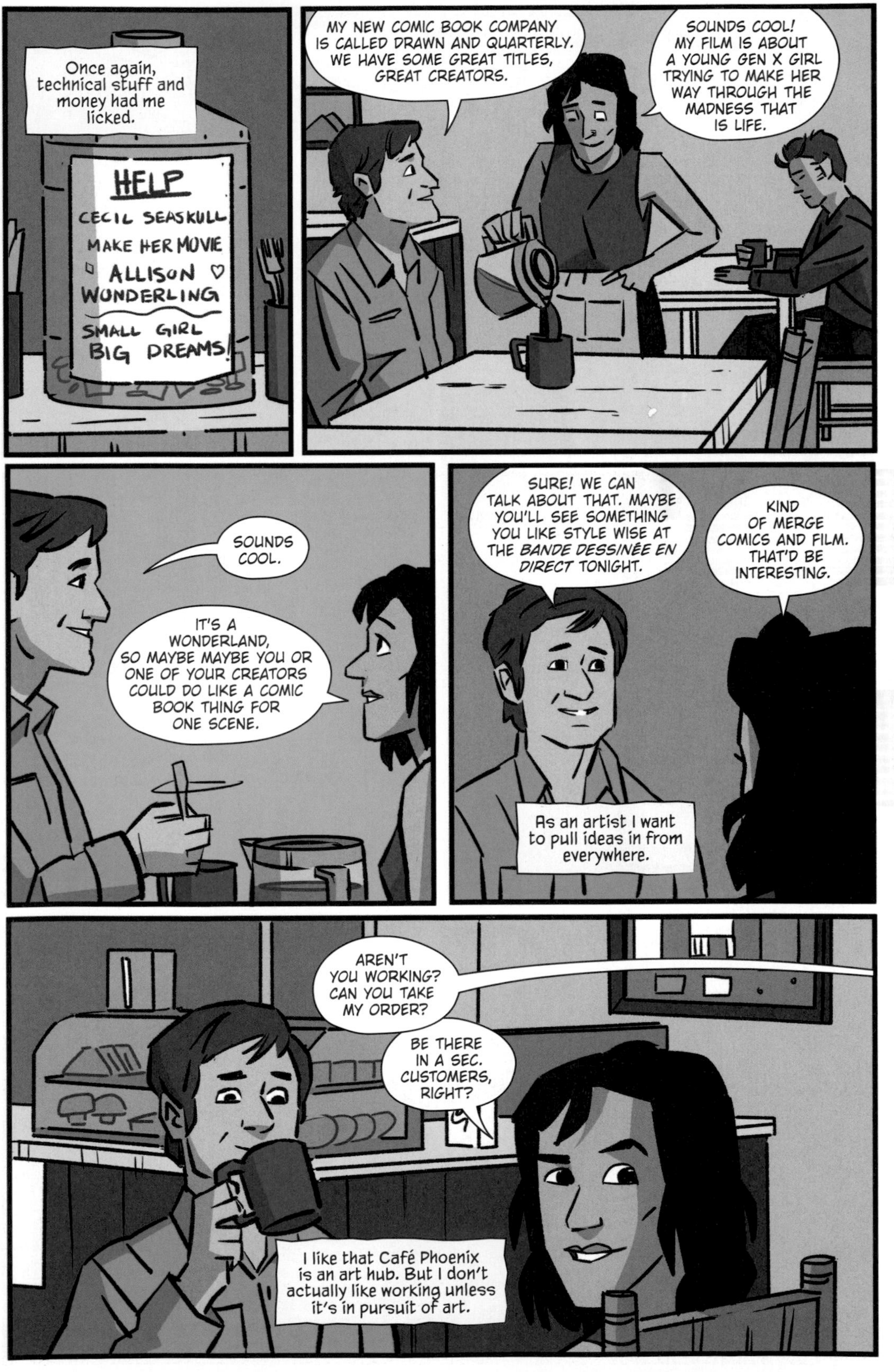
Once again, technical stuff and money had me licked.
HELP
CECIL SEASKULL
MAKE HER MOVIE
ALLISON WONDERLING
SMALL GIRL BIG DREAMS!
MY NEW COMIC BOOK COMPANY IS CALLED DRAWN AND QUARTERLY. WE HAVE SOME GREAT TITLES, GREAT CREATORS.
SOUNDS COOL! MY FILM IS ABOUT A YOUNG GEN X GIRL TRYING TO MAKE HER WAY THROUGH THE MADNESS THAT IS LIFE.
SOUNDS COOL.
IT'S A WONDERLAND, SO MAYBE MAYBE YOU OR ONE OF YOUR CREATORS COULD DO LIKE A COMIC BOOK THING FOR ONE SCENE.
SURE! WE CAN TALK ABOUT THAT. MAYBE YOU'LL SEE SOMETHING YOU LIKE STYLE WISE AT THE *BANDE DESSINÉE EN DIRECT* TONIGHT.
KIND OF MERGE COMICS AND FILM. THAT'D BE INTERESTING.
As an artist I want to pull ideas in from everywhere.
AREN'T YOU WORKING? CAN YOU TAKE MY ORDER?
BE THERE IN A SEC. CUSTOMERS, RIGHT?
I like that Café Phoenix is an art hub. But I don't actually like working unless it's in pursuit of art.

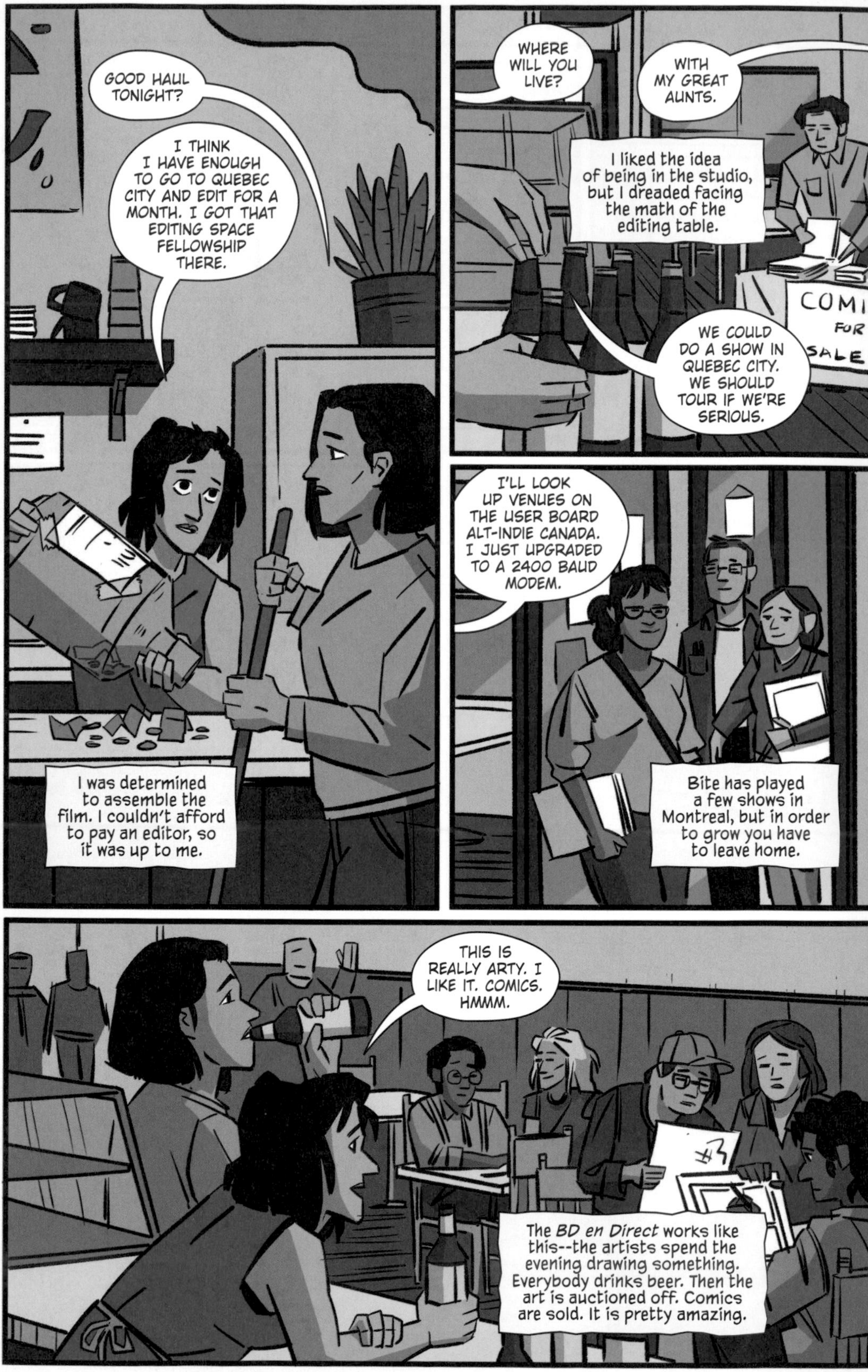
GOOD HAUL TONIGHT?
I THINK I HAVE ENOUGH TO GO TO QUEBEC CITY AND EDIT FOR A MONTH. I GOT THAT EDITING SPACE FELLOWSHIP THERE.
I was determined to assemble the film. I couldn't afford to pay an editor, so it was up to me.
WHERE WILL YOU LIVE?
WITH MY GREAT AUNTS.
I liked the idea of being in the studio, but I dreaded facing the math of the editing table.
COMICS FOR SALE
WE COULD DO A SHOW IN QUEBEC CITY. WE SHOULD TOUR IF WE'RE SERIOUS.
I'LL LOOK UP VENUES ON THE USER BOARD ALT-INDIE CANADA. I JUST UPGRADED TO A 2400 BAUD MODEM.
Bite has played a few shows in Montreal, but in order to grow you have to leave home.
THIS IS REALLY ARTY. I LIKE IT. COMICS. HMMM.
#3
The *BD en Direct* works like this--the artists spend the evening drawing something. Everybody drinks beer. Then the art is auctioned off. Comics are sold. It is pretty amazing.

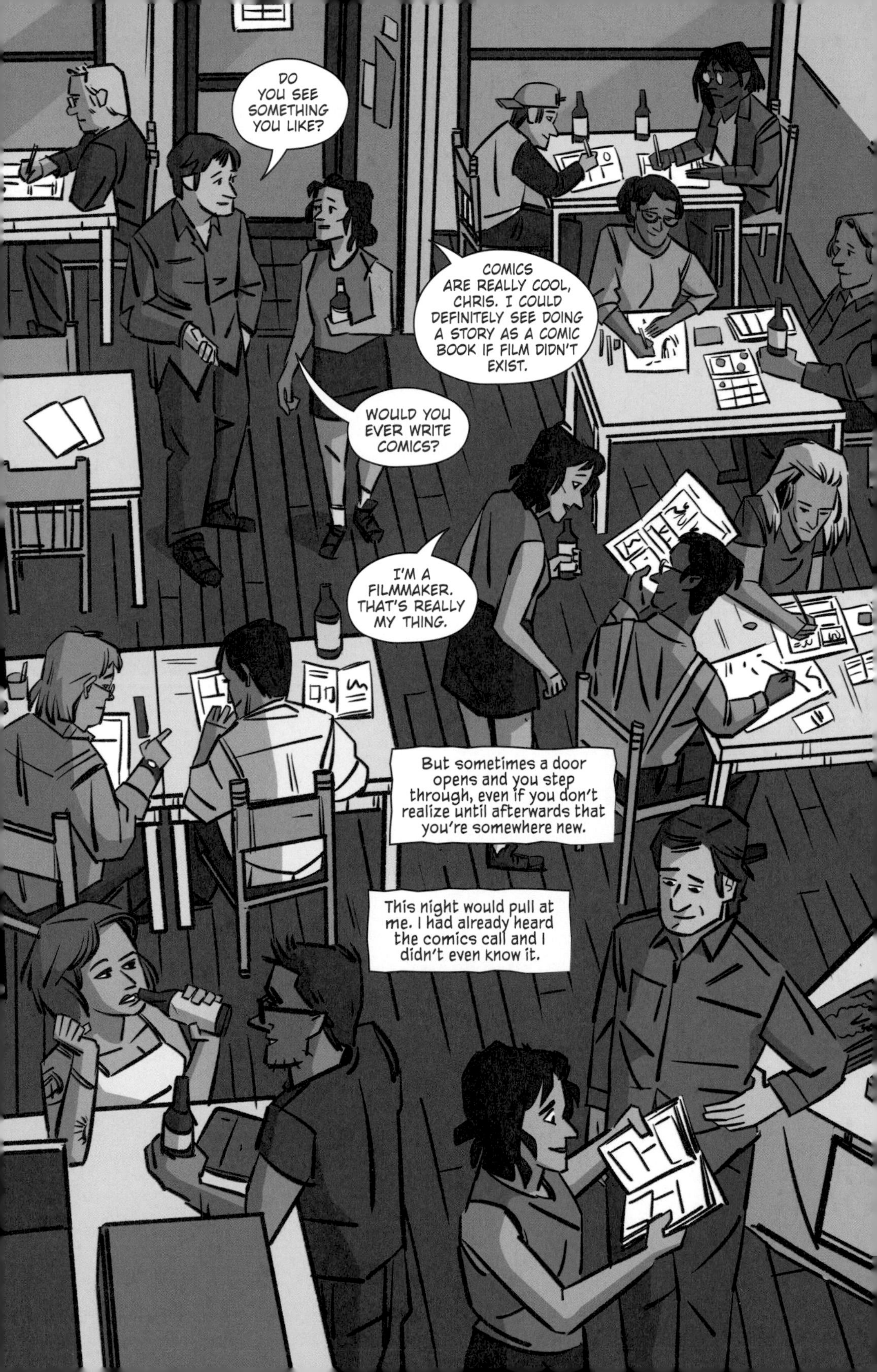
DO YOU SEE SOMETHING YOU LIKE?
COMICS ARE REALLY COOL, CHRIS. I COULD DEFINITELY SEE DOING A STORY AS A COMIC BOOK IF FILM DIDN'T EXIST.
WOULD YOU EVER WRITE COMICS?
I'M A FILMMAKER. THAT'S REALLY MY THING.
But sometimes a door opens and you step through, even if you don't realize until afterwards that you're somewhere new.
This night would pull at me. I had already heard the comics call and I didn't even know it.

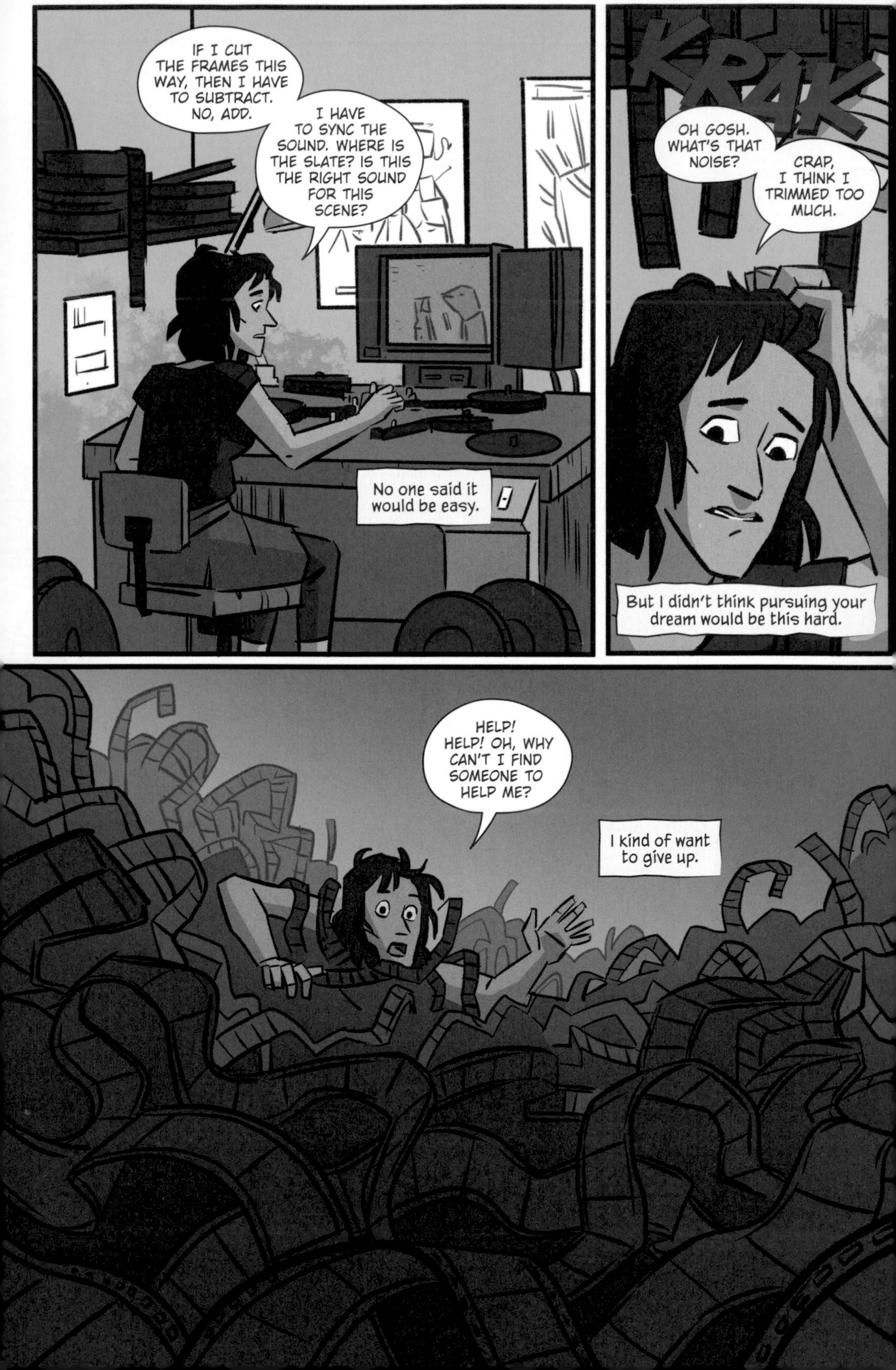
IF I CUT THE FRAMES THIS WAY, THEN I HAVE TO SUBTRACT. NO, ADD.
I HAVE TO SYNC THE SOUND. WHERE IS THE SLATE? IS THIS THE RIGHT SOUND FOR THIS SCENE?
No one said it would be easy.
KRAK
OH GOSH. WHAT'S THAT NOISE?
CRAP, I THINK I TRIMMED TOO MUCH.
But I didn't think pursuing your dream would be this hard.
HELP! HELP! OH, WHY CAN'T I FIND SOMEONE TO HELP ME?
I kind of want to give up.

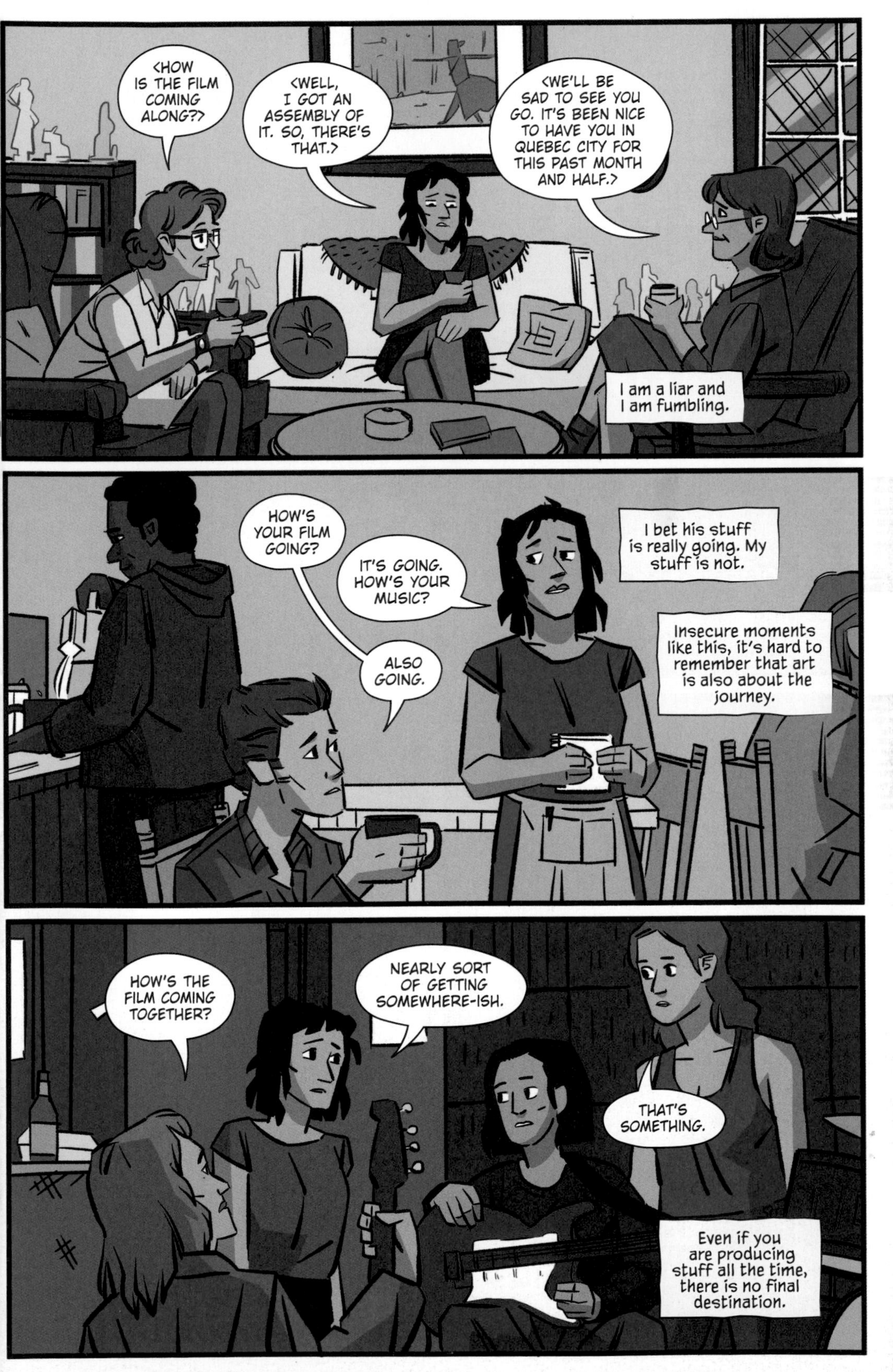

<HOW IS THE FILM COMING ALONG?>
<WELL, I GOT AN ASSEMBLY OF IT. SO, THERE'S THAT.>
<WE'LL BE SAD TO SEE YOU GO. IT'S BEEN NICE TO HAVE YOU IN QUEBEC CITY FOR THIS PAST MONTH AND HALF.>
I am a liar and I am fumbling.
HOW'S YOUR FILM GOING?
IT'S GOING. HOW'S YOUR MUSIC?
ALSO GOING.
I bet his stuff is really going. My stuff is not.
Insecure moments like this, it's hard to remember that art is also about the journey.
HOW'S THE FILM COMING TOGETHER?
NEARLY SORT OF GETTING SOMEWHERE-ISH.
THAT'S SOMETHING.
Even if you are producing stuff all the time, there is no final destination.

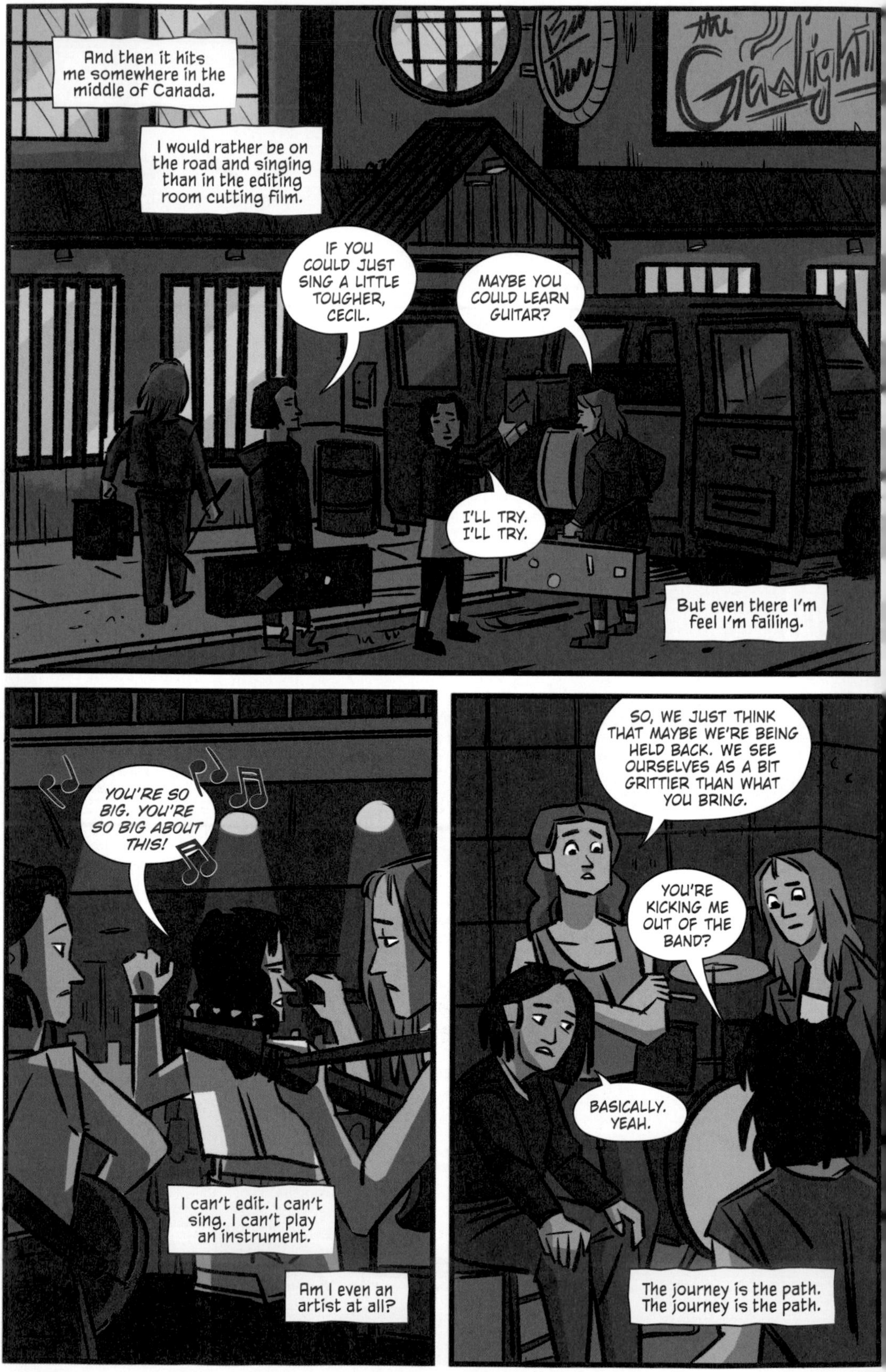
And then it hits me somewhere in the middle of Canada.
I would rather be on the road and singing than in the editing room cutting film.
IF YOU COULD JUST SING A LITTLE TOUGHER, CECIL.
MAYBE YOU COULD LEARN GUITAR?
I'LL TRY. I'LL TRY.
But even there I'm feel I'm failing.
YOU'RE SO BIG. YOU'RE SO BIG ABOUT THIS!
I can't edit. I can't sing. I can't play an instrument.
Am I even an artist at all?
SO, WE JUST THINK THAT MAYBE WE'RE BEING HELD BACK. WE SEE OURSELVES AS A BIT GRITTIER THAN WHAT YOU BRING.
YOU'RE KICKING ME OUT OF THE BAND?
BASICALLY. YEAH.
The journey is the path. The journey is the path.

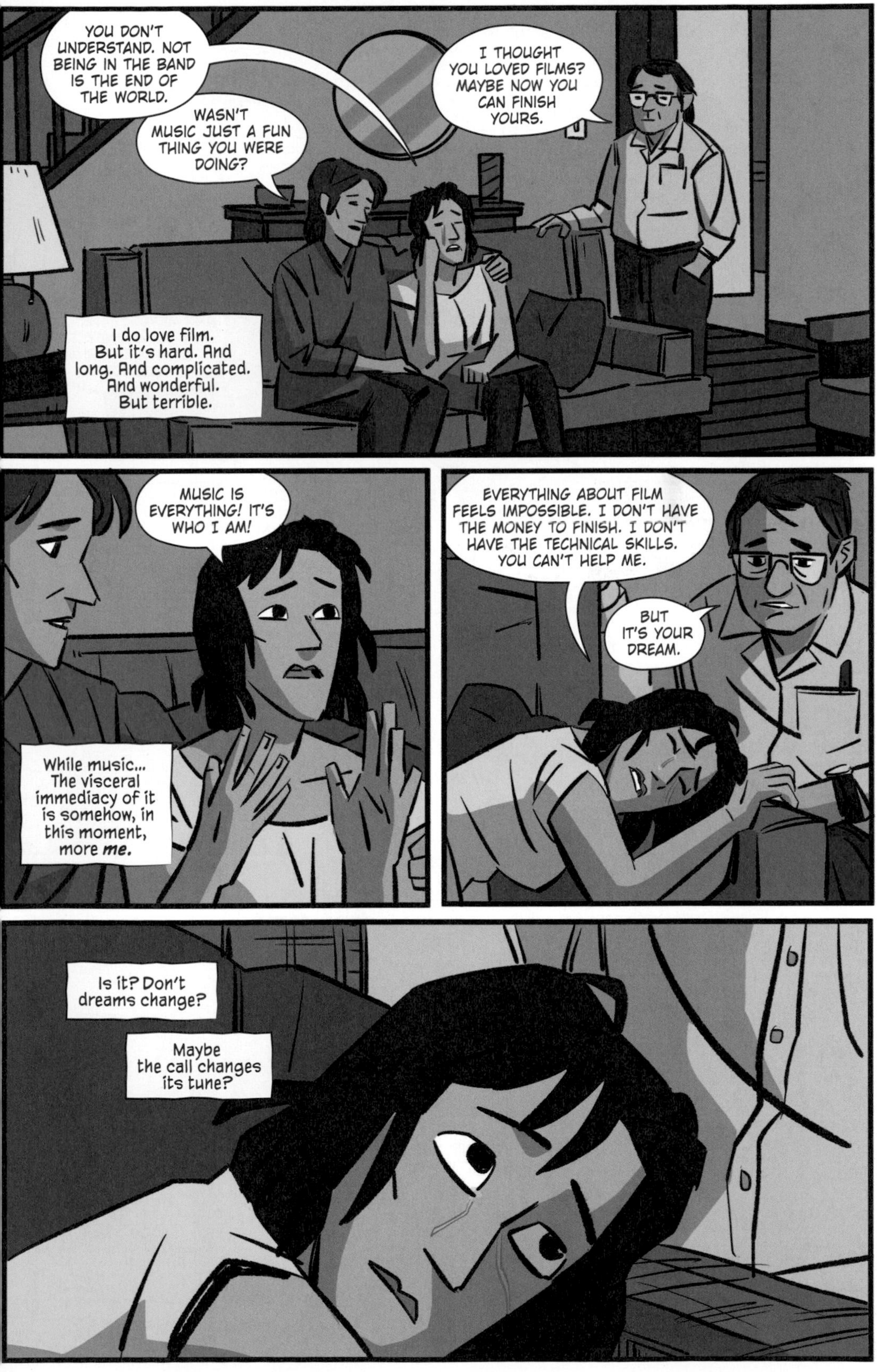
YOU DON'T UNDERSTAND. NOT BEING IN THE BAND IS THE END OF THE WORLD.
WASN'T MUSIC JUST A FUN THING YOU WERE DOING?
I THOUGHT YOU LOVED FILMS? MAYBE NOW YOU CAN FINISH YOURS.
I do love film. But it's hard. And long. And complicated. And wonderful. But terrible.
MUSIC IS EVERYTHING! IT'S WHO I AM!
While music... The visceral immediacy of it is somehow, in this moment, more *me.*
EVERYTHING ABOUT FILM FEELS IMPOSSIBLE. I DON'T HAVE THE MONEY TO FINISH. I DON'T HAVE THE TECHNICAL SKILLS. YOU CAN'T HELP ME.
BUT IT'S YOUR DREAM.
Is it? Don't dreams change?
Maybe the call changes its tune?

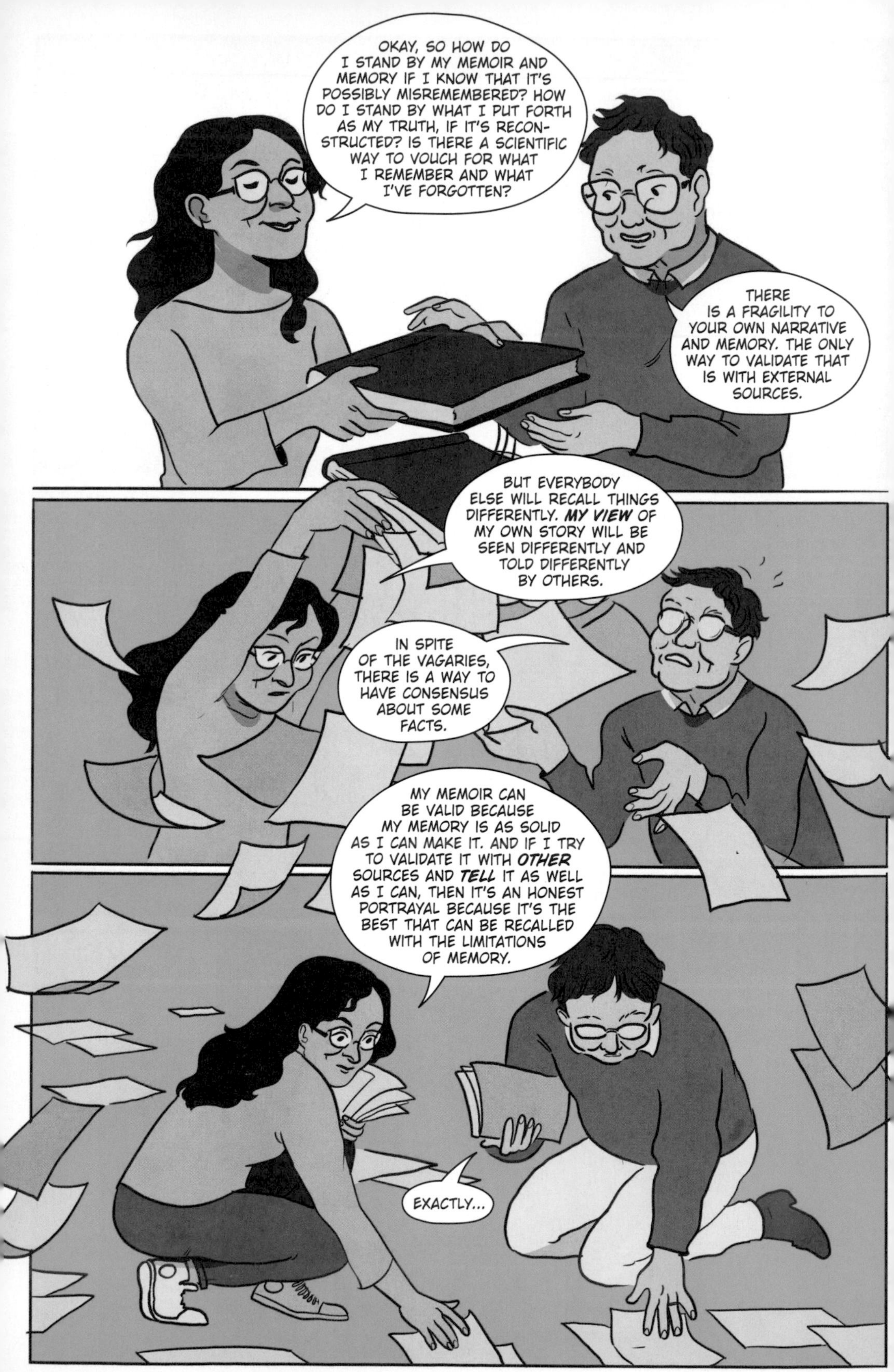
OKAY, SO HOW DO I STAND BY MY MEMOIR AND MEMORY IF I KNOW THAT IT'S POSSIBLY MISREMEMBERED? HOW DO I STAND BY WHAT I PUT FORTH AS MY TRUTH, IF IT'S RECON-STRUCTED? IS THERE A SCIENTIFIC WAY TO VOUCH FOR WHAT I REMEMBER AND WHAT I'VE FORGOTTEN?
THERE IS A FRAGILITY TO YOUR OWN NARRATIVE AND MEMORY. THE ONLY WAY TO VALIDATE THAT IS WITH EXTERNAL SOURCES.
BUT EVERYBODY ELSE WILL RECALL THINGS DIFFERENTLY. ***MY VIEW*** OF MY OWN STORY WILL BE SEEN DIFFERENTLY AND TOLD DIFFERENTLY BY OTHERS.
IN SPITE OF THE VAGARIES, THERE IS A WAY TO HAVE CONSENSUS ABOUT SOME FACTS.
MY MEMOIR CAN BE VALID BECAUSE MY MEMORY IS AS SOLID AS I CAN MAKE IT. AND IF I TRY TO VALIDATE IT WITH ***OTHER*** SOURCES AND ***TELL*** IT AS WELL AS I CAN, THEN IT'S AN HONEST PORTRAYAL BECAUSE IT'S THE BEST THAT CAN BE RECALLED WITH THE LIMITATIONS OF MEMORY.
EXACTLY...

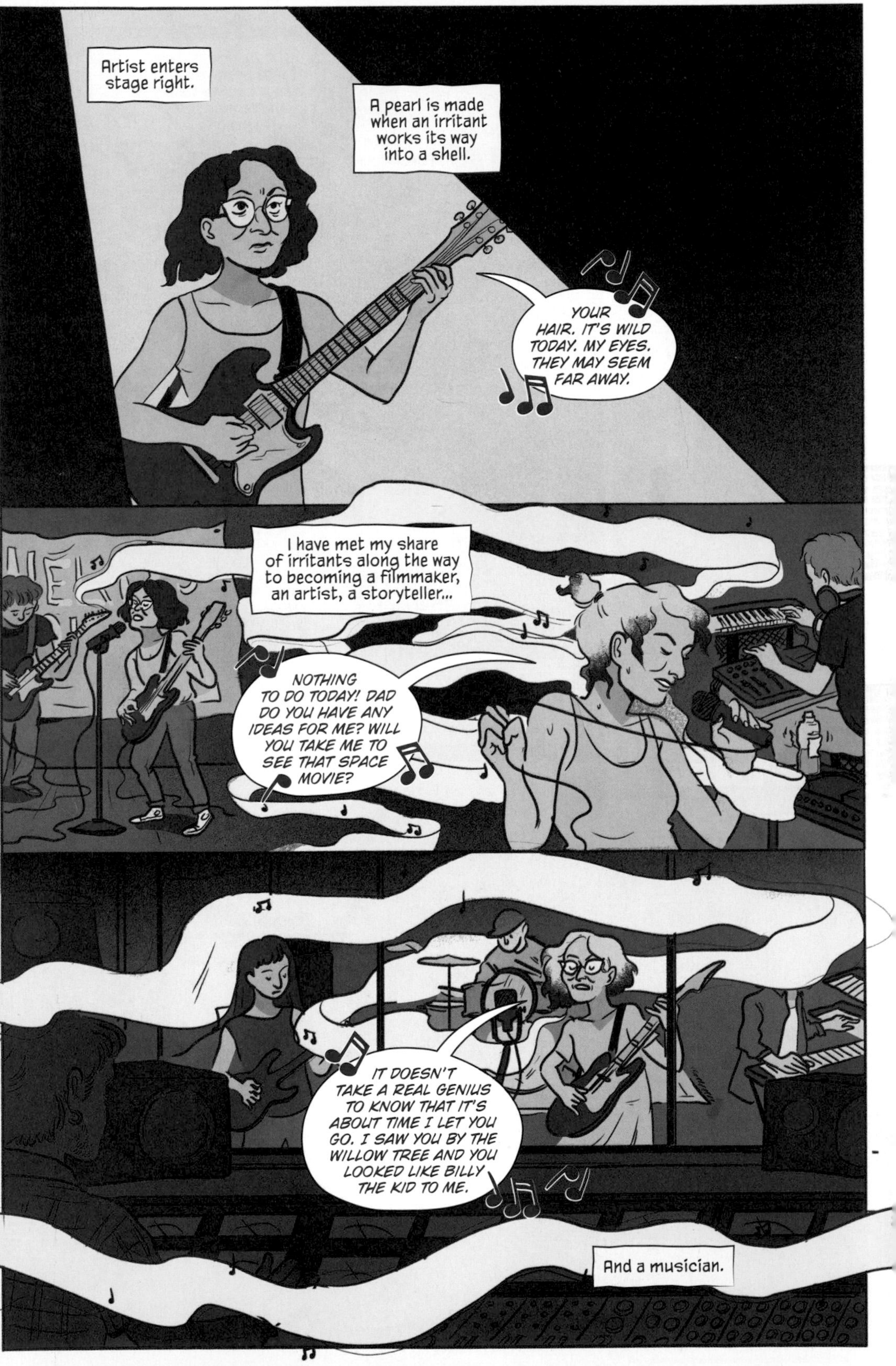
Artist enters stage right.
A pearl is made when an irritant works its way into a shell.
YOUR HAIR. IT'S WILD TODAY. MY EYES. THEY MAY SEEM FAR AWAY.
I have met my share of irritants along the way to becoming a filmmaker, an artist, a storyteller...
NOTHING TO DO TODAY! DAD DO YOU HAVE ANY IDEAS FOR ME? WILL YOU TAKE ME TO SEE THAT SPACE MOVIE?
IT DOESN'T TAKE A REAL GENIUS TO KNOW THAT IT'S ABOUT TIME I LET YOU GO. I SAW YOU BY THE WILLOW TREE AND YOU LOOKED LIKE BILLY THE KID TO ME.
And a musician.

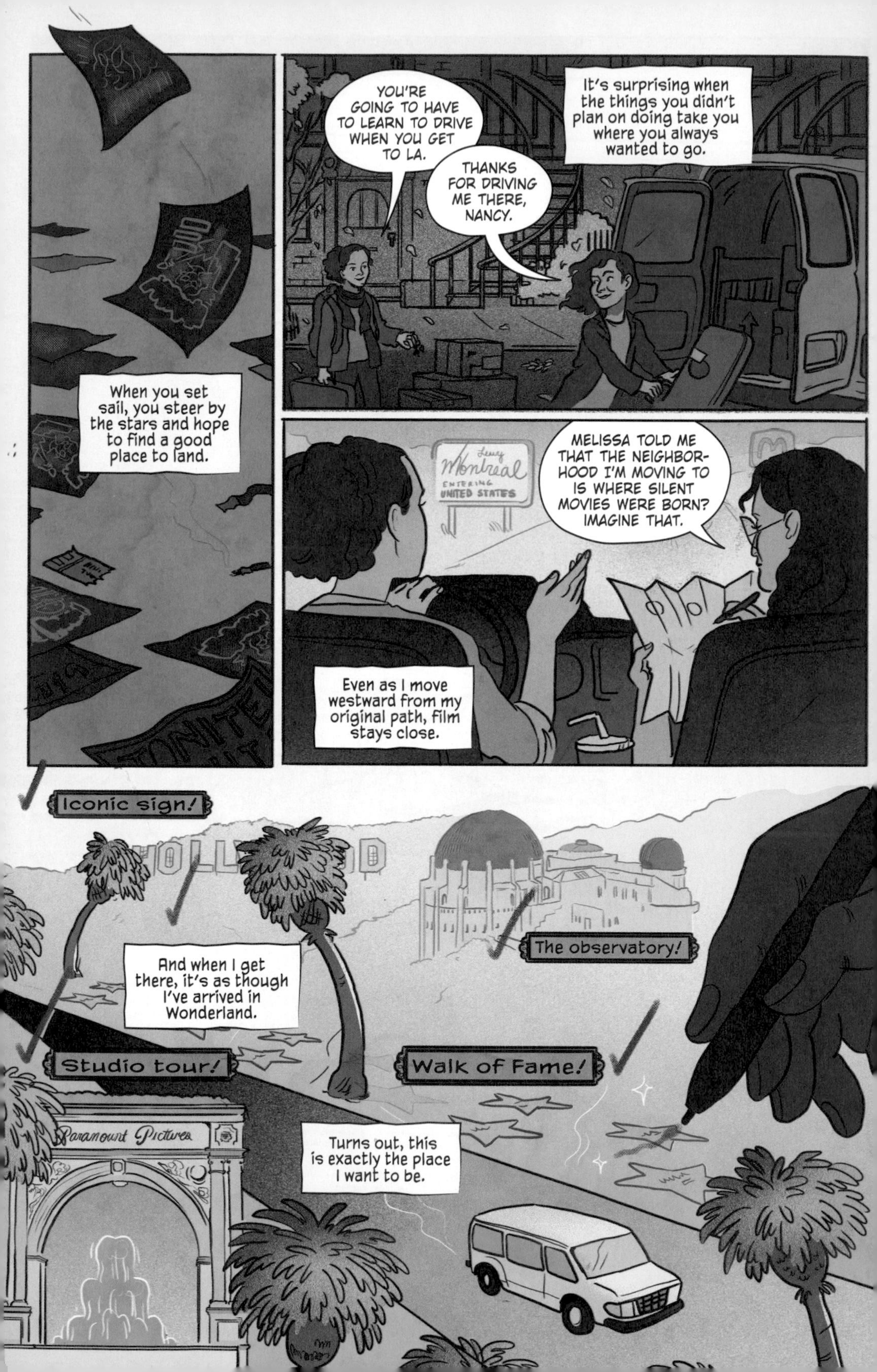

YOU'RE GOING TO HAVE TO LEARN TO DRIVE WHEN YOU GET TO LA.
THANKS FOR DRIVING ME THERE, NANCY.
It's surprising when the things you didn't plan on doing take you where you always wanted to go.
When you set sail, you steer by the stars and hope to find a good place to land.
MELISSA TOLD ME THAT THE NEIGHBORHOOD I'M MOVING TO IS WHERE SILENT MOVIES WERE BORN? IMAGINE THAT.
Montreal
ENTERING UNITED STATES
Even as I move westward from my original path, film stays close.
Iconic sign!
The observatory!
And when I get there, it's as though I've arrived in Wonderland.
Studio tour!
Walk of Fame!
Paramount Pictures
Turns out, this is exactly the place I want to be.

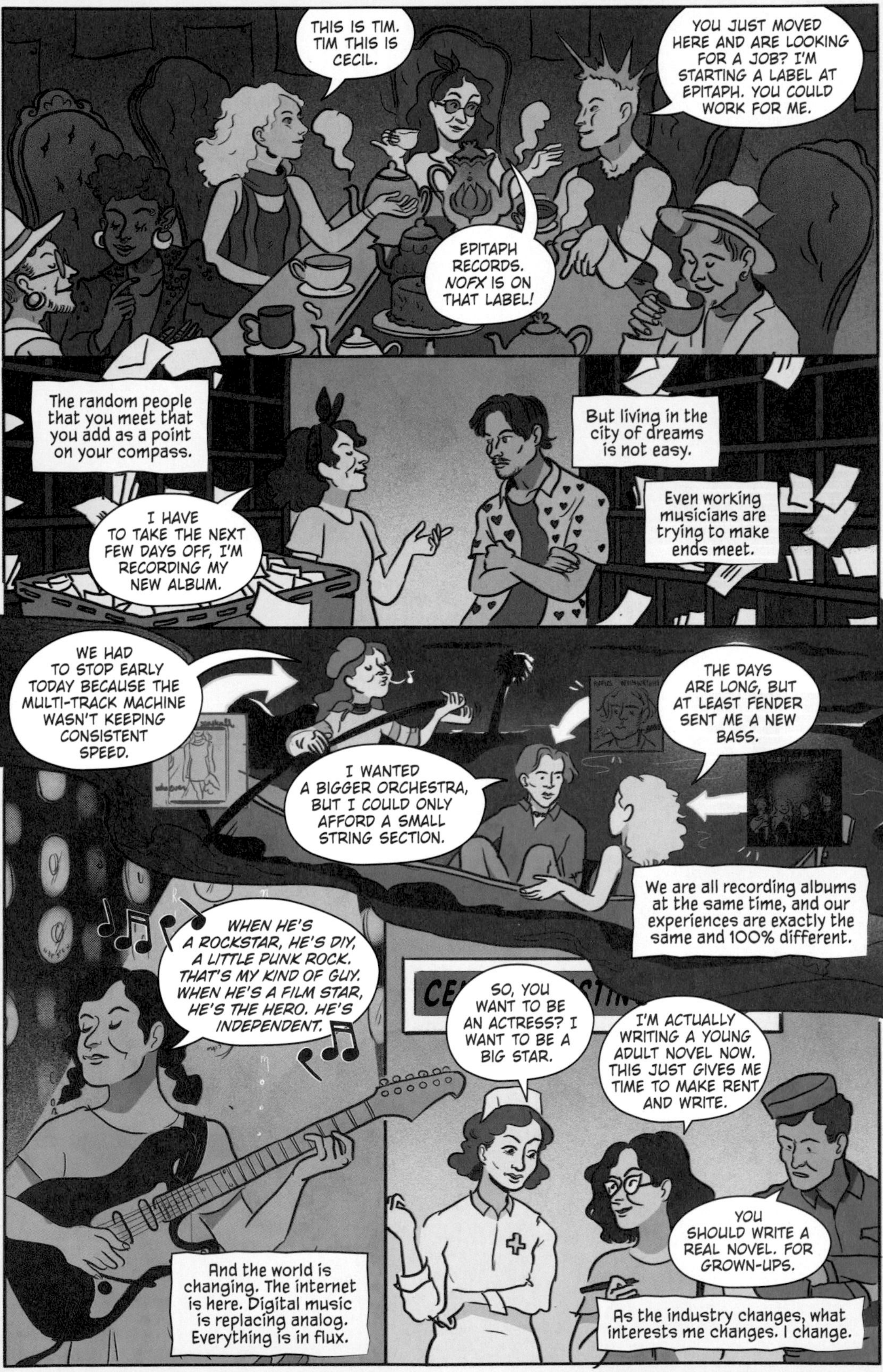

THIS IS TIM. TIM THIS IS CECIL.
YOU JUST MOVED HERE AND ARE LOOKING FOR A JOB? I'M STARTING A LABEL AT EPITAPH. YOU COULD WORK FOR ME.
EPITAPH RECORDS. *NOFX* IS ON THAT LABEL!
The random people that you meet that you add as a point on your compass.
I HAVE TO TAKE THE NEXT FEW DAYS OFF, I'M RECORDING MY NEW ALBUM.
But living in the city of dreams is not easy.
Even working musicians are trying to make ends meet.
WE HAD TO STOP EARLY TODAY BECAUSE THE MULTI-TRACK MACHINE WASN'T KEEPING CONSISTENT SPEED.
THE DAYS ARE LONG, BUT AT LEAST FENDER SENT ME A NEW BASS.
I WANTED A BIGGER ORCHESTRA, BUT I COULD ONLY AFFORD A SMALL STRING SECTION.
We are all recording albums at the same time, and our experiences are exactly the same and 100% different.
WHEN HE'S A ROCKSTAR, HE'S DIY, A LITTLE PUNK ROCK. THAT'S MY KIND OF GUY. WHEN HE'S A FILM STAR, HE'S THE HERO. HE'S INDEPENDENT.
And the world is changing. The internet is here. Digital music is replacing analog. Everything is in flux.
SO, YOU WANT TO BE AN ACTRESS? I WANT TO BE A BIG STAR.
I'M ACTUALLY WRITING A YOUNG ADULT NOVEL NOW. THIS JUST GIVES ME TIME TO MAKE RENT AND WRITE.
YOU SHOULD WRITE A REAL NOVEL. FOR GROWN-UPS.
As the industry changes, what interests me changes. I change.

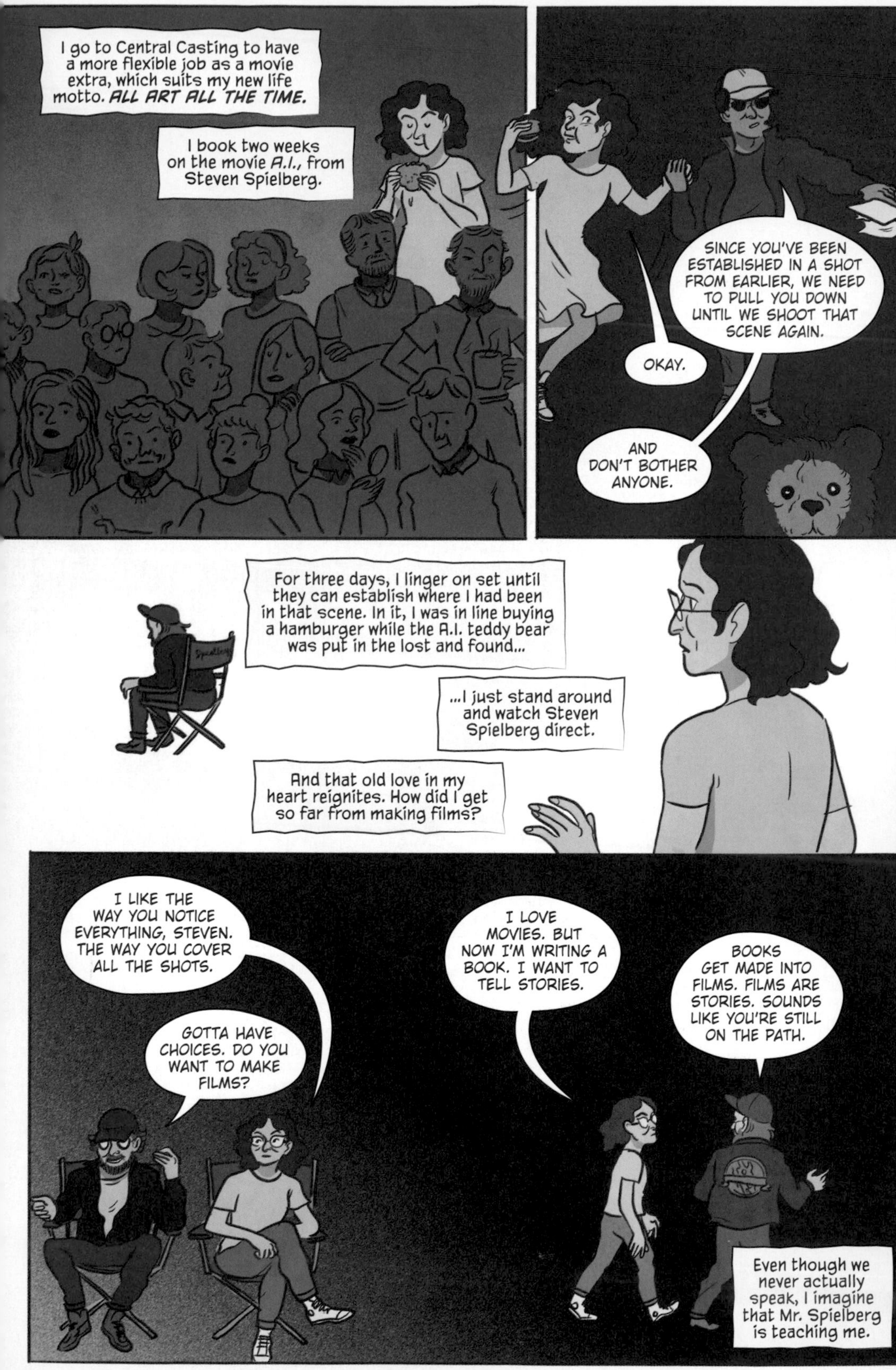
I go to Central Casting to have a more flexible job as a movie extra, which suits my new life motto. ALL ART ALL THE TIME.
I book two weeks on the movie A.I., from Steven Spielberg.
SINCE YOU'VE BEEN ESTABLISHED IN A SHOT FROM EARLIER, WE NEED TO PULL YOU DOWN UNTIL WE SHOOT THAT SCENE AGAIN.
OKAY.
AND DON'T BOTHER ANYONE.
For three days, I linger on set until they can establish where I had been in that scene. In it, I was in line buying a hamburger while the A.I. teddy bear was put in the lost and found...
...I just stand around and watch Steven Spielberg direct.
And that old love in my heart reignites. How did I get so far from making films?
I LIKE THE WAY YOU NOTICE EVERYTHING, STEVEN. THE WAY YOU COVER ALL THE SHOTS.
GOTTA HAVE CHOICES. DO YOU WANT TO MAKE FILMS?
I LOVE MOVIES. BUT NOW I'M WRITING A BOOK. I WANT TO TELL STORIES.
BOOKS GET MADE INTO FILMS. FILMS ARE STORIES. SOUNDS LIKE YOU'RE STILL ON THE PATH.
Even though we never actually speak, I imagine that Mr. Spielberg is teaching me.

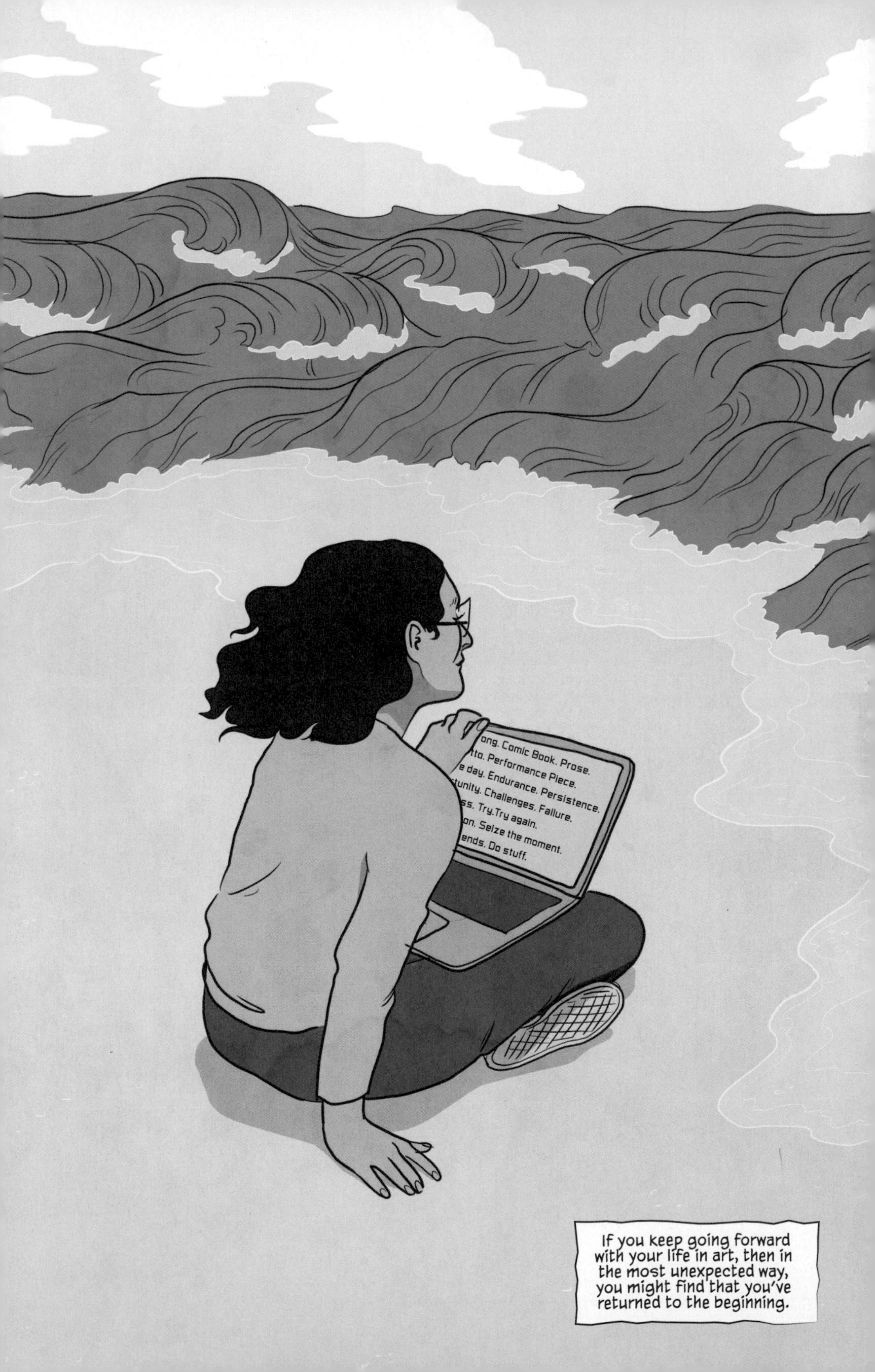
ong. Comic Book. Prose.
tto. Performance Piece.
e day. Endurance. Persistence.
tunity. Challenges. Failure.
ss. Try.Try again.
on. Seize the moment.
ends. Do stuff.
If you keep going forward with your life in art, then in the most unexpected way, you might find that you've returned to the beginning.

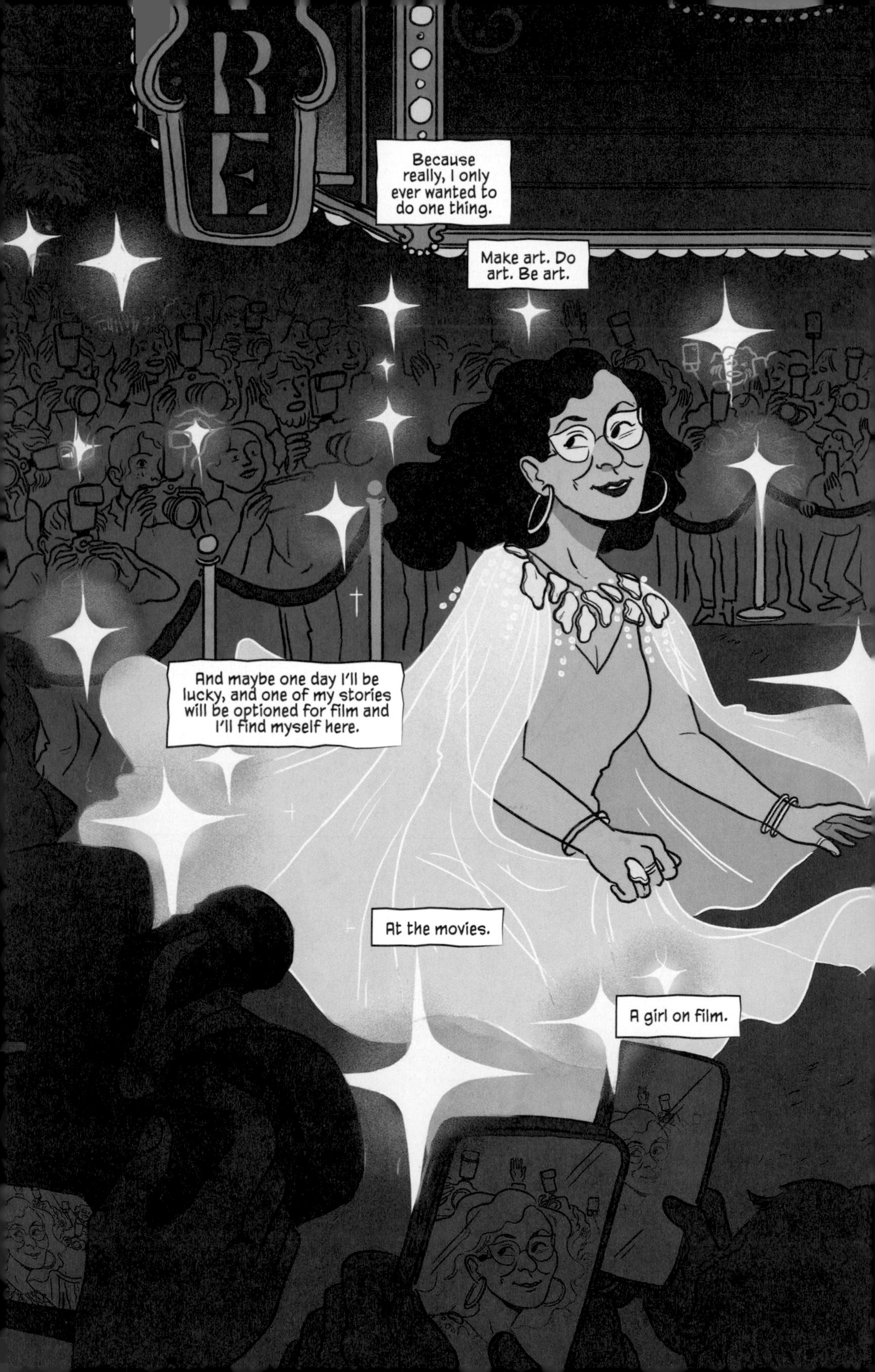

Because really, I only ever wanted to do one thing.
Make art. Do art. Be art.
And maybe one day I'll be lucky, and one of my stories will be optioned for film and I'll find myself here.
At the movies.
A girl on film.

ACKNOWLEDGMENTS

Some people have been altered or changed as happens with memory...

Thank you to editor and friend extraordinaire Sierra Hahn.

Thank you to my fabulous agents Kirby Kim and Eric Reid.

Thank you to Vicky, V, Jon, Duffy and Sophie.

Thank you to Laurent Castellucci, Caz Westover, Steve Salardino and all my friends.

Thank you to all former bandmates in bite, Nerdy Girl and Cecil Seaskull

Thank you to JHS 141, Performing Arts / LaGuardia High School, NYU and Concordia.

Thank you to New York City, Montreal, Paris and Los Angeles.

Thank you to every movie I ever saw and every filmmaker I admire.

Thank you to novels and comics books and opera and theatre.

Thank you to everyone I forgot to remember and remembered to forget.